When Incumbency Fails

The Senate Career of Mark Andrews

Richard F. Fenno, Jr.
University of Rochester

A Division of Congressional Quarterly Inc.
Washington, D.C.

Cover design: Paula Anderson
Cover photo: Newman Outdoor Advertising, Fargo, North Dakota

Copyright © 1992 Congressional Quarterly Inc.
1414 22nd Street, N.W., Washington, D.C. 20037

Printed in the United States of America

Library of Congress Cataloging-in-Publication Data

Fenno, Richard F., 1926-
    When incumbency fails :   the Senate career of Mark Andrews   /
Richard F. Fenno, Jr.
        p.   cm.
    Includes bibliographical references and index.
    ISBN 0-87187-701-5 -- ISBN 0-87187-700-7 (pbk.)
    1. Andrews, Mark, 1926- . 2. North Dakota--Politics and government--
1951- I. Title.
E840.8.A55F46   1992
328.73'092--dc20   92-4049
                                                                        CIP

To Sarah Davidson Fenno

Contents

Preface

This book is about a puzzling case of outstanding political success followed by unexpected political failure. Political scientists know that incumbent members of the U.S. Congress usually win reelection. This book is about one who did not. After twenty-three years of continuous service—seventeen in the House of Representatives and six in the Senate—Sen. Mark Andrews of North Dakota was defeated for reelection. The central questions of the book are: What happened and why? The main method of analysis is a straightforward narrative account. The book's guiding concept is the idea of a political career; its underlying theme is that of political change. Andrews's electoral defeat is viewed as the culminating event in a long political career—a career that was substantially affected by changing contexts in Washington and in North Dakota.

North Dakota is one of the country's smallest and least-known states. That single fact might tempt some readers to close the book at this point. While there may be good reasons for stopping, the tiny population of North Dakota is not one of them. The most important single fact about the Senate is that under the Constitution, each state has the same number of senators—two. Indeed, as students of the Constitutional Convention know, it was at the insistence of the small states in 1787 that the senatorial system of equal representation was adopted. If anything, the Senate is distinctively the haven of small states within our governmental arrangement. In the abstract, therefore, a senator from North Dakota is every bit as newsworthy and powerful as a senator from California. And, in the abstract, the defeat of a senator from North Dakota is as momentous an event—for the operation of the Senate and of the government—as the defeat of a senator from California. It may take a leap of imagination for readers to equate North Dakota with California and to become as interested in stories about one state's politics as the other's. But that leap must be taken if students of American politics are ever to produce generalizations about the U.S. Senate.

This book is an attempt to take the smallest of steps in that direction. It is a case study. As such, it can only suggest certain variables for inclusion in generalizations and raise worthwhile questions. Like several other recent books of mine, this one is a narrative account that relies for its basic outline on the idea of two separable processes of campaigning and governing being played out in two separate contexts, home and Washington, and on the sequential effects of one process on the other in shaping individual senatorial behavior. This governing-campaigning-governing-campaigning sequence helps us supply both definition and structure to the career we are studying. Along the way, the study helps flesh out some of the variables that have long interested students of congressional elections. Constituency size is, perhaps, the most obvious of these. But others include the relevance of previous election margins, the quality of the challenger, the relative impact of national and local issues, the relationship between policy- and candidate-centered variables, and the impact of campaigns on electoral outcomes.

The book makes one major suggestion about the analysis of congressional elections in which incumbents are involved. The suggestion is that the incumbent's vulnerability makes a large contribution to the electoral outcome, that the vulnerability takes shape over time, and that it is necessary, therefore, to study how, when, why, and to what degree incumbents become, or do not become, vulnerable in the period between elections. The analysis of vulnerability can be almost as important to the study of incumbency as the analysis of election results. It has been the habit of political scientists to describe vulnerability primarily in terms of the incumbent's previous election margin, while paying little attention to the interelection period, during which vulnerability assumes its ultimate preelection form. For senators, that neglected period is six years long—far too long a period, we would argue, to leave unattended by closer analysis.

My interpretation of Mark Andrews's career rests heavily on personal observation during visits to North Dakota in 1980, 1982, 1985, and 1986 and during a year, 1981-1982, in Washington. At the outset, it is well to remind ourselves of the considerable limitations imposed by these features of technique and of timing.

Whenever I observed, my perspective was almost wholly the perspective of the senator and his staff. It was, admittedly, a partial and incomplete perspective on the particular event or string of events I was interested in. Because I did not enter the picture until 1980, I was not able to watch Mark Andrews during the most successful time in his political life. Nor were documentary materials available with which to study that earlier time. So the book is centered on one final six-year segment of a career that stretched much further back in time. Moreover, because my observations in Washington were concentrated in one year and confined primarily, therefore, to one committee (Appropriations), I cannot even purport to have gleaned a well-rounded picture of his six years in the Senate. I did not, for example, spend time studying his performance as a member of the Senate's Committee on Agriculture and Forestry, a position of great importance to his home state. I have tried to compensate for my partial and episodic observations by relying on newspaper accounts and on the senator's own discussion of his activities. Notwithstanding these limitations, the following pages contain an amply rich, intriguing, and helpful story of political success and political failure. The reader will have to judge how interesting, how convincing, and how educational that story is.

The lion's share of my thanks goes to Sen. Mark Andrews, who was unfailingly open, accommodating, and enjoyable to be with whether in North Dakota or in Washington. I certainly wanted him to win. Among the Andrews staffers whose friendly cooperation helped ease my task, I wish to thank especially William Wright. I also thank James Austin, Jacqueline Balk-Tusa, Tim Burke, David Crothers, Grace Gronigen, Chip Hardin, Scott Hove, Keith Kraus, Michael Olson, Bruce Post, Ernie Schmidt, David Sorum, and Marjorie Walpole. I thank Sen. Kent Conrad, too, for his willingness to talk with me.

From within the political science community, my deepest thanks go to Morris Fiorina, who gave the entire manuscript an exceptionally helpful reading. For their various sorts of assistance along the way, I thank also Paul Curcio, Tim Fedderson, Paul Harnesen, John Hibbing, Mike Kagay, Ben Meier, Glenn Parker, Wendy Schiller, Barbara Sinclair, David Watt, and Steve Wright. Janice Brown and Rosemary Burnham worked with unfailing good cheer and great skill in transcribing my notes and preparing the manuscript. At CQ Press, my greatest debts are owed to Dave Tarr, Nola Healy Lynch, and Ann O'Malley. I wish also to acknowledge the financial support of the Russell Sage Foundation. And, now that the results of the foundation's support are complete, I wish particularly to acknowledge the indispensable encouragement, from within the foundation, of Byron Shafer. Most of all, I thank Nancy, whose unwavering support has been the one truly essential element of the entire research enterprise.

Incumbency and Representation

THE PUZZLE: SUCCESS AND FAILURE

Mark Andrews, Republican of North Dakota, came to the United States Senate in 1981, after seventeen years of service in the House of Representatives. For the first nine of those years (1963-1972), he was one of the two House members from his state.[1] Following the reapportionment of 1971, he served another eight years as North Dakota's only House member—its representative at large. When he went to the Senate, therefore, Andrews changed offices but kept the same constituency. The response of his constituents to his Senate candidacy was clearly supportive, as it had been during his nine previous elections to the House.

In the best of Democratic years nationwide, Representative Andrews had been challenged by the best politicians of that party, and he had beaten them. He had defeated a future Democratic governor, George Sinner, in 1964, the year of Lyndon B. Johnson's landslide; and he had defeated a future Democratic congressman, Byron Dorgan, in the Watergate year of 1974. In his four elections as North Dakota's only House member, Andrews had averaged 64 percent of the statewide vote. In 1980, he won election to the Senate with more than 70 percent of the vote. It was the highest percentage for a North Dakota Senate candidate in half a century. It was also the largest vote total and the biggest vote plurality in the history of the state.

The maps in Figures A-1 to A-4 trace Andrews's record of success at the polls during his four terms as North Dakota's representative at large (pages 34-37). They depict a gradual increase in his electoral strength during his three most recent elections—from a low of 56 percent in 1974 to a high of 68 percent in 1978. The map in Figure A-5 illustrates the overwhelming and culminating character of his 1980 election to the Senate (page 38).

When he ran for reelection in 1986, therefore, Sen. Mark Andrews could look back on ten consecutive election triumphs and twenty-three years of incumbency in Congress. He could also look back on a recent record of steadily increasing electoral margins. And he was still only sixty years old. Local precedent was in his favor. As North Dakota's top political reporter wrote, "North Dakota voters have shown a tendency down through the decades to leave their U.S. Senators in office for a long time. No incumbent has been defeated in the past 40 years." [2]

National trends were also on his side. It is true that Senate incumbents have not been as safe as House incumbents. But in the years since Andrews had come to Congress, 77 percent of all Senate incumbents running for reelection had been successful—including twenty-eight of thirty in 1982 and twenty-six of twenty-nine in 1984. Furthermore, both recently and throughout the period from 1946 to 1980, incumbent senators from small states had been more likely to be successful at gaining reelection than incumbent senators from large states.[3] And North Dakota is the fifth smallest state in the union. Personal, local, and national trends combined, therefore, to forecast the continuation of a long, unbreakable incumbency.

Yet Mark Andrews failed to win reelection in 1986. Figure A-6, in comparison with Figure A-5, vividly depicts the outcome (page 39). A map that had been solidly black with electoral triumph in 1980 had now turned solidly white with electoral defeat in 1986. Why? Why, with so favorable a past, was Andrews unable to extend his long legislative career? Why was a person who won reelection eight times to the House unable to win reelection once to the Senate? Most senators win reelection; Mark Andrews did not. Why not?

The phenomenon of congressional incumbency has attracted an enormous amount of attention from congressional scholars in recent years—more, perhaps than any other single subject. From David Mayhew, with his pioneering inquiries, to Morris Fiorina and Gary Jacobson, with their influential theories, political scientists have sought to explain "the decline of the marginals" and the increasing "power of incumbency."[4] Most of the empirical analysis has proceeded at the aggregate level—using sophisticated statistical methods to generalize about the electoral performance of a large number of legislators over a long period of time. Typically, scholars have tried to explain the increasing reelection success of incumbent *House* members by weighing a sizable number of candidate, constituency, and national variables. Studies of senatorial incumbency have been strictly a second thought and are only now coming into their own. Leading examples are John Hibbing and John Alford's cross-chamber and cross-state explorations, Alan Abramowitz's study of Senate election outcomes in 1988, and Mark Westlye's analysis of the intensity of Senate campaigns.[5] These Senate studies, like their House counterparts, are primarily cross-sectional, large scale, and statistical.

This book could not have been written without the existing corpus of incumbency-related research; we shall refer to it frequently for guidance. But this study takes a different tack. It focuses on a single incumbent senator, and it follows that senator's activities over time. When an incumbent legislator fails to win reelection, it probably means that something worth looking at has happened between elections. In the case of an incumbent senator, it strongly suggests that there is a six-year success-to-failure story to tell; a six-year story is quite likely to be complicated. It needs a framework our existing studies of incumbency cannot supply. It needs a sequential perspective and a deliberate focus on the entire interelection period. A study of one senator can bring that perspective and that focus to the study of incumbency. Although one senator's journey from success to failure may not allow us to generalize, the approach may encourage students of incumbency to add the analysis of journeys to the analysis of outcomes.[6]

A sequential interelection perspective calls for a sequential interelection idea. This book takes as its guiding idea the notion of a career. It takes for its analytic focus a single six-year slice of one senator's political career. And it provides—with some attention to antecedents—a narrative account of the circumstances, events, activities, and decisions of that six-year career slice. In broadest outline, our narrative follows the typical six-year pattern, both sequential and cyclical, in which a senator's original concern for election gives way to a special attentiveness to policy matters and then flows back again to a preoccupation with reelection. This campaigning-governing-campaigning sequence gives a structure—both topical and chronological—to the chapters that follow. Taken together, the chapters trace the course of one senatorial career from its highest point of electoral victory to its lowest point of electoral defeat.

To emphasize the separable activities of campaigning and governing is to remind ourselves, also, of the essential bifurcation of all senatorial careers. In reality, each senator pursues two careers, one in the home constituency where success depends on campaign activity and constituent support, and one in Washington, D.C., where success depends on governing activity and legislative accomplishment. These two careers are pursued simultaneously—sometimes separately, and sometimes in relationship to one another. Our narrative takes account of

Mark Andrews's career in both respects. We shall think of him as pursuing a constituency career in North Dakota and a legislative career in Washington. And we shall examine these mini-careers both separately and as they affect one another. Our hope is that in both respects, we can illuminate the course of Mark Andrews's six-year senatorial career from its time of success to its time of failure.

REPRESENTATIVE AND CONSTITUENCY

My introduction to Mark Andrews and his constituency came in mid-October of 1980, during a 350-mile campaign swing through south-central North Dakota. Some of the most salient features of the state were easy to see. Its population density of 9.4 people per square mile makes North Dakota the sixth most rural state in the nation. It is a place of few people and much land, of small towns and vast distances, of farms and ranches. With one-quarter of its people engaged in farming or ranching, it is, in Andrews's words, "the most agriculture-dependent state in the union, [agriculture being] responsible for four-fifths of the value of all goods produced." [7]

It seems natural and fitting, therefore, that North Dakota's longtime representative was himself a farmer. Mark Andrews, his 1981 biography tells us,

> operates a farm established by his grandfather in 1881 near Mapleton, North Dakota. Principal crops include wheat, sugar beets, sunflowers, corn and soy beans. Also operates a seed cleaning plant and a feed lot. Cited by Agricultural Extension Service as "one of the best farmers in North Dakota."

He graduated from North Dakota State University with a degree in agronomy, and his private and civic life have been closely intertwined with agriculture ever since. During his years in the Senate, his farming operations were managed by his son. But Mark Andrews made his home at "the farm," and he kept a close weather-eye on its operation. "It's my name that's been on the notes and always has," he says.[8] His incumbency was lubricated and strengthened by his occupational affinities with a large number of his constituents.

Recent studies of Senate incumbency point out the effect of state size on electoral success. Small state incumbents, it is agreed, have a greater likelihood of reelection than incumbents from large states. Among the reasons for this, researchers emphasize, is the greater ability of small state incumbents to make "direct contact" with their constituents. One study concludes:

Compared to their counterparts in populous states, constituents in lightly populated states are much more likely to report having met personally with their Senator and/or with a member of the Senator's staff, to having received mail from the Senator and/or to knowing someone who has met the Senator.[9]

With a 1980 population of only 653,000, North Dakota certainly qualified as a "lightly populated state," in which the opportunity for direct constituent contact—in all its forms—was ever present for its senators.

My first full day of acquaintance with Mark Andrews was a prototypical day of direct and close contact with his constituents. The congressman, his staff aide Bill Wright, and I drove through farmland and prairie to campaign stops in Linton (pop. 1,695), Ashley (pop. 1,236), Lehr (pop. 287), and Edgeley (pop. 888). In the car, there was a flow of farm talk. "We've still got a hundred acres of our beets to dig. If the rain out west moves east, we won't be able to do it. Those thirty ton combines will just churn up the mud." Or, "I wanted you to see some of this rich farmland. We may have forty-below-zero weather and no rain in some parts, but we also have some of the most productive agricultural land in the country." Farm talk, however, shifted smoothly to political talk.

"The votes are far between," Andrews mused, as he described the political landscape.

> We're going to the most Republican part of the state. It's mostly German-Russian—people who left Germany, went to Russia, and then came here. The northern part of the state is more Democratic and the southern part more Republican. They were settled by different people at different points in time. The north was settled by the Great Northern [Railroad]. The southern part was settled by the Northern Pacific. The Great Northern brought in Norwegians; the Northern Pacific brought in Russians, Germans.... Up to a few years ago, there were several German-language newspapers down here. You'll hear a lot of German accents. They are very conservative. The [state] senator from this district ran against me four years ago in the primary. He's a John Bircher. He thought I was a wobbly liberal. But these people are very Republican. If I don't get 75 percent from this area, I'm in trouble.

We left Bismarck to attend a luncheon in Linton (Emmons County), caught an afternoon coffee break in Ashley (McIntosh County), attended a small meeting in Lehr (Logan County), and ended with a Republican rally in the evening in the LaMoure County town of Edgeley. As the electoral maps (especially Figure A-2) make clear, the people of these four counties were among his strongest supporters.

OBSERVATIONS AND REFLECTIONS:
NORTH DAKOTA, OCTOBER 1980

The late afternoon meeting in Lehr seemed to me to epitomize the close representational relationship I found between Andrews and his rural-agricultural constituency. That meeting made a deep and lasting impression on me. In the paragraphs that follow, I shall reproduce my notes describing it.

Lehr is the kind of little one-street town you spot off the highway by its water tower and a cluster of trees. It has a bank, a cafe, a general store, a grocery store, an insurance agency, and a Quonset hut for a community hall. As we get out of the car, Mark says, "Remember the rally we had over there in that hall? It was the last rally of one of my campaigns—I forget which year. They had that place packed with people—must have been a thousand people. It was a great rally." We walk across the street to Krueger's Cafe, up a couple of steps, and in. He is met by a man who greets him, saying, "You're among farmers here."

The cafe is one square room—it has six tables in the center and on the left side. It has five booths running down the right side of the room. And in the back left corner is a counter. Mark shakes hands with the men seated at the tables and gives each one his postcard-sized handout with the recipe for "Mary's bran muffins" on one side and his family's picture on the other. (Mary is his wife.) "Let me give you one of Mary's bran muffin recipes. . . . We're campaigning with these this year." There are about fifteen farmers and local businessmen there, plus Pete, the state senator from the thirtieth legislative district—the one who ran against Mark. Pete greets Mark, and then says to Bill Wright, "I didn't know you were going to be in Linton for lunch." Bill says, "It was a last minute thing." In the car coming over, Bill had said, "Bob [a Linton businessman] organized the luncheon, and he wouldn't invite Pete to anything if he could help it."

The men are sitting around, mostly in overalls, some with caps, one with a big cowboy hat. Some have sport shirts. They are drinking coffee and eating large homemade raisin cookies which the waitress heaps on a plate in the center of each table. Mark sits down at a center table, his back to the counter, and they start chatting about the sunny October weather, about our itinerary for the day, and about "that great rally" next door in the Quonset hut. Other people drift in—two elderly women and an elderly couple. He gets up and greets each one. "Let me give you one of Mary's bran muffin recipes." To the elderly woman, he says, "And there's a picture of the family on the other side." They smile and sit down in one of the booths. The elderly couple stops and the gentleman says, "We thank you for the letter you sent us on our sixtieth anniversary." "That's quite an accomplishment," Andrews says. "Are you still sticking with him after all these years?" he asks the woman. She smiles and says yes. They take a table toward the back. The mood is good.

I take a look around. There is a pinball machine in one corner of the cafe. On the left-hand wall, there are several signs tacked up—an advertisement for Eureka Aerial Sales, a crop spraying outfit. There are two calendars—a big one from the Central Dakota Bank with a picture of some ducks taking off from a marsh, a little one from Ashley Livestock Sales with a picture of a farmyard. The counter is filled with tacked-up notices and signs—most prominently I see "23rd Annual Buffalo Supper" in nearby Kulm alongside two auction notices.

Mark Andrews is a big man—about 6'5", 220 pounds. He has a big crop of silver hair, a paunch, and a soft voice. He is a commanding presence there in the center of the room, and still he seems totally relaxed. He wears a blue polyester suit, white shirt, striped tie. He's a little soft looking to have come right from harvesting. But he looks like he could get back into a farmer's mold pretty quick. He looks, that is, like what he is—a farmer who has been an active politician for eighteen years, but who keeps in close touch with his farm and with farming in general.

He starts talking naturally and slowly, about how important the election is to North Dakota and how important it is to have a farmer in the Senate. "With Milt Young [R-N.D.] and Henry Bellmon [R-Okla.] leaving, I'll be the only farmer in the United States Senate. It's important to North Dakota, the most agricultural state in the union, to have a farmer in there, but it's also important to the country to have someone in there that understands farm export problems." Then he makes a strong pitch for the Republican who is running for Congress to replace him. "Jim Smykowski is a farmer, too. He holds bank notes, he has met a payroll. He's a good family man. He knows what it's all about." (Smykowski's opponent is North Dakota tax commissioner and former Andrews opponent Byron Dorgan.)

Pete, the state senator, asks about the grain embargo. Mark says that it was unfair to farmers, hurts North Dakota, and should be lifted.

> In North Dakota, we either farm or we farm the farmers—there's no doubt about that. If they had embargoed everything, farmers would have gone along with it. They are as patriotic as anyone else. But they continued shipping fertilizer to Russia till some of us stopped it. And they are still shipping Caterpillar tractors to Russia so they can farm better. How silly can you get? Do you think the Russians have been hurt by the embargo? They haven't. They've been picking up grain here and there from other countries. We had these phony CIA reports telling us how much the Russians were hurting. The evidence they gave was that there was no beef in the market. Now, any farmer knows that if you can't get grain to feed your cattle, the first thing you do is rush 'em to market to get the best price you

can. The only people that are hurting are the American farmers. The big companies, Cargil and Continental Grain, were indemnified for their losses, but not the farmers and the farm implement dealers.

Someone asks what the chances are of lifting the embargo. He says a lot of people are trying. "I'll do my best. What we have to explain to our friends in the East is that the embargo hurts them, too. For every $1 billion worth of farm exports we send abroad, we create 15,000 jobs off the farm. That should help persuade members of Congress who come from the cities."

Someone else asks, "Is there going to be a need for food in the world? How about China?" "There certainly is," he says.

We've got to go where the people are. That means Russia, China, and Southeast Asia. Do you know which countries have been hurt most by the embargo: the third world countries. In those countries, people don't have enough food or adequate nutrition. How do you think a mother in one of those countries feels about the great humanitarian United States when her child dies of malnutrition? We are supposed to be the country that feeds the hungry in the world. But these third world countries don't look at us that way now.

Someone else asks him about the recent $20,000 Department of Agriculture award given to an employee of the department for helping the consumer. Another man whistles, "$20,000?" Andrews replies:

Yes, he got an award for turning the Agriculture Department into a consumer agency. That's typical of the problem we've got with the Carter bunch. They're more interested in the consumer than the farmer. They ought to be more interested in the production end of things. We've gotten very good in recent times at unloading the wagon, but we've forgotten how to load the wagon. We've got to provide incentives for farmers to produce. Instead, we have too many government bureaucrats looking over our shoulders. I got an amendment passed this year to get the FTC off the backs of the local co-ops.

He talks briefly about the amendment.

Then he turns to a story about "the crazy environmentalists" who held up for months the construction of a generating plant on the Platte River for fear that its warm water discharge would raise the temperature of the river 250 miles downstream in an environmentally sensitive area. He said:

The water would flow in an area where the whooping crane flies over—going south once a year and north once a year. These environmental experts made the case that as the whooper flies over and looks down at the water he might be "discombooboolated" if that water had lost its cooling power. Basin Electric had to pay $7.5 million to take care of the whooper.

Several of his listeners wag their heads in disbelief.

Someone else mentions the problem with blackbirds eating the sunflower crop. Mark asks them how they are dealing with it, and two or three farmers chime in. One has a cannon set to go off at intervals to drive them out of his field. Mark says, "The problem with that is you drive them into the next farmer's field." Another one says he drops poisoned corn into the field. Mark says, "That only kills the ones that eat the corn. Besides, if you have weeds in the field, the birds can't get at the corn." Another says he went out and shot at a big flock with a shotgun and killed three hundred of them with one blast. Mark says, "The trouble with that, of course, is that it's illegal. And you can't get enough of 'em anyway." There is a technical discussion about poisons. Mark says "One problem is that the blackbird is officially designated a migrating bird and you can't shoot it. If we could get it reclassified as a predator bird, we could kill it." Someone pipes up, "Why don't we get it classified as a bug and then we could spray it with thorazene." Everyone laughs. Mark follows up.

> We need more research; and I got $750,000 for blackbird research put in the agricultural appropriations bill this year. That's an interesting story. Several years ago I got some money for nutrition research at the NDSU [North Dakota State University] nutrition lab in Grand Forks. We know more about pig nutrition than we do about human nutrition. One of the things they found was that eating bran lowers your blood cholesterol. So, you see, the bran muffin recipe I'm handing out has a reason behind it. I showed the results to the Capitol physician, and he checked into it. As a result, we've got eleven members of Congress on bran muffins. And their cholesterol is dropping. One member was so pleased that I traded him my bran muffin information for $750,000 worth of research on blackbirds and sunflowers. Research on human nutrition—that's an example of good spending, not bad spending.

The guy in the cowboy hat asks: "What do you think about Castro letting these thirty-three Americans go? Don't you think he's trying to help Carter get reelected?" Mark says he hasn't got all the facts on who they are; but he thinks Castro has his own reasons and doesn't know what they are. He dodges.

Then a farmer sitting next to Mark who had not yet cracked a smile—a guy in bib overalls, with a Mobil Oil cap on—says, "Maybe we should get rid of that EPA." That's all. The comment seems to have been triggered by the whooping crane story. Mark says:

Maybe you've got a point there. What I think we should do is make the EPA issue an economic impact statement whenever they issue an environmental regulation. We have environmental impact statements; why shouldn't we have economic impact statements? Then we'd see what the cost of some of these crazy environmentalist policies really is.

The man nods, satisfied.

Another man gets up. "I've got to go." Mark says, "I appreciate your taking time out from work to come by. It's good to be with you." Vern Scherbanske, the banker who organized the meeting, says to the farmer, who has reached the doorway, "How about taking a Mark Andrews bumper sticker?" He takes it. Vern laughs: "The next time you come to town, I want to see it on your truck."

One of the elderly ladies comes up and asks, "Where can I get the right bran to make the muffins?" Gene Grenz, the general store owner, says, "I'll show you where to get it." Mark says, "Gene has everything in that store." Gene says to Mark, "Tell them about the underwear." Mark says, "I came down here duck hunting one time and I needed some long underwear. I went into Gene's store and asked him if he had any. He looked and found it." Everyone chuckles. Gene says, "Are you coming to the rally this year?" Mark says "I'm pretty well scheduled for that date, but we'll see what we can do. That was some rally." The mood is good. People shake hands and leave.

The candidate crosses the street to visit with Scherbanske, then back to the other side to visit in Grenz's store. As we wait, Bill Wright exclaims: "Did you see Pete? He just sat there while Mark talked about trading with Russia and China. Four years ago, he would have hit the roof. What a change!" "They are talkers," says Wright as we drive away. "It's neighborly country." And Andrews says: "That's what's fun about campaigning in North Dakota. You never know what part of the grab bag you are going to get." He laughs. "After I spent all that time pushing Jim Smykowski, did you see the guy drive off with the Byron Dorgan sticker on his truck?" And a little later, he reflects on the Cuban refugee question. "It would have been easy for me to say Castro thinks Carter is weaker than Reagan and wants to help him. They wanted me to say that. I won't pander to people's prejudices like that. If I have to do it, the job isn't worth it."

Finally, a few miles down the highway, he closes the book on the Lehr visit. "They'll say, 'ya, he vas here.' Tomorrow, everyone will say, 'Mark Andrews was here.' "

The visit in Krueger's Cafe conveyed a strong and comfortable sense of identification between a representative and his constituents. By his presence and his demeanor, he was saying, "I am one of you, I am working for you"; and by their presence and their demeanor, they were acknowledging—or so it seemed to me—that "he is one of us, he is working for us." He was not a backslapper, presenting himself as "one of the boys." Nor did any such convivial display seem called for. The mood was low key; the communication back and forth flowed naturally; and there was an easy exchange of the constituents' concerns and the representative's responsiveness, of the constituents' respect and the representative's experience. This sense of identification provides an underpinning for constituent trust. And it is this constituent trust that every representative ultimately seeks to achieve. Trust is that benefit of the doubt or that predisposition to believe which, when held by a large enough number of constituents, keeps representatives secure in their job and free to exercise a good deal of personal judgment in performing it.

Constituent trust, however, cannot be taken for granted. It must be constantly rebuilt, renewed, and rewon. In rural, small town constituencies, trust is typically won and held by a person-to-person home style— by frequent and direct personal contact.[10] Andrews's trip was designed to maintain a sense of identification between himself and his constituents through a series of face-to-face meetings on their home ground. He wanted to reassure his listeners that he remained in touch and in tune with them. As he pointed out, his visit would have a ripple effect in the community, reaching those who had not seen him and reaffirming his reputation for accessibility.

It was a trip he had taken often—"seven or eight times or more," he estimated in the case of Ashley. On the way to Linton he ticked off each person he expected to see at the luncheon, with a personal comment about each. On the way home from Edgeley he said, "Edgeley was part of my original district, so I knew almost everyone there. It was like coming home to your family." He was able to recall at least two previous noteworthy visits to tiny Lehr. He seemed to be following a familiar, hands-on routine of constituency visits. He gave every outward sign, too, of enjoying what he was doing. "I like what we are doing here better than I like what I do in Washington," he exclaimed as we approached Lehr on the way from Ashley.

Over the years, I had observed more than twenty campaigns for the House of Representatives at close range, and I had not seen an incumbent House member I deemed—at first glance—to be any more closely attuned to his constituency and any more solidly entrenched there than Mark Andrews. Everything I saw on that trip promised the continuation of a longstanding love affair between the people of North Dakota and their statewide representative. The relationship, indeed, seemed a virtual model of representation in a democracy. For this observer, the meeting at Lehr froze in time a representational relationship that existed in 1980 and seemed so well grounded and so tight a fit as to be indestructible.

THE SENATE CAMPAIGN: 1980

Most politicians' career-in-the-constituency proceeds through two identifiable stages: an expansionist stage followed by a protectionist stage. During the first stage, they reach out to build a winning electoral coalition. Voters and interests must be found and assembled into a voting majority. The earliest goal is simply to gather enough support to win; but the expansionist phase continues until the supportive constituency is large enough and solid enough to secure several reelections. By then, a politician's goal is not to add more voters and interests to his or her majority, but to maintain the electoral support that has already been developed. In this protectionist phase, the politician is less likely to gamble or take campaign risks and more likely to think and act conservatively.[11] Circumstances may, of course, throw this sequence into reverse. But typically, we suggest, a time of building is followed by a time of consolidation. To the degree that consolidation works, continued reelection should follow.

Mark Andrews, when I first saw him, was clearly in the protectionist stage of his constituency career and had been for a number of years. He had undergone two expansionist periods. First, he built constituency support in the eastern half of the state. Later he digested the entire state. In that later period, Andrews's Senate predecessor, Milton Young, had said of the congressman that "he does work hard to maintain contacts with his constituents" and prophesied, further, that this constituency effort would soon make Andrews "the most powerful figure in North Dakota politics."[12] In October of 1980, it looked like Young's prophecy was coming true. Andrews was holding a steady 73 percent to 21 percent lead over his Democratic opponent, and there was not the remotest possibility that he could lose. He was running a campaign of consolidation. That is precisely what the visit to Lehr and the other farming communities was all about.

Consolidation was the purpose too of all the other events I attended during my visit—particularly the three (Edgeley, Washburn, Dickinson) Republican rallies. Andrews's statewide schedule had been constructed to accommodate, as well as he could, the wishes of the party. The party's wish was to hold a rally in as many of the state's fifty-three legislative districts as possible. At each rally Andrews assumed center stage as the head of the ticket, the featured speaker, and the spokesman for the party. His, and only his, introduction produced a standing ovation. His speech contained broad anti-Carter rhetoric—"Let's get that bunch of Georgia characters out of Washington" and "the only thing standing in the way of Jimmy Carter's second term is his first term." He praised Republican presidential candidate Ronald Reagan for his emphasis on economic incentives and a strong national defense. He showered praise on each and every one of the Republican candidates, statewide and local, ending always with the engaging comment: "If you vote for all these other good candidates, I may just slip in there, too." He spoke to and for the party faithful.

In his speeches, as well as in his visits, he touched upon the state's major interests. Everywhere he reminded his listeners that "North Dakota is the most agricultural state in the nation." And he would display, in passing, his familiarity with its major commodities and their associated problems—from technology to price levels to the interest groups that promoted and/or protected them. Informally, he engaged in what he called "neighboring and talking about the crops, the interest rates and the weather." [13]

Everywhere, too, he alluded to the state's energy concerns—from the historic importance of rural electric cooperatives to the more recent development of oil and lignite coal resources. With its 3,700 producing oil wells and its 22 million tons of coal per year, North Dakota had major energy interests. In Dickinson, Andrews spoke of the western oil patch; in Washburn, he mentioned the Great Plains coal gassification plant at nearby Beulah. (His district staff director had driven me out beforehand to see this plant, which makes a coal-based synthetic liquid fuel.) In agricultural and energy matters alike, he portrayed North Dakota as a producing and an exporting state, burdened with all the uncertainties thereof. Several times, too, he mentioned the need for water development, specifically an extremely large, long-term water storage project known as the Garrison Diversion Unit. To underline all these concerns further, he leveled a drumbeat of criticism at "the environmentalists," whose desire for regulations and controls posed a standing threat to his state's delicate economy.

Most striking to the outside observer, however, were not his routine partisan sallies or his intimations of economic problems, but rather the way in which his speeches continually reinforced the bonds of identification between himself and his listeners. As in Lehr, he presented himself largely in terms that said: "I am one of you, I am working for you."

In the western ranching town of Dickinson, he drew on his common experience with ranchers to attack high interest rates.

> All I can speak of, from experience, is as a cattle feeder. I come out every fall and I buy those darn healthy, good doin', wonderful—overpriced—Dickinson calves [*laughter*]. And I go to my banker and I've got to pay him interest on those calves,

even if they're doin' good in the feed lot. We're sellin' 'em right now and we've been payin' 14 percent interest on 'em. And if that isn't cost of production, then maybe I've forgotten what it's all about. Anybody who says high interest rates are the answer to inflation just doesn't know what's going on in this country. It doesn't work in feeding cattle; it sure doesn't work in business; and I know it doesn't work for a working person either [*applause*].

In Edgeley, he found a different locally related link to his listeners to bind his experience to theirs. He elaborated on his amendment (mentioned briefly in Lehr) to "get the Federal Trade Commission off the backs of the [Rural Electric] co-ops."

You ought to see that quarter-page advertisement in the *Washington Post* saying, "Don't vote for that terrible Andrews amendment. He's fronting for the Fortune 500, for the big bad corporations—GTA, Farmland, Land O'Lakes, CF Industries." On the floor, Jim Scheuer from New York City said, "They don't need the protection of Capper-Volstead. They needed it when they wore bib overalls, but they don't wear them anymore." I had him. I got up and told the members about Claire Sandness in LaMoure, head of Land O'Lakes, who puts on his bib overalls and goes out and milks his cows in the morning. Jim Scheuer sat down and we won by a hundred votes. All because of Claire Sandness right over here in [the next town of] LaMoure. I had him. And it's all in the *Congressional Record* [*applause*].

In Washburn, Andrews found his identifying link by reaching into the past. "I look around here," he said,

and I see Dave Robinson, whose family helped settle the Dakota Territory. My grandparents came here, too, a hundred years ago to settle in Mapleton. It was the first white settlement along the Maple River. They came just three years after Custer got clobbered. He was that eastern general who was told by the eastern establishment that if he came out here and clobbered some indians . . . and brought eastern reporters with him . . . it would make him president. . . . But the Robinsons and the Andrews came to build and to make the state better. And we have made it better.

In Dickinson, he elaborated on the "we share a pioneer heritage" theme in a way that made his political point. He began, "We've really got to get back to the idea of incentives in our society. This part of the state was settled about a hundred years ago—a little more than that in the eastern part of the state." And he swung into an illustrative story.

When they laid out the Northern Pacific main line between Fargo and Bismarck, the surveyors found one person, one white person living out there, a woman. A woman by the name of Mary Bishop lived there, in a little log cabin on the side of the Maple River where the railroad was going to cross it. Mary Bishop had been there in that cabin since 1870 or 1871. What a wonderful woman she must have been. Her great-grandson now is farming about four miles from our son. She later became postmistress of Mapleton. But she was out there because she believed in her own ability and in the future of North Dakota.

What kind of a time would she have had if she had to have some inspector come in and tell her how to carve the half-moon in her outhouse door [*laughter*] or where to locate the path, or how you had to lay down the logs? Or if one of these environmentalists got hold of her . . . he would have convinced her that there was no way she could survive out there on the prairie. In fact, if the environmentalists would have gotten hold of our grandparents before they came out to North Dakota, they would have told them all to leave the state the way it was.

Yet they came, they built, they worked together. They had incentives because they were building a better place for their children and their grandchildren. And they turned this state into a productive area that supports, today, three quarters of a million people. And you know, sometimes it's important to get back to basics, to take a look at what went before. We've got to get back to basics, now, a hundred years after our people settled this area.

In all of his speeches Andrews wove a web of community feeling between himself and his audience. They were not partisan bonds. All of it seemed perfectly natural, a matter of consolidating longstanding relationships rather than reaching out to establish new ones. Although the context was less intimate and the mood less palpable than had been the case at Lehr, the intent, the method, and (I thought) the effect were the same.

I have gone to great lengths to emphasize and to illustrate the feeling of close identification I discerned between Mark Andrews and his constituents, because I wish to make a larger and more important point. Namely, this kind of relationship—the "I am one of you, I am working for you"; "He is one of us, he is working for us" relationship—is one of special significance in North Dakota.

Politicians everywhere try to establish and to nurture personal bonds of identification with constituents. But in some contexts it is simply not possible in any broad way. Senators from large states with heterogeneous interests—such as Pennsylvania or Ohio—speak of their states as virtual microcosms of the entire United States.[14] They can neither build nor lay claim to tight bonds of experience and fellow feeling with very many people in their state. And their constituents do not expect it. In North Dakota, however, this kind of relationship is both possible and expected. I do not mean to say that such an expectation would be difficult to meet or would be resisted. Far from it. The politics of identification is, in every sense, the North Dakota norm. And it is made easier for politicians to follow because the state is small, relatively homogeneous, and somewhat isolated.[15]

The norm of identification is also made easier to follow because North Dakotans think of their state as something quite special. *Microcosm* is the last word Mark Andrews would use to describe his home state. "Our roots, our values, our traditions are uniquely North Dakotan," he says.[16] Publicly and privately, as we campaigned in 1980, he spoke always of his state's distinctiveness—its early settlement patterns, its ethnic heritages, its economic history, the variety of its soils and its crops, the harshness of its climate. As he talked, he painted a picture of North Dakota as a community—a distinctive community, one with a very strong sense of place, one for which people developed and professed strong attachments, one from which people could take emotional sustenance as well as political bearings. It was a community that could easily be seen as the measure of all things.[17] He pictured a community in which a strong feeling about the importance of "us" could take root and flourish.

Where "us" becomes especially salient, so does the notion of "them," of people who are outside the community. "We like to say that forty below zero keeps out the riff-raff," says the state's veteran senator, Quentin Burdick. "But we bristle when others attack our state."[18] Listening to Mark Andrews in 1980, one could pick up traces of an "us-and-them" view of the world—the "eastern general" from "the eastern establishment" with his "eastern reporters" who came through the state and got clobbered next door, the congressman "from New York City" whom he bested on the House floor, the House members from "the big cities" who don't understand farm export problems, the "crazy environmentalists" who don't understand the production problems of a crop-producing, energy-producing state. Publicly, he spoke of the visiting political scientist as "an outlander," though privately he would soften his language by telling his friends, "He's like us." There was nothing strident about this. But it was part of a way of thinking that sharpened the sense of "us" and the conviction that being perceived as "one of us" who would "work for us" was crucial to a politician's success in North Dakota.

Andrews's campaign literature embodied this theme. The cover of his main brochure read simply, "Mark Andrews and the People of North Dakota." It shunned claims of "leadership" or "effectiveness" or "vision" in favor of the claim of identification. The brochure consisted of nineteen annotated pictures of Andrews with the widest variety of his constituents. It was modeled after his 1978 campaign brochure, "People with Andrews," which depended just as heavily on images of identification.

SUPPORT AND STRATEGY

Andrews thought of his electoral support in similarly inclusive terms. When asked to describe his "most ardent supporters," he answered, "The people with an interest in agriculture. I'm one of the few farmers in Congress. My name is on a lot of farm legislation. Farmers know I have their interest at heart." He made no distinctions by party. His top district staffer explained that Andrews's first foray into politics had been a close but losing campaign for governor in 1962—a race in which he had been a "self-described 'young Turk' [who had] successfully fought the Republican establishment for a gubernatorial nomination." [19] The staffer went on to explain that Andrews's political strength transcended party. "While he's a Republican, he has always campaigned separately from the Republican party. They haven't helped him all that much. North Dakota is agricultural. He's been elected because he works hard for the farmer and his interest. He knows farming; he lives on a farm; and he's the only working farmer in Congress." Neither Andrews nor his aide thought of the Republican party organization as his primary constituency. If this perception hinted at any difficulty with the Republican organization, nothing of the sort manifested itself in 1980. The aide concluded that Andrews's strength was "not in pockets, but statewide."

Endorsements by Democratic-oriented groups gave evidence of a constituency reach far broader than his core supporters. "The National Farmers Union and the Rural Electrical Co-ops are the backbone of the Democratic party in North Dakota," he said. Yet he had just been named Man of the Year by the national organization of rural electrical co-ops and endorsed by the North Dakota group. [20] He had also won the endorsement of the North Dakota Teachers Association—a first for his career.

> I got a contribution from the North Dakota Nurses Association, and when I looked around to see who else got their award, there was George McGovern [D-S.D.], Frank Church [D-Idaho],

John Culver [D-Iowa], and Birch Bayh [D-Ind.]. There were three Republicans, Jack Javits [N.Y.], Mac Mathias [Md.], and myself. I have no idea why they gave it to me. But here I am wandering around North Dakota with endorsements from the electrical cooperatives, the teachers, and the nurses. I don't know what people will think.

With the exception of the Farmers Union, no single recognizable group seemed outside his statewide circle of support.

In their endorsement of him, the editors of the state's largest newspaper, the *Forum* (Fargo), wrote:

> Andrews did not win reelection to the House over the years because of the help of a great party machine. He won because he has earned the respect of the voters because he is cognizant of the needs of this state. . . . [He] does not fall into any single political category. . . . He is first of all a congressman who wants to represent North Dakota to the best of his ability, and he recognizes that North Dakota voters fall into no one particular pattern. . . . Andrews has a knack for politics, just as he has a knack for handling legislative matters on Capitol Hill." [21]

In the results of the July 1980 survey Andrews commissioned, there was plenty of evidence of widespread support for his behavior in both places.[22] Sixty-nine percent of the electorate could name him as their congressman; and 95 percent could recognize him. In response to a "favorability" question he was ranked as "one of the best" (36 percent) or "favorable" (53 percent) by nearly 90 percent of the electorate and "unfavorable" by only 6 percent. He was, his pollster summarized, "a well known and popular public official."

His "job rating," too, was favorable. And it provides evidence of support patterns that do not vary widely across categories. Residents from the western part of the state—who were also not part of his original House constituency—and self-described independents were slightly less well disposed toward Andrews. But no group—and this held for age and income groupings as well—seemed to have any strong criticism of his performance in office.

Respondents were also asked to rank Andrews on a 5-point scale where 1 meant "He doesn't care about people like me" and 5 meant "He cares about people like me." Sixty-nine percent ranked him 5 (43 percent) or 4 (26 percent), while 10 percent ranked him 1 (6 percent) or 2 (4 percent). This strong sense that he cared surely helped to underpin the sense of identification he was trying to convey. So did the voters' strongly expressed (71 percent) "likelihood of voting for a Senate candidate who was a farmer"—ranked at 5 on the scale by 51 percent

TABLE 1-1   Mark Andrews Job Rating, July 1980

	All	Republican	Democrat	Independent	East	West	Earns Living Farming
Excellent	21%	28%	20%	17%	25%	15%	22%
Above average	31	34	29	33	32	30	34
Average	40	34	36	44	37	45	37
Fair	4	2	7	3	2	6	5
Poor	2	1	5	2	1	3	1
Not sure	3	1	3	2	4	1	1

Source: Dresner, Morris and Tortorello Research, "A Study of Voter Attitudes in North Dakota," July 1980.

and at 4 by another 20 percent. "As a farmer himself," echoed one of his campaign handouts, "Mark knows the problems that affect an agricultural state like ours. He thinks like one of us . . . because he is."

In a strategic sense, Rep. Mark Andrews was running the same kind of a campaign he had always run. He was, therefore, campaigning like a House member in a House member's constituency, although the prize was a seat in the Senate. "I don't worry about the campaign," he explained.

> It will take care of itself. We will do just what we've been doing—the same thing we do during a Lincoln Day recess— drive around, hold meetings, meet with the media, make speeches, get to as much of the state as we can. . . . If I were running for the House, we'd be doing exactly the same thing we are doing now . . . and we'd have the same scheduling problems. There are fifty-three counties in the state and every legislative candidate has to hit as many of them as he can. We won't touch them all . . . but if you don't try, people will say, "He's a big shot. He doesn't care about the people anymore."

Campaign patterns, we might guess, do not change much when the constituency remains the same, regardless of the office being sought. In the smallest states, that is, constituency effects have a greater impact on campaigning than office effects. Senate campaigns in the smallest states will tend to look a lot like the House campaign in those states.

Still, there are some office effects. In Andrews's case, there was a small but perceptible media effect. It registered not by way of free media—in three days, he saw only one reporter, for twenty minutes— but by way of an increase in paid media. "We will spend three times as much as we did in our House races," he said. "I ran [for the House] on a budget of $100,000-$125,000. We'll spend at least $450,000, $250,000 of it on media. That's a difference." He was paying the money, however, not to any big time, outside consultants, but to an ad agency in Fargo, "the same one we've had ever since my first campaign."

A second small difference from his House campaign, he explained, was the decision to pay a few staffers. But he did not alter the nature of his staff. Before this, he said,

> I always had a volunteer campaign committee—my brother-in-law, my uncle, my son, and a few of my old fraternity brothers.... This year, I have hired a campaign manager, a writer, and a field coordinator. And the coordinator has hired five people, for one month, to work for him in different parts of the state, organizing groups, putting up lawn signs, that sort of thing. The three men are old friends of mine.... They have enough talent to stand this state on its ear, if they ran a hard campaign. They have too much talent for what we have them doing. They are paddling in the water, running a relaxing campaign.

Two of the three had already managed earlier Andrews campaigns. The payment of salaries did not seem to reflect much change in what was one more protectionist campaign of identification and consolidation.

The one important office effect on the campaign resulted from his opponent's decision to make Andrews's attempt to change offices the campaign's central issue. In the summer, the Democratic nominee, Kent Johanneson, ran a commercial in which he said:

> Mark Andrews' retirement from Congress shows his apparent lack of concern for protecting the seniority investment that the voters of North Dakota have made with him. By giving up his seat, North Dakotans are being asked to throw away 17 years of seniority and North Dakota's position on the Agriculture [sic] and Appropriations Committee.
>
> I can't believe Mr. Andrews would ask the state to pay this price to realize his ambition to become a freshman Senator at age 55. This notion puts one man's interests ahead of the best interests of 650,000 North Dakotans, and I would like you to help me reject this seniority sell-out.[23]

It was an argument that called attention to Andrews's exceptionally long House service and of his potential for accomplishment as a newcomer in a new institution.

Andrews's pollsters did not take their relatively unknown and inexperienced challenger seriously. They did, however, take his argument seriously; and they surveyed to see how it registered with prospective voters. They found that by large margins, voters felt that Andrews "has earned his chance to be a U.S. Senator" (69 percent), "would be a good U.S. Senator" (68 percent), and that "his experience in Congress will make him a good U.S. Senator" (77 percent).[24] They also found that by a margin of 61 percent to 23 percent, voters rejected the notion that it was Andrews's "ambition" rather than his desire to "do more in the Senate" that motivated him. North Dakotans seemed to view the move from House to Senate as a well-merited, well-motivated personal promotion. Furthermore, the office to which he aspired was vacant. It was probably helpful to him that he was not trying to unseat a well-established incumbent.

The challenger's charge of personal ambition raised, implicitly at least, a more fundamental institutional question: whether Andrews could accomplish more for his constituents in the Senate than in the House. The question has its roots in the most difficult decision of the Constitutional Convention in 1787—what James Madison called "the compromise between the opposite pretensions of large and small states."[25] The system of equal representation in the Senate was the price paid for agreement by the small states. The small states saw the Senate as their special place of institutional leverage and protection within the governmental structure. "There is a peculiarity in the federal constitution," Madison wrote later, which "lies in this, that one branch of the legislature is a representation of citizens; the other of the states: in the former, consequently, the larger states will have the most weight; in the latter, the advantage will be in favor of the smaller states."[26] The question for Mark Andrews's pollsters was whether or not North Dakota voters might see the Senate, still, as a protector of small state interests and view the congressman's move to the Senate in that light.

What they found was a good deal of ambiguity. "Which of the following statements," respondents were asked, "comes closest to your view": "Mark Andrews can do more to help North Dakota in the House by using his 17 years of seniority" or "Mark Andrews can do more to help North Dakota by using his congressional experience in the Senate"? By the barest of majorities (51 percent to 42 percent with 7 percent not sure), respondents chose the Senate alternative. Later in the survey, when asked point blank "Can Mark Andrews do more for the state of North Dakota in the House of Representatives or as a Senator?" the Senate alternative again drew 51 percent, with 35 percent opting for the House alternative and 14 percent not sure.

All in all, the voters seemed very willing to help Andrews move to a more prestigious office if he wanted to; but they were less strongly convinced that the change in offices would be to their advantage. On the other hand, they did not believe that he would be of any less service to them. They did not, it seems, make sharp distinctions between the House and Senate as institutions. They had no well-developed view of the Senate as a distinctive protector of small state interests. They would place the burden of proof equally, therefore, on the individual occupants of both offices as they went about the business of governing in the interests of North Dakota.[27]

Andrews labeled his opponent's charge "negative campaigning," "miserable campaigning," and "mudslinging," and he argued privately: "We're in the 70s [in the polls] and he's in the 20s" because of it.

> That kind of campaign doesn't go over in North Dakota. The last time it was tried was when Tom Kleppe ran against Quent Burdick. And it didn't work. My opponent had a thirty-minute television program ... it was too negative.... If he ran a positive campaign, we'd expect him to be up around 35 percent.

Andrews's answer to the charge was twofold: first, that it was not a matter of personal ambition and, second, that he could be more influential on behalf of North Dakota in the Senate than in the House. When the personal ambition charge came up, he recalled,

> I said the people of North Dakota would decide that. They are the ones who sent me to the House. Petitions started coming in from all over the state. It started in Medora, where the Republican State Committee voted unanimously to ask me to run. There was a consensus I should run.... The Republicans even offered to postpone their convention till I was able to make a decision.... Both senators from Montana had been House members. Both senators from South Dakota had been House members. Quentin Burdick [the other senator from North Dakota] had been a House member. So there was nothing uncommon about it.

As for influence, "A member of the Senate has more power than a House member," he said.

> Besides, the Democrats had done away with seniority [in the House] when they defeated the four committee chairmen. There's no seniority left in the House. The only perk I had was a view of the Capitol from my office, and that's a personal perk. I was the ranking member on an Appropriations Committee subcommittee; but I had no more staff than the day I went on the committee. Every Republican member gets the same. My House friendships will be even more useful to me on the Senate side. Jamie Whitten [D-Miss.] and Bill Natcher [D-Ky.]

and those people will be more helpful to me because they will know that I can help them on the Senate side.

He shared none of his constituents' ambiguity about the special institutional benefits that would accrue to his state. "The Senate delegation from North Dakota," he would tell people, "is as powerful as the Senate delegation from California." North Dakota senators, he told a reporter in Dickinson, "are part of an eleven-state coalition in the West on three issues—energy, agriculture, and water development.... That coalition can pool 22 percent of the Senate's vote on those issues." [28]

In his ads, Andrews swept past charges of misplaced ambition to argue the value of his experience. "The issue in the election," he claimed, "is which candidate has the necessary experience and background to best represent North Dakota in the place where we have the greatest potential for influence." And his ads ended, "If you vote against Mark Andrews, you're just guessing." His campaign button carried the confident slogan, "Today a Great Congressman; Tomorrow a Great Senator."

In 1980, Mark Andrews was a strong candidate facing what political scientists think of as an "unqualified" opponent[29] in "a low key" campaign.[30] "I never had any contact with my opponent during the campaign," he said afterward, "and he never called to congratulate me. Everybody but me thought I was going to win, so there was very little interest in the campaign. It came and went." In November, Andrews won 71 percent of the vote (see Figure A-5). It was the largest Senate win in North Dakota in forty-eight years and the second highest in the state's history. His campaign was not a contest, it was an exhibition.

OBSERVATIONS AND REFLECTIONS:
NORTH DAKOTA, 1982

From the beginning of his term in the Senate, Mark Andrews expressed his intention to keep on doing exactly the same things that had undergirded his long incumbency. In my first interview with the new senator, in March, I asked him whether he valued his new position—as so many former House members do—for its longer, six-year term. He completely rejected the idea. He answered:

I never gave the six-year term one minute's thought. People say to me, "Aren't you glad you're in for six years?" I say no. I always liked campaigning. I always won big in elections. I'll campaign as often as Senator as I did in the House and in exactly the same way. I was back there over the [Presidents'

Day] recess, traveled over the state and made fifteen speeches in five days. Campaigning is the best part of the job. It's the most fun.

His enthusiasm as well as his intentions pointed to more of the same constituency cultivation and more of the same success in his constituency career.

In October 1982, I returned to North Dakota to see for myself. I wanted to compare, as well as I could, the behavior and the outlook of the sitting senator with that of the campaigning House member. I wanted to see how much continuity there was with the picture I had formed two years earlier—a picture of close identification between a legislator and a broad constituency. Before we undertake our analysis of his governing activity in Washington, it will be helpful to our understanding of the story to describe at this point in the story that first, postcampaign, look at Sen. Mark Andrews at home.

During my two-day visit, we drove to the eastern (Valley City, Fargo), northeastern (Grand Forks), and central (Mandan) parts of the state. Andrews joined four Democrats—Sen. Quentin Burdick, Rep. Byron Dorgan, and two state legislators—in a panel discussion of health issues before the North Dakota State Nurses Association; Andrews gave a luncheon talk, "Congressional Issues and Small Business Success," to the Greater North Dakota Association; he gave a dinner speech on education to the Association of Special [Educational] Programs of Region Eight; and he held a press conference on farm issues to help the reelection campaign of Sen. Dave Durenberger, a Republican from neighboring Minnesota. He also attended the homecoming football game at his alma mater, North Dakota State University.

This time, of course, his talks were built around his governing experiences in the Senate, which were centered, naturally, on the work of the three Senate committees of which he had become a member—Agriculture, Appropriations, and Budget. As Andrews talked about a mix of national issues, a sharper sense of his moderate political philosophy came through than had in my 1980 visit. But—and this is the point to be made now—I had the same sense as before of his identification, both comfortable and strong, with a broad, statewide community. I saw no reason to believe that an equal measure of trust was not still being reciprocated by a solid cross-section of the people he represented. He remained, as far as I could tell, in the protectionist phase of a prospectively long political career.

There was certainly no diminishment of effort. He got out of a sickbed in Washington to make the trip home; and he battled a miserable condition of fever and food poisoning throughout the two days. But he met all his engagements. "In twenty years of campaigning," he said during the eighty-mile drive to the press conference, "I've never missed a meeting if I was home. And I told the [TV] crew that there was no way I was going to miss this one." He seemed every bit the same hardy farmer and the same determined representative I had seen two years before.

The trip provided more evidence of his deeply rooted association with the state's basic industry, agriculture. This time, farm talk was punctuated by trips back and forth from his farm home in Mapleton, about fifteen miles west of Fargo. "Andrews Farm," painted in black on a gray grain elevator, announces the farm's presence at the end of a long, flat dirt road, Cass County no. 15. In the distance, "the farm" looks like a tiny settlement, "a small town," as one aide calls it. It consists of twelve to fifteen buildings connected with the business of the farm, some of which are inhabited by the several families who work its 3,000 acres.

The farmhouse is an unpretentious white, ranch-style home, with a windbreak of trees in the rear and a view to the horizon in every other direction. With an estimated million dollars' worth of agricultural equipment, it is, says a local staffer, "a good-sized farm for the [Red River] Valley." While we were there, talk centered on the harvesting conditions in the various sections, quarter sections, and headlands and on the state of equipment repairs in the shop, on the dryer, or on the auger. Whenever we came within range, the senator used the car phone to talk with his son, the farm's manager, and with workers at various farm locations.

At his Grand Forks press conference, Andrews blended a devotion to agricultural price supports and a recognition of legislative practicalities. "I'm known in Congress as the individual who for twenty years has been pushing for the highest possible farm prices. . . . I've never had a farm bill that was as high as I wanted, but I always voted for the farm program that I thought was the best we could get." [31] People who hold out for price supports at 100 percent of parity, he says, "believe in the tooth fairy" or "pie in the sky" and are "pulling the wool over people's eyes." He advocated a measured but upbeat response to obvious farm problems. "As a farmer myself," he continued, "I know things aren't good out on the farm, but we're moving in the right direction." Besides, he added, "I'm not going out there and lead the charge saying farmers are going broke, because that puts more pressure on them to pay up. [The bankers] will just make the farmer buy COD instead of 'buy in the spring and pay in the fall.' "

At the meeting of the Greater North Dakota Association (GNDA) in Valley City, Andrews focused on complaints that the Farmer's Home

Administration (FmHA) had dried up loans to farmers. Andrews told them that there was loan money available. "If that's not getting through to the local level, for gosh sakes, let us know so we can find the bureaucrats who aren't letting it come through." He defended the FmHA administrator and asked people to "take a closer look at some of the [anti-FmHA] talk that's going on." He repeated his view that "scare talk" about the farm situation would·only hurt the farmer. "Here in North Dakota, it's pretty darn good—and we're going to pull out of it. . . . We should be upbeat about North Dakota—a fantastic state."

In the same can-do community spirit, he described two of his current legislative initiatives—both in the Appropriations Committee— to the business development group. The first one involved an increase in the allowable width of trucks on interstate highways. It would, he explained, help in the transportation of agricultural products. The second one involved the provision of a manufacturer's warranty on engines made for military hardware. This idea, he said, was a simple extension from normal warranties on farm equipment to warranties on defense equipment.[32]

Quite apart from their substantive merits, discussing these initiatives, especially in the light of farm interests, was his way of keeping in touch. "Today, with GNDA," he said afterward,

> it was just like dropping around to see some old friends. It was the first time I've tried out my truck width and warranty ideas on anyone. . . . I wanted to see how my ideas would play with my friends. If they didn't play well, I would drop them like a hot potato. But they played well. It's fun to visit with people. It's a style I like, one that I'm comfortable with.

He wanted to make sure that his Washington activity had not gotten out of sync with his constituents' views. To his evident satisfaction, these two undertakings had not.

In his meeting with the nurses in Fargo, there seemed again to be a deep mutual understanding. They had supported him in his 1980 campaign; his Washington activity seemed to guarantee their continued support. "It was my [1981] amendment in the Budget Committee," he told the nurses' group,

> that added $500 million for health programs, including nurses' training education.[33] [On the floor] Strom Thurmond [R-S.C.] wanted to take it away and give it to the veterans. I was just a freshman senator. It was my first Senate fight. I was determined not to get run over by Strom Thurmond in my first fight. Ted Kennedy [D-Mass.] stood with me. The debate raged for a day and a half. All the Democrats supported me, and the

two Republican leaders voted with me in the end, [Howard] Baker [Tenn.] and [Ted] Stevens [Alaska].

"Keep the information coming so we can continue to win these battles," he encouraged them.

The panel discussion uncovered no differences between Republican Andrews and his two Democratic congressional colleagues. "We can't find any hard areas of controversy among the delegation," declared Representative Dorgan. And the moderator echoed, "All three of these gentlemen were tremendously helpful to us last year. They worked on a bipartisan basis." Driving away from the meeting, Andrews commented, "I was the only Republican. Why weren't there any other Republicans on the panel? . . . That's the trouble with Republicans. They don't get out and work with the nurses—or a lot of these other groups either." It was a criticism I had not heard during the 1980 campaign.

Andrews's talk to the regional group interested in special education—whose members came from several states—produced further signs of his moderate brand of Republicanism. He described his participation in the 1981 alliance of four Republicans and seven Democrats on the Budget Committee that won funding for vocational education and education for the handicapped.[34] In 1982, he told them, he had been the only Budget Committee Republican to support a Democratic effort in committee and on the floor to add $300 million to the budget for education—an amendment that ultimately lost, 51-49, on the floor. He attacked the MX missile as wasteful, and he touted his warranty proposal as a defense money saver. "These are the innovative things we can do," he concluded. "When they tell you they can't find the money to fund programs to help our people, you tell them they haven't even begun to imagine how we can find the money." (The next year, he secured a small appropriation for one of the group's projects.)

"They are grand people; but many of them are not from North Dakota," Andrews commented as we began our 200-mile drive home at ten o'clock. He added, "How many times do you suppose a Republican comes to talk to a bunch like that?"

In the context of his sympathetic presentation to nurses and educators, it was easy to see how he had for so long maintained so much across-the-board political support in his home state. But his reproachful comments about his fellow Republicans at the end of each meeting revealed a possible crack in that support—among fellow partisans who might not approve of Andrews's moderation or his outreach to more liberal groups. In the 1960s, he had actively promoted Nelson Rockefeller for president, and he used Rockefeller's defeat to illustrate his views on the party. "Nelson Rockefeller said it best. Someone asked him why he never became president. And he asked them, 'Did you ever see a Republican convention? Did you ever see a Republican headquarters?' The party has a self-destructive impulse." Republicans, Andrews felt, were too conservative and exclusive for their own good.

For his part, Andrews saw himself as both in tune with and responsive to the great majority of his constituents. Several times during the trip he referred to North Dakota as a "liberal" state. On the ride home from his education speech, I asked him why he viewed it that way. He answered:

> I've always thought of it as a liberal state. People are liberal on civil rights. . . . Oh, about 20 percent of them are to the right of Genghis Khan. These troglodytes dominate the Republican convention. But the people are different. They are in favor of openness in government, disclosure, freedom of information, sunshine laws. There's a college in every corner of the state; and they are very insistent that everyone should have an opportunity. They support the kind of programs we saw tonight.

He also saw himself as willing to assert leadership, too, in promoting those views. "I have voted for every civil rights bill on the books," he said later. "My vote for open housing was the only one that really pissed people off. I don't know why. It took me two months of going around the state to turn that one around. You have the obligation to vote right on something as fundamental as that, and then go home and explain."

When I asked him, "Is North Dakota an easy state to represent?" his sense of community and his near-total identification with the state came through more clearly than ever. He used a word I had heard him use in 1980. "If you're *family* it is," he answered.

> But if you're aloof, it would be hard to do it. People here want you to be innovative but not uppity. They want you to do a good job in Washington, but they want you to remember where you came from. They are suspicious of outsiders. They are suspicious of outside government, outside banks, and outside corporations. That's why we have a state bank. That's why farmers can't incorporate in North Dakota.
>
> They expect the whole congressional delegation to come to meetings, like the nurses' meeting last night. . . . And tomorrow at [North Dakota State University] homecoming, all the delegation will be there. It's just a tradition that we go to these things. . . .
>
> When they accept you as *family*, it's easy. But like a family, they could discipline you sternly if they became upset with you. I guess they would; though I've never felt it.

TABLE 1-2   Voter Support Levels: Mark Andrews and Quentin Burdick, 1981-1982

	April 1981		March 1982	
	Andrews	*Burdick*	*Andrews*	*Burdick*
Favorability				
Favorable opinion	83%	64%	78%	76%
Unfavorable opinion	11	14	13	10
No opinion, never heard of	6	22	8	15
Job rating				
Strongly approve	27	27	28	30
Somewhat approve	56	48	50	45
Somewhat disapprove	6	11	7	8
Strongly disapprove	3	2	3	6
Don't know	8	13	13	12

Source: April 1981: DMI, "A Statewide Survey of North Dakota Voters"; March 1982: Dresner, Morris and Tortorello Research, North Dakota no. 2053.

Quite the opposite, he said, after further reflection. "Take the call-in show last week. How many of my colleagues do you think could sit in front of an open line for one hour and get nothing but courteous calls?"

Speaking of his attachment to the statewide family, he summed up: "You have to feel it. You can't fake it. Quentin Burdick feels it, and that's why he's going to win [reelection in 1982]." He believed that both Burdick the Democrat and Andrews the Republican owed their political longevity to their attachment to the community and to voters' recognition of it. "The voters are very independent. If Quent Burdick and I were on the same ballot, he would win by 2 to 1 and I would win by 2 to 1." His polls, he confided, did indeed show him running 2 to 1 ahead of "anybody else."

The poll result to which he referred came from the benchmark "reelect" question, a favorite of campaign consultants who are tracking the strength of an incumbent legislator. "Should Mark Andrews be reelected or is it time to give a new person a chance?" they had asked North Dakota voters in March 1982. By a 59 percent to 29 percent margin (with the rest undecided) the answer had been to reelect.[35] It was a solid margin, which appeared more impressive when compared with the 45 to 44 percent reelect vote given to three-term senator Quentin Burdick—who, it turned out, would be reelected by a 2-1 margin seven months later. From 73 percent of the voters, the new senator received high marks—excellent 30 percent, good 43 percent—for "keeping in touch with the voters back home." And 67 percent of his fellow North

Dakotans gave him good marks—excellent 19 percent and good 48 percent—on "helping to solve the problems of people in North Dakota."

Other poll results, from April 1981 as well as March 1982, conveyed a similar message, that Andrews retained solid and (apparently) widespread support—at least as strong as that of his veteran Democratic colleague.[36] Table 1-2 provides some of these comparisons. One might detect some slippage in Andrews's favorability and job rating numbers from July 1980 to March 1982. This would, of course, bear watching.[37] But the differences were fluctuations within a basic position of strength within the community. The dominant pattern was one of continuity, not change.

CONCLUSION

From my perspective, the 1982 trip was a straightforward extension of the 1980 campaign. Andrews's transition from incumbent congressman to incumbent senator seemed to be going smoothly as far as his relationships at home were concerned. Two years into his term, Sen. Mark Andrews seemed to be as safe and sound inside his North Dakota "family" as Rep. Mark Andrews had ever been.

This conclusion about the strength of a particular legislator-constituency relationship is buttressed by poll data. But it rests most heavily on personal observation. Because the conclusion forms a baseline from which much of the book proceeds, a reminder about the nature of the observational approach is in order. In all cases, the observer watches from a particular perspective and gathers information on a limited number of occasions. My perspective came from over the shoulder of Mark Andrews on two trips to North Dakota. The possibility exists, therefore, that I initially overestimated the strength of the relationship and thus overestimated the amount of change in it over the next six years. Perhaps Mark Andrews's constituency relationships were always quite tenuous; perhaps he was a weak incumbent, after all. One cannot be certain, so a caveat about accepting observation-based evidence is in order.

On the other hand, the observer must begin with self-confidence, adopt a stance about the reliability of the evidence, and proceed cautiously from there. That is what I shall do in the succeeding chapters. In support of the conclusion that Mark Andrews was a strong incumbent, there is his string of electoral victories plus the available, although sketchy, poll data. And Andrews was not the first House member I had observed with constituents.

North Dakota has an unusually strong sense of community, with its shared values and perceptions. The strength of community bonds puts fairly tight boundaries on permissible behavior. An observer can have more confidence in judgments derived from two visits to a lightly populated, homogeneous state like North Dakota than from more visits to a heterogeneous conglomerate like California. As participants in a common culture, North Dakota's politicians are knowable, measurable quantities. They are more neighbors than strangers. They cannot so easily invent themselves for television as politicians in large states can. As Andrews himself put it, they cannot "fake" their relationship with their constituents.

Mark Andrews came across, from these earliest of visits, as a real person with recognizable interests and with community ties that were not hard to discern, understand, and appreciate. I believe it is accurate to conclude that his home state ties were strong, widespread, and in good repair in the early days of his Senate career.

NOTES

1. Andrews was elected to fill a vacancy in a special election on October 22, 1963.
2. Dick Dobson, "Senatorial Security," *Minot Daily News*, June 8, 1985.
3. John Hibbing and Sara Brandes, "State Population and the Electoral Success of U.S. Senators," *American Journal of Political Science* 27 (1983): 809-819.
4. David Mayhew, "Congressional Elections: The Case of the Vanishing Marginals," *Polity* (Spring 1965); Morris Fiorina, *Congress: Keystone of the Washington Establishment* (New Haven: Yale University Press, 1977); Gary Jacobson, *The Politics of Congressional Elections* (Boston: Little, Brown, 1987).
5. John Alford and John Hibbing, "The Disparate Electoral Security of House and Senate Incumbents" (Paper presented at the Annual Meeting of the American Political Science Association, Atlanta, September 1989); John Hibbing and John Alford, "Constituency Population and Representation in the United States Senate" (Paper presented at the Houston/Rice Conference on Electing the Senate, Houston, December 1989); Alan Abramowitz, "Explaining Senate Election Outcomes," *American Political Science Review* 82 (June 1988): 385-403; Mark Westlye, "Competitiveness of Senate Seats and Voting Behavior in Senate Elections," *American Journal of Political Science* 27 (1983): 253-283.
6. Mark Westlye's recent book-length elaboration of his earlier article on "hard fought" and "low key" elections, "Competitiveness of Senate Seats," comes closest of all work on Senate elections to the spirit of our effort here to link journey to outcome. Westlye's research asks why election outcomes should differ at different points in time in the same statewide constituency. He does not trace the activities of any senator over time; but he undertakes his cross-sectional analyses at different points in time. His findings strongly emphasize "the remarkable diversity of Senate election outcomes" and "the

complexity of the dynamics that produce Senate outcomes." Among other suggestions, he urges that researchers "look beyond the static features of the political landscape," expand "our knowledge of what happens in individual Senate races," chronicle "the actions and decisions of incumbents during the campaign," and "further study the vulnerability of incumbents." See Mark Westlye, *Senate Elections and Campaign Intensity* (Baltimore: Johns Hopkins University Press, 1991), 196-202.

7. "North Dakota Admission Day," *Congressional Record,* November 1, 1985, S14607.
8. Patrick Springer, "Mark Andrews," *Forum* (Fargo), December 7, 1986.
9. Hibbing and Alford, "Constituency Population and Representation."
10. Richard F. Fenno, Jr., *Home Style: House Members in Their Districts* (Boston: Little, Brown, 1978), chap. 3.
11. Ibid., chap. 6.
12. Dick Dobson, "Young Could (Kind of) See the Future," *Minot Daily News,* March 23, 1986.
13. *Larimer Pioneer,* January 4, 1984.
14. For example, see Richard F. Fenno, Jr., *The Presidential Odyssey of John Glenn* (Washington, D.C.: CQ Press, 1980), chap. 1; and *Learning to Legislate: The Senate Education of Arlen Specter* (Washington, D.C.: CQ Press, 1991).
15. According to one measure of ethnic and racial diversity, North Dakota had the sixth least diverse population of the fifty states. See "Analysis Puts a Number on Population Mix," *USA Today,* April 11, 1991.
16. "North Dakota Admission Day," *Congressional Record,* November 1, 1985, S14607.
17. North Dakota political scientist (and onetime opponent of Andrews) Lloyd Ohmdal says of the two Dakotas that "We tend to be more like communities than states." *Wall Street Journal,* October 23, 1986.
18. "Celebrating North Dakota Statehood," *Congressional Record,* November 2, 1989, S14539.
19. See Dale Wetzel, "Long Political Career May Be at End," *Minot Daily News,* November 6, 1986.
20. See Bruce Ingersoll, "Lobbyist for Mighty Rural Electric Co-Op Group Pitches the Idea to Give REA a New Lease on Life," *Wall Street Journal,* December 22, 1987.
21. "Andrews Endorsed for Election to U.S. Senate," *Sunday Forum* (Fargo), October 12, 1980.
22. Dresner, Morris and Tortorello Research, "A Study of Voter Attitudes in North Dakota," July 1980. This firm did polls for Andrews in December 1979, July 1980, March 1982, and December 1983. The record of the December 1979 poll was so incomplete as to be useless. The 1980 poll made some comparisons with it. None of the comparisons, however, showed enough of a difference to indicate that it would have added any important baseline information to what we can get from the July 1980 results we have used here.
23. The text was printed in Andrews's July 1980 questionnaire (note 22). Andrews served on the Subcommittee on Agriculture of the House Appropriations Committee, *not* on the "Agriculture Committee." A discussion of the issue and Johanneson's mistakes will be found in Tim Fought, "Senate Race Marked by Anti-Andrews Rhetoric," *Grand Forks Herald,* October 12, 1980.

24. These percentages combine rankings of 5 and 4.
25. *The Federalist* (Washington, D.C.: Hallwell, Masters, Smith, 1852), no. 52, 284.
26. Ibid., no. 58, 268.
27. This may be especially the case in states with a single House member. North Dakota's House member, Byron Dorgan, comments, "Back in the home state, you're not viewed much differently than a senator." Robert Hershey, "Representatives with as Much Turf as a Senator," *New York Times,* May 6, 1985.
28. Dwight Leatham, "Andrews Plans to Have Senate Clout," *Dickinson Press,* October 16, 1980.
29. Peverill Squire, "Challengers in U.S. Senate Elections," *Legislative Studies Quarterly* 14 (1989): 531-547; Sandy Maisel, "Congressional Elections: Quality Candidates in House and Senate Elections" (Paper delivered at a conference at the Carl Albert Congressional Research and Study Center, University of Oklahoma, April 1990).
30. Westlye, "Competitiveness of Senate Seats."
31. Liz Fedor, "Senator from N.D. Criticizes Dayton," *Grand Forks Herald,* October 15, 1982.
32. Both initiatives will be discussed later—the truck width limitation in Chapter 3, the warranty provision in Chapter 4.
33. Transcript of Proceedings, United States Senate Committee on the Budget, "First Concurrent Budget Resolution for FY 1982," April 9, 1981, 550-553.
34. Transcript of Proceedings, United States Senate Committee on the Budget, "Revising the Second Budget Resolution for FY 1981 to Include Reconciliation: S. Con. Res. 9," March 18, 1981, 617-618, 655-657.
35. Dresner, Morris and Tortorello Research, North Dakota no. 2053, March 1982.
36. The April 1981 poll was taken by DMI for the Republican Senatorial Campaign Committee, whose interest was in the upcoming election in North Dakota for Senator Burdick's seat. They included only a few questions involving Andrews. We have tried to exploit such limited comparability as exists between the DMI and the Dresner, Morris and Tortorello polls.
37. Other elements of the March poll will be picked up later in the study.

FIGURE A-1 Percentage of Votes Cast for Mark Andrews for U.S. House, 1972

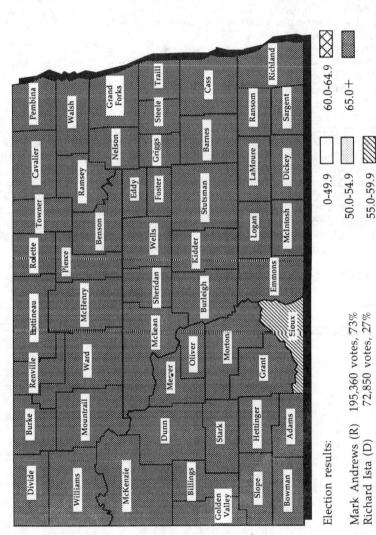

Election results:

□ 0-49.9	⊠ 60.0-64.9	
▦ 50.0-54.9	▦ 65.0+	
▨ 55.0-59.9		

Mark Andrews (R)   195,360 votes, 73%
Richard Ista (D)   72,850 votes, 27%

Source: North Dakota State Canvasing Eoard, "Official Abstract of Votes Cast at the General Election of November 1972."

Note: Bismarck is in Burleigh County, Fargo is in Cass County, Grand Forks is in Grand Forks County, and Minot is in Ward County.

FIGURE A-2   Percentage of Votes Cast for Mark Andrews for U.S. House, 1974

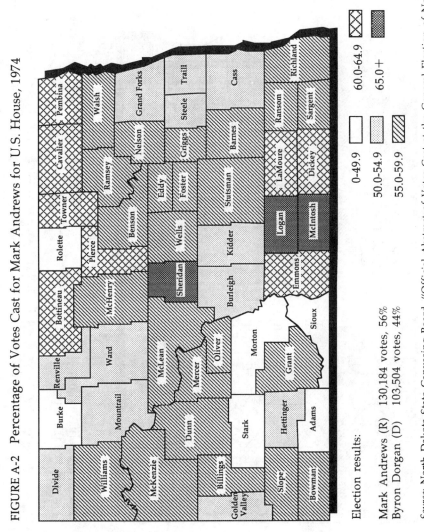

Election results:

Mark Andrews (R)   130,184 votes, 56%
Byron Dorgan (D)   103,504 votes, 44%

Source: North Dakota State Canvasing Board, "Official Abstract of Votes Cast at the General Election of November 1974."

Note: Bismarck is in Burleigh County, Fargo is in Cass County, Grand Forks is in Grand Forks County, and Minot is in Ward County.

FIGURE A-3 Percentage of Votes Cast for Mark Andrews for U.S. House, 1976

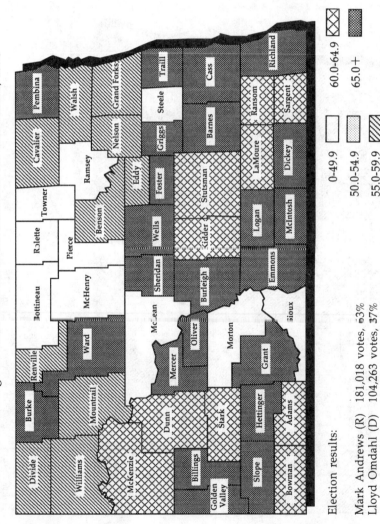

Election results:

Mark Andrews (R) 181,018 votes, 63%
Lloyd Omdahl (D) 104,263 votes, 37%

Source: North Dakota State Canvasing Board, "Official Abstract of Votes Cast at the General Election of November 1976."

Note: Bismarck is in Burleigh County, Fargo is in Cass County, Grand Forks is in Grand Forks County, and Minot is in Ward County.

FIGURE A-4 Percentage of Votes Cast for Mark Andrews for U.S. House, 1978

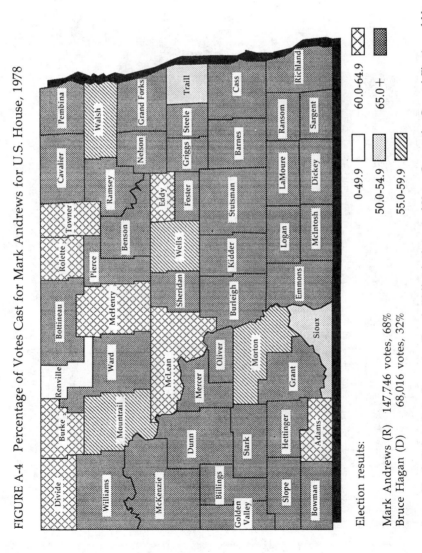

Election results:

Mark Andrews (R)   147,746 votes, 68%
Bruce Hagan (D)   68,016 votes, 32%

☐ 0–49.9	▨ 60.0–64.9
▦ 50.0–54.9	▓ 65.0+
▨ 55.0–59.9	

Source: North Dakota State Canvasing Board, "Official Abstract of Votes Cast at the General Election of November 1978."

Note: Bismarck is in Burleigh County, Fargo is in Cass County, Grand Forks is in Grand Forks County, and Minot is in Ward County.

FIGURE A-5 Percentage of Votes Cast for Mark Andrews for U.S. Senate, 1980

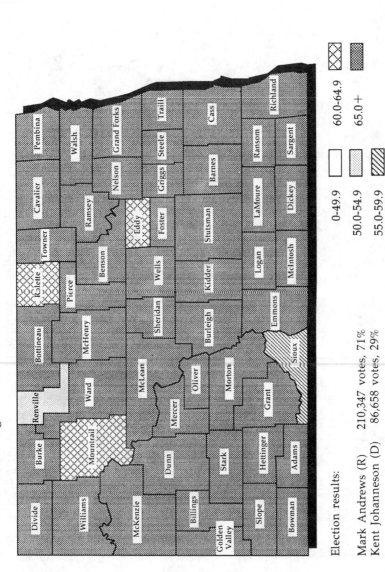

Election results:

Mark Andrews (R)   210,347 votes, 71%
Kent Johanneson (D)   86,658 votes, 29%

Source: North Dakota State Canvasing Board, "Official Abstract of Votes Cast at the General Election of November 1980."

Note: Bismarck is in Burleigh County, Fargo is in Cass County, Grand Forks is in Grand Forks County, and Minot is in Ward County.

FIGURE A-6 Percentage of Votes Cast for Mark Andrews for U.S. Senate, 1986

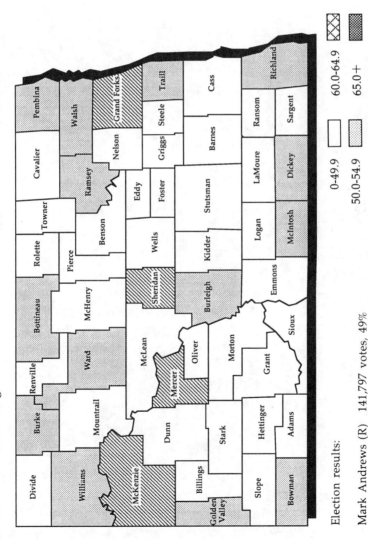

Election results:

Mark Andrews (R)   141,797 votes, 49%
Kent Conrad (D)   143,932 votes, 51%

0-49.9
50.0-54.9
55.0-59.9
60.0-64.9
65.0+

Source: North Dakota State Canvasing Board, "Official Abstract of Votes Cast at the General Election of November 1986."

Note: Bismarck is in Burleigh County, Fargo is in Cass County, Grand Forks is in Grand Forks County, and Minot is in Ward County.

2

Governing Style:
A House Member in the Senate

ADJUSTMENT AND CONTINUITY

During his earliest Senate years, Mark Andrews's successful constituency career was an augury of continued home state support. But what about his Washington career? What kind of a senator would he be? And how, if at all, would his legislative activity in the Senate affect his eventual strength at the ballot box? Our career-oriented perspective assumes some connection between a senator's electoral performance and the governing performance of the preceding six years. Certainly Mark Andrews never doubted the existence of a connection. He believed, to the very eve of his career-ending defeat, that no matter what his other problems might be, his governing activity in Washington would assure him of reelection in North Dakota.

In this chapter and the next, we shall follow him into the Senate, learn what kind of senator he was, and prepare ourselves to assess the relationship between his legislative performance and the election results that came afterward. If, as the senator believed, his governing performance would assure reelection, why didn't it?

It is commonplace for members of the House of Representatives to run for the Senate. In the period from 1960 to 1990, 158 tried and 58 succeeded. But it is not commonplace for longtime House members, like Mark Andrews, to succeed.

In Table 2-1, House members who ran for the Senate in the period 1960-1990 are grouped according to the length of their House service and their electoral success rates. According to Table 2-1, more than half of all the representatives who aspire to the Senate run after two, three, or four terms in the House. Their success rates range from 37 percent for the two-

TABLE 2-1   House Members Running for the Senate: Success and Length
of Service in the House, 1960-1990

Number of Prior Terms in House	Election Outcome		Total
	Won	*Lost*	
1	5 (26%)	14 (74%)	19
2	11 (37%)	19 (63%)	30
3	15 (48%)	16 (52%)	31
4	14 (48%)	15 (52%)	29
5	10 (48%)	11 (52%)	21
6-12[a]	4 (14%)	24 (86%)	28
Total	59 (37%)	99 (63%)	158

[a] Six terms of service won 1, lost 6; seven terms won 1, lost 6; eight terms won 1, lost 6; nine terms won 1, lost 2; ten terms won 0, lost 2; eleven terms won 0, lost 1; twelve terms won 0, lost 1.

termers to 48 percent for those with three or four terms of House service. Five-term candidates are less common, but they do just as well (48 percent) in getting elected. Fewer representatives run after one House term; and they are, at 26 percent, markedly less successful. Cumulatively, these five groupings (one to five terms) account for an overwhelming 80 percent of all House members who run for the Senate. And their cumulative success rate stands at 44 percent. Among the remaining 20 percent who run for the Senate after six or more terms, the success rate drops off precipitously to 14 percent. At some point, increasing length of service in the House appears to dampen ambition and deflate electoral success.

Mark Andrews stands as an exception to these patterns. He was among the very few—seven—House members in this period who ran for the Senate after serving nine terms or more in the House. Of the seven, only he was elected.[1] For at least thirty years—and perhaps longer—no incoming senator had had as much previous experience in the House of Representatives as he. In 1981, he joined twenty-seven other former House members in the Senate. The average length of their pre-Senate experience in the House was a comparatively low 3.5 terms. Indeed, only two of the twenty-seven had served more than four previous terms there: John Breaux (D-La.), with eight terms, and Spark Matsunaga (D-Hawaii), with seven. The Senate's majority leader, Howard Baker, referred to the North Dakotan as "my friend who served in the House of Representatives so long."[2] If ever a first-term senator might be thought of a priori as "A House member in the Senate," it was Mark Andrews. And we shall gain analytical insight into his Washington career by thinking of him in that way.

Previous experience helps to shape the adjustment of newcomers to the Senate; and former House members face a somewhat different mix of adjustment problems than do other newcomers. As Andrews put it, "There are a lot of things you bring with you from the House that you can use in the Senate. But, still, you know you are a freshman." In truth, he was less a freshman than a transfer student. For newcomers without House experience, adjustment problems center on the unfamiliar institutional routines and relationships they encounter. For former House members, on the other hand, adjustment problems are associated with the intensification and the rearrangement of familiar institutional routines and relationships.[3] There is a rationale, then, for examining the adjustment experience of someone who is moving from one branch of the Congress to the other.

There is a rationale also for exploring various dimensions of that experience, such as longevity in one branch and its effect on adjustment to the other branch. For the purposes of that exploration, Mark Andrews is an especially inviting case. As much as anyone ever could, he came to the Senate steeped in, and affected by, the routines and the relationships, the habits and the perspectives, of the House of Representatives.

The early adjustment patterns of all Senate newcomers are linked to their recently completed election campaign.[4] The transition from campaigning to governing is guided by the interpretation that the victorious candidate makes of the events and the outcome of the recent campaign. This interpretation of the election's conduct, issues, and results may help to reinforce certain previously established personal goals, or it may cause some alteration in those goals. Such campaign effects are most pronounced during the early adjustment to the business of governing.

Our exploration of Mark Andrews's career in the Senate begins with these postcampaign considerations. His opponent, we recall, had attacked him most vigorously for seeking the Senate seat to gratify his personal ambition, thus causing North Dakota to lose his seniority-based influence in Congress. If Andrews cared about helping his home state, the argument went, he would have remained in the House, where he had become an influential senior member of the powerful Appropriations Committee. Andrews did not credit the charge; but neither did he forget it. In a low-key, lopsided campaign, there was not much else to remember. So it loomed large in his interpretation of the recent campaign. He mentioned it whenever we discussed the campaign.

Andrews continually asserted that this central campaign charge—and, thus, the campaign itself—had been convincingly laid to rest. The Republican takeover of the Senate, his majority party status, and his committee assignments had combined to do the trick. The campaign, he said in March, "is a closed book."

The campaign is over and done with. As you remember, the main charge against me was that I was giving up my position and my seniority on the House Appropriations Committee. But here I am on the Senate Appropriations Committee, on three subcommittees instead of two [as in the House] and the chairman of one. I'm also on the Agriculture and Budget Committees.

Looking back on the committee assignment process eight months later, he again recalled the main campaign issue—and its short life. "You remember back in the campaign how the other side criticized me for giving up my power spot for North Dakota on Appropriations to satisfy my own ego. When it came right down to it, only one person lobbied me to go on a committee. . . . Nobody cared what committee I went on." By that time, he knew that he had exchanged one power spot in the House for several of them in the Senate.

If there was one thing that Mark Andrews did not have to be reminded about by a campaign opponent, it was the need for a representative of a small, out-of-the-way state like North Dakota to seek and to husband power in Congress. Andrews had coveted a "power spot" from the day he arrived in the House of Representatives, and he had found it fourteen months later, in January 1965, on the House Appropriations Committee. That committee is the repository of the House's most distinctive institutional prerogative—preeminence in the legislature's crucial control of the government's purse strings. It was, in the 1960s, the committee where most of the government's spending decisions allocating money to agencies and programs got their legislative start and received their major legislative imprint. It had long been—and still is—one of the three (with Rules and Ways and Means) most prestigious, most important, most powerful, most sought after, and most exclusive committees in the House of Representatives.

House members in the 1960s overwhelmingly sought election to the Appropriations Committee, they said, because it gave them more "power," "influence," and "importance" than most other members of the chamber.[5] Their influence inside the House derived partly, of course, from their impact on spending decisions in general, but mostly from their ability to help or hurt, to speed up or delay, the requests of their colleagues for appropriations for their districts. We can safely assume that Mark Andrews sought membership on the committee in pursuit of such disproportionate inside influence. And we further assume that it was, excepting only the goal of reelection, his major political goal. Since membership on the committee increased his chances to help his own district, it furthered his reelection goal as well. In short, the House Committee on Appropriations was both a power-producing committee and a reelection-producing committee for its members. Mark Andrews's reading of his 1980 campaign and its message may have reinforced his desire to seek power spots in the Senate; but his goals and his motivation in this respect had long since been settled.

Andrews revealed his goals anew in his first important decision as a senator. Two weeks after the election, he talked about his committee preferences: "I'd like Finance, to do something different. But since I've been on [House] Appropriations for sixteen years, I don't think I could get away with leaving it. So I guess I'll take [Senate] Appropriations." Finance is, of course, the Senate's very influential taxation committee. But—expressing some sense of constituency-related constraint in the matter—Andrews opted for the same committee power base he had enjoyed in the House.

After he had won a place on the Senate Appropriations Committee, Andrews expressed satisfaction with his choice. "I'm happy with my committee assignments," he said at year's end. "Early on, I thought about starting off on a whole new career. But I decided, what the hell, I don't want to do that. I'll stick with Appropriations. I've been doing it for so long and I know it so well that it won't be teaching an old dog new tricks." The continuity would allow him to put to use in the Senate many of the lessons, or tricks, he had learned in the House.

Nothing impressed the North Dakotan more in his earliest days than the magnification of influence that accompanied the move to the Senate. Barely two weeks after his election, sitting in his House office beneath a "Welcome Senator" banner, he exclaimed, "It's a different life style—entirely different. It's amazing. My telephone calls get answered much faster now—even though I've been a senior member of the Appropriations Committee over here. . . . Everything changes, just that quickly." Two months into his term, he embellished the same theme: "There is definitely more power in the Senate. Who cares about a House member? When you are a senator, the White House answers the phone, cabinet members answer the phone. But not for a House member."

In the context of 1981, of course, the senator from North Dakota was twice blessed and his power doubly magnified, since the Republicans had assumed control of the Senate as well as the presidency. "I chuckle," said Andrews as he contemplated this turn of events.

> I chuckle because my opponents attacked me for giving up my power. Here I was, going from the minority party to the majority party. I was going to be ninth on the Senate Appropriations Committee instead of fourth on the House Committee. But I was going from being a ranking minority member to being chairman of an appropriations subcommittee. I went

from fifty-sixth [in chamber seniority] to eighty-seventh here. But what does that matter? I have access to the president and his cabinet. I think to myself, "Boy, I sure am giving up power!"

He had always sought maximum legislative power. Now he had found the most congenial institution for the exercise of it. "It's an exciting time to be in Washington," he said. "And if you are going to be here, you might as well be in the most powerful position you can."

As he related the story in March, it had taken him only a few days in office to begin exercising his newfound influence. Karl Mundt, a former South Dakota senator who had come from the House, once told him "that I'd have more power after nine days in the Senate than I had after nine terms in the House. And he was right." He explained:

> I've been interested in nutrition, as you know—bran muffins and all. Well, in January, the people from Grand Forks called and said they hated to cut off their new nutrition building at three floors, that they needed a fourth floor. But there was no money. I said, "Come on down." We talked about it. I called the Agriculture Department and we found some funds. I talked to my friend [Sen.] Tom Eagleton [D-Mo., member of the Agriculture and Appropriations Committees] on the floor and he signed a letter with me. Then I made a few phone calls. A week or so later, I got a call from Grand Forks. "Whatever you did, it worked. We got the money for the fourth floor." There is absolutely no way I could have gotten that done in the House.

His assessment is correct, notwithstanding his previous position as the senior Republican on the Agriculture Subcommittee of the House Appropriations Committee. While this early success depended upon his experience in the network of relationships governing agriculture politics, it depended equally upon his dual membership on both the authorizing (Agriculture) and the appropriating (Appropriations) committees. This combination of interlocking power spots, so readily available in the Senate, would have been impossible to achieve in the House.

In addition to the magnification of his influence, Andrews faced a second early adjustment: to the magnification of his workload. It, too, represented a quantum change in familiar routines. The federal budget had become the Republican administration's top priority; and two of Andrews's committees—Budget and Appropriations—had put him at the center of that issue. "The workload is heavier than I ever imagined," he said in March.

> When you consider I'm on Budget and Appropriations and all the subcommittees, and if you overlay that with the revolution

Reagan is trying to bring about on budget cutting ... I don't have any time left.... I'm working Saturdays and Sundays just to catch up with the week's work. In the House my desk was clean by Thursday night. And I have the same staff plus six new ones—all good.

There was, of course, his additional assignment to the Agriculture Committee—the policy area of paramount importance to his constituents. "There is no time," he mused.

I don't think I realized the workload would be so much heavier [than in the House]. I haven't been disappointed here, but the committee workload is so heavy, I'm not so sure I'll like this job any better than I did the House. We'll have to wait till the dust settles. Come back in a couple of months. . . .

These several changes brought with them, he added, a quantum increase in the interest of outsiders. His spread of committees had tripled and his voting power had grown from one in 435 to one in 100. "I get a lot more requests from outside the state," he said. "So much so that we have a rule in the office that no one from outside the state gets through to me—not unless they are very persistent." He mentioned requests from the *Boston Globe*, from Eunice and Sargent Shriver, and from San Francisco Mayor Dianne Feinstein (all accepted). He concluded, "If you aren't careful you can fritter away two hours a day on that kind of stuff."

These last comments suggest an effort to manage his time to remain as available as possible to the people of his home state. Whatever else changed in his move from House to Senate, his constituency did not. In 1980, North Dakota was one of six states in which a single House member shared constituencies with two senators.[6] For all other House members, the move to the Senate meant adjusting to an enlargement of their constituency, a change in its makeup, and a more complex set of home relationships. As Andrews pointed out in March,

Senators who took on larger constituencies may have a problem, but I don't. I have the same constituents, and I'm sitting here getting the same mail I always did—no more. The same people come to me as always came to see me. Right now, everyone in North Dakota is focused on the [state] legislature. So we are in the same hiatus we always have. By April, they'll get interested in the federal government again, and we'll get busier.

At every turn in our conversation, he gave evidence of his continuing devotion to the service of North Dakota constituents and to the continuing closeness of his relationship to them.

Amid changes in power and workload, therefore, the new senator foresaw a strong set of career continuities. He retained the same major appropriations committee assignment in Washington and the identical statewide constituency at home. As he began his Senate career, he could seize the opportunity deliberately to alter his legislative behavior, or he could hew pretty closely to work patterns he had developed in the House. Although we have not yet examined his governing activity in the House, these first-year conversations point more toward continuity than revision, a direction that seemed intentional.

Near the end of his first year, I asked Andrews, "What kind of a senator do you want to be?" He answered:

> I guess I'll have to be myself. I've gotten along pretty well in the House just by being myself, so I'll have to stick with it. A farmer from a farm state comes to the Senate with some pretty fixed notions. Maybe in the House you ask yourself what kind of a member you want to be; but by the time you get to the Senate, that's pretty well determined. So I'll be the same as always.

His emphasis on continuity gives further support to our tentative characterization of Mark Andrews as a House member in the Senate.

TWO COMMITTEES

Any continuities in Mark Andrews's legislative outlook and behavior would show up in his committee activity. Most legislators, after all, spend most of their time in committee work. In Andrews's case, moreover, two of his Senate committee assignments—Appropriations and Budget—were directly related to his longtime committee assignment in the House. For sixteen years, from 1965 to 1980, he had served on the House Appropriations Committee. And we would expect to find his governing behavior on the Senate Appropriations and Budget committees to bear some imprint of his committee experience in the House.[7]

When he came to the Senate, we shall argue, Mark Andrews brought with him a strongly held set of beliefs and a set of ingrained habits, the product of his long service on the House Appropriations Committee. From the 1950s to the 1970s, including the period when Andrews was a neophyte member, that committee dominated congressional spending decisions. Its members shared a distinctive and stable body of supporting perspectives and practices which the veterans passed along to the newcomers and which the newcomers—with an interest in preserving the committee's power—accepted. Altogether, life on the committee was an intense and effective learning experience. The result, for most members, was a working knowledge of the appropriations process, skill in manipulating that process, and devotion to its primacy in the work of the Congress. By the time Andrews left the committee for the Senate, he had long since become a prototypical, functioning, believing member of the group. Appropriating money, he avowed, "is a whale of a lot more important than passing a bill." [8]

The reform of the congressional budget process in 1974 brought a new committee—the House Budget Committee—into the domain of the House Appropriations Committee. Members of Appropriations accurately perceived the change as a threat to their traditional preeminence. As one senator recalled later, "They opposed openly, relentlessly, this budget process. They did not want it. It takes away, it diminishes their power." [9] At the least, Appropriations members dragged their feet, seeking at every turn to minimize the intrusion. In some instances, they succeeded in weakening the House Budget Committee—by limiting its actions in the first budget resolution to setting spending "targets" rather than "ceilings," for instance, and by saddling it with rotating and overlapping membership requirements. [10] The degree to which the House Appropriations Committee subsequently declined in stature and in influence deserves a good deal more research. On balance, available evidence indicates some loss, some capacity for self-protection, and some continuing tensions. [11] For our purposes, it is important only to note that Mark Andrews came to the Senate with a veteran House Appropriations · Committee member's view of the reformed budget process. That view— suspicious and rivalrous—colored his Senate committee work.

The appropriations and budget committees to which he came in the Senate had a much different relationship to one another than did their counterparts in the House. Members of the Senate Appropriations Committee had taken an extremely cooperative view of budgetary reform in 1974. They viewed the new Senate Budget Committee less as a pretender than as an ally. Never having staked a claim to the unique institutional importance of their handiwork, they welcomed budget reform as an opportunity to put the Senate on a more equal institutional footing with the House in money matters. They left negotiations largely to others in 1974. And they lent their support to the creation of a strong Senate Budget Committee with membership requirements that permitted normal long-term career involvement. In the Senate, therefore, influence over money decisions tended, after 1974, to flow away from Appropriations and toward Budget to a greater degree than in the House. There were, naturally, tensions between the committees but not like what occurred in the House.

The Senate Budget Committee to which Mark Andrews came, therefore, had developed a good deal of institutional running room. Its members were aggressively optimistic about their overall influence in money matters and relatively unencumbered by the Appropriations Committee in their chamber. Andrews's view of the Budget Committee, however, was colored by the jurisdictional suspicions he brought from House Appropriations colleagues; he did not share the expansive outlook of his new committee colleagues. On the Senate Budget Committee, we shall argue, continuities with his past made for a difficult and incomplete transition.

On the Senate Appropriations Committee, however, the continuities with the past yielded a smoother, more conventional transition for Andrews. After we have examined Andrews's move from House Appropriations to Senate Budget, we shall examine his move from House Appropriations to Senate Appropriations. In both cases we shall find his governing activity in the Senate to be markedly affected by his past governing activity in the House.

THE SENATE BUDGET COMMITTEE

"I probably shouldn't have gone on the Budget Committee," Andrews said in March. "But they wanted me to take it, so I did. . . . I don't think the budget process is all that helpful. It can all be done in the appropriations process." In December, he repeated:

> I went on the Budget Committee, because [Chairman] Pete Domenici [R-N.M.] and one other senator—[John] Tower [R-Texas], I think—asked me to. They said they wanted me because I was familiar with the appropriations process. I told them that my experience on the House Appropriations Committee taught me that if that committee did its job, the Budget Committee would be unnecessary. They laughed and said that's why they wanted me.

The following May he returned to the theme. "I told Pete Domenici, 'I'm not sure I believe in the budget process. I've been fighting alongside [House Appropriations Committee Chairman] Jamie Whitten for years telling the Budget Committee to keep its hands off appropriations.' But Domenici said he wanted someone on the committee who understood appropriations. So I said, 'Just so as you understand.' "

Doubtless, Chairman Domenici, who saw his main job as the promotion and protection of the reformed congressional budget process, lived to regret his request.[12] What he got was an unsympathetic—if not unreconstructed—House Appropriations Committee member on the Senate Budget Committee. Indeed, Andrews had to keep repeating the story of his assignment in order to explain his maverick behavior as a Budget Committee member.

At a time when Republican cohesion on the Senate Committee and on the Senate floor held the key to the success of President Reagan's budget-cutting program, Andrews proved to be the least reliable, most free-wheeling, most unpredictable Republican on the committee. In the Ninety-seventh Congress (1981-1982) he voted with Chairman Dome-nici only 46 percent of the time in committee. The average support level for the other ten Budget Committee Republicans was 78 percent; and for its five other freshman Republicans the average was 86 percent. Andrews's record was partly the result of votes in opposition to Domenici, and partly the result of absenteeism. He missed *forty-seven* of *eighty-seven* committee votes in 1981 and *thirteen* of *twenty-six* votes in 1982. With the exception of John Tower, whose chairmanship of the Armed Services Committee kept him away from Budget Committee meetings, Andrews's combined support-and-absenteeism record was the poorest among the Republicans on the committee—and 27 points lower than that of the next lowest GOP colleague.[13] The North Dakota senator felt no responsibility to preserve the budget process, and he displayed little discipline in implementing it.

To the contrary, Andrews exploited budget making for his own purposes—to register his dissenting views on policy, to extract whatever benefits he could for North Dakota, and to protect his interests as a subcommittee chairman of the Senate Appropriations Committee. Some glimpses of his Budget Committee behavior in his first two years will be offered in support of this enlarged picture of a House member in the Senate. Indeed, the enlargement shows a House committee member at work on a Senate committee.

BUDGET COMMITTEE BEHAVIOR, 1981

At the inaugural meeting of the Senate Budget Committee in March 1981, Andrews was the first member (and the only Republican) to comment adversely on his chairman's opening remarks. "I hate to correct what the Chairman said at the outset," he began, and he proceeded to put his own twist on "the challenge that faces this committee...."[14] A little while later, Chairman Pete Domenici suggested that a committee staffer walk the members through one substantive area to familiarize them with the content of the budget books they would be working with. The committee's task would be to "instruct" each of the other Senate committees on the savings they would have to enact under the reconciliation process. Domenici chose the materials related to the Senate Committee on Agriculture, Nutrition and Forestry. It was a very bad choice. After a few minutes of exposition, Andrews again was the first to interrupt. This time, he spoke as an expert. "I think the staff has done a great job on this," he said, "but . . . let me point out one of the things the staff has failed to do. You have failed to bring up the question of linkage." He went on to explain that some of the programs scheduled for cuts had been put in place to compensate farmers for losses due to the export embargo on grain—an embargo still in place and still hurting his constituent wheat farmers.

When the chairman tried to turn Andrews aside and to support his Budget Committee staff, Andrews persisted.

> SENATOR ANDREWS: Now, as a farm representative from a farm state, I would certainly go along with these cuts if they are linked to doing away with the export embargo on grain sales to the Soviet Union. If it is not, then what the federal government has done is it has compensated the corporations and it has gone back on its promise to the farmers. So I think I would like to have the staff delve a little bit into why these programs were put on the books. . . .
>
> SENATOR DOMENICI: Senator, let me just say that if you will at your leisure—not now—
>
> SENATOR ANDREWS: I did not want to get into specifics, but you brought it up and I wanted to point out that in many other programs, I am sure there is linkage.
>
> SENATOR DOMENICI: Well I think the staff has provided the linkage wherever they can determine it and you will find in the back-up material that linkage is provided with reference to that issue that you just raised.
>
> SENATOR ANDREWS: I looked in the back-up material, and it does not say it is tied to any type of lifting of the export embargo on grain to the Soviet Union. . . .[15]

By the end of day one, the newcomer had established his outspoken presence, his agricultural expertise, and his political independence on the Budget Committee.

Mark Andrews never became a regular participant in Budget Committee meetings. His interventions in 1981 (and 1982) remained infrequent. But they were not aimless. They were always purposeful; they were usually timely; and they almost always reflected a political interest. They reflected his tendency to want to keep those with whom he was working a little off balance, uncertain about what he might do. In his office he kept a large teddy bear on the couch. "See that teddy bear?" he asked one day. "It's pretty disconcerting to these military types. It 'discombooboolates' them when they see it. They don't know quite what to make of it. I love to see their faces." He liked to appear unpredictable and to gain a negotiating advantage thereby.

Agriculture was his primary concern. Within that policy area, he gave the highest priority to protecting the Rural Electrification Administration (REA) and its capacity to make loans to electric and telephone cooperatives. These home-grown, locally run North Dakota enterprises helped to develop and maintain family farming; they have long been of economic, political, and symbolic importance in the state. Normally these organizations supported Democrats, but, we recall, they had endorsed Andrews in 1980. The Reagan administration had targeted their loan funds for severe reductions.[16]

No sooner had Andrews been assigned to the Budget Committee than he called into question the initial REA figures prepared by Budget Director David Stockman.

> When Stockman sent over his black book, I found a couple of mistakes in the areas I know about. He had one figure at 175 million when it should have been 4 million. He swore I was wrong. Then, later, he called, said he'd buy me a steak dinner, and apologized. It turned out they used interns to research these things during the transition. Stockman doesn't know details.

Steak dinner or no, the senator saw the budget director as an enemy of REA and remained openly critical of him from that point forward.

During the last hours of the Budget Committee's four-day marathon on reconciliation (in which each committee would be instructed to make spending reductions within its jurisdiction), Andrews moved to seek ironclad protection for REA in the face of administration efforts to reduce federal funding and force the co-ops into the private borrowing market.

> SENATOR ANDREWS: Is this Committee going to do anything with these off budget functions?
> SENATOR DOMENICI: No sir.
> SENATOR ANDREWS: In other words, there is going to be no action taken by the Budget Committee to limit loans to the Rural Electrification Administration.
> SENATOR DOMENICI: No. . . . Those would be taken up if we see fit in the First [Budget] Resolution.
> SENATOR ANDREWS: But not at this point.
> SENATOR DOMENICI: No sir.[17]

Later in the day, Andrews pressed for further assurances.

> SENATOR ANDREWS: I would like to establish some legislative

history and maybe correct a misunderstanding I have. Three hours ago ... I asked the Chairman if he had any intention of taking up this page of off budget savings recommended by the President, having to do specifically with the REA.

SENATOR DOMENICI: Yes sir.

SENATOR ANDREWS: The Chairman assured me he would not.

SENATOR DOMENICI: I will not.

SENATOR ANDREWS: I think we have the votes in here to defeat that type of approach, if it were taken. But now I look at Section 10 ... and I just want to make it crystal clear that we are in no way, in Section 10, patting the President on the back for ... taking away money availability to build power generating plants by rural electric coops.

SENATOR DOMENICI: ... I can assure you that there is no off-budget item contemplated in Section 10. ...

SENATOR ANDREWS: I just wanted to make that point, Mr. Chairman.

SENATOR DOMENICI: I understand your concern about REA.

A few minutes later Andrews spoke up for the third time. He repeated his bottom-line warning that he had the votes if necessary by reminding his Democratic allies out loud that "we do not have to go to a vote with it, as long as we have the assurance of the Chairman and we have made parliamentary history that we are not messing around in that field here today." Chairman Domenici said, "I am opposed to it, too." After explaining why, he added, "Does that satisfy you?" Andrews replied, "We just wanted to make sure that the snake we have been trying to kill stays dead." [18]

A month later, when the committee took up the agricultural function in the Budget Resolution, Andrews intervened again to keep the REA out of harm's way.

SENATOR ANDREWS: Is there any inference in the mark [that is, numbers] that you have proposed, Mr Chairman, about the funding for rural telephone service which the President also suggested to be eliminated? I would imagine that your mark would call for the elimination of funding for rural telephones.

STAFFER: No, it does not. The REA is off budget and not in this function.

SENATOR ANDREWS: I did not think it was, but I wanted to make sure.

The next day, Chairman Domenici mentioned "Senator Andrews' fantastic success heretofore" on REA. Later, during the discussion of off-budget items, Andrews proposed the "restoration of present borrowing power by rural electric co-ops and rural telephone co-ops" by making loan money available through the Federal Financing Bank. With the support of the committee's southern Democrats, who were his sturdiest allies on all matters affecting the REA, his proposal passed by voice vote.[19]

At the end of his first year, Andrews looked back with satisfaction at his ability to exploit his multiple committee memberships to protect REA from the Reagan budget cuts. "My committee assignments were perfect for protecting rural electrification," he explained.

> We used the Budget Committee to track what Stockman and company were doing early on, so we could stop him on reconciliation and the budget resolution. Then we kept him from cutting during the appropriations process. And we could protect the program in the authorizing committee [Agriculture]. I had all three legs of the three-legged stool. It wasn't a matter of expanding the program. It was a matter of keeping it from being cut.

Andrews's "three-legged stool" gave him virtual legislative hegemony over the Rural Electrification Administration.[20]

It was not just his three committee positions, however, that explained the influence of Mark Andrews: it was his willingness and his ability to use those positions.

> If I can sit here with four four-star generals and an assistant secretary of state asking me for $4 billion for a weapons system, then I ought to be able to ask $300 million for rural electrification loans. . . . What could be better than to make North Dakota self sufficient in heating and at half the price of oil.

He seized every opportunity to make his case.

Sitting in his office in October, I listened as he took a call from the White House to sound him out on the critical upcoming vote to send AWACS planes to Saudi Arabia. Andrews's end of the conversation went, in part, like this:

> The best thing everyone could do is just lay off. The more pressure I get to vote for it, the more I'm going to have to vote against it. . . . No, I've had all the input I want to have on AWACS. I've had more input on that in the last two weeks than anything else since I've been here.
>
> Well, if you want to talk about other considerations, the administration is telling us we have to sell AWACS to Saudi Arabia to protect our oil supply in the Middle East and keep us energy independent. Then Stockman comes up and recommends we cut subsidies to energy producing cooperatives in my state. . . . If you are interested in energy independence— and you should be—why not help the people in this country

who are also working toward energy independence? How inconsistent can you be? There's no quid pro quo here. We ran over you on the rural cooperatives twice before this year and we'll do it again. But that's something you might want to consider. . . .

When he got off the phone, he said, "AWACS is taking two hours a day—all that time for an issue that doesn't mean a rat's ass in North Dakota." He had taken the occasion to try to make the process meaningful for North Dakota, however, by lecturing the administration on the substantive merits and the political support for his REA interests.

Similarly, when the Budget Committee met on the day after David Stockman's doubts about Reaganomics had been shockingly revealed in the *Atlantic* magazine, Andrews jumped in to further undermine the director's credibility, using the matter of REA. "I always thought," he said, "that Stockman was long on style and short on substance. He was dead wrong on the REA co-ops. He said I didn't know what I was talking about. But he had to call later and apologize. . . . We have one apple in the barrel that is a little overripe." Chairman Domenici, not Stockman, deserved credit for budget cutting, Andrews said, adding: "Down on the farm, we have the bull that paws the ground and the one that delivers the calf." [21] Other Republicans on the committee rallied to Stockman's defense. Andrews, instead, moved just as quickly to further discredit a major antagonist on a matter of prime concern to him. In both these instances, he had aggressively seized opportunities to further his REA interests in situations that did not call for such behavior.

Andrews's outspoken opposition to the administration on rural electrification drew early notice from journalists. So, gradually, did his success. When I arrived in Washington in the fall of 1981, a leading congressional reporter on the Budget Committee beat told me, "You can tell that Andrews has had more experience than the [other freshmen]. They don't know what they're doing. He knows his way around and he has hit the ground running." Andrews himself soon took to describing his new life as "same zoo, different cage." [22] In January, a second national reporter tagged Andrews as one of the few "budding stars" of his freshman class for his "artful way of bailing people out when they begin stumbling over their questions and losing their trains of thought." [23]

In December, Albert Hunt of the *Wall Street Journal* delivered the first year end scorecard on the sixteen Republican newcomers.

Senior senators [are] especially disappointed with the six freshman Republicans who previously had served in the House. None have made much of a legislative impression in the

Senate, although North Dakota's Mark Andrews sometimes is an effective champion of parochial interests such as rural electrification and farm subsidies. . . .[24]

It was a comparatively favorable judgment.

When Andrews read it, he was content. "I don't know how successful I've been," he said.

Our senior colleagues may think we're a bunch of dolts and dummies, but they come around and ask us for a bridge or a rail line. They seem to appreciate the help, too. At least they say they do. I don't know who that reporter talked to. . . . I came off pretty well—as an effective champion of rural electrification and farm subsidies. They called me parochial. Well, *parochial* may be a damning word in the *Wall Street Journal*, but it's a favorable word in North Dakota.

That seemed like a reasonable enough verdict on the budgetary preoccupations of his first year.

BUDGET COMMITTEE BEHAVIOR, 1982

In 1982, I was able to follow budget making first hand, off and on, from start to finish. Mark Andrews continued to use the budget process—infrequently but tenaciously—for his own purposes. His tactic was disconcerting to those more devoted to that process than he. When, for example, Director of the Congressional Budget Office Alice Rivlin came to testify about the needs and operations of her office, Andrews steered her directly to agricultural matters. Chairman Domenici gently admonished him.

"Senator Andrews, you can get into substance if you wish, although this was supposed to be an oversight hearing." Andrews replied, "I'm getting to that . . . I thought this would add something, that it would be a fun deal" [*laughter*]. At that point he proceeded to question the director about the pending farm bill. When she had difficulty responding, he said, "We know these things backwards and forwards. Don't you have the experience, or is this a low priority?" He asked her to "drop me a note" explaining how the budget office interpreted "commodity loans" and "target prices," and he asked her to "send me a report on peanuts and sugar." [25] It was a blunt and independent-minded intervention. But, except to Andrews himself, it was not helpful.

Andrews's behavior throughout the budget-making activities of May 1982 vividly displayed the maverick-style pursuit of North Dakota's interests. On the morning of May 4, we talked just prior to the Budget Committee's meeting to begin its markup of the budget resolution.

Calling this time "the zoo season here" and predicting nothing but "a big hoorah," he seemed to be keeping his distance from all proceedings. "I don't think we'll get anything accomplished," he predicted.

> We had a meeting with the president yesterday, and we couldn't agree among ourselves. The Republicans are meeting now in Domenici's office. I don't want to go there. And I don't want to know what they are saying. I had a talk with the chairman at breakfast. I know what the script is. I can make more productive use of my time than sitting here this morning. But I have to show up and sit here for a while.

Once the committee meeting got under way, he stayed for half an hour and left—and was the first senator to do so.

The next morning, on the day of the climactic budget negotiations, Andrews came to the committee meeting late and immersed himself in a newspaper. He spoke once—to register his personal desire to repeal the third year of the Reagan tax cut—and then went back to his newspaper reading. "I'm getting sick and tired of the signals we are sending out to the general public," he said. "Last year, this Congress voted for $750 million in tax cuts [and] that is too damned high." [26] It was a strongly held policy position, and it stemmed from his belief that the tax cut was keeping interest rates high and hurting his constituents. "There are only three things my constituents are interested in now," he was saying privately. "The first is interest rates, the second is interest rates, the third is interest rates. They aren't even interested in the farm bill."

Rehearsing the May 3 visit of committee Republicans to the White House, he said:

> I told the president that people thought he started on the right track and had things going well until the big tax bill, that people feel he went off the track there and has had his head in the sand ever since. I said people felt he had to do something— and getting rid of the third year of the tax cut would be a start. . . . I told him that, and he nearly flipped. . . . No one else was as blunt as I was.

Eventually, Andrews would be the only Republican to vote in committee to repeal the third year of the tax cut. It was a constituency-based view embedded in a populist's distrust of the corporate beneficiaries of tax cuts and a fear of high interest rates for the ordinary citizen.

"There isn't anything more basic to what this country is all about," he declaimed, in discussing his tax cut vote later,

> than the opportunity for people to obtain long-term credit—to build a small house, or start a small business, or buy a small

farm. Interest rates are so gol darned high—16 1/2 percent—
that long-term borrowing is impossible. People can stand it for
one year, maybe two. But if we don't bring interest rates down
and make long term borrowing possible again, there will be a
wrenching in this country worse than anything except an
invasion by the Russians. And, frankly, I don't know which
would be worse.

He was using the Budget Committee as a platform for expressing and
voting what he believed was an identity of policy views—and emotions—between himself and his fellow North Dakotans.

His Budget Committee behavior was not, however, making Chairman Pete Domenici's decision-making job easier. Far from it. Domenici
had spent May 5 negotiating with committee members and the administration over his proposed budget plan.[27] The strength of his bargaining
position with the administration depended entirely upon the unified
support of his twelve committee Republicans. When he had reached a
tentative agreement with the president, Domenici convened an early
evening caucus of the Committee Republicans to firm up their support
for the overall bargain. But, again, Andrews did not show up at his
party's caucus. As it turned out, he was waiting to intervene at the
eleventh hour, at the crucial moment of full committee decision making.

Chairman Domenici opened the May 5 evening meeting with the
dramatic announcement: "The president will support this budget." It
was a high point of Chairman Domenici's budgetary leadership. No
sooner had he finished handing out copies of the agreement, however,
than Andrews broke in: "Mr. Chairman, I have a problem—not with
your logic nor with the great work you have done in bringing the White
House around. But I have a serious problem that I think we ought to
bring up tonight on how you figure the baseline [for transportation]."[28]
In this case, he was acting in his capacity as chairman of the Subcommittee on Transportation of the Appropriations Committee, to protect his
subcommittee's segment of the budget. The problem was that money
deferred from 1981 to 1982 and spent in 1982 was not being counted as
part of the baseline funding level for 1983. It amounted to $800 million;
and Andrews wanted it put back into the transportation section of the
budget.

He had shrewdly chosen the very moment of the chairman's political
triumph to pose his threat. He knew he would catch everyone off balance;
and he knew that would be his time of maximum leverage. "I can't sit
here," he said, "as much as I am intrigued by the package that my good
friend from New Mexico has worked out, and not bring this to the view
of the committee." He called it "a unique misfortune"; and he punctuated
his complaint by reminding his committee colleagues that they and the

White House were at that very moment importuning his subcommittee for more highway and Coast Guard funds for their districts.

Four times he asked the chairman for "assurance that we can handle this one way or another." All he got from Domenici was: "I can tell you that we can surely work on it. I can't promise you that we can handle it." Andrews concluded, "If we can make that adjustment, fine. I think you have done a great job." "Thank you very much, Senator. I appreciate it," said Domenici. "I'm sure you do," replied Andrews, to the laughter of the spectators.[29] Both men knew that the chairman's leadership hung in the balance. "Mark Andrews hadn't come to our caucus," Domenici said when it was all over. "He scared the hell out of me."

Domenici joined Budget Committee Staff Director Steve Bell and Appropriations Committee Staff Director Keith Kennedy in a huddle with Andrews in the corridor. Andrews turned up the pressure. He was, he told them, speaking also on behalf of committee Republican Bob Kasten [R-Wis.], who faced a similar problem. "We reached an understanding," recounted Andrews a couple of days later,

> that $800 million of appropriations money would be earmarked for my [transportation] bill. That took care of me. We also took care of a little for Kasten. When we got back in the meeting, I said, for the record, that I appreciated the accommodation the chairman had made. And I asked Kasten to say he appreciated it too. We did it publicly . . . [otherwise] the staff people may forget it—on purpose or not.
>
> If it's in public, everyone understands what has been done. Domenici knew what I was doing. The Democrats knew what I was doing. Most of the people around the table had a bridge or a highway or the Coast Guard or something they wanted in that [transportation] bill. The bottom line was that Domenici could count.

With a committee ratio of twelve Republicans and ten Democrats, everyone understood that two defections would surely be fatal.

After their hallway huddle, Chairman Domenici told the committee that "there is one slight item of disagreement . . . you know, the one Mark Andrews raised. . . . I want to negotiate that tomorrow." But Andrews, making certain there was no misunderstanding about the stakes, reasserted his position:

> I would just like to point out, since I brought up the question of deferred funds in the baseline—and there are two or three of us on this side of the table who feel the same way I do and a number on the other side—that the Chairman has assured us that he will do his dead level best tomorrow to negotiate out this problem. . . . Am I wrong in that statement?

"No" replied the chairman, "you are absolutely right."[30]

After the committee adjourned, a satisfied Senator Andrews talked about "the good deal we made." He explained: "You understand what we did, don't you? There were two votes he didn't have, and we became the rally points. We got what we wanted." The next day a third committee member, whose vote Andrews had held in reserve, proposed an amendment to do for his program interests what Andrews's deal had accomplished for his. He did not succeed; Andrews did not support him. "I don't know what he'll do," said the North Dakotan. "But that's his problem. That's the way it goes. I never thought much of [his] program anyway." So much for the principle of the thing. He needed two votes to protect his subcommittee's budget, and two votes was all he cared about.

The next evening, May 6, the Budget Committee met to vote on a series of Democratic amendments and to pass the Domenici budget. Early on, Andrews (and he alone) voted twice with the Democrats—for the repeal of the third year tax cut and for a $300 million boost in funding for education programs. After the second of these votes, he sought a public commitment from the chairman that "there will be reference protecting the rural electric cooperatives' access to the FFB [Federal Financing Bank] . . . just as we had in our report last year. That is the understanding I have with the Chairman." And, again, he reminded the chairman of the political bottom line and his easy relationship with committee Democrats. "My colleagues Senator [Bennett] Johnston [D-La.], Senator [Lawton] Chiles [D-Fla.] and, I am sure, Senator [Ernest] Hollings and Senator [James] Sasser [D-Tenn.] certainly are as interested as I am. The Chairman has been a great supporter of this amendment. I just wanted to make sure it did not fall through the cracks this year." "It will not," responded Chairman Domenici.[31]

Having won all his points, Andrews left the room, thereby missing the last nine committee votes. "When Jim Sasser said he had to leave, and asked unanimous consent to be recorded against the budget resolution," said Andrews, explaining his departure,

> I jumped in and said I had to leave and asked unanimous consent to be recorded for the resolution. I had already voted twice with the Democrats. And I probably would have voted with them several more times. That would have displeased my Republican colleagues. So Sasser gave me a graceful way out.

His absenteeism, in this case, should probably be interpreted more as dissent than lack of interest. He continued:

> I guess I'm a marked man around here. I was the only Republican to vote to rescind the tax cut and the only Republi-

can to vote for the Hollings motion on education. . . . On the
Hollings motion, I just believe in those programs.

The latter vote was one he subsequently talked about with the educational group back home in October (Chapter 1).

From the perspective of his Republican colleagues, Mark Andrews
was notably unpredictable on budget matters. And he would remain so.
When the budget resolution came to the floor, he used his unpredict-
ability once again to bargain for his interests—this time with his party
leader. The day after his maverick committee votes, Majority Leader
Howard Baker came around to nudge his stray member into the corral.
"Howard Baker came up to me today," Andrews recounted with a
chuckle,

> and said "We've got to get the budget resolution through
> without any amendments." I said I agreed that we had to get a
> budget resolution passed. He said, "You've been voting with
> the Democrats." I told him, "I've been voting for those pro-
> grams since before you came to Congress, Howard." He said, "I
> know, but we've got to get this budget resolution through." I
> said I didn't know whether I'd vote for amendments or not.
> Then he said, "What do you want?" I said, "I want this REA
> deal and a couple of other things." He said, "You've got 'em."

Nonetheless, when the resolution came to the floor, Andrews's vote
contributed to his committee's only defeat—on an amendment he
supported to restore certain railroad retirement benefits.

Two of Andrews's staffers explained that vote as a constituency
matter pure and simple. "The railroads used to be the biggest employer
in North Dakota. Maybe they still are," said one. "I think we have more
railroad retirees than any other state in the union. We got a horrendous
amount of mail from them." Another explained: "A lot of the mail came
from people who used to be section hands. They are the people who
went out and pulled the ties and pounded the spikes. They never did
make very good wages, so their pensions are small. So the mail was
skewed to the low income end of the scale. Mark responds to such
people." In a conflict between party and constituency, he had sided with
his constituents.

In their back rooms, Budget Committee staff members took a less
sympathetic view of Andrews's defection. They had expected him to
stand up to constituency pressure in order to protect the committee. "He
was the biggest disappointment. He doesn't have to run again for four
years, and he'll never be beaten," said one. "He's a little flaky," said
another. "He gets along OK with the other members, but he doesn't
always do what he promised he'd do." Another one generalized about

the North Dakotan's committee behavior: "You can watch Mark Andrews run circles around everyone else. He knows more about how the system works than anyone. You can watch him lean on people. He likes to do that. The staff thinks he's the worst manipulator in the Senate. They love it when he loses." After Andrews had voted twice more against the committee on the Senate floor, and after the fiscal year 1983 budget had passed the Senate, he wanted to be named to the Senate-House conference committee. But Chairman Domenici, worried about Andrews's unreliability, finessed that.

The next time I talked to Andrews about the budget resolution, it had come back from conference and he was unhappy about the outcome of the REA deal he had struck with Baker. He was now using his position on the Appropriations Committee to pressure the chairman of the Budget Committee. "I was just in Baker's office with [Senate Appropriations Committee Chairman Mark] Hatfield [R-Ore.]," he said,

> fussing about the budget. Domenici was there. Unless they change it, I'm not going to support it. I spoke up in the [Republican] policy meeting today. Do you know what the conferees did? For the first time in history, they put on a credit allocation ceiling. Any loans above that ceiling will be subject to a point of order. Domenici said they set the ceiling high enough so that the provision would not be triggered this year. I said "I know, but what about next year? What will happen to rural electrification loans?" It's between Budget and Appropriations. I brought in [Appropriations Committee member Arlen] Specter [R-Pa.] for reinforcement. We have the votes to defeat the conference report. . . . Our staffs are trying to work something out. Everything's up in the air.

In the end, he accepted some verbal assurances and voted for the budget. But he had held up the conference report in order to extract one last REA concession from the Budget Committee.

At the end of the year, the senator from North Dakota could once more point with pride to his legislative efforts on behalf of REA:

> I enjoy shepherding things through the process. On REA, it was my amendment that saved it in the Budget Committee, my amendment that saved it in the Ag[riculture] Committee, and my amendment that saved it in the Appropriations Committee. Of course I didn't do it alone . . . [but] you have to go pretty far down on the Republican side to find REA support. All the Democrats are strong supporters.

Writing at the same time, the *New York Times* reporter covering the Budget Committee, Martin Tolchin, concurred.

The Rural Electrification Administration ... was targeted by the White House, but survived intact largely because of the efforts of Senator Mark Andrews, Republican of North Dakota. "We got nowhere on that," said Edwin L. Dale, Jr., a spokesman for OMB. "Not only did we not succeed, but Congress mandated that REA loans for new power plants be financed through the Treasury." As a freshman senator, Mr. Andrews is an unlikely protector. But the senator previously served in the House and knows his way around Congress.[32]

Much of Mark Andrews's behavior surely traces back to his strong North Dakota roots and to an ideological independence nurtured there. But much of his success surely traces, also, to legislative skills developed during his long tenure in the House. His frequent alliances with the Democrats were the product of his many years of bipartisan cooperation on the House Appropriations Committee. His membership in the minority on that committee had not been polarizing, either ideologically or with regard to policy. His shift to the majority was effortless. These experiences set him apart from the other five Budget Committee freshmen, who came to the committee predisposed to close ranks and go down the line for the administration's requests. Andrews came to the Budget Committee knowing when, where, and with whom to intervene in the legislative flow in order to get what he wanted.

Much of his Budget Committee behavior also traces back, we have argued, to his strong distaste—as a deep-dyed House Appropriations Committee veteran—for the entire reformed budget process. "A lot of the old-time Appropriations types would just as soon do away with the budget process," said a committee colleague in 1982. "Mark Andrews would probably be willing to do that." Just before he cast his vote in the Budget Committee in favor of the 1981 reconciliation package, Andrews lectured his colleagues on their fiscal pretensions. "The only way I can characterize it," he said,

is it is the damnedest display of arrogating into ourselves that I have ever seen a committee in Congress do. We are not the whole show.... This is not the only committee in Congress. What the Budget Committee, as I understand it, is supposed to do is put some broad strokes on the canvas to show the other committees on which we serve, in the Appropriations Committee, the Finance Committee or the rest what they are coming to ... we are not the only act in town.[33]

It was hardly a call to collegial responsibilities.

Back home in the fall of 1982, in his speeches to business groups and to educators there (Chapter 1), he made his preferences clearer still.

"We need a Budget Committee like we need another hole in the head. . . . The press got the idea that Congress should have a Budget Committee, so we have a whole new set of inexperts overseeing the whole thing. . . . The authorizing committee can't do it like the Budget Committee does it. The Appropriations Committee can't do it like the authorizing committee does it. Nobody did it so nobody does it." Further, "The budget process is a mess. It slows everything down." It is, he said, "a rinky-dink idea that has made things worse." The addition of the budget process to the already time-consuming authorization-appropriations process, he told his constituents, has put Congress in "a functional slowdown" and "in the last stages of cholesterol filled arteries." His preference was to "clean house" and return to a more appropriations-centered process. (One week after his defeat in 1986, he called publicly for the abolition of the Senate Budget Committee.)[34] Small wonder he was not a model member of that committee.

Because he believed the work of the Budget Committee to be eminently dispensable, Andrews did not concern himself with implementing or protecting its broadest mandate—the introduction of a comprehensive macro-level perspective into a traditional process deemed to be excessively fragmented and micro-oriented. Unlike several of the other committee newcomers, he never prepared his own comprehensive budget plan for the scrutiny of his colleagues. By going his own way and exploiting his Budget Committee membership for his own purposes, he was behaving contrary to the spirit of its charter. While he did occasionally—as with the tax cut—observe the macro-level injunctions of the budget process, he slipped those constraints whenever he believed it to be in the interests of his state or himself to do so. Most of the time, therefore, he operated at the micro level in pursuit of his personal goals. His attitude and his behavior often put him at odds with his fellow Republicans on the committee. His considerable success in these disruptive pursuits probably exacerbated a sense of discomfort and lack of fit on all sides.

THE HOUSE AND SENATE APPROPRIATIONS COMMITTEES

Mark Andrews's Budget Committee behavior can be explained in part by his lack of allegiance to the explicit macro-level injunctions and the implicit committeewide constraints of its charter. But that is a negative explanation. A more positive explanation derives from his oft-stated devotion to the traditional budget process in which, as a member of the House Appropriations Committee, he participated for so long.

For the first ten years (1964-1974) of Mark Andrews's service there, the House Appropriations Committee was the central institution in congressional budget making. It was the first committee to pass judgment on the president's budget, and it typically set the overall pattern for the congressional response. Its members saw themselves as the most regular overseers of agency spending and the front-line guardians of the federal treasury. Their decisions took the form of an incremental balancing of budget reductions and allowances for growth, with careful attention to the distribution of constituency benefits to individual House members. Insofar as the committee had a special mission, it was to make executives walk the hard road to get their money and to reduce their budgets where possible. Committee members did their work within a sharply defined subcommittee division of labor. Subcommittee specialists engaged in a close, line-by-line, micro-level scrutiny of executive requests.

Members arrived at their decisions privately, in a style that featured nonideological, bipartisan compromise. "Appropriations Committee politics is back room politics," said the House Education and Labor Committee's top staffer in the mid-sixties. "They accommodate to you; you accommodate to them. They don't pass a bill the way other committees do—with public discussion, public arguments, and then appeals to support groups to put on the pressure to get you the votes." With deference and reciprocity operating between, as well as within, subcommittees, each one was able to carry its decisions confidently to the floor. Sometimes the committee would invade the jurisdiction of an authorizing committee, write "legislation on an appropriations bill" and win protection on the floor for their rule-breaking aggressiveness. The system provided for no comprehensive planning or summary supervision. Whatever the specialized subcommittees produced would, in the normal course, constitute the national pattern of expenditures.[35]

By the same token, whatever an individual subcommittee member could accomplish within his or her small work group stood a good chance of becoming law. For a representative like Mark Andrews, from a small state and in the minority party, it was an ideal context in which to participate actively, work across party lines, have a detectable impact on spending, and secure benefits for his constituency—benefits that were more certain since he sat on the agriculture subcommittee and rose to become its senior Republican member.

With the coming of congressional budget reform and the Budget Committee in 1974, the House Appropriations Committee found its primacy gone, the presumption in its favor reversed, its ability to set congressional budget patterns reduced, and its budget-cutting zeal undermined. Now the committee had to operate within funding limits given to it by the Budget Committee, and each Appropriations subcommittee had to operate with the amount of money allocated to it by the full Appropriations Committee.[36]

We cannot know how Andrews responded to these changes while he was still on the House committee. But we do know that as a member of the Senate Budget Committee he maneuvered constantly to protect the Senate Appropriations Committee from the effects of new budgetary constraints.

In the Senate, Andrews's legislative domain became the Sub-committee on Transportation of the Senate Appropriations Committee— of which he became the chairman. And he worked, within the Budget Committee, to protect his domain. He pressed, for example, for higher ceilings. "I put together an amendment in the Budget Committee that saved Amtrak in the budget resolution"; and "it was my amendment as a member of the Budget Committee that increased funding [for transportation] by some $400 million." [37] He worked also in the Budget Committee to maintain maximum budgetary leeway for the parent Appropriations Committee. "The mark that I propose is the mark that is supported by Senator Hatfield and by the staff of the Appropriations Committee. . . . we think we need that much additional leeway." [38]

When conflict between Budget and Appropriations broke out in 1985, Andrews fought aggressively on behalf of his subcommittee. In the Budget Committee he voted against the budget resolution, which called for $800 million in "unspecified savings" from the Transportation Subcommittee. Having lost, he proceeded to engineer the required savings by cutting his subcommittee's two most popular programs— Coast Guard and FAA—knowing that they would eventually be restored in conference with the House. And, adding insult to injury, Andrews also eliminated an important $16 million highway project of Budget Committee Chairman Pete Domenici from his subcommittee bill. That action prompted Domenici to take the Senate floor and ask his colleagues for restoration of the funds. The thoroughly unpleasant floor fight resulted in a 56-40 amendment victory for Domenici. But he had been forced to walk a very hard road to get it.[39] And that lesson was probably not lost among Andrews's Senate colleagues.

Another Republican newcomer, one who served with Andrews on both the Budget and Appropriations Committees, described his own loyalties and preferences by saying, "I wear my Budget hat in the Appropriations Committee much more than I wear my Appropriations hat in the Budget Committee. . . . I'm closer to Pete Domenici than I am to Mark Hatfield." Mark Andrews wore his hats, however, in the contrary fashion. He harmonized more naturally with Hatfield than with Domenici. And between the two committees, there was never any doubt where his head and his heart were located.

In one important respect the House Appropriations Committee's operation did *not* change after 1974 and did not call for any adaptation on Andrews's part. That was the committee's ability to make decisions allocating benefits to individual House members. The committee's traditional decision-making pattern—incremental, dollars-and-cents decisions rather than philosophical ones—had always been perfectly suited to piecemeal, constituency-oriented decision making. And in the period after the budgetary reforms, constituency-oriented decision making became an increasingly prominent committee activity. Indeed, the committee's constituency orientation became the most attractive feature of the committee to its newest members.[40] Observers came to see Appropriations as the premier House committee through which Congress "goes about its unglamorous, basic business of trading [and] cutting deals" and "returns direct benefits to home districts and states."[41] House Appropriations committee members had a continuing opportunity to sharpen their constituency-oriented skills in the postreform years between 1974 and 1980.

For all of his sixteen years on the House committees, therefore, Mark Andrews worked to steer federal money toward North Dakota. When he came to the Senate he was a strongly constituency-oriented legislator, well-practiced in achieving constituency-related goals through the appropriations process. And he would find the Senate Appropriations Committee to be an even more congenial arena in which to pursue those goals.

The Senate Appropriations Committee never expressed the pretensions to budgetary primacy traditionally held by its House counterpart. To the contrary, its members had *always* thought of their committee as the optimal location in the Senate from which to look out for constituency interests; and it was this feature that had always attracted senators to it. In the mid-sixties senators routinely explained their membership on the committee by saying, "I know I can get more for my state on this committee than on any other committee" or "on Appropriations I can, realistically, get more benefits for my state" or "on Appropriations you can ... get things for your state you couldn't get otherwise."[42]

In the late 1980s, observers were still describing the Senate Committee as "the insiders' world of Appropriations [where] partisanship [is] rare, as members swap support to steer federal dollars to their home states."[43] In 1982, a senator who sat on both the Appropriations and Budget Committees made the comparison.

> Appropriations people are traders. They are split-the-difference guys. "I'll give you this if you give me that." "You owe me one." "I'll give you a bridge if you keep a Coast Guard station

open." They are the people who decide most of what gets
spent. . . . On the Budget Committee, there is no trading. There
is this feeling that we're going to solve this great big problem
and make the government work.

For Mark Andrews, the transition from a committee of traders in the
House to a committee of traders in the Senate was effortless.

Within the Senate Appropriations Committee, member expectations
regarding benefits tend to focus on the business of their subcommittees.
As Andrews's own subcommittee staff chief put it:

If the Senate is a club, then each [Appropriations] subcommittee
is a junior club. Membership conveys access and prerogatives. If
you are a member, you can get things from the subcommittee
that other people can't. The main thing is access. The members
don't think of their subcommittees as decision-making bodies,
although they are. They think, "I'm a member of this subcommittee, so I can get something done in this area."

The best subcommittee position from which to operate is the chairmanship.

Mark Andrews became chairman of the Subcommittee on Transportation by a process of elimination, as Republican committee members
chose their subcommittee assignments in order of seniority. The subcommittee presided over a piece of legislation with about $12 billion in
yearly appropriations decisions and more than twice that in yearly
expenditures. It provided money for such matters as roads, bridges,
subways, airports, railroads, and traffic safety and for such agencies as
the Coast Guard, the Federal Aviation Administration, the Urban Mass
Transit Administration, and the Federal Highway Administration.

Observers of the transportation subcommittees in the contemporary
House and Senate describe them as among the most constituency-
oriented of all appropriations subcommittees.[44] A high proportion of
subjects within their jurisdiction contain development and construction
grants with requirements for broad geographical dispersion—the perfect combination for legislators eager to bring bricks and mortar, jobs
and publicity, to their home constituencies. When the Reagan administration's record-breaking budget reduction effort ended in 1981, one
analyst concluded:

It still barely scratched the surface of most transportation
projects, one of the most lucrative parts of the congressional
pork barrel. Many of the same senators who joined the assault
on a wide variety of domestic programs continued to vote for
costly new highways, subways and money-losing railroads in
their states.[45]

"This [transportation] subcommittee is different from some others," agreed a top Andrews staffer: "It is basically a pork barrel committee." So Mark Andrews, a constituency-minded senator, became chairman of one of the most constituency-minded subcommittees on one of the most constituency-minded committees in the Senate.

Our explanation for Mark Andrews's conspicuous lack of team play on the Senate Budget Committee gives special weight to his strong attachment to the prereform appropriations process in which he was steeped during his lengthy service on the House Appropriations Committee. We can test further for this explanation by examining his behavior on the Senate Appropriations Committee—which provides the closest match with the House Appropriations Committee and which was, for that very reason, Mark Andrews's first committee choice. Such an exercise would buttress our general idea that Mark Andrews's senatorial behavior can best be understood as the continuance of behavior patterns he learned in the House.

If our argument is correct, we would expect to find the North Dakota senator more enthusiastic, more participatory, more influential, and altogether more at home on the Senate Appropriations Committee than he was on the Senate Budget Committee. We would not necessarily expect these differences to flow from any change in his highly individualistic and particularistic governing style. Rather, we would expect to find a consistent set of goals and strategies that ran *against* the grain in one committee context but *with* the grain in the other committee context. In the more congenial, more familiar, and more facilitating environment of the constituency-minded Senate Appropriations Committee, we would expect to observe the more authentic and more constructive committee performance by our House member in the Senate. That governing performance is the subject of Chapter 3.

NOTES

1. Andrews, as mentioned in Chapter 1, fell ten months short of nine full terms. The only nine termer to try besides Andrews was James Broyhill of North Carolina, who was appointed to the Senate but defeated for election to it, both in 1986.
2. *Congressional Record*, December 20, 1982, S15757.
3. Richard F. Fenno, Jr., "Adjusting to the United States Senate" in *Congress and Policy Changes*, ed. Gerald Wright, Leroy Rieselbach, and Lawrence Dodd (New York: Agathon Press, 1986).
4. Ibid.
5. Richard F. Fenno, Jr., *The Power of the Purse: Appropriations Politics in Congress*

(Boston: Little, Brown, 1965).

6. The other states with a single House member were Alaska, Delaware, South Dakota, Vermont, and Wyoming.

7. I did not observe him at work on the Agriculture Committee or, later, on the Select Committee on Indian Affairs, of which he became chairman. I touch upon his Agriculture Committee work at various points, but the treatment of his committee work is confined to Budget and Appropriations.

8. Alan Ehrenhalt, ed., *Politics in America, 1984* (Washington, D.C.: CQ Press, 1984), 1153. A full description of committee beliefs and practices in the period will be found in Fenno, *The Power of the Purse.*

9. Sen. Ernest Hollings (D-S.C.), in Transcript of Proceedings, United States Senate Committee on the Budget, "Revising the Second Budget Resolution for FY 1981 to Include Reconciliation: S. Con. Res. 9," March 19, 1981, 785.

10. Allen Schick, *Congress and Money: Budgeting, Spending, Taxing* (Washington, D.C.: Urban Institute, 1980); John Ellwood and James Thurber, "The New Congressional Budget Process: The Hows and Whys of House-Senate Differences" in *Congress Reconsidered*, ed. Lawrence Dodd and Bruce Oppenheimer (New York: Praeger, 1977); and John Ellwood, "House-Senate Relations and the Budget Process" (Unpublished manuscript).

11. The Budget-Appropriations picture as of 1981 is described in Richard Cohen, "Budget Express Leaving the Station Without the Appropriations Committees," *National Journal*, July 4, 1981; the situation later in the eighties is described in Joseph White, "The Functions and Powers of the House Appropriations Committee," unpublished manuscript, University of California, Berkeley, 1989; and Diane Granat, "House Appropriations Panel Doles Out Cold Federal Cash, Chafes at Budget Procedures," *Congressional Quarterly Weekly Report*, June 18, 1983.

12. See Richard F. Fenno, Jr., *The Emergence of a Senate Leader: Pete Domenici and the Reagan Budget* (Washington, D.C.: CQ Press, 1991).

13. Calculations by the author.

14. "Revising the Second Budget Resolution," March 19, 1981, 18.

15. Ibid., 40-42.

16. Harry Anderson, "Reagan Readies the Axe," *Newsweek*, February 16, 1981.

17. "Revising the Second Budget Resolution," March 19, 1981, 804.

18. Ibid., 934, 940-941. See also George Will, "Government: Not a Klutz," *Washington Post*, March 26, 1981.

19. Transcript of Proceedings, United States Senate Committee on the Budget, "First Concurrent Budget Resolution, FY 1982," April 8, 1981, 311; April 9, 1981, 562, 581-593.

20. To the end of his term, Andrews continued to act as the watchdog-protector of REA funding. For the 1985 story, see Elizabeth Wehr, "Bipartisan Budget Headed for Senate Floor," *Congressional Quarterly Weekly Report*, March 22, 1985. For the 1986 story, see *Congressional Record*, October 17, 1986, S16937.

21. From my notes taken at a Senate Budget Committee markup session, November 12, 1981. A similar attack on the Senate floor can be found in *Congressional Record*, September 10, 1982, 23152.

22. Al McConagha, "Mark Andrews Gets Senate Reputation by Riding Lone Trail," *Minneapolis Tribune*, May 8, 1983.

23. Eleanor Randolph, "The Best and the Worst of the U.S. Senate," *Washington Monthly*, January 1982.

24. Albert Hunt, " 'Popsicle Brigade': New GOP Senators Impress Their Seniors,

Though Not Favorably," *Wall Street Journal*, December 14, 1981.

25. From my notes taken at a Senate Budget Committee hearing on the Congressional Budget Office, February 5, 1982.
26. "First Concurrent Budget Resolution, FY 1982," May 5, 1982, 374-375.
27. The story of the 1982 Budget Committee effort is told in Fenno, *The Emergence of a Senate Leader*, chap. 3.
28. "First Concurrent Budget Resolution, FY 1982," May 5, 1982, 466.
29. Ibid., 467-473.
30. Ibid., 502, 534.
31. Ibid., May 6, 1982, 614.
32. Martin Tolchin, "Where the Budget Cutters Didn't Want to Cut," *New York Times*, October 3, 1982. See also Ward Sinclair, "Reagan Budget Gothic: Rural America Sees a Horn of Unplenty," *Washington Post*, April 4, 1981.
33. "Revising the Second Budget Resolution," April 9, 1981, 646-647.
34. Associated Press, "Andrews: Senate Too Slow in Acting," *Bismarck Tribune*, November 11, 1986.
35. This description can be found in detail in Fenno, *The Power of the Purse.*
36. See Schick, *Congress and Money.*
37. *Hearings*, FY 1987, April 9, 1986, 27; *Hearings*, FY 1984, pt. 2, April 27, 1983, 1068.
38. Transcript of Proceedings, United States Senate Committee on the Budget, "Revising the Second Budget Resolution for FY 1981 to Include Reconciliation: S. Con. Res. 9," March 19, 1981, 748ff.
39. Jonathan Rauch, "Senate Budget Panel Leaders Wage War on 'Budget Busting' Appropriations Bills," *National Journal*, November 11, 1985; *Congressional Record*, October 3, 1985, S13168-S13875.
40. Steven Smith and Christopher Deering, *Committees in Congress* (Washington, D.C.: CQ Press, 1984), 93-95.
41. Dan Morgan, "The Triumph of Geography over Ideology," *Washington Post National Weekly Edition*, August 21-27, 1989; Dan Morgan, "The Power to Spend Is the Power to Get Reelected," *Washington Post National Weekly Edition*, June 5 11, 1989.
42. Fenno, *The Power of the Purse*, chap. 10; Richard F. Fenno, Jr., *Congressmen in Committees* (Boston: Little, Brown, 1978), chap. 5.
43. Jackie Calmes, "Byrd Wields Power Quickly as New Committee Chief," *Congressional Quarterly Weekly Report*, December 9, 1989.
44. White, "The Functions and Powers of the House Appropriations Committee," chap. 4; John Yoo, "As Highways Decay, Their State Becomes Drag on the Economy ... Congress Pork-Barrels Along," *Wall Street Journal*, September 30, 1989.
45. Howie Kurtz, "Budget Knife Only Nicks Road and Harbor Projects," *Washington Post*, January 26, 1982.

Governing Style:
The Subcommittee Chairman

In January 1981, Mark Andrews took up his duties as chairman of the Subcommittee on Transportation of the Senate Committee on Appropriations. We shall view his governing performance as chairman from two angles. From one angle, he can be seen carrying out the chairman's basic tasks and responsibilities in a manner to which his years on two House subcommittees had accustomed him. From the other angle, he can be seen using his chairmanship to protect the interests of North Dakota and to steer as many tangible benefits in that direction as he legitimately could. This, too, he did in the familiar pattern of a House Appropriations Committee member.

HEARINGS

Because every senator has multiple governing involvements, every subcommittee chairman carries a lopsided burden of work and responsibility in his or her domain. Andrews slipped into the chairman's harness without a trace of difficulty. From his House experience, he was totally familiar with the micro-level routines of the job—interrogating the same executive branch officials in order to make the same line-by-line, dollars-and-cents decisions. He often stated his belief that "Congress is at its best in the hearings process." From that premise we can begin to chart his governing behavior.

"I've got a very interesting subcommittee," he said after a year on the job.

On the Republican side, I don't have a single person who ever served on an appropriations committee before. And on the Democratic side, I have a bunch of "rookies" like Lawton Chiles, John Stennis [Miss.], and Bob Byrd [W.Va]! They came to the first few meetings and they have not been back since. They came to see whether I could do the job, and I guess they decided I could. . . .

It's a lot easier to chair a Senate subcommittee than a House subcommittee. In the House, all the other members of the subcommittee come to the hearings. They all want to ask questions and you have to sit through a lot of repetition. Here, you get to ask all the questions you want to ask.

On the five occasions when I dropped in on his subcommittee hearings, the chairman was alone and asking a lot of questions. As he told one newcomer, "I have found that the more questions we get on the record, the better job we can do." [1] He was knowledgeable, comfortable, and in charge.

In most everything he did, moreover, Andrews revealed a strong attachment to his former committee. He talked constantly about it. "I have learned, in the 16 years that I have been on this side of the table in appropriations testimony . . ." he would say to witnesses. Or, "in the old days over in the House, we always used to find . . ." And he would describe the House committee as "the group I was brought up in." [2]

Over and over—especially in his early years—Andrews would draw on the wisdom of his first appropriations subcommittee chairman, John Rooney (D-N.Y.) "who coached me in this business." [3]

- "I had a friend by the name of John Rooney who taught me what I know, on the Appropriations Committee 16 years ago."
- "When I first started on Appropriations, John Rooney, my first chairman 16, 17 years ago told me, never ask a question you don't know the answer to."
- "Chairman Rooney taught me about running a committee some 16 years ago. I haven't forgotten some of the lessons he imparted to me way back when."
- "I had a subcommittee chairman years ago by the name of John Rooney who always said [that witnesses] never get into trouble if they don't stimulate a couple of extra questions."
- "I learned long ago from my friend John Rooney from Brooklyn—he was my first subcommittee chairman—he told me better make sure you get all the facts out." [4]

The nonpartisan inoculation administered by veteran Democrat Rooney to newcomer Republican Andrews in the 1960s obviously took—and lasted well into the 1980s.

Early on, Andrews remarked privately: "I'm going to miss the close friendships I made on the House committee. You worked day after day with the same small group of people on your subcommittee. Frankly, that was a plus. You worked in anonymity and you learned your subject. You knew what you were talking about." In the Senate hearings, he reminisced, too, about those "close friendships." He spoke especially warmly of the senior subcommittee Democrats with whom he had worked.[5] They were the same people—Jamie Whitten and William Natcher, for instance—with whom he had predicted effective future working relationships during his election campaign (see Chapter 1).

In the hearings, Chairman Andrews hewed to an interrogation pattern that was familiar to students of the pre-1974 House committee. He questioned executive branch witnesses closely and pressed them for operational and budgetary detail. "Hearings based on the maximum information possible are the best hearings to have," he would tell them. "The main thing we want to do" he would explain, "is to establish as factual a record as we can, so all this slip-sliding, duck-around-the-end kind of stuff gets out and we deal with cold, hard facts."[6] Should executive officials fail to come fully prepared with the relevant facts and figures he would remind them of the committee's authority by threatening to postpone the hearing and/or cut back their funding request.[7]

Or he would send them back to the drawing board.

> SENATOR ANDREWS: On the Appropriations Committee, we sort of sit with our green eye shades and have to look at the figures you give us. And you are asking for a capital account you say is going to pay dividends.... Yet when we ask you where the dividends are going to be saved ... it ain't there.
>
> [AGENCY HEAD]: It sounds like we could go back and try to give you some actual numbers. I do not think we have done a good enough job of our calculations.[8]

Agencies caught between allegiance to the Office of Management and Budget and compliance with a committee recommendation would hear the frustration of the longtime appropriator with the budgeters, "those turkeys who hide away in their dark closets and send down their edicts."[9] Then a lecture on the primacy of the legislative appropriations process would follow. "You are living in a very unreal world," he lectured one administrator.

> Let me point out that under this constitution the Congress still appropriates the funds that run this government. Now let me also point out that we could care less what the Office of Management and Budget said or did or intimated along the

way. Your instructions were instructions in the appropriations
bill signed into law by the President.[10]

Occasionally, he would continue his attack on the leader of the
institutional opposition, "that great budget wizard . . . our friend Davey
the Stockman." [11] In his emphasis on "cold hard facts" and in his
emphasis on committee prerogatives, his hearings activity adhered to
the traditional patterns of the House Appropriations Committee.

More than anything else, Chairman Andrews's performance in the
hearings reveals the breadth and depth of his constituency relationships
and the degree to which North Dakota was, as we have said, the measure
of all things. Sometimes his own experiences or those of his constituents
became the evidential base from which he worked his way toward
broader judgments about agency performance. Sometimes he used his
constituents to describe a larger class of citizens that needed help.
Sometimes he singled out specific constituent interests that needed
direct agency attention and pressed the relevant official to provide it. In
the abstract or in the concrete, few executive officials could fail to notice
his concern for North Dakota's interests or the doggedness with which
he pursued them in his questioning.

One constant theme of his questioning was his belief that deregulation in the transportation field had been a failure. Not that he had a
theory about it: he had originally supported airline deregulation. But on
the evidence, it simply had not worked for North Dakota. He used the
hearings to make agency officials aware of the evidence, to test for their
responses, to encourage the search for remedies, and to vent his
frustration and fears. Witnesses connected to air travel were each year
confronted with his personal experiences, and then pushed on that basis
to broader questions. "When I first came to Congress, I could fly round
trip to Fargo, North Dakota, for $106. Now I can't do it for less than
$450. . . . Would you say deregulation is working? Are you happy with
this child of yours?" [12]

A classic statement of the inductive mode of questioning was the
following colloquy with the administrator of the Federal Aviation
Administration.

> SENATOR ANDREWS: I can leave Fargo at 6:50 in the morning and fly
> to Minneapolis and routinely we have 20-25 minute delays. Mr.
> Administrator, Fargo is hardly a traffic choke point and those 20-25
> minute delays are getting to be more and more customary. . . .
> [ADMINISTRATOR]: Before the chairman leaves I just want to tell
> him . . . that Fargo, North Dakota is not being discriminated
> against. . . .
> SENATOR ANDREWS: Let me assure my friend that Fargo had better

darn well not be discriminated against. Let me go one step further. The only way you can use practical working examples for what goes on out in the world of airway control is to use the examples of where you have been. When I see regular 20-25 minute delays going from Fargo to Minneapolis, I know something is wrong.[13]

The administrator probably knew that the North Dakota example should be taken as illustrative of a larger problem of air traffic delays. But he would also learn that he ought not to ignore the problem in North Dakota.

Andrews had far more than his personal experience in mind, however, in thinking about deregulation. He used his experiences as a handhold to help him think about a statewide problem. "We get a little gun shy up there," he told another agency head,

because prior to airline deregulation, we had seven cities in my state served by major airlines. After airline deregulation—that great wonderful bill that was supposed to bring us more service—we now have four cities served by airlines. . . . Not only that, but the four cities that are served are paying twice as much as ever before for an airline ticket. . . . So far as serving the public, I take a real dim view of it.[14]

On the basis of that evidence, he would push officials for remedies: "The aircraft loan guarantee program was designed to assist carriers providing service to small communities. . . . What is going to happen to those small communities that have been kicked out in the cold?" [15] In this case, he was working to get leverage on his state's problems by thinking in terms of small communities in general.

Much of his questioning proceeded in this vein, where North Dakota became the lead example in a broad category of cases.

- "Well, let us talk about equity in taxation, equity for the small, more rural states particularly . . . the rural parts of this country have unique transportation problems all their own."
- "I would like to find out if for one minute, the freedom of movement for . . . those living in the rural areas of this nation was ever considered." [16]

In the case of the Greyhound company's plans to cut bus service, Andrews included the states of other subcommittee members, to add political reality to his general argument about small towns. He addressed an official from the Interstate Commerce Commission:

Looking at the [Greyhound] map, there are members of the subcommittee from these states—it shows that Mississippi [Stennis] is going to lose Greyhound service to 14 small towns.

West Virginia, whose senator happens to serve on this sub-committee [Byrd], is going to lose 40 small towns. The state of New York [D'Amato] is going to lose 53. Yes, even North Dakota is going to lose 25 small towns. . . . Is this map accurate? Does Greyhound intend to drop service to 25 towns in North Dakota?[17]

In this line of questioning, North Dakota's problems are synonymous with the problems of "rural areas" or "small communities" or "small towns" or "medium-size towns" in general.[18] The state is one case within a larger category. But it is a prototypical case, and the broader discussion can always be punctuated with a specific North Dakota application.

North Dakota's transportation problems were, for Andrews, a barometer of his state's well-being. Clearly, he concluded that the recent movement to deregulate the transportation industry had not helped. He expressed a lot of frustration.

I didn't vote against airline deregulation. That's where I made the big mistake. I did vote against rail deregulation and bus deregulation. You know I may be a little slow, but eventually I get smart. This darn deregulation was cracked up to be a whale of a lot more than it turned out to be.[19]

He also worried about his state.

Deregulation has led to an awful lot of rail abandonment in the less densely populated areas of the country. . . . In the case of trucking deregulation, we have a lot of small towns that probably won't get any trucking service based on deregulation now. We have towns in my state that used to have airline service that no longer have airline service because of this type of deregulation. Is this going to continue? Are we going to find that under deregulation, the smaller towns and rural America are just going to be abandoned by the railroads, by the truckers and by the airlines?[20]

As Andrews saw it, his constituents needed a lot of help; and he used the hearings in whatever ways he could to get it.

He had no difficulty linking the subject matter of transportation to his state's dominant industry—agriculture. They were, after all, the two shaping forces behind the state's economic development.[21] There were the constant references to his own background:

- "This is just a plain farmer speaking, but . . ."
- "I'm not much of a mathematician, I am just a farmer, but . . ."
- "You know, back on the farm, we don't really understand . . ."

- "Mr. Riley, you are talking to an old farmer."
- "Any farmer in North Dakota knows that ..." [22]

Another chairman of this same subcommittee would doubtless have put a very different twist on his questions. In Andrews's hands, agricultural experiences frequently provided his test probe into a transportation agency's activities. Meanwhile, he pressed the case for his farm constituency.

The railroads, for example, had profound effects on prairie farmers, as he explained to officials of the Interstate Commerce Commission.

> North Dakota is dependent on its agricultural industry. Efficient transportation of agricultural commodities is essential to the economic viability of my state. North Dakota shippers, however, are rail captive. Over 73 percent of all the shipments out of state are by rail. Under the grain marketing system, transportation charges are borne by the farmer. When small grain elevators are exploited by high freight charges or abused by discrimination in the areas of rates and services, farm families suffer. [23]

Consider these farm-related comments to officials of the Federal Highway Administration:

> You can have the best damn roads in the area, but if you come to a bridge that you can't cross, the roads don't do you any good. . . . The problem that bothers me in this whole bridge thing is that those of us who are used to driving on dirt roads or gravel and fighting through the mud or one thing and another, can make do, but we can't make do if all of a sudden we come to a bridge that isn't there or a bridge that has a 5 ton limit when we are trying to haul a load of wheat out to the elevator to join in the overall commerce of this country. That's where the problem is. [24]

> In small rural states similar to the one I represent, we have some inequities in the excise tax, particularly on trucks. . . . The Federal excise tax on trucks makes no differentiation between farm use trucks which run maybe 5000 or 6000 miles a year and never get on an interstate highway and regular trucks. . . . Often they [farm trucks] are 15 years old; the farmer buys a chassis, sticks a tandem on behind it and uses it for hauling potatoes or wheat or whatever over township roads largely. [25]

> I farm, or rather my son does, but I am still pretty much involved. You get these fuel economy standards on a pickup truck . . . and that is wonderful except for the people that use pickup trucks to work with. . . . When you take a load of wheat

out of a wheat field, the truck you buy now you have got to
specify two engine sizes larger than you used to have to specify
10 years ago, to haul the same 200 bushels of wheat. This really
isn't progress.[26]

With these sorts of comments, the chairman sought to impress upon
those who implemented national transportation policy that many of
their allocations and regulations made no sense for an agricultural state
that was not a microcosm of the country and that North Dakota needed
relief from nationwide transportation formulas that placed an undue
burden on its farmers. Privately, Andrews expressed his belief that the
Senate was the institutional protector of small states. Publicly, he acted
as if one of his missions was to make that principle a reality.

His protective thrusts reached well beyond the agricultural area. He
asked for a waiver of the rule that 10 percent of highway contracts be
awarded to minority business because "in a state like mine, you can't
find that number of minorities, so the local firms can't bid." He
protested that the formula for returning the gasoline tax to the states
shortchanged less populous states, when "to us northern weather . . . at
40° below . . . is damn tough on highways . . . [and] they break up. . . .
[But] those heavy trucks need a stable road bed." He often used the
harsh weather to argue for North Dakota as a special case. A regulation
requiring that buses be "wheelchair accessible" did not solve the
problem "in Fargo, North Dakota, where the wind chill factor four
months of the year is 70 below zero [and] you don't go in your
wheelchair down the snowy sidewalks to wait at a bus stop for a bus."
Ordinary seatbelt construction fails, too. "You ought to try the fun of
getting a car started when it is 45 degrees below zero out in North
Dakota and that damn ignition interlock does not work. You have to go
around and try to lift up the hood in a blizzard and jiggle the thing to
make it work." [27]

The record of the subcommittee hearings overwhelmingly conveys
the impression that if any North Dakota angle could be found within
the bailiwick of a witness, the chairman would find it. And the
executives who came to testify before him knew what things were, as
Andrews often put it, "close to my heart."

"If there is anything that I've found of witnesses," said Andrews in
1983, "it is that they are fairly well prepared on the points that affect
North Dakota." [28] One of his subcommittee staffers put the matter
succinctly: "Make no mistake about it. North Dakota is in the front of his
mind—all the time."

At the most particularistic level, of course, Andrews used the
hearings to protect or promote discrete benefits. He would engage

witnesses in conversation on such matters as a projected office closing at Bismarck, airport construction at Grand Forks, bridge construction at Mandan, a Coast Guard station at LaMoure, air service for Williston, rail service for Rugby and Minot, bus service for Casselton, the effects of the Northwest-Republic airline merger on Jamestown and Devils Lake, increasing the low percentage of North Dakota grain handled by the St. Lawrence Seaway, maintaining access roads to recreational lakes, and building a program at the Aerospace Sciences Facility at the University of North Dakota.[29]

A couple of examples, of style as well as purpose—one with the Coast Guard and one with Amtrak—are illustrative.

> SENATOR ANDREWS: Another initiative from 2 or 3 years ago that impacts our immediate area, your light signals on Lake Sakakawea are for navigation out there. No news is good news. You put them in. We have not heard any complaints, so I assume you are keeping those lights on, and you are keeping those navigation markers going out on Lake Sakakawea. Is this the case as you understand it?
>
> ADMIRAL GRACEY: I do not know the answer, Senator, but I would like to answer with a generality. . . .
>
> SENATOR ANDREWS: The only thing is, the only aids to navigation that the chairman of the subcommittee is interested in are on Lake Sakakawea. [Laughter]
>
> ADMIRAL GRACEY: The point I was going to make, Mr. Chairman, is that we are doing such a good job, everything goes fine. I am sure they are working fine.
>
> SENATOR ANDREWS: That will be reassuring to our friends who enjoy the recreational facilities on Lake Sakakawea. That is a big body of water, and that is a key and important safety feature, what you are doing up here. We think you are doing a great job. We want to keep it that way.
>
> ADMIRAL GRACEY: We may be contracting those out some time, Senator.
>
> SENATOR ANDREWS: If it works, do not fix it. It is working pretty well now, so let's keep it the way it is going. We like it.
>
> ADMIRAL GRACEY: I am making particular note of that comment, Senator. Thank you. [Laughter][30]

> SENATOR ANDREWS: The Burlington Northern in early February announced that it was reducing its signal apparatus at Devils Lake Depot. . . . Are you aware of that decision . . . you will maintain someone at Devils Lake to take care of ticketing and checking luggage and parcel receipts and the rest? This does not mean that you are going to shut down that depot? . . . There is no way you are going to eliminate that stop at Devils Lake?

MR. CLAYTOR: No sir, no way we will eliminate that stop.

SENATOR ANDREWS: I just wanted to make that crystal clear, Mr. President.

MR. CLAYTOR: No way we are going to eliminate that stop and no way we are going to eliminate that station.

SENATOR ANDREWS: That is good. Or no way you are going to eliminate the Empire Builder either [the Amtrak train that runs across North Dakota]. . . .

MR. CLAYTOR: No, no the Empire Builder is one of our key long distance trains.

SENATOR ANDREWS: One of your favorite trains, too, isn't it, Mr. Claytor?

MR. CLAYTOR: Yes, sir, it is indeed. [Laughter]

SENATOR ANDREWS: We want to keep it that way; and we appreciate the speed at which you moved to rehabilitate the station facilities at Fargo. I was at the dedication last Saturday and it was a good show.[31]

Both colloquies testify to one legislator's impact on specific projects. The navigation aid and the railroad depot were protective actions; the station renovation had been a promotional one. Andrews's Fargo initiative would be a lasting one. But it seemed doubtful that the Lake Sakakawea and the Devils Lake projects would long survive the chairmanship of their well-placed protector.

ANTICIPATING THE FLOOR

In addition to satisfying his budgetary and constituency purposes, the hearings reveal the chairman's anticipation of further stages in the appropriations process. First, as an agent of the parent chamber, Andrews anticipated the reaction of his colleagues on the floor, so he pushed for the most complete and detailed information he could get. That is the chairman's currency when he goes to the floor to exchange his work product for votes. "Our point in making this record is not to just satisfy the curiosity of the subcommittee," he told the witnesses. "We want to have this information when we go to the floor and somebody asks a question about what progress we are making." [32] On another occasion he explained:

We just want to get a record that's pretty well defined because, when we go to the floor with this bill, after markup, we have to have the backup and the information to convince our colleagues of the necessity for the money that we are putting in here, and your candor helps a good deal in making as strong a case as possible when we get to the floor of the Senate and when we are in conference with the House.[33]

The down-to-earth, matter-of-fact, dollars-and-cents quality of the chairman's currency is a hallmark of appropriations committee discussions. He wants, he tells witnesses, "Factual information that we can base these projects on because we have had more darn rumors, innuendos and pie-in-the-sky concepts." [34] Or, "We want to have as many statistics as we can to show that what we are doing is not pink cloud stuff but based on straight-out dollar figures." [35] The worst thing that can happen to a subcommittee chairman, Andrews's House experience had taught him, is to be caught on the floor without an adequate explanatory record. Loss of policy, loss of prestige, and loss of confidence may follow.

The hearings reveal a second form of anticipation that is of equal importance for the chairman's ultimate success. He must know the concerns and priorities of each member of his subcommittee, and he must speak to executive officials on their behalf. His dominance within the subcommittee rests ultimately on colleagues' acquiescence and support. "The other members of the subcommittee don't come to the hearings," said Andrews.

> They can't. They are spread too thin. But their presence is felt, always. The people sitting in back of me [at the hearings] aren't my staff. They are the staffs of the other members. Senatorial courtesy works. They expect me to watch out for them—just as I expect them to look out for me [in other Appropriations subcommittees].

Andrews's interrogations are peppered with references to the constituency concerns of other subcommittee members.

- "Senator Chiles my good friend and colleague, the ranking member of the subcommittee . . . has one question that he wanted to make sure we asked. . . ." (about beltway construction around Orlando).
- "I have one question that Senator [Alphonse] D'Amato who was here and had to leave wanted to have me ask orally [about] a new school ship for the New York State Maritime Academy."
- "In other words . . . you have no plan to close . . . a couple of them [airport towers] that happen to be in areas of Missouri, [and Senator Eagleton] is a member of the subcommittee."
- "We have to address . . . poor air service to smaller communities and no air freight service to some of the small communi-

ties in North Dakota, Mississippi [Sen. John Stennis], West
Virginia [Sen. Robert Byrd] and I am sure upstate New York
[D'Amato]." [36]

The following excerpt from subcommittee hearings on the FAA
budget captures the link of anticipation that binds subcommittee chairman and subcommittee member.

> SENATOR ANDREWS: Let me ask one other question on something
> we have discussed before. Time after time, you know, my interest
> and Senator Byrd's interest in keeping air traffic control towers,
> airport control towers specially, operating—I am specifically
> interested in Minot and Bismarck, N.D. Senator Byrd has interests
> in West Virginia, as you know so well. Are you continuing the
> policy of keeping in operation all of those traffic control towers
> that are now in operation?
>
> MR. ENGEN: We are, sir.
>
> SENATOR ANDREWS: And there is no plan in the system to shut
> down or cut back the operation of that airport control tower in
> Minot or in Bismarck or in the ones in West Virginia?
>
> MR. ENGEN: There is no plan in the mill at all. Give me one out, if
> you will, please. Please do not say that I can never change—make
> me say—that I can never change the system.
>
> SENATOR ANDREWS: No; we are not saying . . .
>
> MR. ENGEN: There is no plan.
>
> SENATOR ANDREWS: Never is never; but there is no plan rattling
> around there that should cause either Senator Byrd or myself any
> concern during the foreseeable future.
>
> MR. ENGEN: There is not.
>
> SENATOR ANDREWS: Fine.

Later in the hearing the following exchange occurred.

> SENATOR ANDREWS: Senator Byrd, I mentioned that we have
> already solved the problem of control towers in West Virginia
> and North Dakota.
>
> SENATOR BYRD: Yes; and I am very grateful for your having asked
> the question. Let me just be sure that I understand that the answer
> was what I hope it was.
>
> SENATOR ANDREWS: You want to hear it with your own ears.
>
> SENATOR BYRD: Yes.
>
> SENATOR ANDREWS: That proves that you are indeed and in fact
> the excellent Senator that every one of us knows you are.
>
> SENATOR BYRD: I hope I can get that excerpt from the minutes that
> are being taken down. [Laughter]
>
> SENATOR ANDREWS: You know how the system works.

SENATOR BYRD: Plato thanked the gods for having permitted him to live in the age of Socrates. I thank the benign hand of destiny for allowing me to live and serve on this subcommittee at the time that the very distinguished Senator, Mr. Andrews, presides over the subcommittee with a degree of efficiency and ability as rare as a day in June.[37]

Each year, when he took his bill to the floor, Andrews received the same kind of flowery praise from Byrd and other subcommittee Democrats.[38] But it had a basis in the realities of his governing style.

DECISION MAKING

In the hearings, the search for information was directed toward a possible reallocation of funding among programs within the totals given them in the budget. With evident satisfaction, Andrews described the results of his subcommittee's action in 1981.

We came in under the original budget, but we reallocated among the programs within the total. We changed the money for Amtrak and the Coast Guard and put some innovative ideas in the bill. That's what the Appropriations Committee is for, in my opinion. We should be allowed to say how the money should be allocated. We hold the hearings; we know what we are doing; we have the expertise; we know where the waste is. Of course, Stockman fought against our reallocations. We won. We did what an Appropriations Committee should do.

Within the restricted scope of the new congressional budget process, the chairman wanted to view his subcommittee's deliberations as an independent and positive force—which they doubtless were.

At a time (1981-1982) when policy making in Washington was at its most partisan in years, Andrews continued to work closely with the Democrats on his subcommittee. He governed, that is, in the bipartisan manner that had been the trademark of his years on the House Appropriations Committee. In his first year, for example, when he found out that Minority Leader Robert Byrd had a bridge construction problem—as Andrews also did—he reacted: "We are both caught in the same net. Maybe we can scrape together some money and take care of both of us." [39] He did so—packaging $15 million for the North Dakota bridge with $4 million for the West Virginia bridge and inserting the package into the next appropriation bill.[40] At the end of his second year, he commented: "I get more votes from the Democrats than the Republicans. It's five to four. Most of the time I can count on the four Democrats and one Republican besides myself."

Andrews found it easier to accommodate the constituency-oriented Democrats than the more partisan Republicans. "But that will change," he continued. "The Republicans are shaping up. And the one who shaped up the quickest was Al D'Amato. Now it's 'Yes, Mr. Chairman, yes, Mr. Chairman.' When he wants to impress people on mass transit, we give him a hearing to conduct so he can impress them." Andrews gave D'Amato special opportunities in Washington and New York. "He wants to do it," said an aide one day when D'Amato was presiding over the subcommittee hearing in Washington. "There's nothing in our bill that means more to him than mass transit. So we arranged for the chairman to have something else to do this morning at ten o'clock." On other occasions D'Amato held mass transit hearings, in the name of the subcommittee, by himself in New York City.[41] Andrews had made a masterful accommodation to the interests and the project-oriented governing style of the freshman New York senator.[42] D'Amato spoke of his chairman as "a big bear, one of the good guys, a real straight shooter."

"He likes to work quietly in the committee and settle things there," a subcommittee staffer generalized. "He believes that you get your work done in committee, not on the floor." In his first year, Chairman Andrews did not even wait for the subcommittee markup to work out his accommodations. When I asked him if I could sit in on the markup, he replied,

> We do it in a pretty Teutonic way. I don't bother with the fancy fine points [of procedure]. I talk with the staff on the run. We had a preliminary markup all done and put it on hold when the president's second round of budget cuts came down. I don't know what we are going to do now or when we will do it . . . it may come up suddenly.

It did come up suddenly, and I missed it. But Andrews commented afterward: "In my bill everyone was accommodated within the realm of possibility and we still came in under the House bill. That's an accomplishment." The accomplishment, as Andrews knew from his House experience, would mean subcommittee satisfaction and support at subsequent stages in the process. In 1982, I missed the subcommittee markup again. But a staffer's description of the event indicated that nothing had changed: "It took about twenty minutes. It's a very low-key, nonpartisan subcommittee. There's a lot of pork in the bill. And there's something in there for every member of the subcommittee. It's all worked out beforehand. If there's a quarrel in the subcommittee, it means I haven't done my job."

In the case of the 1982 supplemental appropriations bill, the chairman did not even hold a subcommittee markup before presenting his recommendations to the full committee chairman. "A supplemental is a different bill than a regular bill," explained a top aide.

> Since there wasn't anything controversial in the bill and there weren't many items in it, there was no need for an actual subcommittee markup. I began by putting together a list of all the things that had been requested—by the administration, by the groups, by senators—a fairly comprehensive list, just in case. Then we got a notice from Chairman Hatfield's office that the bill was to be considered a truly urgent supplemental, that there were veto problems, and that the bill was to be kept as clean as possible. With that instruction, I immediately took out most of the requests and made a list of the provisions I thought were urgent. I got a lot of input from [ranking subcommittee Democrat] Chiles' staff on what he wanted. Then I gave it to Mr. Andrews. He made some changes, approved it and we sent it to Chairman Hatfield. He accepted it and it became the chairman's bill.... The first time subcommittee members saw it was when it came from the printer. Of course, if there had been something they wanted, they would have made their wishes known.... "The boss and I are proud of our subcommittee markups. They are so quick, they are painless.

Quick enough, I might add, that I never saw one! If that is the case for a determined, on-the-scene observer, then surely this theater of operation—so important to the legislative success of Andrews—was totally obscured from the gaze of his North Dakota constituents. They would have to depend entirely on his word that he did what he said he did in the Senate.

I was able to watch in 1981 when Andrews took his bill to the full Appropriations Committee for approval. It took twenty minutes. Most of the time was consumed by the effusive praise of Sen. Lawton Chiles for his chairman's "experience, ... willingness to consider whatever suggestions other members made, ... completely bipartisan manner, ... and lean budget." The rest was pro forma. So far as I know, only once in the first two years did Andrews lose control over anything his subcommittee did. It was in the 1981 conference committee. As he told it afterward:

> The buddy system is very important when you go to conference with the House. The House members are there and they are all experts. Your members haven't any idea what it's all about. So they have to be willing to give you their proxies. If they decided to go it alone, it would be a disaster. [In the conference] on one matter, I didn't have one proxy I thought I

had. One of my members voted against me on the 406 [airline] subsidy issue. So I couldn't do all that I wanted to do to get rid of that program. I made sure he'll never do that again. We talked; and you can be sure that won't happen again. Next year we'll get rid of the 406 program. I'll make damn sure I've got all my proxies.

And that is exactly what he did in 1982.[43]

In 1982, I watched Chairman Andrews at work in the full Appropriations Committee while its members wrestled with the crucial matter of allocating their total budget among the thirteen separate subcommittees. A last-minute hitch indicated that $200 million would have to be taken out of the domestic subcommittees and given to the defense subcommittee. Committee Chairman Mark Hatfield started around the table, asking each subcommittee chairman in turn to defend his existing allocation. The criterion Hatfield applied was the degree to which a given subcommittee's existing allocation was greater than that already passed by the House. Andrews's transportation subcommittee allocation was already $800 million above the House figure, making his among the most vulnerable of the subcommittees to a further reduction.

He did not wait for his turn to come. After two subcommittee chairmen had argued that their total was already below that awarded by the House, Andrews jumped in from far down the table:

In my office today there were twenty-three people from the states of five members around this table. We've got to explain the facts of life to these people and stop them from coming around trying to add funds to these bills. We've got to tell them they can't come over and try to add more on the floor. . . . If we take any more out of my bill we won't be able to fund the improvements in the Coast Guard. I don't see where we have any wiggle room at all.

Hatfield agreed that it was important to hold the line on the floor, and diverted his attention to that subject. Whoever made the later sacrifice, it was not Andrews.

It was, I thought, an impressive move. Andrews had taken the offensive preemptively, altering the nature of the discussion. In so doing, he had eliminated his subcommittee's special vulnerability. By emphasizing the extreme constituency-oriented pressure he already faced—and in the process reminding his colleagues of their stake in his bill—he was able to change the question at issue. He made further cutting seem unthinkable, and made the existing allocation untouchable; and the only problem left was how to hold the line in the future. His interruption reminded me of his behavior in the Budget Committee:

making an unpredictable move, one calculated to throw the people around him off balance, and succeeding. It was the straightforward, blunt-speaking farmer pushing past protocol to get to the heart of the matter, but acutely aware of his own interests as he did so. "Nothing namby-pamby about him," said a subcommittee staffer, grinning, on the way out. "He's very effective." I agreed.

The following year he achieved another allocational victory for his subcommittee during full committee negotiations. As he said afterward:

> We were successful in getting an additional $200 million added to the transportation function in the last little meeting of the Committee before we reported the bill out. I hate to say it out loud, but our section probably did as well as or better than any of the other sections.[44]

It was the kind of inside effectiveness, the ability to use the legislative process to his own ends, that I had become accustomed to seeing whenever I watched the North Dakota senator in action.

An equally striking aspect of Andrews's actions, however, was the difficulty of observing them. Even granting the episodic nature of my efforts, there was simply not much to see. Formally and ostensibly, the entire appropriations process was public. Actually, most appropriations business was conducted out of the limelight. Or it came into view very briefly—as witnessed by Andrews's pleasure with speedy floor action in 1981. "When the bill came to the floor, it zipped through in a few minutes. I'm grateful for that. It's the kind of recognition you cherish around here." On another occasion: "We passed the conference report in three minutes. That's not bad."

Subcommittee hearings were easy to attend; but in the five mornings I sat there, only one television camera ever came—to film about an hour of testimony one morning. The three full committee markup sessions I attended were held in small rooms, without television and without the familiar Capitol Hill reporters in attendance. Andrews's transportation bills did not linger on the Senate floor; and the one conference committee I attended, as we shall see, was an extremely low-key affair. In the words of a recent observer, appropriations decision making is

> silent, hand to hand, night fighting. Many of these battles are never seen. They are fought in a realm of congressional politics that is difficult to illuminate, since Appropriations Committees work quietly. When they are over, the casualties of the infighting do not issue press releases announcing their wounds.[45]

It is an apt summary of my experience.

All this was in the sharpest possible contrast to my experience watching the Budget Committee in action. That committee met in large rooms, before a bank of television cameras, with reporters lining the press tables, with spectators packed in the room, with an overflow crowd outside waiting to get in. The members performed for the public—making speeches, grandstanding, and arguing. They debated, to no firm conclusion, large issues of national policy and priorities. Appropriations settled the short-run, bread-and-butter issues of how much money, to whom, for what, and for how long. The contrast in the two committee worlds helps clarify the contrasting outlook and behavior Mark Andrews displayed toward those worlds. Appropriations, not Budget, was the world in which he felt most at home; it was, therefore, the world in which he performed at his legislative best.

REPORT LANGUAGE

When an appropriations subcommittee takes its dollars-and-cents recommendations to the full committee, the subcommittee prepares an accompanying report explaining, justifying, and elaborating its decisions. Typically, the report is ratified, along with the subcommittee's funding recommendations. It then becomes a *Committee Report*, and it accompanies legislation to the Senate floor. In the six years of Andrews's chairmanship, 1981-1986, the annual reports of the transportation subcommittee averaged a hundred pages. The language of the report constitutes evidence of subcommittee members' thinking and intentions that goes beyond their aggregate dollars-and-cents decisions to reveal their ideas about the distribution of money within the aggregates.

Through a device known as earmarking the subcommittee can express its desire to have specified sums of money spent for specified projects in specified locations.[46] Formally, earmarking can be accomplished in the text of a bill. In a less formal, less binding, and more common form, earmarking is accomplished in the language of the committee report—language in which the committee "directs" or "instructs" or "intends" the agency to allocate some portion of its funds in specified ways. Not surprisingly, the language of each final committee report follows closely the thinking and the intentions of the person who chairs the subcommittee involved.

"Report language" does not have the force of law, but it has the force of politics. An agency head who ignores the committee's desires— conveyed in delicate gradations of intensity—risks retribution by that same committee at funding time next year. The transportation subcommittee report threatened agencies on two such occasions:

- "The FAA can expect swift and decisive action if it continues to 'stonewall' the directive of the Congress."
- "Any efforts initiated by the FHWA [Federal Highway Administration] to use this money in another manner than expressly indicated by this Committee would be considered a serious breach of congressional intent, and not judicious in view of FHWA's ignoring the 1984 congressional earmarks." [47]

It is the chairman speaking. Although the agency head may find it undesirable or even impossible to comply with earmarks in committee reports, there is a powerful incentive to do so.

To the degree that the language of a committee report reflects the ideas of the subcommittee chairman, the committee reports on transportation provide evidence of Mark Andrews's efforts to use his position to channel transportation-related projects and money into North Dakota. Such instances are numerous. In the section of the 1981 report on the FAA funding of airport facilities we find, for example, the flat statement: "An ILS [Instrument Landing System] is also to be provided at Dickinson, North Dakota." In the same section, in 1982, we find stronger language: "The Committee directs that an instrument landing system be immediately established at Devils Lake, North Dakota." In the 1981 section on FAA grants-in-aid for airport development, we find: "It has come to the Committee's attention that there is an acute need for a parallel runway at the Grand Forks Airport as well as for terminal relocation or reconstruction and expansion and apron and taxiway construction. Consequently this Committee directs that the Department gave the highest priority to the projects at the Grand Forks Airport." [48]

One of Andrews's favorite projects was the development of an airway science program at the University of North Dakota (UND). In Andrews's first year as subcommittee chairman, the committee report suggested that $4 million be divided between the FAA facility in Oklahoma and UND for this purpose. But by the time the bill was passed into law, he had succeeded in placing an earmark in the law itself. To an appropriation of $285 million he added, "Provided that $4,000,000 shall be available only for the design, engineering, construction and equipment for an air traffic control training facility at the University of North Dakota at Grand Forks." [49] In later reports, in one form or another the committee earmarked $4 million (1985) and then $3 million (1986) for the airway science curriculum at the University of North Dakota; and there was another provision for $2.2 million for atmospheric research at the same school. Another committee report earmarked $1,750,000 for a pedestrian walkway demonstration project in downtown Fargo.[50] Eventually, all these projects were carried out by the agencies involved, and the money flowed into the state.

Because earmarking is so easily associated with pork barreling and because pork barreling is so often criticized as substituting political for more rational criteria, Andrews's straightforward defense of the practice is noteworthy. When elements of his bill—in this case the appropriations for the Urban Mass Transit Administration—came under attack on the floor for "excessive earmarking" Andrews expressed this view:

> There is in fact a choice, Mr. President; either we do it or the bureaucrats downtown do it. We held committee hearings. Senators from various states—and I might assure the Senator from Idaho that there are no earmarked transit funds for North Dakota in this bill—made their case in public hearings. That is where the earmarks came from. It has been done for years, long before I came to this body and I think it is a preferable way to do it.[51]

Whatever the objective merits of executive versus congressional decision making on individual projects, the latter method gave members of Congress a special advantage. An even greater advantage accrued to those members whose legislative positions—like the chairmanship of an appropriations subcommittee—gave them privileged access to decision making.

Andrews talked about it in the context of his senatorial efforts to get construction funds for a project he had begun pushing as a member of the House committee. At the administrator's first appearance before his Senate subcommittee, the following colloquy took place.

> SENATOR ANDREWS: Last year's report directed that priority be given to the Missouri River Bridge between Bismarck and Mandan. . . . What is the status of this?
>
> [ADMINISTRATOR]: As you said, Mr. Chairman, in the 1981 appropriations bill the bridge did receive legislative history. By that act, it became more eligible for inclusion in the discretionary bridge program. . . .
>
> SENATOR ANDREWS: In other words . . . the report mentioned it, but no money was set aside in the bill itself.
>
> [ADMINISTRATOR]: No, sir. The bill itself did not designate specific money for this bridge. . . .
>
> SENATOR ANDREWS: What happens next?
>
> [ADMINISTRATOR]: Well, sir, this bridge will be given consideration at the beginning of the next fiscal year for the overall funding for the Nation's needs, and it will be given consideration along with all other bridges we receive requests for. . . . I don't think I could guarantee anything at this point in time.[52]

Convinced that only a formal earmark in the law itself would ever guarantee agency action, Andrews placed a proviso in the FY 1982 transportation appropriations bill specifically authorizing the expenditure of $15 million for the North Dakota bridge together with $4 million for Robert Byrd's West Virginia bridge.

When, however, the transportation bill was folded into the omnibus continuing resolution at the end of the session, that provision was lost. At the beginning of 1982, with an urgent supplemental appropriations bill making its way through the House, Andrews talked about the progress of his two-bridge package, and about earmarking:

> I've got 15 million for a little bridge in North Dakota. Bob Byrd has one; Pete Domenici has something in New Mexico; John Glenn [D-Ohio] has something he wants. We've got all these special deals. When you operate under a continuing resolution, it's a lot more difficult to earmark these little deals. You have to be pretty nimble. I was [last year]. But I didn't get them all. Under a continuing resolution, the executive branch has a lot more discretion to do what they want. But Congress is the people's house, and I think it does a better job of earmarking these projects. We know who has gotten what in the past, who has been waiting in line, and we follow cost benefit formulas. When the supplemental comes up, we'll try to do some earmarking for a few of the special deals we didn't get last year.

At the subcommittee level, he inserted the following statement in the section devoted to the Federal-Aid Highway Program: "an additional amount not to exceed $19,000,000 in obligational authority to carry out Section 310(d)(3) of Public Law 97-102." As we walked over to the full committee meeting, a subcommittee aide noted:

> There is money in there for two bridges—North Dakota and West Virginia. There is also some money for highways, the greatest portion of which is for New Mexico. The authorizing committee isn't happy with these provisions. Andrews's fall-back position is that if they take out the money for bridges, they'll also take out the money for Domenici. . . . From a good government standpoint, the bridge provision is lousy. We should have to fight it out with all the others. But that's the pork barrel aspect.

Nothing happened. Andrews's $19 million earmark survived the Senate and the conference intact and was enacted into law on July 16, 1982.[53] The chairman also kept watch over programs that benefited the larger class of communities into which North Dakota fell. He used report language in these cases, too. The 1983 report, for example, read,

"The committee directs the FHWA to continue the rural transportation assistance program at a $5,000,000 level." In 1986, the committee provided $750,000 for a "study on air service for communities most severely affected by airline deregulation." It asked that the study identify "the smallest and most remote areas which risk transportation dislocation without some form of community air service" and specified four states whose "aeronautical representatives" were to be consulted— including North Dakota.[54]

Every year for six years, the committee report noted that the administration requested zero funds for the Local Rail Service Assistance Program; every year the committee appropriated funds for the program, "helping to alleviate shipper and community dislocations caused by branchline abandonment." When a hearings witness told Chairman Andrews, "The local rail service assistance program is extremely important to your state. . . . It receives $500,000 whereas 27 states receive only $200,000," Andrews replied, "Don't mention that or I will get in trouble." [55] Not in North Dakota.

Nor would Andrews be likely to get in trouble when North Dakotans found out about his ability to win funds from a small FHWA program for repairing "access highways to public recreation areas on certain lakes." In 1981, money for only four access roads, all in North Dakota, was earmarked in the report. In 1984, money for only six projects was earmarked in the appropriations bill itself; again, all six were in North Dakota—in six different counties.[56]

Not all of the chairman's efforts were successful. In every one of his subcommittee's reports, for example, in the section on FAA grants-in-aid for airport development, we find the following language: "Within the obligational [funding] level recommended, the Committee directs that priority be given to grant applications involving the further development of the following airports," which are listed. In 1983, the committee began to make an explicit ordering of these airports; North Dakota received priority rankings grossly out of proportion to any considerations of urgency or merit. In 1983, five of the thirty-four airports given priority were in North Dakota, ranked 4, 8, 12, 16, and 20. The comparable North Dakota figures for 1984 were six of twenty-two airports, with rankings of 6, 7, 8, 9, 11, and 12; and in 1985, the numbers were three out of twenty-four airports, ranked 1, 3, and 10. In 1986, seven of twenty-three airports were in North Dakota, and they ranked 1, 5, 6, 7, 9, 10, and 11.[57] Other subcommittee members had priority airports, too. But no other state came close to tiny North Dakota's dominance on these lists.

The FAA, like any agency, could find plenty of reasons—in this case prior commitments, agency-created criteria, safety, or traffic volume—

for establishing its own priorities. Apparently the agency did just that. Three of Andrews's original five (1983) airports, including the two largest, at Bismarck and Fargo, remained on the priority list to the end. There were, it seems, some limits to the chairman's power.

For our purposes, the size of the chairman's appetite is enough to know. As we sat in the subcommittee's offices one day, a staffer talked about the 1982 bill.

> Keith Kennedy [staff director of the parent Appropriations Committee] came through that door the other day saying, "oink, oink, how much pork have you got in there this time?" That reflects Mr. Andrews's way of operating. He's an old timer. He'll put lots of things in there, knowing that he won't get it all.

Doubtless, Andrews was pleased with what he got and surprised at what he didn't get. Doubtless, he would take credit at home for everything he could and keep on trying.[58] Doubtless, too, transportation agency executives would know what North Dakota projects remained "close to my heart," would continue to feel his pressure, and would never be sure that they could emerge unscathed when the next year's appropriation was at stake.

LEGISLATIVE HARDBALL

It was part of Mark Andrews's inside effectiveness that he was quite prepared to play legislative hardball—you help me, I help you; you hurt me, I hurt you. He often used this distinguishing dimension in evaluating his colleagues. "He's got some moxie; he's one of the savables"; "he's a nice man but a babe in the woods"; "he needs more guts"; "he's a wimp." He praised a state party leader as "hard nosed," and he berated a D.C. lobbyist who capitulated to a senatorial whim as "lily-livered."

The day before he took his 1981 bill to the Senate floor, I sat while he worked to head off a colleague who had promised a floor amendment mandating an Amtrak stop in his state. Andrews called Amtrak's president. "We've got a good agreement to have only two hours of debate" he began.

> The transportation bill is like a piece of meat hanging out there and the longer it's there, the more inviting it looks. If one amendment passes, it might open things up. I'd appreciate it if you would talk to Senator _____. Lay some magic words on him so he will feel that he's being listened to and will feel that he

doesn't have to offer his amendment ... [and] get the arguments to me by tomorrow morning so that if I have to play hardball with him on the floor, I can do it.

He did not want to do that, and he did not have to. His bill took about seventy-five minutes to pass the Senate, during which time he fended off the only two amendments with lopsided votes. The first proposed to eliminate a famous Amtrak train, the Cardinal—a well-known passion of his cooperative colleague Robert Byrd, and one which Andrews had happily protected with an earmark in the bill.[59] The second amendment was a 4.1 percent across-the-board cut.

The chairman's willingness to play hardball was well illustrated, however, on the proposed 4.1 percent cut. A young liberal Democratic admirer, and a former House colleague of Andrews, told me afterward:

Mark Andrews did something today that only a man with legislative experience, with a deep loyalty to the legislative process, would do. He was managing the transportation bill and someone offered an across-the-board cut. One of the other freshmen, a man with House experience but very little of it, voted for the cut. Afterwards, Mark gave him a taste of what it's like to face someone who is going to play hardball with you. He told him: "When we go to conference, we are going to have to cut some projects. I am going to put your projects up for cuts. And I'm going to use your vote as an indication of your lack of interest." The other guy started to protest. Mark told him that was the way it was going to be—no anger, no recrimination, just a statement. Now that's my kind of guy!

It was another example of the chairman's bargaining style. Again, it had been the prevailing style among members of the House Appropriations Committee.[60]

In 1982, President Reagan vetoed a supplemental appropriations bill; and he suffered his first major congressional defeat when the veto was overridden. Andrews became deeply involved in the override effort—speaking critically of the president both on and off the Senate floor.[61] On the regular appropriations bill later that year, he played hardball with a senator whom he had previously helped but who had rejected his entreaties for support on the veto override. Republican Charles Percy of Illinois was requesting more money from a certain highway program than anyone else in the Senate. The program—interstate transfer grants—bundled unused funds from the major highway building program into a fund that was then spread around pretty much at the discretion of the Appropriations Committee. In the words of a subcommittee staffer, it is "the biggest pork barrel in the bill." When I asked him how the subcommittee allocated the money—$375 million in 1982—he replied:

> We make professional judgments as to which projects are nearest completion or most certain of completion. That still leaves us with far more projects than we can fund in any one year. So we try to spread the joy around. We see who is up for reelection, who makes the best case for assistance. In the end, it becomes a completely political process. The amount of money involved can fund some pretty big, pretty sexy projects, projects which have a big impact in a city.

In 1982, Percy wanted just such a project for the Chicago area. But he had supported the president's veto of the supplemental bill, and the senator from North Dakota was unhappy about it.

In its 1982 report the transportation subcommittee recommended eighteen transfer grants, with these words: "The Committee directs that the $375,000,000 recommended in the bill be allocated as follows. . . ." Working from the amounts allocated to the eighteen locations in the appropriations bill already passed by the House, the Andrews subcommittee held six projects at the same level, increased four, and decreased eight. Exclusive of the Illinois project, the seven proposed decreases averaged 21.4 percent. The median decrease was 12.0 percent. The recommended decrease for Senator Percy's Illinois project, however, was 66.0 percent.[62] It was the largest percentage cut of all. It was also the largest dollar cut, from $150 million to $51 million. It was the chairman's effort to teach his colleague a lesson. A subcommittee staffer explained:

> Percy supported the president, and Andrews thought he shouldn't have. Andrews thought a lot of Republicans were sticking their necks out, that there was a lot in the bill for Illinois and that Percy shouldn't get a free ride. When we were marking up our regular bill, Chicago's figures dropped. A lot of the others dropped; but Andrews instructed us to drop Chicago's. The result was very costly to Illinois. They may put some back [in conference]. But they lost a lot of money.

When the subcommittee allocation of transfer grants came to the full committee for approval, Sen. Daniel Inouye [D-Hawaii] read from a letter from Chicago Mayor Jane Byrne asking for restoration of $45 million. Andrews defended his subcommittee's action by laying great stress on the pressure placed on him during "a long conference in my office with the secretary of transportation and his many minions who pointed out that we had to get much closer to [the administration figure] of $150 million." He continued:

It wasn't easy to do. I looked down that list. I couldn't really see much sense in cutting Oregon [home state of full committee chairman Hatfield]. And I couldn't see a whale of a lot of sense—incidentally, there are none of these funds for North Dakota—a number of other places didn't make much sense. It was hard to see where we could cut. We figured Washington, D.C., was always overlooked and we gave them an increase.

I happened to read the *New York Times* just before meeting with the secretary. I read in an article where the president had called one of our colleagues from Illinois and assured him that if *he* voted with him to sustain a veto, he would take care of the interstate transfer funds for Illinois. I thought if we cut that to make the adjustment, then the president would probably send up a request for $150 million for the overall pot. . . . There is nothing arbitrary in getting close to the point where the president will sign the bill and then making adjustments in Congress. Maybe, in the meantime, the president—having made that pledge—will send up a request for more funds for Illinois.

Andrews was stating his disapproval of Percy's actions more obliquely by making the president his target. But the effect of this more whimsical approach was the same. No one in the room challenged his defense or spoke in support of the Byrne-Percy position. In the Senate, at least, he was playing winning hardball.

In 1981, the subcommittee chairman delivered the same hard-nosed message to a group outside the Senate—on a matter of concern to him and to North Dakota. For someone whose history lessons encompassed the railroad domination of agricultural life on the prairies in the nineteenth century, the abandonment of railroad branch lines in the twentieth century could only be described as "a plague in our area." [63] In a long introductory overview of transportation problems, his subcommittee's very first report, in 1981, included this sentence:

Railroad deregulation has made it ridiculously simple for a railroad to abandon branchlines just about wherever they want to, without concern for the impact of grain shippers, country elevators and the many other concerns in rural parts of the country which are dependent upon freight movement. [64]

Andrews expressed his suspicions often during subcommittee hearings:

- "You work from history. If you don't take a look at history, you really suffer. One hundred years ago the robber barons of the railroads were gouging certain towns and giving sweetheart deals to others, gouging certain companies and giving

low rates to others."
- "I remember the railroads all came in and supported railroad deregulation and then they raped all the small towns and the branch lines."
- "I wouldn't trust any railroad as far as I could throw a General Electric locomotive." [65]

Year in and year out, Andrews reserved a populist-style questioning for the Interstate Commerce Commission. And in 1985, he introduced a bill to "curb uncontrolled monopoly power" in the railroad business.[66]

In the 1981 hearings, Andrews prophesied: "In the West ... this summer, we are going to see some of the biggest branchline abandonments that anybody could possibly imagine." At about the same time, the Burlington Northern Railroad announced that it "planned to abandon 1,201 miles of railroad branchlines in the State of North Dakota out of its total of 2,221 branchlines in that state." [67] Andrews later said: "That's an awful lot of track. It was murder, really—a slaughter—which would have done great damage to the state." He decided to put pressure on the railroad to back down. Calling it a proposal for "massive and unprecedented abandonments," his subcommittee reported out a provision which "prohibits any such branchline abandonments in North Dakota in excess of 350 miles." [68] It was passed by the full committee and the Senate. "We thought," said Andrews afterward, "that Burlington Northern would say that they were withdrawing plans to abandon two-thirds of those lines. Then we would claim that the amendment had had its effect; we would withdraw our amendment in the conference committee, and the episode would be a deal." But that is not what happened.

"A vice president of the railroad attacked me," said Andrews, "and attacked the amendment as 'special interest' legislation. He used some choice phrases—the staff has them all. It was so dumb." A top assistant picked up the theme:

> What a dumb son of a bitch he was to issue the statements he did—that the provision was self-serving, special interest legislation. He kept at it. He wouldn't shut up. Mark just got madder and madder and madder. Finally the guy said, "I didn't know Mark Andrews owned all the newspapers in the state." He should have known better.

"His attack stimulated my imagination," recalled Andrews. "We changed the wording so that *no railroad anywhere in the country* could abandon more than 3 percent of its total track in any one state. We changed it [in conference] from special interest legislation to national interest legislation. And it passed the Senate." [69] His assistant reported:

I knew what Mark was thinking when he came back from the conference. He said to me, "show me that clipping again." I showed it to him. He said, "I fixed that son of a bitch so he won't be talking about special interests anymore." You should have seen those lobbyists swarm in here the next day—in twos and threes and in waves. They called the president of Burlington Northern and said to him, "Who's that dumb bastard you have working for you?"

Another staffer described Andrews's mood going into the conference as: " 'You ain't seen nothin' yet.'. . . The whole railroad lobbying community came to Mark's office. There was standing room only. . . . I was told by some railroad men that this was the biggest railroad issue this year. The slurry pipeline was second."

Andrews completed the story.

The railroad executives were having a weekend conference at some foxy resort in Virginia with their ladies. They canceled their conference and came up here to lobby against the Andrews amendment. They appeared out here in the hall, en masse. I spoke to them briefly and went off to a Budget meeting. Two of them walked with me—the VP of the Southern Railroad and another one. We bumped into John Warner [R-Va.] and I said to him, "John, I know you'd be happy to vote against the Andrews amendment calling for restrictions on rail line abandonment, wouldn't you?" And he said, "Are you nuts? I'd never vote against an amendment like that." We ran into two or three other colleagues too. Those railroad men were in shock. Their chins were resting on their navels by the time we got to the Budget Committee.

They soon came around to the position that they didn't care what we did to Burlington Northern so long as we didn't apply it to them. They asked us to change the legislation back from national interest to special interest legislation! We did—in the continuing resolution.[70] And we worked some more magic. We not only said none of the money could be used this year, but we said no money could ever or hereafter be used to process the abandonment of more than 350 miles per year in North Dakota. That word *hereafter* is a wonderful word.

It's outrageous that a healthy railroad should try to abandon that much track of such vital importance to a state like North Dakota. If what we did is special interest legislation or an abuse of power, then so be it.[71]

"We had a fun deal with Burlington Northern," he concluded. "Fun deal" was a description he often used when he had combined inside maneuver and insider power to win a legislative victory.

A LEGISLATIVE INITIATIVE

Mark Andrews's broadest legislative initiative, and his most interesting fight as subcommittee chairman, came over his sponsorship of a 6-inch increase—from 96 inches to 102 inches—in the mandatory limit on the width of trucks on interstate highways. The idea was not new. By all accounts, it had been bouncing around just off the agenda for some time. In 1981, the Senate Commerce Committee had recommended that a permissible 102-inch limit be enacted, but had withdrawn it from the budget reconciliation bill at the last minute.[72] When Andrews—for reasons unknown—became seized of the issue in 1982, it had stalled out in the Commerce Committee. In early July, as he opened a letter from Commerce Committee Chairman Robert Packwood [R-Ore.], he described the issue briefly and then showed me the letter. It had three sentences: (1) Thank you for your offer to include the 102-inch width in your appropriations bill. (2) "For a variety of reasons," I have decided not to accept your "generous offer." (3) I appreciate your notifying me of your interest in matters that fall within the jurisdiction of my committee. "I know what's bothering him," said Andrews. "He knows that if I put it in an appropriations bill—which I can do—that Hatfield, who is chairman of the Appropriations Committee, will get all the credit with the timbering interests out west. They want the bill very much; but the bill is languishing in Packwood's committee."

Alongside the timber interests, the grocery industry was an equally ardent supporter of the legislation. Both used trucks to transport their products, and both wanted their trucks to carry bigger, money-saving loads. They were not pressing it as a North Dakota issue. Clearly, however, the senator from North Dakota was preparing to take up their cause.

The Andrews proposal emerged on September 9 in the 1982 Appropriations Committee Report, which stated that "the bill provides that funds under the 1956 Highway Act may not be apportioned to a state with a vehicle width limitation other than 102 inches." The report defended the idea:

> In summary, current 96-inch trailer restrictions are archaic, artificial and economically unjustified. Productivity improvements in terms of billions of dollars saved and millions of gallons of fuel conserved can be realized; improvement of truck equipment would be enhanced nationally; there is no evidence that 102-inch trailers are unsafe; 22 states now allow some permitted overwidth loadings and/or trailers; and permissive state standards destroy uniformity and are dysfunctional.[73]

Early opposition came from the Teamsters Union, concerned with the effect on jobs, and from the American Automobile Association, concerned for safety. Later opposition came from associations of state legislators and governors arguing for state option, and from environmentalists fearful of the effects of highway deterioration. But concerted interest group opposition never appeared.[74]

When Andrews took his subcommittee bill to the parent Appropriations Committee on September 16, Senators Harrison Schmitt (R-N.M.) and Thomas Eagleton, the latter a subcommittee member, zeroed in on the 102-inch provision. Schmitt argued that it was "an inappropriate effort on the part of this committee. . . . It very simply is beyond the priorities of this committee. . . . We shouldn't be trying to preempt state law in this area. . . . [New Mexico] has narrow state roads. We have a deteriorating highway system." Eagleton noted that the proposal remained on the Commerce Committee calendar. He noted further that the three most senior members of the Public Works Committee "have written a letter to members of this committee expressing their strong objection to this kind of legislation on an appropriations bill." Calling it "the starkest form of legislation on an appropriations bill," Eagleton threatened a point of order.

Andrews spoke at length—launching his rebuttal by invoking the constitution, Chief Justice John Marshall, the case of *Gibbons v. Ogden*, the commerce power, committee prerogative, and congressional responsiveness.

> I think this is clearly within the purview of the committee. We are designated by the Senate to decide where we shall apportion the funds of this government. There is no better way to decide where to apportion than through our highway legislation. I think it goes back to the beginning of our country, to the Constitution. . . . I have heard senator after senator refer to the Constitution on the floor of this great body. . . . We've gotten into trouble whenever we're backed away from that.
>
> None of us is a virgin from the standpoint of putting appropriations through with directives that can be construed as legislation on appropriations. We have done it in the Hyde Amendment [on federal funding for abortion] and a whole lot of things. Some voted for it, some voted against it. We've never really worried too much about it, because we do in fact have the responsibility to make sure this money is wisely expended.
>
> We sit here talking about raising money, yet we are running empty trucks back and forth over the roads of this country. . . . The Department of Transportation has no objection to this particular piece of legislation. . . . I have driven heavy trucks in my day; and it is safer to have a truck with a 102-inch

trailer than with a 96-inch trailer because you have a lower center of gravity and you have less fishtailing on the icy roads we encounter in the north or on roads with curves.

I know there are other committees of Congress that have been looking at this for quite some time; and I know they have been postponing and postponing. But I would suspect, Mr. Chairman, that the people of Oregon feel like the people in North Dakota. It is about time we got off our duff and did something.

Our subcommittee saw an opportunity to save $4 billion in transportation costs, enhance safety, move into a new era when we do have 24-foot roads. The old 96-inch trailer was made for 22-foot roads. We'll have more space, a lower center of gravity and we'll save the consumers money. I think this amendment is a necessary one.

And let me conclude by telling my colleagues they didn't elect me back in North Dakota to come down here and dance around politely and say so and so should have the jurisdiction and so and so should do this. They hope, when they elected us ... that we come down here and try to do the best we can to help consumers meet the high cost of living, ensure safety, and do the sensible adjustment that needs to be done.

He drew immediate support from the senior committee Democrat, John Stennis, a member of his subcommittee. "I'm pretty much a stickler for no legislation on appropriations bills but ... I think the senator made a remarkable statement. . . . I am supporting his position."

Chairman Hatfield asked Eagleton not to press his point of order in the committee. "The committee does not have detailed rules governing these matters," he said. "I would not like to set a precedent of getting into a point of order problem at the committee level. I think we get enough of that on the floor and I would like not to have to get into a complex set of rules for committee action." Schmitt argued that "this bill, this transportation appropriations bill, is in jeopardy of not passing the Senate because of this amendment." Hatfield replied: "We have that information transmitted to the committee. I don't think we should be intimidated by that, though, because the committee has taken other action that was very controversial, such as abortion." Eagleton protested that the provision "shouldn't be whisked through this committee. . . . I wonder where are the states' rights advocates today on that issue. This is a steamroller of the states. . . . This amendment will accelerate and intensify the already preexisting rapid rate of [highway] decay."

Andrews had the last word.

A wide truck width will cut back on road deterioration according to the engineers in our highway department. Let me point out why. I am not a highway engineer, I am a farmer. But if I drive out on a soft field, I want to get those tractor tires spread as far apart as I can. I don't want them close together. If you broaden the width of a trailer, you get your duals farther apart and you enhance the kind of traffic that will hold up the road.

The subcommittee provision passed in the full committee, 18-4.

When the highway authorization legislation came to the floor two weeks later, on the last day before adjournment for congressional elections, Andrews offered his proposal as an amendment. He noted that it had passed the Appropriations Committee, 18-4, but argued that it was appropriate to the authorization bill as well. After a brief debate—three speakers pro and three con—it was voted down, 45-47, in favor of a substitute that made the 102-inch width permissible but not yet mandatory.[75]

A couple of weeks after that, I watched Andrews try out the idea before business and education groups in North Dakota (Chapter 1). He talked about it under the rubric of "things we can do to help solve our various problems." As we rode around, he talked often and enthusiastically about his losing Washington effort. "I only needed one more vote; so I came close on that one."

We were losing 2-1. I started going around and saying, "I'd appreciate it. In the end we lost by only one vote. . . . We lost 45-47. But we found out who our friends are and who our enemies are. And for once we had a really good debate. My provision is still safely tucked away in the Transportation Appropriations Bill.

The committee of jurisdiction got ticked off because we did it on our bill, but they've been sitting on it for years without doing anything. People didn't send me down here just to suck my thumb and say how terrible things are—or put my head in the sand and do nothing about it.

The following week, he added, he was going to Portland, Oregon, to talk to the Boise Cascade Company. "They have an interest in my truck width amendment—the lumber industry." The next time I talked to him, his appropriations bill was nearing the Senate floor.

Andrews's trip to Oregon in October was not a routine effort at persuasion. The chief Washington lobbyist for Boise Cascade, Jacqueline Balk-Tusa, had been one of the earliest—if not the earliest—and one of the steadiest promoters of the idea.[76] "It's been five years since I started," she said. "I began with the authorizing committees and got nowhere. Then I took it to Andrews, who saw it as a challenge." When Andrews's staff speculated on the origins of his interest, they did not dispute her claim. "Nobody knows where he got the idea," said an aide.

> Hatfield's staff told me that Hatfield thinks the idea came from Andrews and Packwood, and that Packwood thinks it came from Andrews and Hatfield. Maybe Andrews thinks it came from Hatfield and Packwood. . . . Maybe Jacqueline suggested the idea some time ago and it appealed to him as a common-sense, matter-of-fact idea. That's the way he's selling it.

By October, Jacqueline Balk-Tusa of Boise Cascade had become the outside manager of the legislative campaign, working closely with the subcommittee chairman on strategy. When he and I spoke briefly on December 1, the two of them were in his office preparing for an expected floor fight the next day.

Andrews mentioned that he had called the Grocers Association and urged them to divide up the membership and get cracking.

> I'm for it because it's good for agribusiness. But all I can do is provide the framework. She [Balk-Tusa] and the grocers and the farmers who think it's important to them have got to go out and get the votes. If they want a vote from South Carolina, they've got to convince their people to convince Fritz Hollings that it's a good thing. I can't go to my good friend Fritz and ask him to vote for it. If it were something in North Dakota that I wanted, I would go directly to him and seek his support. But it's not up to me to do that in this case. At least that's the way I see it. . . . I don't even want to know how she has been trying to turn the votes around. We provide the vehicle. They have to want it badly enough.

That didn't mean, however, that senators might not come to him to talk about it. Minutes later he said, "I just picked up two votes from Kentucky. It seems they want a new airport control tower in Owens-boro. If they could just have that tower, there is nothing they would rather do than vote for the 102-inch truck width." (On the floor, the next day, the Kentucky senators extracted a public statement of support from the subcommittee chairman.)[77]

Balk-Tusa said she had begun by solidifying and reinforcing the support of those who voted with them in October. Then, she added, "We've turned around three votes either because it was the end of the session or because they didn't know what they were voting for." Andrews worried that "the whole thing has been muddied up now with the gas tax bill." With a proposed five-cent increase in the gasoline tax tied up in the Finance (or taxing) Committee, an argument had emerged that the truck width should be taken up in that bill in order to extract support from the truckers. The two strategists also said they were expecting the initial vote to come on Eagleton's promised point of order, that their proposal was legislation on an appropriations bill.

On December 2, the Transportation Appropriations Bill for FY 1983 reached the Senate floor.[78] Eagleton proposed his point of order. He reminded his colleagues that they had voted on the same issue in October and "turned down the amendment to impose a mandatory 102-inch wide truck standard on all the states." He argued that any reconsideration should come as an integral part of the regular highway bill, "not separate and apart from everything else as a little section of an appropriations bill." Andrews argued that the Senate had done this before, and he counterattacked by calling for a vote on the germaneness of the issue.[79] He was upheld, immediately, by a vote of 67-27. This procedural vote forecast the outcome by revealing strong support for Andrews's position. But a brief debate "on the merits" of Eagleton's motion to strike the provision followed. Eagleton and Schmitt rehearsed the arguments they had used in the committee, buttressed now by the notion that the Andrews proposal should be coupled with the gas tax bill. Bob Dole [R-Kan.], chairman of the Finance Committee, chimed in with that argument. Bob Stafford [R-Vt.], Chairman of the Environment and Public Works Committee, protested—as he had in October—that "clearly this action at this time is an invasion of the jurisdiction of the committee ... which I have the privilege of chairing."

Andrews, calling it "a consumer amendment," rehearsed his arguments—emphasizing the number of people and groups that would benefit, touting $3.5 billion in savings, and rejecting arguments about road deterioration. "If I heard anything when I was back home in October," he concluded, "it was that people back home are getting tired of us sitting here talking to each other, beating our breasts and doing nothing about the problems. . . . I'm a country guy," he said, "but we have to be practical in the country, too." As he had told his constituents, he saw it as a "thing we can do," and he believed Congress should do it. The final vote, in favor, was 62-31. When the vote was announced, Eagleton walked up to Andrews, shook his fist, laughed, and said in a loud voice, "Bong, bong"—as if his bell had been rung. It had. When I bumped into him in the hallway afterward, Andrews said simply, "They all came around nicely, didn't they?" It was a moment of success.

From the gallery, I was able to chart Andrews's activity on the floor during the fifteen or twenty minutes it took for the Senate to vote on each roll call. Notwithstanding his reluctance to approach colleagues on a non-North Dakota issue, he appeared to be engaged in a good bit of instant one-on-one activity. Some of it was, no doubt, random. The Senate floor, especially down front in the "well," is a buzzing confusion,

TABLE 3-1   Contacts Made by Mark Andrews During Senate Voting: Two Roll Calls

	Point of Order		*Passage*	
	Republicans	*Democrats*	*Republicans*	*Democrats*
Contacted by Andrews (total)	21	15	13	14
First contact	—	—	7	9
Second contact	—	—	6	5
Voted with Andrews				
Yes (total)	15	13	12	11
No (total)	6	2	1	3
Yes (first/second contacts)	—	—	7/5	6/5
No (first/second contacts)	—	—	0/1	3/0
Votes switched to Andrews[a]				
No to yes	1	6	2	3
Yes to no	0	0	0	0
No vote to yes	0	2	—	—
No vote to no	0	0	—	—

Note: Total senators contacted: 52; total switched to yes: 14.

[a] On the point of order vote, the "switch" is from a senator's position on the October vote; on passage, the "switch" is from the point of order vote.

with senators coming and going, bumping into one another accidentally, mingling and swirling. It is also a bazaar in which brief encounters produce exchanges—of information, attention, favors. For a senator with a purpose, there is less randomness then meets the eye. Some proportion of Andrews's encounters seemed purposeful. Table 3-1 charts his contacts during two votes.

While the first, procedural, motion was being voted on, he spoke briefly to thirty-two senators. In addition, he gave the thumbs-up sign to three others. When another senator rushed in to cast a last-minute vote, Andrews called loudly to him, "Vote aye." Of the thirty-six contacted, fifteen were Democrats and twenty-one were Republicans. The Democrats voted 13-2 in favor; the Republicans voted 15-6 in favor. Since these proportions were slightly better than the proportions for the two parties as a whole—Democrats voting 2-1 and Republicans 3-1 in favor—he seemed to have concentrated his attention disproportionately on those he considered favorable or potentially favorable, especially among the Democrats. Of the thirty-six he contacted during the vote, seven of them—six Democrats and one Republican—changed their October vote from no to yes, and none changed in the other direction.

Two others with whom he talked had not voted in October but voted with him this time.

We cannot know, of course, what he said to each person, whether he was reinforcing or persuading—or just explaining the germaneness vote. But he had some time to do all of that. On votes like this one, where party positions are not at stake, reliance on cues from the manager of the bill or the sponsor of the amendment increases. In any case, the bill's manager could be seen moving about and hard at work.

During the second and final vote, Andrews talked briefly to twenty-seven senators. A majority of this group—sixteen senators—were new contacts. In the half hour or so consumed by the two votes, therefore, Andrews had been able to catch a word or give a signal to a majority (fifty-two) of the senators. His conversations during the second vote also seemed to form a pattern. Among his new contacts there were more Democrats (nine) than Republicans (seven). Six of the nine Democrats voted with him, a higher proportion (2-1) than the proportion of supporters (4-3) among Democrats as a whole. Of the six who voted with him, three had been opposed to him on round one. He also lost a number of Democrats who had voted with him on the first vote. Two of those were people he had talked to on round one; but he did not talk to them during the second vote. They were on loan for the procedural vote only, and he seems to have understood that. The five Democrats with whom he talked during both votes voted with him on both.

Among his Republican contacts on the second vote, six out of seven of the new ones and five out of the six old ones were repeat supporters. But in the other two cases, he turned votes of no on round one into votes of yes on round two. In one case, he talked to the same person four times during the two votes; in the other case, my notes say that Andrews made "a special plea" and showed the senator the wording of the provision. Persuasion as well as reinforcement did take place.

Combining the two periods of activity, Andrews appeared to be as attentive to Democrats as to Republicans—especially to Democrats who could be persuaded to switch from their opposition in October to support now. By the final vote, twelve senators switched their October votes from no to yes on Andrews's proposal. Four others who had not voted in October voted yes on the final vote. During the thirty or forty minutes he had to work the floor during the two votes, he had contacted fourteen of the sixteen. Despite the confusion and babble in the chamber during the voting, Andrews had, from all we can tell, used his last minute cue-giving opportunities purposefully. It was further evidence of inside legislative skills.

By shepherding his truck width proposal through the Senate, he had demonstrated legislative prowess and won a legislative victory. He had also demonstrated, once again, how deeply committed he was to the appropriations process he had been engaged in for so long and how well suited his experience and his talents were to the kind of politics generated by that process.

After Andrews's December triumph, only one major congressional hurdle remained—the conference committee. On December 9, five senators and nine House members from their respective transportation subcommittees gathered in a small room (S-126) on the Senate side of the Capitol to resolve their differences. The senator from North Dakota was in the chair. He was among his former House committee colleagues, people with whom he naturally felt at ease.

In the previous year, Andrews's House counterpart in the business of conferencing out the transportation appropriations bill had been Indiana Democrat Adam Benjamin. When he reminisced about his 1981 dealings with Benjamin, Andrews defined his idea of a good legislator operating in a small legislative space:

> We sat [in conference] and completed our business in twenty minutes. And we did it on the basis of facts—without any b.s. I suppose there's a little b.s. in every politician. But it is enjoyable when you can deal with someone straight from the shoulder, without doing a minuet or waltzing around. When you sat down with Adam, everything was on the table. You knew exactly what he wanted, and he knew exactly what you wanted. If you've been around here any length of time, you know just where you are going to come out anyway. Of course, some people still don't know where they are going.

Benjamin was all business, and he was someone you could do business with. He was knowledgeable and experienced. He would not posture. He would not, as one of Andrews's favorite metaphors would have it, "trade horses for rabbits." He would talk straight, give and take, cut a deal, and keep his word. In Andrews's view, that described the ideal conference committee legislator—at least for an appropriations conference. Andrews saw himself, I believe, in that same light.

Adam Benjamin had passed away in the summer of 1982 and had been replaced by Florida Democrat Bill Lehman as chairman of the House subcommittee. Andrews liked Lehman. He "has bent over backwards to be accommodating," said Andrews, adding by way of praise, "Together we once ran over one of his own colleagues." The senior Republican on the House Appropriations Committee—who was present at the conference ex officio—was Silvio Conte [R-Mass.], a long time colleague. Conte's determined and colorful opposition to "the pork barrel" in water and agricultural projects had often put him in opposition to Andrews. But Conte, too, was known as someone who was exceptionally adept at channeling money to constituents, in his case, in western Massachusetts.[80] And Andrews savored their history of legislative arm wrestling.

Looking forward to the conference, he laughed in reminiscence.

> I remember when Sil Conte was getting ready to amend something in the agriculture appropriations bill. Jamie Whitten [subcommittee chairman] and I were worried that the amendment would pass. I told Jamie that when the section came up I'd go over and talk to Sil about ducks. In the House, if they read a section of the bill and you don't get your amendment in before they finish with that section, it's tough. When the time came, I went over to Sil and started talking to him about duck hunting. Then I suggested we leave the chamber and have a cup of coffee. When we got back, the clerk was just finishing reading the section he wanted to amend. He was mad as hell. Then he started to laugh because he knew he'd been had. And I laughed because I knew he'd been had. It wasn't a major amendment—just some crazy idea of his.

Andrews liked Conte personally and respected him as a legislative professional. Certain established personal relationships added, therefore, to the informality of the conference committee setting.

One of the striking things about the December 9 conference committee meeting was, once again, how far removed it seemed from the public gaze—no television cameras, no recognizable media faces, with the spectators nearly outnumbered by the legislators and their staffs. Most of the matters to be resolved had already been worked out by the staffs. Once Andrews opened the meeting and turned over the task of reading off the agenda items to a member of his staff, the action moved swiftly, and informally. Generally it took the form: "Here's what the staffs propose on this item. Are there any objections?" Conferees moved through the agenda quickly. Like so much of the subcommittee's decision making, most of the work had been done behind the scenes and the public part of it was preordained and swift. That, of course, is in tradition of the prereform House Appropriations Committee, and it reflected the established stylistic preference of its longtime member from North Dakota.

Twenty minutes into the proceedings, Rep. Martin Sabo [D-Minn.]—who was going to manage the conference report on the House floor[81]—initiated the following exchange.

> REPRESENTATIVE SABO: About this 102-inch truck width: Isn't it involved in another bill?

SENATOR ANDREWS: It's important that we get it out as early as possible. The gasoline tax bill is not a certainty. It's going to produce savings of $3.5 billion.

REPRESENTATIVE SABO: If no one else has any objection, and the senators are all agreed, I'll let it go. But I think it's the wrong place to do it.

SENATOR ANDREWS: I appreciate that.

That was it. It was over. Andrews had what he wanted. The conference rolled on.[82]

Five minutes later, Andrews was the only senator left. The meeting continued for another half hour, while he sought agreements and announced agreements with a combination of good humor and dispatch. He was, after all, among friends, members with whom he had worked in committee as recently as two years before.

- "Is everybody happy? OK."
- "You're convincing. Sold. Why don't you quit while you're ahead."
- "You're your usual eloquence. We'll split the difference."
- "I and my colleagues, represented by the proxies in my pocket, accept your figures."
- "The administration is having fits over this one. So if your legislative committee doesn't agree, then maybe we'll throw it out."

The meeting was over in one hour. "Good to do business with you," Andrews said to his counterpart, Representative Lehman. Representative Conte echoed the sentiment: "I hope you all get something for Christmas in this bill. It's been a pleasure doing business with you."

When I congratulated Andrews on the way out, he expressed his pleasure.

You don't think we're mean and nasty, do you? We slipped that 102-inches through before anyone knew what we were doing. We let [Senate staffer] Chip [Hardin] read because he reads fast. Bill Lehman would have read too slow. Look at all the proxies I had in my pocket. I never needed them.

Some legislators love to tell stories about tricks of the legislative trade; others do not. Mark Andrews was one who did.

GOVERNING STYLE

The truck width conference was the last time I saw Andrews operate in a legislative setting. But the episode was an appropriate one to remember him by. The setting was ideal for an inside player—one who knew what he wanted, who had the skill to get what he wanted and who, in his words, "enjoy[ed] shepherding things through the process." An appropriations conference committee—with its routines of bipartisan accommodation and its piecemeal focus on matters not likely to attract widespread public attention—was the kind of legislative setting in which Mark Andrews was most at home. It was typical of the settings where appropriations politics is played. In "shepherding" things through the appropriations process Mark Andrews was as knowledgeable and as capable as any legislator on Capitol Hill.

Near the end of 1982, I asked him how people got their reputations in the Senate. "I don't know," he answered. "They [senators] will listen to you or they won't. That happens—but I don't know how it happens— in the first year or two. I know they don't like showoffs. I've been pretty lucky so far." Judging by some of his legislative successes—the protection of the Rural Electrification Administration, the channeling of projects into North Dakota, the truck width proposal—his colleagues would listen to him. Clearly, from my observation, he worked hard to make certain that they would listen.

The major elements of his governing style, we have argued, were the ingrained product of his long experience in the House, as a member of its Appropriations Committee. His House experience underpinned his victories in the Senate. The depth of his commitment to appropriations committee power and to its distributive decision processes brought him success in that particular domain. But it impeded his success in other, less circumscribed domains. In the Senate at large, however, the husbanding of his bargaining power, the preference for deal making, and the willingness to play hardball kept him from winning any popularity contests. "You have to buy him for everything," a Republican insider complained. "He has a House minority mentality—all he cares about is trying to squeeze some little pork barrel out for his state." [83] While other collegial judgments might not be as perceptive, the level of exasperation was common to many who contended with his unpredictable individualism on the Budget Committee or with the jurisdictional aggressiveness of his appropriations subcommittee.

In the case of the truck width provision, his invasion of the jurisdiction of another committee via legislation on an appropriations bill reaped considerable disapproval, if not hostility.[84] A subcommittee staffer discussed Andrews's first October amendment to the highway authorization bill. "He has no idea how much people resented his sticking it on the highway bill at the last minute. We shed a lot of blood at the staff level; and we reaped a lot of ill will because he had it stuck in his craw. Once he becomes possessed of something like that, he won't stop. It becomes a big thing with him."

After Andrews's December victory on the Senate floor, a top aide to Majority Leader Howard Baker ventilated the collegial disapproval.

> I don't want to talk about him. But I'll tell you what I don't like about him. I don't like what he's trying to do—turn the Senate appropriations process into what it is in the House. He wants to act like Jamie Whitten. We may not have the greatest process here, but it's a hell of a lot better than what the House has. Andrews says to Bob Stafford, "I don't give a god damn what your authorizing committee did, I'm going to put your legislation in my appropriations bill. I'm going to shove this down your throat." That's what the Appropriations Committee does in the House. It leans on authorizing committees. I'm an authorizing committee man. I'm completely opposed to what Andrews is trying to do. He just wants to sit and cut deals.

The aide was expressing the broad perspective of the leadership, for whom House-style appropriations politics was fragmenting at best and institutionally debilitating at worst. He was expressing the view of people who instituted the macro-level congressional budget process to counterbalance the micro-level, deal-cutting appropriations process.

The leadership aide had put his finger on the problems generated for the leadership by the legislative perspective of deep-dyed, free-wheeling, deal-cutting appropriations politicians like the senator from North Dakota. People like that made it difficult to manage the business of the institution. But this aide's rhetoric, at least, gave Mark Andrews too much credit. The North Dakotan had no grand design. He didn't want to make over the Senate in the image of the House. He was just doing what came naturally—what he had always done ever since he had come to Congress: he was behaving very much like a House member in the Senate.

Our analysis of Andrews's Senate governing behavior makes it clear that the part of the world that mattered most to him was not the Senate, but North Dakota. Most of what he did in the Senate, he did with North Dakota in mind. He wanted his Senate performance to bring favorable judgments from his constituents, not from his colleagues. Without a doubt, he channeled a lot of money into North Dakota; and he prevented even more money from being taken away from North Dakota. He certainly believed that delivery of these tangible benefits would carry great weight with his constituents. It always had. Still, the ultimate assessment of his governing performance—its success, its shortcomings, and the weight it would be given in a final calculus—would not be known until November of 1986.

NOTES

1. Senate Subcommittee on Transportation, *Hearings on Department of Transportation and Related Agencies Appropriations for Fiscal Year 1986,* Committee on Appropriations, Washington, D.C., March 19, 1985, 580. Hereafter, hearings before Andrews's Transportation Subcommittee will be cited as *Hearings,* in the fiscal year (FY) noted.

2. *Hearings,* FY 1982, pt. 1, February 26, 1981, 82; FY 1984, pt. 1, February 24, 1983, 201; and FY 1982, pt. 1, March 10, 1981, 565.

3. *Hearings,* FY 1982, pt. 2, April 6, 1981, 685. For a very instructive profile of Rep. John Rooney and his appropriations subcommittee behavior, see Peter Wyden, "The Man Who Frightens Bureaucrats," *Saturday Evening Post,* January 3, 1959.

4. *Hearings,* FY 1982, pt. 1, March 3, 1981, 250; March 23, 1981, 808; FY 1982, pt. 2, April 6, 1981, 299; FY 1983, pt. 2, March 24, 1982, 688; and FY 1983, pt. 1, February 17, 1982, 34.

5. *Hearings,* FY 1982, pt. 2, March 27, 1981, 15; April 3, 1981, 274; April 6, 1981, 582; and FY 1984, pt. 1, February 17, 1983, 38, 127.

6. *Hearings,* FY 1987, pt. 1, February 19, 1986, 27; FY 1986, pt. 1, March 19, 1985, 514.

7. *Hearings,* FY 1987, pt. 1, March 19, 1986, 628.

8. Ibid., 758.

9. *Hearings,* FY 1984, pt. 2, April 14, 1983, 647.

10. *Hearings,* FY 1986, pt. 2, March 28, 1985, 40. See also April 18, 1985, 674.

11. *Hearings,* FY 1984, pt. 1, February 17, 1983, 124; FY 1986, March 5, 1985, 341.

12. *Hearings,* FY 1982, pt. 1, March 3, 1981, 237; see also FY 1983, pt. 1, March 29, 1982, 814-815; and FY 1987, pt. 1, February 19, 1986, 30, 46.

13. *Hearings,* FY 1987, pt. 2, May 8, 1986, 604.

14. *Hearings,* FY 1984, pt. 1, March 3, 1983, 690.

15. *Hearings,* FY 1982, pt. 2, March 27, 1981.

16. *Hearings,* FY 1987, pt. 2, April 23, 1986, 394; and FY 1986, pt. 2, April 4, 1985, 369.

17. *Hearings,* FY 1984, pt. 1, March 15, 1983, 687.

18. *Hearings,* FY 1983, pt. 2, March 29, 1982, 876.

19. *Hearings,* FY 1984, pt. 1, March 15, 1983, 687.

20. *Hearings,* FY 1983, pt. 1, March 24, 1982, 556.

21. Kevin Murphy, "Prairie Towns. Transportation, Agriculture Changes Decided Their Fate," *Forum* (Fargo), November 9, 1986.

22. *Hearings,* FY 1983, pt. 1, March 9, 1982, 100; March 11, 1982, 218; FY 1984, pt. 1, February 17, 1983, 28, 34; February 22, 1983, 134; FY 1986, pt. 1, March 19, 1985, 581; FY 1987, pt. 1, March 5, 1986, 320.

23. *Hearings,* FY 1987, pt. 1, March 26, 1986, 745. Andrews's introduction of a bill to remedy his complaints can be found in the *Congressional Record,* October 31, 1985, S14484.

24. *Hearings,* FY 1983, pt. 1, March 24, 1982, 761.

25. *Hearings,* FY 1982, pt. 1, March 25, 1981, 938.

26. *Hearings,* FY 1982, pt. 2, March 27, 1981, 23.

27. *Hearings,* FY 1987, pt. 1, March 5, 1986, 326 and 324; FY 1982, pt. 1, March 10, 1981, 474; and FY 1983, pt. 1, March 24, 1982, 666.

28. *Hearings,* FY 1984, pt. 1, March 15, 1983, 688. On Andrews's "close to my heart" comment, see *Hearings,* FY 1982, March 25, 1981, 941.

29. See *Hearings*, FY 1982, pt. 1, March 3, 1981, 216; March 23, 1981, 792; March 25, 1981, 949; FY 1982, pt. 2, March 27, 1981, 127; FY 1983, pt. 1, March 15, 1982, 584; FY 1984, pt. 2, March 17, 1983, 355-356; FY 1986, pt. 1, February 28, 1985, 360-361; FY 1986, pt. 2, April 4, 1985, 434; FY 1987, pt. 1, March 12, 1986, 541-556, 854; FY 1987, pt. 2, April 9, 1986, 213-215.

30. *Hearings*, FY 1986, pt. 2, April 24, 1985, 832.

31. *Hearings*, FY 1987, pt. 2, April 9, 1986, 31.

32. *Hearings*, FY 1983, pt. 1, March 11, 1982, 323.

33. *Hearings*, FY 1982, pt. 1, March 25, 1981, 961-962.

34. Ibid., March 23, 1981, 798.

35. *Hearings*, FY 1987, pt. 2, April 9, 1986, 27.

36. *Hearings*, FY 1986, pt. 1, March 5, 1985, 342; FY 1987, pt. 1, March 19, 1986, 857; *Hearings on Federal Aviation Administration Office and Facility Consolidations*, Subcommittee on Transportation and Related Agencies, Committee on Appropriations, U.S. Senate, January 4, 1985, 25; and *Hearings* FY 1984, pt. 1, February 17, 1983, 17-18. (A similar exchange will be found on p. 28.)

37. *Hearings*, FY 1986, pt. 2, March 28, 1985, 195, 204.

38. *Congressional Record*, November 3, 1981, 26313-26314; July 15, 1983, S10115.

39. *Hearings*, FY 1982, pt. 1, March 25, 1981, 957.

40. *Committee Report*, Department of Transportation and Related Agencies, Appropriations Bill (FY) 1982, Committee on Appropriations, October 27, 1981, 95. Hereafter cited as *Committee Report*.

41. For example, *Hearings on Transit Systems—New York*, Senate Subcommittee on Transportation and Related Agencies, Committee on Appropriations, U.S. Senate, New York City, April 14, 1981; *Hearings on Crime in Mass Transit Facilities*, Senate Subcommittee on Transportation and Related Agencies, Committee on Appropriations, New York City, January 18, 1984.

42. See Tom Goldstein, "D'Amato, at Home in the Senate," *New York Times Magazine*, February 13, 1983; Michael Kramer, "Battlin' Al: D'Amato the Senator as States Man," *New York Magazine*, reprinted in *Rochester Democrat and Chronicle*, March 16, 1986.

43. *Committee Report*, FY 1983, September 16, 1982, 3.

44. *Hearings*, FY 1984, pt. 2, April 26, 1983, 835.

45. Dan Morgan, "All's Fair in Love, War and Appropriations Bills," *Washington Post National Weekly Edition*, November 27-December 3, 1989. Interestingly, this article centers on a public dispute between the House transportation subcommittee and another House committee in 1989.

46. An excellent early study of earmarking in the appropriations process is Michael Kirst, *Government Without Passing Laws* (Chapel Hill: University of North Carolina Press, 1969). A recent critique is James D. Savage, "Saints and Cardinals in Appropriations Subcommittees: Academic Pork Barreling and Distributive Politics in an Era of Redistributive Budgeting" (Paper presented to the Annual Meeting of the American Political Science Association, Atlanta, August 31-September 3, 1989).

47. *Committee Report*, FY 1984, July 14, 1983, 37; FY 1985, July 17, 1984, 42.

48. *Committee Report*, FY 1982, October 27, 1981, 80; FY 1983, September 16, 1982, 33; and FY 1982, October 27, 1981, 82. In 1984, the Grand Forks Airport was appropriately renamed the Mark Andrews International Airport.

49. *Committee Report*, FY 1982, October 27, 1981, 80; Public Law 97-102, Department of Transportation and Related Agencies Appropriations Act, 1982, December 23, 1981, 95 Stat. 1445.

50. *Committee Report,* FY 1986, October 4, 1985, 32; FY 1987, August 19, 1986, 28, 33; and FY 1985, July 17, 1984, 39.
51. *Congressional Record,* October 3, 1984, S12967-S12971.
52. *Hearings,* FY 1982, pt. 1, March 25, 1981, 949.
53. *Congressional Record,* July 15, 1982, S8345. P.L. 97-102 was the final FY 1982 Transportation Appropriations Act, combining the transportation appropriations bill as originally passed and the relevant provisions of the continuing resolution. The act was signed at the very end of December 1981. Section 310(d)(3) of the original bill remained intact in the final act; but the effect of the provisions of continuing resolutions on the section was unclear. So, while the bill could be used as reference, new legislation was needed to trigger spending.
54. *Committee Report,* FY 1984, July 14, 1983, 49-50; FY 1983, September 16, 1982, 39; FY 1987, August 19, 1986, 9-10; and *Committee Report,* FY 1982, October 27, 1981, 118.
55. *Committee Report,* FY 1985, July 17, 1984, 52; *Hearings,* FY 1984, pt. 1, March 15, 1983, 1036.
56. *Committee Report,* Supplemental Appropriations Bill, May 14, 1981, 339; *Hearings,* FY 1986, pt. 1, March 5, 1985, 360-361; and *Committee Report,* FY 1986, October 4, 1985, 49.
57. *Committee Report,* FY 1984, July 14, 1983, 39; FY 1985, July 17, 1984, 32; FY 1986, October 4, 1985, 36; and FY 1987, August 19, 1986, 35.
58. Two examples of such credit-claiming press releases are: AP, "$25.5 Billion Tied to Transportation Bill," *Bismarck Tribune,* August 8, 1986; David Lindley, "Congress OK's UND Money, Liquor Bill," *Grand Forks Herald,* October 20, 1985.
59. *Congressional Record,* November 3, 1981, S26312; Public Law 97-102, December 23, 1981, 95 Stat. 1451. The story of the Cardinal will be found in Howie Kurtz, "Budget Knife Only Nicks Road and Harbor Projects," *Washington Post,* January 26, 1982.
60. The style still prevails on the transportation subcommittee, see Morgan, "All's Fair."
61. Off the Senate floor, see interview on CNN, November 23, 1981; "Behind the Budget Battle," *Newsweek,* December 7, 1981. On the floor, see the *Congressional Record,* September 10, 1982, S11252-S11253.
62. *Committee Report,* FY 1983, September 16, 1982, 47.
63. *Hearings,* FY 1983, pt. 1, February 26, 1982, 105.
64. *Committee Report,* FY 1982, October 22, 1981, 41.
65. *Hearings,* FY 1984, pt. 1, February 17, 1983, 18; FY 1983, pt. 1, March 15, 1982, 590; and FY 1984, pt. 1, March 15, 1983, 698.
66. *Congressional Record,* February 20, 1985, S1580-1581.
67. *Hearings,* FY 1982, pt. 1, March 25, 1981, 802; *Committee Report,* FY 1982, October 27, 1981, 122.
68. *Committee Report,* FY 1982, October 27, 1981, 122.
69. Public Law 97-102, December 23, 1981, Section 311, 95 Stat. 1460.
70. When Andrews made this change, in full committee, November 17, 1981, it went through without a comment (from personal observation).
71. Public Law 97-102, December 23, 1981, Section 402, 95 Stat. 1465. A later newsletter devoted to this battle and its results—only 187 miles of abandoned track in four years—will be found in "Senator Andrews Talks on B-N Abandonment," *New Rockford Transcript,* August 14, 1985.

72. Judy Sarasohn, "Timber, Trucking Industries Continue to Back Allowing Wider Trucks on Interstates," *Congressional Quarterly Weekly Report*, September 5, 1981, 1664.
73. *Committee Report*, FY 1983, September 16, 1982, 43-45.
74 Sarasohn, "Timber, Trucking Industries Continue", *Congressional Record*, October 1, 1982, S26786-S26792; Judy Sarasohn, "Turf Fight Results in Limited Highway Funds," *Congressional Quarterly Weekly Report*, October 9, 1982, 2635-2636.
75. *Congressional Record*, October 1, 1982, S26786-S26792.
76. Sarasohn, "Timber, Trucking Industries Continue."
77. *Congressional Record*, December 2, 1982, S13774.
78. The account that follows is from the *Congressional Record*, December 2, 1982, S13773-S13785.
79. A useful discussion of the procedural relationship between the point of order and the germaneness provision in Senate rules will be found in the *Congressional Record*, November 18, 1981, S13616.
80. On Conte's constituency-oriented style, see David Nyhan, "Silvio Conte Dies at Age 69," *Boston Globe*, February 9, 1991; *Congressional Record*, February 19, 1991, S1874-S1887; February 27, 1991, S1231-S1240.
81. See the *Congressional Record*, December 16, 1982, H9992ff.
82. The conference report passed the Senate. *Congressional Record*, December 16, 1982, S15001-S15004.
83. Ronald Brownstein, "Mark Andrews," *National Journal*, April 12, 1986.
84. Other cases involving the Andrews subcommittee are found in the *Congressional Record*, November 18, 1981, S13616-S13617; October 3, 1984, S13007-S13008.

Governing Style and Constituency Career

STYLISTIC CONTINUITY

When Mark Andrews came to the Senate in 1981, he had already spent a full political career in the House of Representatives. The governing style he displayed in the Senate was heavily influenced by the governing style he brought with him from his eighteen years on the House Appropriations Committee. That style emphasized the maximization of his influence inside the legislature in order to serve his constituents at home. It was rooted in a strong sense of identification between the legislator and his constituency. And it was prefigured by the way he defined that constituency—as atypical and distinctive rather than representative or microcosmic.

The distinctiveness of North Dakota, Andrews believed, required distinctive policies, which tended to be limited in scope and targeted in impact. Inside his committees, as we have seen, Andrews used the legislative process with relish and skill to work out bargains for his constituents in the fields of agriculture and transportation. In return, he sought the home state judgment that "he is one of us" and "he works hard on our behalf." When I traveled with him in North Dakota in 1980 and 1982, there seemed little reason to doubt that he had won the judgment he sought and that his inside-playing, home-oriented governing style—so successful in keeping him in the House—would serve equally well to keep him in the Senate.

One could, of course, ask whether the voters of North Dakota expected a different governing performance from their senators than from their House member. There are several reasons, however, for believing that they did not.

First, when voters in a national sample were asked in 1978 to rank the importance of five basic job expectations, their orderings were virtually the same for members of both institutions. For the activity of particular interest to us—"making sure the district gets its fair share of government money and projects"—14 percent of the voters ranked it the most important activity for House members and 15 percent ranked it at the top for senators. In the rank orderings for both sets of politicians, this pork-oriented expectation ended up in fourth place overall.[1] Speaking generally, America's voters do not differentiate between the job of a House member and the job of a senator.

Second, when statewide samples of voters were asked in 1988 to rank the same five job expectations for their senators, North Dakota voters gave noticeably strong support to the pork-oriented expectation. Table 4-1 compares North Dakotans with respondents from the other single-district states and with those from the remaining states.[2] It indicates that North Dakotans differ from each of the other groups in the importance they attach to the business of "bringing home the bacon." It is enough of a difference to encourage North Dakota's legislators to aspire to reputations as devoted providers of pork. It indicates that Mark Andrews had substantial constituency support for continuing his House member behavior patterns when he went to the Senate.

Third, there is evidence that "bringing home the bacon" was a well-established constituency expectation of North Dakota's senators. Andrews's predecessor in the Senate had been another farmer, Republican Milton Young. As one reporter generalized: "His name did not become a household word, but he amassed power on the Hill."[3] Upon his retirement, Young told people "that his proudest accomplishments included having obtained funds for seven water projects and seven federal research laboratories in North Dakota." His Senate career was spent in "tireless advocacy of his state's farm products . . . [and] as a champion of the wheat farmers and ranchers of North Dakota." "He seemed to lack glamour and diversity," wrote an observer. But deliberately so. "I have always tried to stay close to the people," explained Young. "In North Dakota, to be elected and to stay on, you have to know the farmers and stay close to them." For this pattern of thought and action Milton Young had been rewarded with the nickname "Mr. Wheat" and with six consecutive elections to the U.S. Senate.

Andrews's current Senate colleague, Democrat Quentin Burdick, was cut from the same cloth as Young. He had been rewarded with a fourth consecutive term in 1982. (And a fifth term in 1988.) One profile stated:

TABLE 4-1 Citizens' Prescription of Senators' Job: The Importance of Securing Pork

| | Importance of Pork | | | | |
| | Extremely Important | | Somewhat, Not Very, and Not at All Important[a] | | |
Residence of Respondent	Percent	(n)	Percent	(n)	Total N
North Dakota	87	(62)	13	(9)	(71)
Other states with single representative (5)	77	(262)	23	(78)	(340)
All other states (44)	75	(1,998)	25	(646)	(2,644)

Source: National Election Studies, 1988 Survey of Senate Voters.

Questions: "Here is a list of some activities that occupy U.S. senators as part of their job. We want to know how important you think these activities are, or should be." "How about making sure the state gets its fair share of government money and projects?"

[a] Don't know and not applicable have been eliminated from the calculation. They totaled 3 percent of the sample and did not vary among the three categories of states used.

> In a town of political peacocks, [Burdick] is a rare bird. Despite his 26 years in the Senate . . . his primary legislative focus has been a North Dakota water project. He eschews the national news media in favor of the Fargo (N.D.) *Forum* . . . and remains so comfortably obscure that he lists his Washington telephone number. . . . He has given primacy to constituency work over the years, often playing down the burning national issues of the day.[4]

Inside the Senate, said a lobbyist with whom he worked, Burdick "plays the Senate game—the way the Senate functions, the way favors are traded, the way chits are saved up and dispersed."[5] In the face of electoral threats, Burdick advertised his inside influence. "I'll be able to do more for the state in my position than [any opponent] will be able to do in 15 to 20 years."[6] His campaign brochures asserted: "Burdick's clout is North Dakota's."[7]

In a rank ordering of senators' voting records on one group's "pork barrel and subsidy index" for 1985-1986, Burdick ranked second highest and Andrews ranked third highest in pork barrel support. As a delegation, the two North Dakota senators combined ranked second highest in pork barrel support.[8] For at least a quarter of a century, it seems, North Dakotans had expected and had rewarded a behind-the-scenes, vote-trading, homestate-centered governing style.

Our description of Mark Andrews's behavior on the Budget and Appropriations Committees places his style well within this established tradition. During an interview in December 1982, one of his transportation subcommittee aides talked about his style at some length.

> He once told me that you don't score any points in North Dakota for being a national senator. If it's something for North Dakota, he'll go one on one with other senators.... If it's something with a national sweep, he prefers to let others do it.... Make no mistake about it. North Dakota is in the front of his mind—all the time.... He likes to work quietly in committee. He believes that you get your work done in committee, not on the floor.... He doesn't speak out a lot on the floor. He's very independent. But he doesn't see himself as a national senator.... He worked very hard behind the scenes with Secretary of Transportation Drew Lewis, to get some exemptions for farmers on the highway tax. They don't use the main highways very much—mostly back roads. He had long sessions with Lewis on that. He's helped farmers everywhere, but he won't take any credit for that among the farmers nationwide.... He'll send a press release to North Dakota. That's the way he prefers to work.

The description could also be used for the Young-Burdick pattern. That is not surprising, since the three legislators served the exact same constituency—small, self-conscious, and homogeneous—throughout the 1970s.

In her superb study of the U.S. Senate in the 1980s, Barbara Sinclair corroborates this picture of Mark Andrews's low-profile, committee-centered, constituency-oriented governing style. According to her measures of each senator's breadth of policy interests and the extent of each senator's participation in floor activity, Andrews ranked in the bottommost category in both respects. Andrews was among the most specialized in terms of his policy interests and among the least active on the Senate floor. In 1981-1982, he was one of only nine senators who chose not to offer a single floor amendment; in 1983-1984 he was one of only fourteen senators in that same category. In 1985-1986, he offered two amendments, a total exceeded by seventy-seven of his colleagues.[9] Since Sinclair's measures of policy breadth rest on the number of different committees and the number of different issues involved in each senator's amendments, Andrews's lack of amending activity places him at rock bottom as a policy generalist and at the top as a policy specialist. His scores, that is, reveal someone who did his work in committee and stuck to the business of his committees. While the merging of the two measures may exaggerate the narrowness of his policy interests somewhat, Sinclair's profile differs little from what we would have expected.

Sinclair's book is *The Transformation of the United States Senate.* She argues that during the 1960s and 1970s, changes in the environment of the Senate—"an expanded issue agenda, the explosive growth of interest groups and the increased role of the media in the policy process"— produced a quantum change inside the institution. Agenda setting and decision making became more open, more public, more media-dominated, more competitive than previously. Individual senators saw new opportunities and new incentives "to become broadly active across a variety of issues and in multiple arenas." [10] And that is what most of them did.

The result was a changed senatorial style, one Sinclair calls "unrestrained activism." She writes:

> The typical senator offers large numbers of floor amendments and is little concerned with whether the bill at issue originated in a committee on which he serves. He participates in a broad range of issues. During the 1970's, freshmen increasingly adopted the style of unrestrained activism as soon as they entered the chamber. The new style is not conditional upon a senator's status. A large proportion of the membership—regardless of seniority, ideology, party or region—has adopted the new style.[11]

One of those who did *not* adopt the new style, however, was Mark Andrews.

Sinclair's comparisons help us to point up the salient features of Andrews's governing style. But it should be emphasized that her study does not argue that his style is an unproductive one. One of her major conclusions is that where unrestrained activism prevails, "maximum accommodation of the individual member has become the overriding expectation." Each senator is given a large piece of the action and plenty of running room. Furthermore, the emergence of the Senate floor as an arena for important decision making still leaves the great bulk of the decisions to be made inside the committees. "Most of the decisions made in committees stand," she writes. "Consequently, if a senator wants to influence policy in a given area on a sustained basis, the committee with jurisdiction over that area provides the best arena for doing so." And she gives special mention to the Senate Appropriations Committee as one that "gives its members and especially its subcommittee chairs the opportunity to make large numbers of spending decisions, most of which will not receive serious review in full committee or on the floor." [12] That, of course, was precisely the realm where Mark Andrews worked, was accommodated to by his colleagues, and accomplished much for his constituents.

It is, nonetheless, true that some elements of Andrews's governing style were distinctly atypical of the Senate in which he served. To some degree this difference may be traced to the constraining expectations of his North Dakota constituents. But we know from other studies that legislators who take strong initiatives can change constituents' expectations in districts the size of North Dakota.[13] A broader explanation for his atypical style, we have been arguing, lies in the length and the timing of his career in the House.

In the mid-1970s, the House of Representatives reformed itself and began the same transformation that the Senate had begun in the mid-1960s. Much has been written about "the new breed" of House member that changed the decision-making processes of the House and brought a new, issue-oriented, publicity-wise, floor activist style to that chamber. If it was, as Sinclair says, the Senate class of 1966 that broke the mold there, it was the class of 1974 that broke the mold in the House. Burdett Loomis's fine study of that reformist class of 1974 is aptly entitled *The New American Politician*.[14] Mark Andrews, however, did not fit the new image. He came to the House eleven years too soon to be much affected by its changing styles. But he came to the Senate fourteen years too late to be much affected by the changing styles there. The sequencing of his career caused him to miss the impact of both transformations.

Andrews developed his insider governing style in the pre-1974 House, and he brought an old breed, old politician style with him to the Senate. Our description of him as a House member in the Senate could be amended to read, "a House Member of the 1960s in the Senate of the 1980s." That amended view pictures a political career that had gotten doubly out of sync—generationally in the House of the late 1970s and institutionally in the Senate of the early 1980s. The timing of his career move from House to Senate was such that at no point did he have an incentive to change his governing style. If he had come to the House later or to the Senate earlier, he might have altered his style and thus have been a different kind of senator.

The question which remains, of course, is this: Would it have made any difference if Mark Andrews had been a different kind of senator? If he had seized upon a national issue and publicized his leadership on that issue, would it have helped him in the final reckoning? Might not some record of issue activism have brought him an extra increment of support when he most needed it? Such speculation will be postponed. It is a question that will not go away, in large part because Andrews raised it for himself. He was well aware of the alternatives posed by the prevailing senatorial style, and he worried about them.

STYLISTIC WORRIES: THE NATIONAL ALTERNATIVE

The Senate of the 1980s was, as Sinclair tells us, one in which members increasingly won inside reputations and outside recognition by laying claim to national issues, developing expertise in their content, and leading legislative battles for their resolution. The more this "unrestrained activism" took hold as a dominant governing style among senators, the more did national problems command Senate attention and the more did purely regional matters get relegated to secondary status. A region-oriented or state-oriented issue activism became almost a contradiction in terms. A senator whose overriding legislative goal was to help constituents get their share of what the government had to give would have a difficult time accommodating to the stylistic alternatives.

Mark Andrews recognized this difficulty, and he tried to cope with it; but he never overcame it. It will be recalled that he showed a good deal of sensitivity to the *Wall Street Journal*'s assessment of his freshman year accomplishments as "parochial." It was his first nationally delivered scorecard. While he expressed some satisfaction that "parochial may be a damning term in the *Wall Street Journal* but it's a favorable word in North Dakota," he also added, "besides, I happen to think those programs are good for the nation, too; but they never let us talk about that side of things." Clearly the term "parochial" rankled.

Throughout that same December 1981 interview he kept coming back to the notion that he was not merely parochial. Speaking about his recent effort in conference committee to keep $300 million in the appropriations bill for the Coast Guard, he said:

> Dave Stockman fought us every inch of the way on it, but I got it in the [Senate Appropriations] Committee and last night [Rep. Joseph] Addabbo [D-N.Y.] agreed to put it in the final bill. There's nothing parochial about that. Those Coast Guard cutters aren't built in North Dakota, aren't stationed in North Dakota, and don't patrol in North Dakota waters. That's in the national interest as I see it. What kind of a senator would you say that was?

And as I left, he fired his parting shot. "That's what you've been hired for—to look out for the interests of your state and, you hope, for the nation as a whole. To coin a phrase, 'What's good for North Dakota is good for the nation.'" It sounded like some self-administered reassurance.

The following year, Andrews began publicly to emphasize his support for the U.S. Coast Guard as evidence of his national, nonparochial outlook. In subcommittee hearings, he would say:

- "We do not have a whale of a lot of navigable waters in North Dakota—that is probably why I can be about as objective as anybody in the Senate on Coast Guard operations."
- "Might I say there is nothing parochial or pork barrel in this because, unfortunately, we have no sea coast in North Dakota."

On the Senate floor, he would argue similarly.

- "This is not a matter of parochial interest to me.... Coming from North Dakota, which has all kinds of advantages, we even have to admit we do not have much Coast Guard, so this is not a personal thing for the people of North Dakota. But it is a very important thing to the people of this nation."
- "It is not a parochial issue with me. There is no Coast Guard search and rescue station in the whole state of North Dakota." [15]

He was at pains to identify a national dimension in his thinking.

While he used his support for the Coast Guard to demonstrate his national perspective, he was also using his solicitude for the agency to accumulate bargaining chips. When he found he could use his pursestring controls over the Coast Guard to trade constituency benefits with other subcommittee chairmen, he did so. To my question as to how he came to be so supportive of the Coast Guard, he combined both a public and a private rationale:

> Just the facts and the arguments and the responsibility you accept when you become a subcommittee chairman. No one can accuse me of bias there, because I don't have Coast Guard installations in the state. But it sure helps when you want a small business loan for the Fort Totten Indian reservation and the chairman of the subcommittee [Lowell Weicker of Connecticut] handling those loans just happens to come from a seacoast state and just happens to be interested in the Coast Guard and just happens to have the Coast Guard Academy in his state and wants funding for the Coast Guard band. And it sure helps to get the attention of people like Lawton Chiles, Fritz Hollings, and Bennett Johnston [from the coastal states of Florida, South Carolina, and Louisiana].

However persistent his protestations of objectivity and national concern, they neither subsumed nor stopped his never-ending effort to find and to wield inside legislative leverage for the benefit of North Dakota.

Interestingly, there did exist a tiny Coast Guard signal beam station in LaMoure, North Dakota, hometown of former senator Milton Young.

In 1980, Andrews drove out of his way to show me what he called that "monument to the power of a senior United States senator." And he had laughed at the ridiculous sign, "Senator Milton Young Way," on the little dirt road leading up to the one-room building in the middle of a wheat field. But, ironically, he lived to defend that installation. As subcommittee chairman, he defended it vigorously when a Coast Guard official had the temerity—and the bad judgment—to suggest that North Dakota lacked "the political clout" to keep the station, and its $250,000 payroll, open.[16] The "parochial" tag might rankle, but the protection of a federal investment in North Dakota—no matter how bizarre or how small—came first.

When we met at his farm in October 1982, the first thing Andrews did was show me a *New York Times* story crediting him with saving the Rural Electrification Administration (REA).[17] It was the second national judgment on his performance. But he still remembered the earlier judgment in the *Wall Street Journal*. "The newspapers don't think much of us freshmen, you know. But look at this." Later, in the car, he came back to the subject. "What did you think of that *New York Times* article?—only a freshman." Still later, when his top staff aide joined us from Washington, Andrews gave him the article.

> SENATOR ANDREWS: I thought you'd like this.
> AIDE: Did they call you 'parochial'?
> SENATOR ANDREWS: You couldn't have written it better yourself. It's from an unbiased source, the *New York Times*. I thought you'd know how to use this with your friends. I'm the only freshman they mention. Do you think you can use it? It's the *New York Times*.

Several times during my two-day visit, Andrews and his aides referred with evident pleasure to the article in a nationally read newspaper, and they speculated on how they might use it as a counterweight to the notion that he was parochial.

It was not just the *Wall Street Journal* scorecard that had kept Andrews's sensitivity alive. In March 1982, his administrative assistant, Bill Wright, told me:

> We're working off some polls we took that showed our people want a little more of a national leadership image. We're doing a very good job of representing the people, but they expect a little more leadership, on national issues, from their senators. So that's on his mind now.

In their March 1982 poll, 71 percent of the North Dakotans surveyed had ranked Andrews's performance as "excellent" (30 percent) or "good" (41 percent) "on keeping in touch with the voters back home." [18]

But only 55 percent had ranked him "excellent" (12 percent) or "good" (43 percent) for his "leadership on important national issues." The contrast had made an impression on senator and staff. They did not believe that the voters were suggesting any diminution of his North Dakota-centered efforts; they took the results as a call for augmentation—for a legislative orientation that we might characterize as "pork barrel plus."

The response of the Andrews enterprise was to organize a May 1982 hearing on energy policy before one of Andrews's Agriculture Committee subcommittees. Said Wright in March:

> North Dakota is a big energy exporting state. We don't mind contributing energy to the rest of the country. But we're sick and tired of the other states not doing anything. The nuclear industry is just about shut down. . . . Nobody is worrying about energy sufficiency . . . what our energy policy should be, not what it is. . . . The [REA] co-ops will orchestrate the hearings.

And in May he said: "Our aim is to show that we have no national energy policy, that the industry is overregulated, and that we are headed for a brownout situation if we ever have another crisis." The issue had a strong North Dakota slant; and it had been a major topic of discussion in Andrews's campaign two years earlier. The two days of hearings, May 25 and 26, were advertised in the *Washington Post* as a "review of the energy needs of rural communities." [19] They went entirely unreported in that paper; without Washington coverage, Andrews could not hope for national recognition.

In July, I rode the Senate trolley with his transportation subcommittee staff chief. He was carrying the current *Newsweek*, with a cover story called "The Decaying of America." It was the story of the collapsing national infrastructure, much of which—roads, bridges, rails—fell within the subcommittee's jurisdiction. "That's good press," he exclaimed. "When a national magazine has a cover story supporting your bill, you couldn't do better than that." He opened the magazine and pointed to a paragraph on Andrews. The paragraph he pointed to, however, was *not* about the scope of the national effort that was required, but rather about the discouraging fact that "the pork barrel is alive and well in Congress." In a critical segment headed "How Congress Slices the Pork," subcommittee chairman Andrews was cited for his $15 million bridge.[20]

I suggested that the issue of the nation's infrastructure was a natural for Andrews and for his subcommittee, that it was a no-lose issue, that it would counter the pork barrel image, and that he should seize it and make it "his" issue in the Senate and in the country. The staffer nodded agreement but said only, "It's hard to push it when you don't have the money to do anything about it." They did nothing about it. Even when he was put right next to a "good" national issue, an issue waiting for leadership, Andrews had managed to get himself on the "bad" pork barrel side of it. And there was nothing in his stylistic repertoire to predispose him to enlarge the scope of his activity. Mark Andrews did not think that way. He did not "see himself as a national senator." He "did not think you could score any points in North Dakota for being a national senator."

Nor did he surround himself with staffers who would encourage him to pursue leadership on the national issue. With respect to policy, Andrews was slow to understand the staff's potential for helping him do his job. He brought his agriculture specialist with him from the House, to take care of the most sensitive issue area. But when he hired his first legislative director—and he did not do this until early 1982—he reached into Sen. Robert Byrd's staff to hire a person whose only claim to fame was managing the successful effort to keep Amtrak's Cardinal running through West Virginia.[21] Faced with the opportunity to fill the staff position calling for the broadest legislative perspective, his instinctive choice was an accomplished pork barreler.

When we talked about his staff in the summer of 1982, Andrews was becoming aware that his instincts and his choices had not served him well in his new office. "We'll have a couple of months more of shaking down, and by the beginning of next year the transformation should be complete," he said.

> I thought I ought to learn to be a senator first. It's a different discipline. I didn't think it would be. I thought I could continue to do just what I did in the House, but I can't. When I stood up to debate in the House, I was debating my colleagues. I think I did pretty well, too. But when I stand up in the Senate, I'm debating a senator who has one staff person on one side and one on the other. They probably both have Ph.D.'s and law degrees. I may be the smartest man in the Senate, but I can't compete against all of them.
>
> I'm still looking for a person who's an expert in city problems. Coming from a rural state, I don't get much call for that. But if you're going to be a senator, you have to take a national perspective. So I want to get someone who knows where the bodies are buried in the urban area.

He admitted to a fair amount of internal turmoil.

> It hasn't been easy. There's been quite a hoorah and a lot of groaning among the staff. We've gotten rid of several people

who were not very competent. Old "Fire and Brimstone" went
to work. I think we've got a fine Senate staff now.

But not a settled one, it appears. By the beginning of 1983, his first
legislative director had been fired. It would be another year before a
replacement was found. And, true to form, the replacement was a
constituency-contact specialist from within his Senate office.

He was, indeed, learning to be a senator, but hesitantly and very
sporadically in the national legislative area. He worried about it. But
when action was called for, neither the senator nor his staff possessed a
natural appetite or a sustained interest in a nationally oriented issue
activism. So he continued to operate somewhat against the grain and
against the thrust of the institution of which he was a member. Thus he
passed up at least the possibility that he might score points in North
Dakota by behaving differently.

STYLISTIC WORRIES: THE DORGAN ALTERNATIVE

An even more immediate cause of Andrews's stylistic worries was the
political context at home. Throughout his Senate term, there was a
young and successful North Dakota politician who was the embodiment
of the newer governing style—living proof that longstanding constituency expectations could be changed by an entrepreneurial newcomer.
He was a Democrat; and he had taken over Andrews's seat in the House
of Representatives. With his statewide constituency and his national
political office, he posed a standing threat to Andrews's Senate career.
With his highly visible new politician's activism, he displayed an
attractive alternative approach to a career in North Dakota politics.

We will not elaborate on the political activity of Rep. Byron Dorgan.
Our intent is to see Byron Dorgan through the eyes of Mark Andrews—
the better to understand the political life of the senator. For, given the
politics of the situation, any political analyst could predict that the two
men would be natural competitors.

From Andrews's perspective, two events of the past gave added
weight to this prediction. First, Dorgan had tried to take away Andrews's
House seat in 1974, and Andrews had defeated him by 27,000 votes—a
solid 56 percent victory (see Figure A-2 on page 35) in that best of
Democratic years. Someone who had challenged him once and lost might
very well be spoiling to try again. Second, in the later years of his own
service as the state's only congressman, Andrews had coveted—more or
less actively—the Senate seat of Milton Young.[22] Andrews's assessment
of Dorgan's ambitions could easily have been sharpened by remem-

brances of his own senatorial ambitions when he had been in Dorgan's shoes.

From the beginning of his term, Andrews viewed Dorgan as his natural rival and his likely opponent in 1986. Three weeks after he was sworn in, he mailed to some of his supporters a copy of Dorgan's 1980 fund-raising results, as reported to the clerk of the House. He noted that Dorgan had spent "far more than we ever raised for a House race" and that Dorgan had raised more money from individuals than had the Andrews for Senate Committee. "Every year," said Dick Morris, the man who did Andrews's 1982 and 1983 polling, "we tracked Dorgan. He was certain that Dorgan would be his opponent." The results of these polls made it very clear that Dorgan, gaining steadily in local esteem, would be a formidable challenger.

During our Washington conversations, I never asked Andrews about the congressman, but he frequently broached the subject without prompting. In March 1981, talking about his committee choices and his increased power, he said: "If the opposition is so interested in keeping my power [in the House], why didn't Byron Dorgan try to get on the Appropriations Committee? He could have. But . . . nobody even asked Dorgan that question." Again, in an October interview about his life in the Senate, he repeated the criticism. "Byron Dorgan, whose side was making all that [campaign] noise, didn't even try to get on the Appropriations Committee. And there were five vacancies." In March 1982, a senior staffer commented: "We've drafted a [Republican] candidate to run against Dorgan. . . . He'll give Dorgan some trouble and take some of the glitter out of him. We'll spot weld his halo so he won't be a threat to Mark Andrews." The "threat" did not subside. In 1982 Dorgan won reelection with 72 percent of the vote; and he won a seat on the most broadly powerful and most coveted of all House committees—its committee on taxation, Ways and Means.

As Andrews voiced his worries about Dorgan's political strength, he began to point up the stylistic contrast between them. As Andrews saw it, Dorgan's biggest asset was his ability to get publicity. As described by North Dakota's only Washington reporter, the congressman's outreach operation was formidable.

> He has one of the most sophisticated communications operations in the House. He puts out a three-color newsletter with punchy writing that other lawmakers are copying and calling the "People" magazine of the Hill.
> He's built up mailing lists of North Dakotans by occupation, and he churns out up to 2,000 personalized letters a day asking opinions and offering information about activities in Congress that pertain to their occupations and interests.

In his first two terms, he held some 150 community forums across North Dakota, and he frequently stops in various cities on weekends for televised press conferences.[23]

An editor of one of the state's smaller dailies wrote that "Rep. Dorgan's organization is by far the best of the three in leading the media by its collective nose. Andrews and Burdick do the same thing, however, but not as well." [24] Andrews believed that this was the area of his own greatest weakness.

He first expressed these views in the course of an end-of-the-first-year assessment of his staff, in December 1981.

> I'm still working to fill in spots on my staff. I've been a little slow to build up the staff because I wanted to learn things myself first and then fill in where I need help. Transportation is well covered. The staff is doing a good job for me there. My Budget Committee is going well and my Agriculture person is good. The constituency operation—I brought it over from the House—is going pretty well. Our PR is weak—compared to what Dorgan gets. But that has been my lowest priority.
>
> My Republican friends are worried that Dorgan gets so much publicity, and they want me to get more. But I think you can oversell yourself if you aren't careful. I believe you can flood the market. People will get tired of it. We've only sent two newsletters out this year; that's partly because I've been too busy. I was talking to Jim Abdnor [R-S.D.], and he hasn't sent any out. Dorgan contradicts himself all over the place. First, he's on one side of the issue, then on the other. But he certainly is getting blazing headlines. If that's the way you have to play the game, we'll do it. We've got time. PR is our main weakness. But it's still my lowest priority.

These ruminations betray a little apprehension but no serious soul searching about upgrading his own efforts to publicize his activity. Indeed, they reflect a good deal of skepticism about the long-term benefits of a souped-up publicity-gathering effort.

It is not surprising that Andrews's first explicit evaluation of Dorgan's strength should have come during his thoughts on staff and that they should have focused on publicity. For legislators who adopt the style of "new politicians" or "unrestrained activism," two essential resources are staff and publicity. They cannot live without a staff to broaden their impact on policy or without a public relations capacity to make their performance visible to the outside world. In both respects, Dorgan's staff was reputed to be a good one.[25]

Andrews had no press secretary among his initial appointees. His press relations were handled by one of his former campaign managers, a man who had run for office several times in North Dakota. He was called the executive secretary. After a year and a half, he was replaced by a professional reporter from North Dakota's public television station, who was given the title of press secretary. The replacement was still new to the job when I traveled with him and the senator back home in October 1982. In their conversations, one could detect the senator's continuing concern about the narrowness of his own image and his competition with Dorgan.

Andrews asked the newly appointed press aide, for example, to prepare a new standard biographical brochure to hand out to interested parties at home or in Washington. The old one, said Andrews, "is too slanted toward agriculture. It doesn't play up that I'm a member of the Budget Committee." He seemed to be seeking a broader reputation. They talked, too, about the aide's recent enrollment in a computer course; they were hoping to make the office's publicity operations more efficient. "You'll be able to run rings around Dorgan," exclaimed Andrews. "He gets one newsletter out every month and lots of press releases. His press secretary worked for the *Forum* [Fargo] and was the person who screened press releases. So he knows how to do it." In these conversations, I detected a more active concern for the broadening and promotion of his public image than I had observed ten months earlier. A year and a half later, this press secretary would be let go because "he couldn't keep pace with the publicity machine of Rep. Dorgan." [26] And the senator would try two more press secretaries before the end of his term.

Mark Andrews had a great deal of turnover on his personal (noncommittee) staff in Washington. It began early and it continued throughout his term. From 1981 through 1985 the staff averaged a 49.4 percent turnover from one year to the next. To be sure, Senate staffs normally display a good deal of turnover. Still, Andrews's figures seem abnormally large. The eight other senators whom I was studying during that period averaged only a 30.5 percent turnover of their personal Washington staffs. In any case, after a couple of years, political observers in North Dakota began to pick up on the problem. "This revolving door syndrome," wrote one columnist, "has become a subject of some gossip and speculation in North Dakota." And another reporter described Andrews as "trying to stabilize his staff which has experienced a flood of unhappy resignations in recent years." Their explanations emphasized personal factors, that Andrews had an "abrasive style" and was "something of a bear to work for." [27] Although there may well have been some personal difficulties, our overall explanation of the phenomenon is quite different.

As a House member Andrews had experienced, according to local account, very little staff turnover. The abnormally high Senate staff turnover rate, we would argue, reflects the new ambiguities of his Senate career and his difficulty in determining what kind of a senator he wanted to be and what style he wanted to settle on. Basically, as we have said, he behaved very much like a House member in the Senate. Every member of his 1980 House staff save one came over to the Senate with him in 1981. But he recognized that he needed a different staff makeup; by his second year half of his House staffers were gone.

Andrews could not decide how much different his Senate staff should be. So he kept shuffling both his legislative and his public relations people, until the end of his term, as it turned out. His uncertainties about staff produced his staff turnover. And his uncertainties about staff grew out of the ambivalence generated by his long career in the House and his late arrival in the Senate. Staff turnover, we suggest, was yet another derivative of the anomalous, unsynchronized, ambivalent career of a House member in the Senate.

My October 1982 trip (see Chapter 1) provided the only opportunity I ever had to watch Mark Andrews and Byron Dorgan (as well as Quentin Burdick) together on the same platform, and to compare their presentations of self to voters. The occasion was the North Dakota Nurses Association Convention; the format was a question-and-answer session with the state's two senators, its congressman, and two of its state legislators. Joint appearances by the state's entire three-person national delegation are (we noted earlier) commonplace in this small state. Dorgan stressed their accessibility to the community. "It's not true that in all states you can get to see your United States Senator. In North Dakota you can get to see your United States Senator anytime. It's a tradition in North Dakota." The moderator was able to say, "All three of these gentlemen were tremendously helpful to us last year. They worked on a bipartisan basis." On the concerns of the evening—nurses' training and education, home health care, catastrophic health insurance, equal pay for equal work, FTC regulation—there was no disagreement. "We can't find any hard areas of controversy among the delegation," said Dorgan. And the nurses continued to support all three in their next elections.

The three men did not differ on the issues; but in their approach to governing, as they articulated it, they differed. Quentin Burdick answered each question in a halting manner, bluntly and briefly. "I believe in this idea or this program and I will support it"—no elaboration, no frills. If you want to help, he said, organize and send money. It was a meat-and-potatoes message. Dorgan's answers were the same substantively but packaged thematically and delivered smoothly. They were broad-ranging philosophical and sociological musings about "the condition of American society" and "the changing structure of the medical profession." They were seeded with lots of relevant facts and punctuated by expressions of agreement with his senatorial colleagues. Andrews's comments differed markedly from those of the other two. They were blunt like Burdick's but long like Dorgan's, and his mode of delivery fell somewhere between theirs. Altogether, his remarks spoke volumes, I thought, about his governing style.

If you want to help, said Andrews, in answer to the first question, send us information. "People in Washington are looking for answers. We are not the experts. You are. We need information." From that point on, he answered every question in terms of the legislative process and with reference to something he had accomplished by working that process. "I serve on the Budget Committee. It was my amendment in the Budget Committee [in 1981] that added $500 million for health programs, including nurses' training.... It was my first Senate fight.... We won based on facts. So keep the information coming so we can continue to win these battles." He discussed his losing vote in the Appropriations Committee to increase educational funding in 1982. On each issue, he gave the details of the legislation he had cosponsored and with which senator. At one point, Burdick recognized an amendment he, too, had cosponsored—a Warren Rudman (R-N.H.) amendment on FTC regulation of the medical profession. "I'm a cosponsor of that one, too," he broke in. "We'll call it the Rudman-Burdick-Andrews amendment," Andrews countered. "He's my senior colleague." Everyone chuckled; but even this humorous gesture was a senator's inside joke.

Andrews's answers were not abstract, nor were they filled with statistics. They consisted of "this is what I've done in the Senate in this area," punctuated by other relevant personal testimonials—an experience with home health care in the case of his wife's illness, an appreciation of equal rights for women from the three generations of professional women in his family. What the nurses saw was what they got: a low-key, down-to-earth legislator whose keenest interest lay in working the legislative process for their benefit. That evening, Mark Andrews was the only one to present himself to his listeners as a *legislator*—as someone who knew how to legislate and who spent his Washington days immersed in legislating.

It was not Andrews, however, but Dorgan who received the only sustained, heartfelt applause from the group. Asked a question, near the close of the session, about the state of the economy, he delivered a ringing reply along the lines: "These are tough times, the [Reagan] administration is pursuing the wrong policies, but this is a great country." The sentiments of the youngish group of women were clearly with him, and with the broad sweep of his analysis. Doubtless, Andrews sensed this. Riding away in the car, he said: "What a tame bunch we were. I wanted to pop Dorgan after what he said about Reagan ruining the economy. We had 21 percent interest rates when he took over. But I decided that was not the place to do it." He knew that nurses were supportive of him—after all, he delivered the goods. He also knew they were not his crowd. In a partisan confrontation, he could not count on them. So he kept quiet.

Throughout the October trip, his attitude toward Dorgan was a combination of worry and puzzlement. He understood that his rival was popular and strong; but he still viewed Dorgan as something of a curiosity and only partly as a serious threat. When I asked him where Dorgan's strength was greatest, he answered "everywhere.... Everybody likes him. They think he has the best constituency operation in the delegation. We always thought ours was the best. I still think it is."

A similar note of doubt crept into his final and more basic assessment of the congressman. After his lengthy description of North Dakota as "a liberal state" (Chapter 1), the senator added,

> These attitudes make it very easy for someone like Byron Dorgan to come along and mouth all these nice-sounding liberal ideas. Pretty soon, though, he'll have to produce something. So I think he's a passing phase. But maybe not. Times are changing.

It was Mark Andrews's fundamental conviction that the name of the governing game was the ability to accomplish something—that actions taken, decisions influenced, deals consummated paid off in constituent service and constituent approval. He believed that producing something counted more than talking about it; and he believed that he was a producer, while Dorgan was a talker. He believed, deep down, that in any final reckoning, North Dakotans would honor the difference.

Those were the beliefs that had validated his legislative career. But his comment also reflects the nagging sense that he might be caught on the cusp of change, and that just possibly his past practices and his established governing style might not be enough to guarantee the continuance of that career. The question was whether his North Dakota constituents—notwithstanding their longtime attachment to deliveries of federal bacon—were not also becoming increasingly attracted to the issue-oriented, publicity-oriented governing style that was being introduced by Byron Dorgan. It was a question he might well have to face if he confronted the congressman at the polls.

PUBLICITY AND STYLE

Whether or not the voters of North Dakota would, as Andrews believed, honor him for getting things done in the legislature depended in large part on what they knew about his legislative activity. In turn, their information depended on what was reported to them by Andrews himself or by the media. We do not have access to any files or summaries or indices to describe for us the full array of information available in North Dakota. We have pieced together, however, material from a variety of sources—interviews, newspaper files, national indices, and casual reading—to provide some tentative notions about the kinds of information that North Dakota voters had available to them.[28] The question whether the voters picked up or interpreted or used any of the available information will be postponed. But it seems very likely that a governing style that emphasizes inside play and neglects public relations is not the easiest one to present to the voters.

Throughout his term—at least until his reelection campaign began in earnest—local newspaper stories contained occasional glimpses of Andrews's governing style. Many of his own published comments reveal his aptitude for Capitol Hill politics, his preference for bargaining, trading, and accommodating. When asked to explain an unpopular vote, he explained, "You don't not go along with the subcommittee chairman when he is being accommodating to you." When asked to prescribe a course of action on farm problems, he explained, "We need to do business with our rice growing friends and our peanut growing friends and a host of other farmers." When a reporter questioned a checkered series of votes, he explained, "You have to realize that a lot of this is an exercise. When you come from a small state, legislation is the science of maneuver and accommodation." [29]

His reasons for voting for Sen. Ted Stevens for Senate Republican leader, reporters noted, were that "they have been friends in the Senate and Stevens has backed Andrews on a number of issues, including Garrison Diversion." When Senator Dole won that election, Andrews responded: "He supports farm programs and Garrison Diversion. . . . I don't have to explain to him about target prices, loan rates and such. He knows them as well as I do. . . . A good clean hard scrap is what it's all about, and this was one of the cleanest scraps I've known." Similarly, after a bitter fight with the president, he wanted to get back to business. "I guess the honeymoon's over. But in this business, you work item-by-item." [30]

The local papers bore occasional testimony, also, to his willingness to use his resources to cut deals favorable to his constituents. When he became chairman of the Select Committee on Indian Affairs in 1982, he called his promotion, characteristically, "another leg up for North Dakota," and he focused on the inside leverage he had gained. "I think we'll be able to do some things with the Wahpeton Indian School now that we wouldn't have been able to do otherwise. It'll be no cinch, but I've learned that you have a lot better crack at things when you're in a position like this." [31]

One year later, he was able to announce in a front page *Forum* story, that the secretary of the interior had reversed his prior decision and would not close the Wahpeton Indian School. Five hours of committee hearings, plus a site visit by the assistant secretary, plus a "one on one conference" with the secretary caused him "to realize that the bureaucrats and the BIA hadn't given the right information on which a decision was based," said Andrews.[32]

When Senator Thurmond (R-S.C.) pushed a $27.5 million amendment for an Air Force hospital in Minot, North Dakota, through his Armed Services Committee, credit was given locally to Andrews. "Although there was no 'tradeoff' as such," said the newspaper report,

> Andrews' office noted that Thurmond is a strong supporter of rural electric cooperatives and Andrews is recognized as the leading spokesman for the Rural Electrification Administration in Congress. Thurmond has invited Andrews to come to South Carolina and speak before the co-ops there.... The REA question has led to a close sharing of views between the two senators, and this in turn influenced Thurmond's decision to help Andrews get the Minot hospital ... according to Andrews' aide.[33]

Three months later, at a picnic in Minot, the mayor introduced Andrews with the story of the hospital. "Mark started without a bill. It wasn't even in the Defense Department Budget. But he is getting it done.... [Ten projects had to be dropped to make room for Minot] but Mark got that done." The local papers credited him with "the instrumental role in getting the hospital authorized." [34]

Doubtless Andrews imbibed these stylistic precepts and patterns as a member of the House. And doubtless—though we have not researched his House tenure in this regard—that is why the state's largest paper in its 1980 endorsement praised his "knack for handling legislative matters on Capitol Hill.... Rep. Andrews has been able to work easily with the Democratic House members in an effort to get North Dakota programs approved in his branch of the Congress." [35] Doubtless, too, the newspapers had revealed the same elements of his governing style during his tenure in the House.

As the foregoing quotations—widely separated by time—illustrate, however, an insider style is hard to convey in any thematic, continuous, or widely available way. Episodic snapshots of face-to-face legislative prowess are hard to grasp and retain as durable guides to voting. A researcher who searches for them will find some. A voter who wants the information to form an impression will not.

As for the more concentrated bursts of publicity he received as a senator, we shall divide them into two periods—an earlier one when local publicity was favorable and a later one when local publicity was unfavorable. Together, they reveal midcycle trends, from 1982 through 1984, that were not helpful to his constituency career.

FAVORABLE PUBLICITY: 1982-1984

VISIBILITY AND INDEPENDENCE

The smaller size of the Senate together with the increased importance of his position within the institution could be expected to produce an automatic increment of publicity for the freshman senator from North Dakota. And it did. In Andrews's own words, in 1983, visibility "goes with the territory . . . given the events that have come before Congress. . . . Unless you are hiding your head in a sack, you are bound to be visible." [36] Even an incremental increase in visibility achieved through his senatorial status would constitute a big change from his national obscurity during his years in the House.

Andrews got his first taste of national publicity in December 1981. The occasion was President Reagan's hairbreadth victory in his effort to sell sophisticated AWACS surveillance planes to Saudi Arabia. Andrews's vote became pivotal when he switched from opposition to support late in the game—thereby attracting national media attention. A camera crew from NBC followed him around the day of the vote; he appeared on the McNeil-Lehrer news show that evening; and the next morning he was interviewed live on CNN. It was obviously a new experience for this veteran legislator.

His reaction to the McNeil-Lehrer appearance was revealing. "I didn't prepare anything. I walked in and saw John Glenn with his notes all in front of him, and I said to myself, . . . 'What are you doing here playing with the big boys?' " The reaction he got at home again revealed the newness of the experience:

> I went home to a football game, and all the people who came up said they liked my vote. At the dinner, it was the same. Their main reaction was, "We saw you on the McNeil-Lehrer

Report. We saw you on a national news broadcast. It's the first time we've ever seen a North Dakota senator on national television."

Nobody noticed, apparently, that on the program, Andrews had been introduced as a senator who had been a *four-term* representative![37] One year into his Senate term, it seems, he remained an unknown. "The national media treated me fine," he said afterward. "They didn't know me from Adam's off ox, even though I've been down here for eighteen years. A congressman from North Dakota isn't very newsworthy from a national point of view." It was a natural consequence of his eighteen-year preference for an inside, committee-based, low-profile governing style. He had come to the Senate with a national publicity quotient of zero.

Over the next couple of years, Andrews reaped occasional national press attention. According to the National Newspaper Index compilation of articles in five major newspapers, Andrews made those papers twice in 1982 and ten times in 1983.[38] In nine of the twelve stories, he was critical of the administration, while the rest were progress reports on matters before his transportation subcommittee. In Stephen Hess's ranking of all senators in 1983 in terms of national media attention— newspapers and television—Andrews ranked sixtieth among his colleagues.[39] Although that ranking placed him thirty-six senators ahead of Quentin Burdick, it did not qualify him as a national media attraction.

Stories of his independence, however, did appear in the press. More than any others, these filtered back to his home state. In *National Journal's* analysis of ten key Senate votes in 1983, Andrews voted more often (six times) against the views of the administration than any other Republican senator. This marked a major change from his voting record in 1981 and 1982.[40] And the change in voting record was accompanied by a greater willingness to criticize his own administration publicly. In hearings before the Agriculture Committee's Subcommittee on Rural Development in 1982, for example, his criticism of the Agriculture Department's programs took the mild form "Rural America is suffering from bipartisan neglect." A year later, however, he blasted the department's report on rural development as "fluffery": "It's a travesty. What makes it worse is that this was done by my party. . . . We don't want the troglodytes to say the job is done. And that's what they're doing." [41] His picture accompanied both these stories in the *Washington Post*.

Similarly, Andrews's dissatisfaction with administration decisions, which we described earlier as simmering inside his budgetary committees in 1981-1982, broke into the national press in 1983. Not surprisingly, the first occurrence was an attack on his favorite target, OMB Director David Stockman, who came before the Appropriations Committee proposing cuts in nutrition programs. Andrews exploded, "Of all the dumb ways of saving money, not feeding kids is the dumbest." The unplanned outburst landed him twice in the *Washington Post* and on the Associated Press (AP) wire.[42] "That's what you get for speaking your mind," he reflected a few days later.

> I got so pissed off at Dave Stockman at the hearing. What happened was that I took the time to go down on Friday to visit one of these volunteer church groups that is feeding the hungry in the city.... They go down to the market and go through the dumpsters to find food that has been thrown away. They find they can use about one-third of the green peppers and one-third of the tomatoes. Then they get some chicken backs and try to put together a meal. But they have no wheat in that meal, no pasta products, and no milk products. We have huge surpluses of all these products. Then Stockman comes before the committee and says we have to cut all our food and nutrition programs.... I got mad. And that's how I got all this press attention.

In the *Post* he was quoted as saying to Stockman, "After two years, it's inexcusable we sit here and say there's no need—the needs are there. [Your view is] a bunch of garbage and you know it." [43]

Two weeks after the Stockman contretemps, the *Washington Post* Senate reporter, Helen Dewar, enlarged her original story on the hearing into an article about the "restive" Republican freshman. Again, it featured criticism by Andrews and was accompanied by his picture. President Reagan, he was quoted as saying, "started off in the right direction [but] refuse[d] to make the mid-course corrections that needed to be made" and now had "his feet frozen in concrete; his head in the sand, whichever way you want to look at it." He argued that it was cheaper to feed pregnant women than look after a disabled child. "If you don't want to do it on the basis of humanitarianism, if you're too flinty eyed and tough and uncaring to do it that way, then damn it you'd better do it on the basis of watching the dollar sign." [44]

Dewar concludes her article with Andrews's interpretation of the 1980 election. "As far as I could see," he said, "people in 1980 were saying 'restructure the government so the government can help us.' I'm afraid that's a far different signal than some of the people over at the White House got." The Washington press corps, which had been kept on the defensive for most of 1981-1982, was delighted to find critics of the president within Republican ranks. The North Dakotan obliged; and he became, for a brief time, an interesting figure in Washington.

The nutrition contretemps reverberated beyond the beltway and into North Dakota, courtesy of the Associated Press. Only one North

Dakota newspaper has a reporter in Washington, and he works for a syndicate. The state is, therefore, entirely dependent on the wire services. All ten of the state's daily newspapers subscribe to AP, and seven of these subscribe to no other wire service.[45] If, therefore, a story is to get widespread play in North Dakota, it has to be picked up and carried by AP. The stories with the biggest impact are what we might label AP stories.

As far as I can tell, looking through his office's newspaper files, the first general appraisal of Mark Andrews's Washington performance to gain wide currency in North Dakota came via reporter Tom Raum's AP story triggered by the nutrition episode. It was carried in the two largest papers—the *Forum* (Fargo) and the *Grand Forks Herald*—and some of the others. It was printed in North Dakota on the same day Dewar's story on the "restive Republicans" was printed in Washington.

The gist of the AP appraisal appears in its opening paragraphs.

> He rarely makes speeches on the Senate floor, issues press releases or holds news conferences, but when Sen. Mark Andrews gets officials of the Reagan administration before him, he eats them up.
>
> Andrews has emerged as one of the severest critics of the President among congressional Republicans.
>
> "I wasn't elected to come down here and represent the White House" says Andrews ... an independent-minded Republican from North Dakota [who] has been making life miserable for top Reagan aides [with] his blunt criticism.[46]

The article features the food and nutrition controversy which is, after all, about agricultural surpluses as well as health. But it also records Andrews's criticism of the three-year tax cut program and excessive defense expenditures. The senator's independence is treated as a basic matter of governing style alongside—if not competing with—his low public profile.

Back home in Fargo, a month later, Andrews assured an AP reporter that he had suffered no "disfavor" or "estrangement" among his Senate colleagues because of his criticism.[47] The resulting article rehearsed the several anti-administration positions Andrews had taken and added a more recent one—his vote in the Budget Committee against the third year of the Reagan tax cut. "My reason for voting against the tax cut is very simple," explained Andrews. "In North Dakota, the toughest tax of all is high interest rates. . . . It's a nonpartisan position. We've got to get these deficits down. It's extremely important to North Dakota. The farmer gets a double whammy from high interest rates." In general, Andrews argued that he had been elected "to use the best judgment I can in voting for things that are important to North Dakota."

The next month, a lengthy profile on Andrews appeared in the *Minneapolis Star Tribune,* the closest thing to a North Dakota newspaper beyond its borders.[48] One theme was the same as the major AP story— that Andrews was "blazing away at a government run by a man his state voted for by a 2-1 margin." Once again, "all those unkind things" Andrews was saying about the administration were toted up, with new episodes being added to the expanding list. "Not long ago, the outspoken North Dakotan left a meeting filled with ranking White House staff members to observe . . . that Reagan's men were like onions, heads in the ground, feet waving in the air, going nowhere." And he was also quoted as saying, "It is not comfortable going eyeball to eyeball with the President telling him his [defense] figures are wrong. . . . Nobody likes the messenger when the messenger brings bad news. So I suppose I was somewhat controversial."

In this article, the reporter was able to incorporate the publicity Andrews had received earlier and to pursue a larger theme—the North Dakotan's growing national visibility. His opening paragraph pictures Andrews "striding over Capitol Hill making all those headlines, taking pot shots at the Reagan administration." Andrews, he writes, "casts a large silhouette in the Senate after nearly two decades of low visibility in the House." And he quoted a "former top aide" to Milton Young as saying, "This emergence so early is remarkable. In my opinion he has the potential to be a power in the Senate for years to come." That remained to be seen. But in the spring of 1983, Mark Andrews was doubtless getting something of a reputation at home for his independence in Washington. The *Star Tribune* reporter expressed the view that "Andrews' independence has hurt him little with his colleagues or with the voters, in a state known for its maverick politics." That judgment, too, would take a longer time to prove itself. But the existence of a favorable senatorial publicity increment—one that emphasized his home grown independence—seemed evident.

THE GARRISON PROJECT

If there was any single activity of Mark Andrews that would have been on the minds of North Dakota's citizens during his early years in the Senate, it would most likely have been his continuing battle to resuscitate the state's beleaguered $1.1 billion Garrison Diversion water project. It was a project with a long history and an equally long record of support by the politicians in this water-poor state. In Andrews's words, "Every North Dakota governor, every member of the U.S. House, of the

U.S. Senate, every North Dakota Legislature—all irrespective of party—
have supported Garrison Diversion since statehood." [49] Andrews spoke
for the politicians and for a large segment of North Dakotans when he
said of the project, in a widely reported statement:

> Garrison Diversion is not just a water project. It is our fu-
> ture. . . . Unless you understand what it means to be a North
> Dakotan, whether city dweller or farmer, to live and struggle to
> survive in an environment plagued by the vagaries of a climate
> that is submarginal for rainfall during most years, you cannot
> fully appreciate the value of the benefits offered by putting
> Missouri River water to work for the people of our state. [50]

For Senators Young and Burdick and Representative Andrews—with
their seats on the appropriations committees—funding Garrison had
been a career-long preoccupation.

The results of Andrews's own 1982 poll reveal that the voters of
North Dakota *did* know more about his fight for Garrison than any other
particular thing he was doing. [51] But the poll also reveals how few voters
knew it. When asked to name an accomplishment of his, 6.4 percent said
he "supports Garrison." Only his support "for farmers" (7.8 percent), for
"the farm bill" (2.5 percent), and "other non-negative mentions of
farmers" (2.9 percent, for a total of 13 percent pro-farm) drew more than
1 percent of the answers. Sixty-nine percent of North Dakota's voters
had no answer. Another 1982 poll showed, however, that when asked
directly, 90 percent of the voters did have an opinion on the Garrison
project—with 63 percent in favor and 27 percent opposed. [52] Such
publicity as he received would build on a small but relatively important
base of knowledge and a strong but not solid base of opinion.

The project involved pumping water stored behind the Garrison
Dam to irrigate 250,000 acres of the state's farmland and to provide
additional water for twenty-two of the state's municipalities. It had been
authorized in 1940, reauthorized in 1965, and funded regularly from
1965 to 1977. At that point the Audubon Society initiated a lawsuit that
stopped construction and funding until a federal judge finally lifted the
ban in 1982. At that time, the project was only 15 percent completed. In
North Dakota, the main battle lines involved environmentalists and
agricultural interests. In Congress a broader battle formed around
representatives from places especially sympathetic to constituency-
oriented "projects" and an administration-congressional alliance pro-
claiming the evils of "the pork barrel." [53]

In each of his first two years in the Senate, Andrews—with help
from Burdick—pushed pro-Garrison amendments through the Senate
and/or the conference committee. Without his skillful activism, none

would have passed. In 1981, his vehicle was a provision to nullify the court order and allow construction to proceed and to spend $4 million. The *Washington Post* reporter studying the Appropriations Committee gave Andrews the credit for this success. "Andrews pushed an amendment through the Senate" he wrote, "directing the Bureau of Reclamation to ignore a court order and spend $4 million on the project anyway." And he quoted Democratic Committee member William Proxmire: "That is sheer, unadulterated pork. But Andrews went around telling people, 'It's in my state and we need it.' "[54] The provision—which survived in the conference committee report—was rejected by the House.

In 1982, after the judge had lifted the court order, and after the $4 million appropriation had been rejected by the House, Andrews pushed the appropriation—the first since 1977—through the House-Senate conference committee. *Time* magazine described this exploit.

> The King of Pork, as North Dakota's Mark Andrews is known to his colleagues, persuaded a House-Senate conference committee to reinstate a water diversion project back home after it had been overwhelmingly defeated in the House. "Those guys knew damn well Andrews would stop their pet projects in the future" says Conte. They ran like scared rabbits.[55]

Garrison was apparently a case of Andrews, the home state legislator, at his best as an insider battler.

Time's "King of Pork" description quickly became an AP story and as such spread widely across North Dakota. Along with Andrews's reaction, it was carried in January 1983 under these headlines:

- "Andrews Not Upset by King of Pork 'Tag' " *(Forum)*
- "King of Pork Title Doesn't Bother Senator" *(Minot Daily News)*
- "Andrews Says Actions Aided North Dakota" *(Bismarck Tribune)*

The AP article began: "Sen. Mark Andrews (R, ND) says he's in Washington to bring home the bacon for North Dakota, so *Time* magazine's label for him as 'The King of Pork' doesn't disturb him."[56] The senator took the opportunity to claim credit for more than Garrison. "We had a whole deck of things in that bill," he said. His provision forgiving a $120 million debt owed by the St. Lawrence Seaway to the government, he pointed out, would save eight to twelve cents a bushel on grain moving through the seaway.

Explaining his Garrison Diversion victory, he first said: "Generally you get your projects by making your points. . . . I used reason and logic and the merits of the project." Then he added: "You bet we were hard nosed on the conference committee. I may well have given the inference that if they didn't see the reason and good logic of our projects, then I might have trouble understanding theirs." A House staff participant commented on Andrews's effectiveness in conference. "Andrews carries a lot of weight, especially considering he's a first term senator. Everybody depends on him for their state's transportation projects." [57] Once again, we glimpse the North Dakotan's willingness to play tit-for-tat legislative hardball in order to funnel federal dollars into North Dakota.

Andrews's Senate Garrison victories, when compared with a string of defeats in the House, gave him a further opportunity to discuss the contrast between his legislative success and the failures of House member Byron Dorgan. Andrews took this opportunity to lecture Dorgan publicly. He told reporters:

> Anytime we had a Garrison issue on the floor over the years, when [former representative and governor] Art Link was my colleague in the House and when I've been in the House by myself representing North Dakota—because of the importance of this project to the future of our state and its people, I've never felt the project should rise or fall on what I do myself. We always invited bipartisan delegations from the legislature, the governor, the attorney general, top Democrats and Republicans. We've always had 15-20 of them down to help talk about the great need in North Dakota for the project and we always won by comfortable votes. I don't know if Byron felt it wasn't important enough to get that type of team together or whether he felt he had it handled or what. . . . It had to be that the issue wasn't presented properly. [58]

Andrews followed these lessons about legislative support with some lessons about legislative timing.

> Here he is, a Democratic congressman with a Democratic Speaker. You'd almost think he would say, "Hey, postpone this thing a week. We've got it moving on another vehicle." But now we've got a vote that's 314-67 and trying to keep it in another vehicle becomes that much more difficult. By bringing it up when he did—at the worst possible time—he's made it extremely difficult for us to carry it through on the continuing resolution. . . . Had he just kept it off the floor another 24 hours, we would have been through, and I can't imagine why he didn't do that. [59]

With Republican officials calling the episode "glaring proof of how little influence" Dorgan had in Congress, and with the state's largest paper suggesting that Dorgan might be more interested in press releases than legislative solutions, Andrews knew he had Dorgan on the defensive.[60] He touted his own legislative savvy as he poured it on his prospective rival. When the judge lifted the ban on Garrison construction in 1982, Andrews said, with some pleasure, privately, "It vindicates the provision Quent and I put in the Senate bill and in the conference version last year. Of course, Byron Dorgan called it a horse shit provision—after he lost it in the House four to one."

In 1983, Andrews and Burdick faced the first direct Senate attack on Garrison—and an appropriation of $22.3 million—and defeated it on the floor by a vote of 62-35. This time, however, Dorgan kept the House from instructing its conferees to "insist" that no money for Garrison be allowed. According to one observer, the congressman "appealed personally to virtually everybody" in the House. "Face to face or by telephone," he wrote, "Dorgan had spent day and night lobbying Republicans and Democrats alike, telling them 'It's important to me and important to North Dakota.'" Majority Leader Jim Wright (D-Texas), fearful that it could cost Dorgan his seat, "worked the door" to the chamber urging people to vote for the project. Another observer called it "the most striking maneuvering ... [brought about by] Democratic sympathy for the state's lone congressman."[61]

At the end of three years, therefore, Andrews's ability to deliver had been proven three times over; but finally, Byron Dorgan, too, had a personal legislative success—albeit a holding action—to his credit. The freshman senator dominated the process; but the congressman would not go away, or be blown away.

DEFENSE WARRANTIES

A few months later Mark Andrews received another burst of highly favorable publicity, first nationally and then locally, for a legislative proposal that was his alone. It demonstrated the political potential of a genuinely national legislative initiative. It planted a seed among attentive people in North Dakota that Mark Andrews might become a national figure. Judging by their favorable response, North Dakotans wanted their senator to achieve such a stature. It was the capstone of the first half of his term and, we shall argue, represented the high water mark of his senatorial career-in-the-constituency. This favorable run of publicity came in the first months of 1984—after which point the publicity he reaped and the local reputation that went with it took a definite downward turn.

This noteworthy national venture was the Andrews provision, passed in 1983, requiring warranties on defense weaponry. As a member of the Subcommittee on Defense of the Senate Appropriations Committee, Andrews had listened to critical testimony concerning weapons that failed to meet specifications. Engines, for example, wore out long before they shou!.! have. When Andrews learned that the M-1 tank transmission was the same as the one in his tractor on the farm, but that the tractor transmission came with a three-year warranty and the tank transmission came with none, he wondered why civilian standards could not be applied to the military. "If we can get and expect warranties on our civilian purchases, from TV sets to washing machines and air conditioners, why not when we buy the machinery to protect our freedom?" He inserted just such a provision in the Defense Appropriations Bill, and it sailed through to easy passage. But by early 1984, the Pentagon and the defense contractors were seeking repeal of what they regarded as a wholly restrictive and unworkable idea.[62]

For Andrews, the original idea was a bonanza. It fit perfectly with his favorite themes of "let's use some common sense" and "let's get back to basics." As he told Pentagon officials who were pushing a gun that failed to work in cold weather,

> You're buying lemons. On my farm I need feeding machinery that will start and operate at 40 degrees below zero or my cattle will starve. Unless the Army plans to fight only in balmy 70° temperatures of early summer, this [weapon] is far from satisfactory.[63]

The warranty fight pitting the down-to-earth farmer against the mammoth Pentagon and its big business allies gave him an unassailable position in populist-leaning North Dakota. Well before it even passed, a campaign aide was exultant. "People love the warranty issue. That one can get us reelected. Mark can run as the man who brought common sense to the Defense Department. That's the kind of issue you can ride back into the Senate." The issue did show Mark Andrews at his best and at his strongest—as a successful legislator, as a resourceful North Dakotan, as the little guy standing fast against the big guy, as "one of us" standing fast against "them."

In February, the emerging warranty controversy received wide coverage in North Dakota. In news stories and editorials, Andrews was pictured as a tough fighter for a good cause. Headlines read:

- "Andrews Prepares for Challenge to Warranty Law" (*Minot Daily News*)
- "Andrews Vows to Fight Arms Warranty Effort" (*Forum*)
- "Andrews Fights the Pentagon" (*Grand Forks Herald*)

Andrews's words reflected his battle posture. "We are playing major league ball here, because the defense contractors don't want their cozy relationships with the military to end." Or, "The Pentagon and its contractors have had an incestuous relationship for 35 years and they want to continue business as usual. It will be a tough fight to stop them."[64]

Editorials adopted him as their champion and cheered him on.

> Senator Mark Andrews has his big farmer mitts on the military industrial folks and he won't let go.... [He] uses his farmer logic well when he talks about product warranties or guarantees.... It just makes good sense.... Maybe it takes North Dakotans to put the Defense Department on the defensive. Someone's got to do it.[65]

> Senator Mark Andrews of North Dakota is getting in one heck of a fight on his bill to force the military to get warranties for its weapons. The Pentagon bureaucrats are wriggling and squirming to get out of it.... The bill is simplicity itself, and Andrews got it passed into law last year.... Makes sense to us.... It's time civilian common sense was applied to military procurement.[66]

Statewide coverage ran from favorable to laudatory.

Judging by the National Newspaper Index of five leading papers, Andrews received more national attention for the warranty issue than for any single story during his first five years—seven stories in all.[67] Three related stories identified him as part of the military reform movement in Congress. At a time when issues surrounding defense spending were especially prominent, Andrews's subtheme was a natural. Shortly after he unveiled it at home in October 1982 (see Chapter 1), an NBC camera crew came to the farm to do a story for the "Today" show and a couple of articles appeared in 1983. But most of the national publicity occurred at the same time as the statewide publicity. And the very fact of this national coverage—modest though it was—made a strong impression on the newspapers in North Dakota. For the first time in his Senate career, Mark Andrews began to be viewed as a national political figure.

The state's most respected political columnist, Dick Dobson of the *Minot Daily News*, set the standard in a mid-February article entitled "Andrews Draws Notice." His theme was that of the eleven North Dakotans who had served in the U.S. Senate, only one could be called a national senator, with two others coming close. He described Milton Young, for example, as "a 'regional senator,' who seldom attracted the notice of the national media."

> But now it appears that a North Dakota Senator, Mark Andrews, is edging into the national limelight. He is showing up

frequently on national television and in such publications as the *New York Times,* the *Washington Post* and the *New Yorker.* . . . Much of his work is national in scope. . . . It is probably too early to call Mark Andrews just 'Mark Andrews' on national television. But he is receiving quite a bit of notice beyond the borders of North Dakota.[68]

Other local journalists echoed the same theme.

- "Andrews has become one of the leaders in the Defense Reform movement . . . [and] Andrews' motives seem to most Washington insiders to be genuine prairie populism."
- "It is doubtful any North Dakota senator, at least in recent memory, has received the exposure currently being given to Mark Andrews in what is considered the most prestigious press in the nation."
- "In the Senate, Mark Andrews has attracted a lot of attention. Perhaps some of it is due to his imposing physique, some to his plain talk. . . . Another reason is Andrews' independence." [69]

Andrews's performance on the defense warranty issue provided a glimpse of what might be accomplished at home by seizing on a national issue in Washington. A local reputation for national leadership—for "pork barrel plus"—seemed achievable. Two and a half years later, in September 1986, with an election campaign under way, 6 percent of North Dakota's citizens mentioned the defense warranty issue when asked to specify something Andrews had done that they liked. Only the 13 percent who mentioned "doing a lot for farmers" ranked higher among specific constituent recollections. The memory lingered despite the short life of the issue in early 1984. Andrews did not massage the specific warranty proposal for more publicity, nor did he enlarge the issue into any broad-scale attack on Pentagon waste and spending. With additional cultivation by Andrews and his staff, this noteworthy amount of citizen recollection might have been increased substantially. It was an opportunity glimpsed; but it was an opportunity lost.

MIDTERM WEAKNESS

In the early months of 1984, with his Garrison and defense warranty efforts making favorable headlines, the outward signs of electoral security were extremely favorable for the incumbent senator. The private signs, however, were decidedly mixed. Andrews's own survey of

December 1983 showed continued strength when the incumbent was considered in isolation, but a worrisome weakness when he was compared with his likely opponent, Byron Dorgan. The poll numbers provided convincing evidence that Andrews's concerns about the Democratic congressman—his activist style and its constituent appeal—were justified. Indeed, survey respondents seemed sufficiently enamored of Dorgan's legislative style to give it the status of an independent criterion in their voting calculus.

On the basic tracking question, whether the senator deserved reelection or whether a new person should be given the chance, his grades of 60 percent to 27 percent remained strong and virtually unchanged from the previous year. His job rating, which drew a 74 percent approval figure when last taken (as a House member) in July 1980, now stood higher, at 82 percent. On the other hand, his favorability ("one of the best" or "favorable") score, of 78 percent, was lower when compared with the July 1980 score of 89 percent. All these scores remained high, especially since his disapproval or unfavorability scores, in all cases, remained at 10 percent or less. In these general respects, the Senator appeared to be in no special difficulty—except that while he was doing quite well, so was Byron Dorgan, with favorability and approval scores both at 81 percent.

More worrisome, however, were the signs of slippage in voter perception of Andrews as "one of us, working for us." In December of 1979, when Andrews was a congressman and still unannounced for the Senate, 76 percent of the voters had given him high marks on the question whether "he cares/doesn't care about people like me." [70] In July of 1980 his high scores on the same question dropped to 69 percent. In March 1982 they were 54 percent; and in December 1983, they were 53 percent. His low marks had risen from 11 percent in July 1980 to 15 percent in December of 1983. On a new question, in December 1983, calling for a similar 5-point ranking, 28 percent of the respondents gave Andrews low marks for having "lost touch with people." The picture was one of some erosion in the sense of identification that had been so basic to his constituent support.

Moreover, when the pollsters asked point blank whether Mark Andrews had "done better" as congressman or as senator, by 34 percent to 28 percent, with 37 percent not sure, North Dakotans said he had done better as a congressman. And when asked "which one did the better job as congressman," by 42 percent to 31 percent they named Andrews over Dorgan. The implication could be drawn from these responses that some kind of transition had to be made from House member to senator, that voters would make some kind of reassessment of the familiar person in the new position, and that Mark Andrews had not yet been entirely successful in negotiating the transition. Alternatively, he was now being compared, as a senator, with Byron Dorgan and was being found wanting.

Andrews's pollster from 1979 to 1983 was Richard Morris. Long afterward, Morris recalled his worries about the trending of these postelection results:

> When he was in Congress, his constituents had the greatest intimacy with him. It was more than name recognition. It was a tremendous depth of intimacy. I had never seen anything like it. They could tell you lots about him. . . . In 1980, there were any number of candidates who began their races with a 70 percent margin. Andrews, however, was the only one who kept it to the end. But year by year, you could see that intimacy flake away. In fact, when we asked them whether they thought he was a better senator or congressman, by three to one they said he had been a better congressman. He had had such a long-term intimacy with the people and it had raised expectations so high that they almost had to be disappointed.[71]

It is not Morris's faulty recollection of the 3-1 margin or his notion that voters were doomed to disappointment that is of interest here—only his pollster's sense that constituent satisfaction with Andrews seemed to be eroding over time.

Another set of answers in the December 1983 survey added to the sense that some slippage—in what pollster Morris called intimacy and we have called identification—was taking place (see Table 4-2). Byron Dorgan's consistent lead in all "keeping-in-touch" categories could not fail to impress. Dorgan had an obvious ability to fashion connecting links with the voters. Given Andrews's own strong performance as a congressman, one could imagine that Dorgan's impressive showing was attributable to the office he held as much as to himself. But given the widely recognized publicity-generating activity of this "new politician," our view is that most of the credit belongs to the alternate style Dorgan exemplified.

During our 1982 trip, Andrews had offered the opinion that his constituent operation was still the best in the North Dakota delegation. In 1983, there was scant survey support for that judgment. There was every good reason to believe that Andrews's inability to adopt a publicity-oriented governing style was costing him dearly in his head-to-head comparisons with the activist congressman. Andrews conceded, of course, that he was no match for Dorgan in terms of ability to generate publicity. But even where the senator believed he was especially strong, Dorgan held 2-1 leads in the polls. Dorgan's activist style seemed to dominate all other considerations in the voters' minds.

TABLE 4-2 Keeping in Touch with North Dakotans

	Andrews	*Burdick*	*Dorgan*	*Not Sure/No Answer*
Whom do you get more mail from?	24%	21%	31%	24%
Whom do you read about more in the papers or see on TV?	21	10	55	14
Whom do you call when you have a problem with a government agency?	24	19	52	5
Who is doing more to obtain federal funds?	19	14	37	30

Source: Dresner, Morris and Tortorello Research, North Dakota Survey, December 1983.

Andrews believed, for example, that he was an effective user of the franking privilege to mail items to his constituents—by one calculation the biggest per voter spender in the U.S. Senate.[72] When asked whether they had received any mail from him (in the same survey), 80 percent of his constituents answered yes. Even so (see Table 4-2), Dorgan was perceived to be doing more in that respect. And—the unkindest cut of all—North Dakota voters gave Representative Dorgan more credit for securing federal funds for the state than they gave Senator Andrews. Above all, the message Andrews had wanted to convey was about getting money for his state. Securing and protecting funds is what Andrews had spent his years in the Senate doing. His reputation for getting and keeping the money is what Andrews believed would underwrite his reelection in 1986.

In the light of these survey results, it seems unlikely that the episodic, insider-oriented newspaper publicity we discussed earlier had actually penetrated the consciousness of the average North Dakota voter. In Washington, Andrews might have been known as a superior pork barreler, but at home, even that reputation seems not to have been firmly enough established to give him the edge over Dorgan.

The December survey itself provided additional support for skepticism about the impact of local publicity. In one sequence of questions, the voters were asked whom they would vote for, Andrews or Dorgan, in a head-to-head Senate race. Then they were read a series of editorials concerning Andrews's senatorial independence—his general record on budget cuts, his opposition to the president, and his attack on the administration for cutting nutrition programs. Then the voters were asked, "How would you vote after reading these editorials?" The result was a switch from a trial vote of 47 percent to 41 percent in favor of Dorgan to a second vote of 49 percent to 35 percent in favor of Andrews. If people knew what Andrews had done, they would react favorably. But they did not know. The favorable publicity Andrews had received in the local press in 1983 had not yet registered with his constituents. He had failed, therefore, to gain the increment of constituent support he might have expected to gain from what we have called his purely senatorial increment of publicity.

At year's end in 1983, and from the perspective of the incumbent senator, voter preferences remained at best unstable and uninformed, and at worst a source of worry. Andrews and his likely challenger both showed a good deal of political strength. But Andrews seemed not yet as firmly established as a senator as he had been as a congressman. He seemed a little less closely identified with his constituency than he once was and a little slower in communicating his senatorial governing accomplishments than he wanted to be. Byron Dorgan seemed to be getting far more mileage out of his governing activity than Andrews was getting out of his. Put differently, the voters seemed to be responding to a governing style that Mark Andrews—the old style House member in the new style Senate—was not yet giving them. All in all, the incumbent could have used a more commodious cushion of constituent trust and support as he headed into what was to become a time of troubles.

UNFAVORABLE PUBLICITY: 1984

THE MALPRACTICE SUIT

In the spring of 1984, the senator received the heaviest dose of statewide publicity he would ever receive for a nonpolitical activity. The publicity had a political impact, however, an impact that was not helpful to him. It quickly displaced the flattering press notices of February; it accelerated the worrisome trends of December's private poll; and it marked the public beginning of a downturn in his political fortunes.

The publicity came from a nine-week, April to June, malpractice trial in Fargo. Mark and his wife Mary sued some of North Dakota's best-known doctors, its best-known hospital, and its best-known clinic, alleging negligence in their care and treatment of Mary Andrews for an illness that had left her permanently disabled. They asked a Cass County jury to award them $16.9 million (later reduced to $10.2 million) in damages.[73]

On a plane ride from Washington to Fargo in November 1979, a change in cabin pressure had given Mary Andrews a severe headache, followed a few days later by the onset of bacterial meningitis and in February 1980 by brain surgery. Despite intensive and exhaustive physical therapy ever since, she remained confined to a wheelchair, with only partial control of her motor functions and considerably impaired speech. Her memory and intelligence and spirit were unaffected. Both sides called in experts to theorize about what happened and when; the medical issues were left in dispute. After thirty-nine days of testimony from ninety-odd witnesses, and three days of deliberation, the jury found negligence on the part of some defendants, but awarded the Andrewses no damages—on the grounds that the negligence did not contribute to Mrs. Andrews's illness. The verdict was regarded by participants and observers alike as a victory for the doctors and a loss for the Andrewses. Shortly thereafter, the senator and his wife filed an appeal asking for a new trial, a move that guaranteed a reminder, later on, of whatever negative publicity had accrued the first time around.[74]

The trial was heavily covered locally and regularly covered statewide. Two of Fargo's TV stations kept a continuous watch; and the *Forum* published a lengthy account of each day's testimony. The Associated Press provided the state's other dailies with a steady supply of reportage. Amid the technical arguments, a good deal of emotion surfaced—all of which guaranteed a lot of interest.

The Andrewses charged the doctors with negligence. The doctors claimed their treatment had been "equal to the best in the world, not the country, but the world." The Andrewses accused the doctors of altering or destroying medical records; the defense replied that the doctors "are not liars, are not cheaters, are not falsifiers." Senator Andrews testified that "Mary was not only my wife, she was my best friend. We've always done things together. Now we can't." Mary Andrews, seated in a wheelchair "her head bobbing," "struggled" to write three words. Videotape showed her doing rehabilitation exercises in the newly constructed pool at the farm. When it was over, one of the defendants said, "The personal attacks and the derogatory manner in which they treated the physicians, were uncalled for." And Andrews said, "What is tough to take is the celebration, joy and frivolity on the other side. . . . They are laughing all the way to the bank."[75] Excerpts such as this appearing regularly in the press—and, we assume, on television—were bound to generate public interest and public opinion.

The immediate political effect of the lawsuit was to divide Fargo, the state's largest community and Mark Andrews's home territory, sharply and emotionally. "No other lawsuit in recent memory has commanded such intense interest or created such a division in the community," one journalist wrote in May.

> For the Andrews are part and parcel of the Fargo and the North Dakota establishment. The Senator is a wealthy, third generation landowner, born to affluence and influence. The people they are suing are lifelong friends, schoolmates, social, business and political intimates and associates and allies.
>
> In addition, the city's medical establishment is renowned for the extent and quality of its services. This is a source of great local and regional pride and of considerable comfort.
>
> The hostile view is that the Andrewses have turned on friends and attacked local institutions, that the matter should have been settled without a trial.
>
> The supportive view is that a well-liked woman, wife of an extremely popular man, has suffered permanent and costly damage.

The author quoted the *Forum*'s publisher to the effect that "Nearly everybody in town has a connection. We're all touched by it." [76] A local minister spoke of the "significant and profound effect" of the trial. He added, "I meet people who formed strong opinions well in advance and they seem to be undeviating. A kind of anti-Andrews sentiment." [77] One of the senator's veteran Fargo employees described a direct effect of this sentiment.

> The Andrewses belonged to the [Fargo] country club. Mary always came over to play bridge. She loved bridge, and she was an excellent player. After they filed suit, she would come over and the players would stick her way over in the corner playing with the little old ladies. She wasn't invited to play with the people she had always played with. Finally, she stopped coming over.

"A lot of latent prejudice has been released," said the minister. "There are those who vehemently hate the Andrewses, and there are those who feel every doctor is on the take." [78] This kind of polarization is surely distressing to doctors, but it is positively life-threatening for politicians.

The political threat to Andrews was that the lawsuit would do damage to the strong sense of identification he had developed with a broad North Dakota constituency and displayed, once again, in his overwhelming 1980 election. His public reputation rested heavily on the sentiment, from both sides of the representational relationship, that "he is one of us." That sentiment rested, in turn, on the existence of a sociocultural homogeneity, a commonality of interests, and a feeling of community that were unusual in their statewide scope. It rested, too, on the notion that such a unifying fabric was best treated as a given and left undisturbed by protective politicians. If there was to be conflict, the idea was that it should be conflict between "us and them," between North Dakotans and outsiders.

In this context, the Andrews lawsuit had been internally divisive— quite certainly in Fargo and perhaps statewide as well. It was treated by the local establishment more like the act of an outsider than the work of a community member. To some of them, Andrews seemed now more like a traitor than a member of that family of which he had for so long considered himself a part. Andrews's choice of a Los Angeles lawyer— regularly identified as such in the press—to battle a bevy of North Dakota's homegrown litigators was surely no help in maintaining his communal ties. It seemed clear, at the end of the trial, that the senator had received some bad publicity and that bad publicity would hurt him. But it was impossible to know how much, among whom, and for how long.

When I had finished looking in Andrews's office files for newspaper reports of the trial, I noticed there was almost no expression of public opinion on the matter. So I asked his staff if they were keeping editorials and expressions of constituent opinion in a special file. No, they said, there just were no such things to be found in the public press. It would be a while before anyone knew for sure what the ultimate political effects might be.

Difficulties in assessing public opinion did not mean there was none. It meant only that private opinions were being privately exchanged. In a fairly homogeneous state made up of small towns, private exchanges of opinion can be potent influences on public opinion. Word of mouth gossip can do serious damage to a public figure. With a few shreds of evidence and much speculation, we can suggest one line of private discussion that had the potential to hurt Andrews. It is the notion that a public official, because he is powerful, should be held to a different standard in his private life than the ordinary person. However much his public acts may confirm the idea that he is one of us, in his private actions he will be viewed differently. His private actions are judged in terms of character traits they reveal. He is expected to display self-restraint, not to exercise his power, not to seek advantage, not to advertise his status, not to indulge his emotions. As one example of the "how" and the "what" of this process, Andrews said after the election: "When I filed the lawsuit, certain members of my own staff ... began talking to others and calling others, saying, 'Mark Andrews is getting greedy. Who does he think he is?' It only takes a hundred calls like that and pretty soon everybody knows about it." Needless to say, he fired the disloyal aides; but the communitywide damage had been done.

From the few comments that did reach the press at the time, one can find the sentiment that Andrews should not have pressed the lawsuit and/or shouldn't have asked for so much money. The sentiment took several forms: that he was greedy; that he only wanted to buy more land; that he wanted something for nothing; that he should do something for his state and not for himself; that his action would raise health care costs for everyone else; that he should take his lumps like everyone else.[79] A public official, in short, should not seek unusual benefits for himself, should not act like a big shot. Andrews's status as a well-to-do farmer, which stamped him as doubly privileged, did not help.

"In Andrews's case," said one observer much later, "it was a rich man and a powerful one taking on the doctors. . . . The doctors won because in the North Dakota imagination, wealth should not challenge wealth. Instead, the rich and the powerful should be content with their lot whether they've been wronged or not." Never mind that he is legally entitled to act as any other private citizen can act—"to exercise my constitutional rights," as Andrews put it. When he does so, it may trouble the citizenry.[80]

"It's somewhat difficult to understand why this lawsuit has developed such strong feelings against the senator, but there's no question that it has," began an editorial in the *McLean County Independent*, from north-central North Dakota. Under the title "Politics, Pursuit of Damages Don't Mix," the editor explored these incompatibilities, which, he noted, "are not talked about publicly . . . [and] never surfaced publicly."

> Perhaps there is no way that a political leader in North Dakota could bring a lawsuit for malpractice without destroying his own image. Maybe it's because while we get disgusted with high medical costs, we still keep doctors and their institutions on a pedestal, sacred cows of sorts. Or maybe it's because the retaliatory nature of a lawsuit just is contrary to what we North Dakotans believe in. Or maybe it's because we sense that someone is trying to profiteer through misfortune. . . . Whatever the reason . . . Andrews probably can't pursue rewards of the court and politics at the same time.[81]

There is nothing definitive about these varied and scattered sentiments. But they all boil down to a single concern: the character of the incumbent. The doubts they express are doubts about the judgment, the values, and the ethics of Senator Andrews.

Character issues, when and if they enter an election campaign, can mean serious trouble for an incumbent. For they can weaken the kind of representational bonds I saw enacted at Lehr. An editorial in the *Emmons County Record*, from the south-central part of the state, not far from Lehr, put the problem just that way. "For Senator Andrews, whose relationship with the people of North Dakota implies that he has their values and their interests, this is an action that refutes the good relationship." This editorial was reprinted without comment at the state capital, in the *Bismarck Tribune*.[82] To the degree that doubts of this sort existed in North Dakota, they would by no means be confined to Fargo. They would work to undermine the sense of identification between Andrews and a much broader constituency.

On the other hand, it was possible to imagine a more empathetic and sympathetic constituency reaction, both in and out of Fargo—the reaction that the Andrews family had been dealt a devastating financial and quality-of-life blow and that the lawsuit was a normal, understandable response under the circumstances. That reaction would have signaled an acceptance of Andrews's own comments that "this wasn't a money grubbing thing. This was a conscious decision on my part to do what I should do: take care of my family needs"; "Your private responsibility comes before your elected responsibility . . . Mary is going to need a lot of care for the rest of her life." [83]

That same reaction would have given some consideration to the central importance of Mary Andrews—"my chief adviser and best friend in politics," "the closest political adviser I've ever had"—in Mark Andrews's political life, and to the severity of that loss. "I have never known a couple as close politically as the Andrewses," wrote one newspaper editor.

> Mary Andrews took part in every one of her husband's campaigns for the U.S. House. She gave him political advice. She interrupted interviews to suggest how he should answer questions. She helped him remember names. She appeared on TV with him on every election eve. In every way, she was a political help-mate. She also was a great political asset. She gave him good advice.[84]

His comments provide a convincing measure of Andrews's political loss.

From the earliest moments of my 1980 visit to North Dakota, the relationship between Mary Andrews and Mark Andrews's political life was a constant topic of conversation. It was intertwined with his very decision to run for the Senate.

> I decided to run in April. I waited till then because of my wife's illness. The Republicans even offered to postpone their convention till I was able to make a decision. In April the doctor said Mary would be walking normally by July. She wasn't. She walks now with a walker. If I had waited till July, I might not have run. The decision to run was a vote of confidence in her

recovery. If I had decided not to, she would have felt that it was because of her. That wouldn't have helped. She's making progress. But you learn the word *patience*. I think when we get back to Washington and she gets with her buddies again, that will help. She's been active in congressional wives' activities and has a lot of friends in Washington. They're awfully good to her.

At that time, she was undergoing physical therapy at the University of North Dakota Hospital in Grand Forks. "I have been home every weekend this year," he said, "not to campaign but to be with Mary at the Rehabilitation Center."

In every previous campaign, she had traveled with him. In 1980, she was unable to do so. The Associated Press reporter covering that campaign made her absence the theme of his major campaign story. "Campaigning for us has always been a family thing," Andrews told him. "We've been in politics since the beginning. She's been a great source of strength. . . . This is kind of a family business. It means a lot to Mary. It means a lot to me. . . . She tells me when I'm not hitting my best points." [85] The reporter noted something I had noted, too—that wherever Andrews went, people inquired about Mary and in every talk he gave he told people how she was getting on, as if they expected it. Recall how he campaigned in Lehr with "Mary's Bran Muffin Recipe." More than once, I heard people say, "She is the real campaigner in the family." As the senator put it himself, "We joke that I've been doing her thing for 25 years." [86]

In everything he said and did, he seemed determined to encourage her comeback. As his staff saw it, he always put the most optimistic face on her painstakingly slow recovery. Most important, in 1980, he was planning their traditional election eve "Mark and Mary Show."

> Mary wants to do it. Her speech is 90 percent of normal. In the morning, she is good. Later on, when she gets tired, her speech gets slurred. We'll do it Monday morning. If parts of it need to be redone or dubbed, we'll have time to do that. We just sit in the living room at the farm with the family, looking through an album, talking about where we've been and what we've done. [The idea is:] "With all the backbiting and mud slinging, isn't it nice to see a family sitting around the fireplace reminiscing?"

"The Mark and Mary Show," wrote another reporter "is a staple of North Dakota politics . . . corny maybe but endearing." [87] And the show did go on.

Whenever we talked, during his early years in Washington, comments about his relationship with his wife always entered in at some point. In his earliest evaluation of life in the Senate, in March of 1981, he commented:

> It's hard to compare my situation now with what it would have been in the House because the baseline changes. With Mary still recuperating, it means that instead of her looking after me, I look after her. She was always a producer—taking me to work, picking me up, helping me back home. Until she becomes more transportable, I may not go home as much—at least on weekends.

Describing his decision-making process on one of his most important votes later that year, he said:

> I sat down with Mary—who is, as you know, the political adviser in the family. We made a checklist zip zip zip on one side, zip zip zip on the other side. She asked me, "Well, what do you think it adds up to?" I said, "It looks like I ought to support the president." She said, "I've been wondering why it took you so long to reach that conclusion." And she knew it wasn't a good political vote.

At the end of the year, he summed up. "I'm comfortable in the Senate, but not as comfortable as I would have been if Mary was around. When we are in session at night, she and I would have gone off to a piano and violin deal and then come back to work. . . . Mary's health is improving, but it is not improving a whole lot." A week after that interview, they filed the lawsuit.[88] But that was something he never mentioned to me until well after the trial had taken place.

GARRISON REVISITED

In the fall of 1984, there was even more negative publicity in store for the North Dakota senator. For three years, we recall, he had battled as hard as he could to fund the Garrison Diversion irrigation project in the Senate and in conference committee. His efforts had kept it alive. But the fact was that for three years, no money had been appropriated for the project in the House of Representatives.

The only way an appropriation for Garrison could pass the House was to have it brought to the floor by the back door of a conference committee decision. Representative Dorgan's one victory had come in defeating a motion made in the House to insist that the Garrison appropriation be eliminated in conference. On a straight up-or-down vote to appropriate the money, Garrison could not get a majority in the House—or so Andrews believed, and both Burdick and Dorgan subsequently agreed with him. At least, they supported his proposal that Congress establish a review commission to revise the project—with all the appropriated but unspent money to be held in escrow until the commission made its recommendation. In June 1984, Congress established the Garrison Diversion Unit Review Commission and directed that it report back with a plan in December.[89]

The proposal for a commission, as Andrews presented it to Congress, had been negotiated beforehand with the Audubon Society and the other environmentalists with whom he had for so long been at loggerheads. But Mark Andrews was nothing if he was not a deal cutter and a compromiser. Indeed, much in the style of his Senate activity, Andrews and his aides had negotiated with the environmentalists in private. When the proposal came to light, he drew early criticism for this procedure. In the words of one editorial:

> That some proponents of the diversion project are understandably upset with the state's junior senator isn't surprising. After all, the senator appeared to assume godlike powers (true to his personality) boldly going ahead with the compromise without consultation with other governmental leaders of this state.[90]

Despite the editorialist's conclusion that "perhaps that's the only way any compromise could have been achieved," the portrayal of Andrews's "godlike" behavior as "true to his personality" is another small indicator that his reputation as "one of us" might be getting less secure than it had been previously.

When the commission began its work and some of its preliminary blueprints started circulating around the state, criticism of Andrews escalated. The report in November that commission plans called for cutting irrigation from 250,000 acres to 108,000 acres and eliminating one of the dams involved drew "the gloomy prediction that Garrison diversion, as North Dakota has known it for decades—is doomed."[91] The elimination of the dam—the Lonetree Dam—was widely believed to have come about when some Andrews staffers and some environmentalists suggested the outlines of a plan they believed would most easily pass Congress.

Immediately, one of the state's most prominent Democrats, former Governor William Guy, launched a blistering attack on Andrews for selling out and betraying the people of his home state. "I think the trail is clearly marked back to Mark Andrews' office. I think it's very obvious that Andrews' office . . . was behind this sellout of North Dakota." On another occasion, he said: "I don't see how any North Dakotan could be other than outraged, stunned and with a feeling of total deception and betrayal."[92] Guy, too, criticized Andrews's failure to consult. He was soon joined by the Garrison Conservancy District Board, the officials immediately overseeing the project—a board on which Andrews had long sat. Altogether, these critics mounted the sharpest, most personal attack on the senator within the reach of my research.

Not surprisingly for a child of the legislative process, Andrews defended himself in terms of that process.

> Garrison as it stood hasn't gotten by the House of Represen-
> tatives for three years. It's long time past for the whiners and
> the gripers and the bellyachers to try to get together and work
> constructively.... We had to put a commission together, be-
> cause we had no other choice. Without it, we wouldn't have
> seen dollar one.... I could design a wonderful project for
> North Dakota; but it wouldn't go anywhere in Congress.[93]

Press headlines of November 30 placed him clearly on the defensive:

- "Andrews Defends Support of Garrison Proposals" *(Jamestown Sun)*
- "Andrews Rejects Sellout" *(Devils Lake Journal)*
- "Andrews Defends Garrison Proposal" *(Minot Daily News)*
- "Andrews Denies Sellout of Garrison" *(Williston Daily Herald)*

It was a further blow when his colleague Quentin Burdick, feeling the heat of opposition to the emerging plan, parted company. "I don't like to have to oppose him," said Burdick, "but I am convinced this plan is no good." [94]

Opposition to the commission's preliminary plan came quickly to center on the tentative elimination of the partially built Lonetree Dam, the largest water storage facility in the project. Andrews had expressed some uncertainty about the prospects for congressional approval of any plan that included this dam. When his most closely involved staffer testified to a similar sense of uncertainty to the commission, other witnesses in attendance gave him a punishing reception. Headlines on December 5 read:

- "Water Users Jeer Aide to Andrews" *(Jamestown Sun)*
- "State Water Users Group Taunts Andrews' Aide" *(Grand Forks Herald)*
- "Water Users Group Jeers Andrews' Aide" *(Dickinson Press)*
- "Andrews' Aide Jeered by Two Water Groups" *(Bismarck Tribune)*

It was not a helpful episode for the senator. After a brief interval, he fired the offending staff member.[95]

Shortly thereafter, a bipartisan group of statewide officials and

notables—including the Republican governor and the Democratic gov-
ernor-elect—sent a telegram to the commission asking that the Lonetree
Dam be kept in the project. But Andrews, for reasons that were never
clear, declined to sign the telegram. Another spate of unhelpful headlines followed on December 5:

- "Andrews Declines to Sign Pro-Garrison Telegram" *(Minot Daily News)*
- "Andrews Refuses to Sign Garrison Note" *(Grand Forks Herald)*
- "Andrews Won't Back Telegram over Garrison" *(Bismarck Tribune)*
- "Andrews Won't Sign Garrison Telegram" *(Dickinson Press)*

In these articles he was quoted to the effect that "unless the commission comes up with a project that will receive the support of both
houses of Congress, North Dakota will end up with nothing." [96] But
he was pictured in the press as pursuing a course in isolation and
at odds with the other pro-Garrison leaders of his state—"twisting
in the wind," in the words of "one of the state's leading politicians." [97]

"Politically," one reporter summed up in early December, "it is
downright hot in North Dakota, where Andrews has been taking the
beating of his political life." By his actions, the reporter continued,
Andrews had "allowed Guy to frame the issue of retaining Lonetree as a
test of loyalty to the state" and had "allowed himself to become
associated with the possible loss of Lonetree." Sensing this dilemma,
Andrews quickly "made a 180 degree turnabout" and "threw his
wholehearted support behind the restoration of Lonetree Dam." [98]

One week after the statewide headlines had publicized the humilia-
tion of his staffer, a new set of headlines appeared, on December 14:

- "Andrews: I Will Try to Get Lonetree Back" *(Bismarck Tribune)*
- "Sen. Andrews Says He'll Try and Restore Lonetree" *(Minot Daily News)*
- "But Andrews Hasn't Given Up" *(Jamestown Sun)*
- "Andrews: 'I'll Insist on Reservoir'" *(Grand Forks Herald)*

These articles reported Andrews's disavowal of anything his aide might
have said to the contrary on Lonetree.

"I have gotten my head beat in on something that's a damn phony"
protested the senator. "If [my staffer] has been telling people we can't
get a project with Lonetree through Congress, he sure as hell hasn't been
reflecting my point of view." The commission idea, he continued, "gave
the ones who wanted to raise hell with me politically an opening as big
as all get out." He confessed to being "damn sick and tired of being

ragged around about Garrison." And somewhat later, he said he was "damned sick and tired" of the charge that the commission was "cooked up in my office closet." [99]

He sought to recapture the high ground of concern for the state by counterattacking his critics.

> They've undercut North Dakota by fussing with the Commission. The 50-50 chance we had of getting a project when the Commission was set up has deteriorated to one in three because of the crazy antics of people who should have known better. . . . I make mistakes, but if somebody wants to make a case of me being against Garrison, that's a flimsy damn case.

He repaired always to his legislative process defense. "I resent being set up this way. I stand by my belief that this commission approach was the only way there would have been any chance for Garrison." He summed up, "I will not stand for a bum rap on this thing and this is a bum rap." And he added, hopefully, "The people in North Dakota resent bum raps." Lest anyone think his troubles had paralyzed him politically, he took the occasion to declare his intention "if the Lord is willing and my health is OK" to run for another term.[100]

The heated language of Andrews's remonstrances suggests a greater than normal anxiety. He had been put on the defensive on an issue to which he had devoted his political career. What was equally upsetting to the experienced legislator was that he had lost control of a legislative-style deal he had engineered. Garrison Diversion had turned—temporarily at least—from a source of favorable publicity to a source of unfavorable publicity.

This turn of events and Andrews's enormous frustration with home state interpretations lends support to an earlier suggestion that Mark Andrews's insider governing activity was difficult to convey to voters. It could be portrayed in small, unconnected doses, but it was lacking in sustained impact. And when it was conveyed in a concentrated dosage—as in the Garrison episode—the legislative maneuvering involved was too easily portrayed as lacking in steady conviction. An insider legislative style may be especially remote from the voter, especially hard to fathom by the voter, and very easily characterized by opponents as unprincipled. Even when understood, it may be an especially difficult style to defend. As a source of difficulty in constituency relations, this publicity problem dogged him in settings that were even more important than Garrison.

As his problems with Garrison grew, state politicians suggested that in his eagerness to negotiate a settlement, he might have lost touch with sentiment at home. "I am totally bewildered by what Mark is doing," said one. "I think it has kind of gotten away from him," said another.[101] Editorial speculation hinted at the unthinkable. Referring to Andrews's huge 1980 election margin, the editor of the state's second-largest paper wrote, "It is hard to imagine that it could be eroded away in disagreement over a water development project. This is the Garrison project, however, a project near and dear to the powerful in North Dakota."

Even more unsettling was the editor's observation that the Garrison flap might have compounded the problem begun with the malpractice lawsuit. "This is the second time Andrews has offended parts of this state's establishment. A lawsuit about his wife's illness alienated the medical community." [102] For a senator whose constituency career had featured a relationship of closeness, sensitivity, and responsiveness, activities that "offended" and "alienated" more than one group of community leaders could put his normal election margin in serious jeopardy. Furthermore, with the lawsuit scheduled to come up for appeal and the Garrison Commission recommendations still languishing in Congress, neither of these difficulties was likely to disappear any time soon.

As his fourth year in the Senate came to a close, a politician who had enjoyed a long, successful, and peaceful tenure in office had become involved in controversy. Controversy always commands attention. Controversy also creates uncertainty, as new issues come to the fore and old patterns of support are put in jeopardy. Public controversy, public attention, and uncertainty combine to threaten political success. In our view, the lawsuit was the event that triggered controversy. Until that event intervened, Andrews remained, publicly at least, on a familiar political course. His weakness had remained private and potential—private in the poll results of March 1982 and December 1983, potential in the candidacy of the person who had exposed those weaknesses.

The lawsuit severely threatened the underpinning of voter identification and confidence that had sustained his political career. It magnified those doubts that the comparisons with Dorgan had already revealed privately. And it made people more predisposed than before to interpret succeeding events like the Garrison deal negatively. Like a "string of [bad] votes" inside the legislature, a string of unfavorable reactions at home carries large political costs. The negative response to Andrews's actions on Garrison, following on the heels of the lawsuit, bore all the earmarks of such a costly string.

NOTES

1. Barbara Hinckley, *Congressional Elections* (Washington, D.C.: CQ Press, 1981), 48-50.
2. On the small state-large state difference, see John Hibbing and John Alford, "Constituency Population and Representation in the U.S. Senate" (Paper presented at the Houston/Rice Conference on Electing the Senate, Houston, December 1989).
3. Richard Pearson, "Former Sen. Milton Young Dies," *Washington Post*, June 1, 1983. The rest of this paragraph depends on this article and on the *Congressional Record*, March 12, 1980, S2432; June 13, 1983, S8228.
4. Michael Weisskopf, "Burdick, a Rare Bird, Heads Flock for First Time," *Bismarck Tribune*, December 3, 1986, reprinted from the *Washington Post*.
5. Ibid.
6. AP, "Burdick: I'm Fit in Politics and Gym," *Bismarck Tribune*, February 17, 1986.
7. Dirk Johnson, "Burdick of North Dakota Runs Against G.O.P. and Age Issue," *New York Times*, October 13, 1988.
8. "CEI Pork Barrel and Subsidy Index, 99th Congress—1985-1986," Competitive Enterprise Institute, Washington, D.C., 1987 (on the twenty-six issues in the index, Burdick cast twenty-five pork barrel votes, Andrews twenty-four); "CEI Statistical Summary and Analysis, 99th Congress," Competitive Enterprise Institute, Washington, D.C., 1987 (the Hawaii delegation ranked first).
9. Barbara Sinclair, *The Transformation of the United States Senate* (Baltimore: Johns Hopkins University Press, 1989), Table 5:4, 80. I am indebted to Prof. Sinclair for supplying me with the specific totals for Andrews.
10. Ibid., 51, 70.
11. Ibid., 88.
12. Ibid., 138, 158.
13. Richard F. Fenno, Jr., *Home Style: House Members in Their Districts* (Boston: Little, Brown, 1978).
14. Burdett Loomis, *The New American Politician* (New York: Basic Books, 1988).
15. Senate Subcommittee on Transportation, *Hearings on Department of Transportation and Related Agencies for Fiscal Year 1983*, pt. 1, March 30, 1982, 957; Subcommittee on Transportation, *Hearings*, FY 1984, pt. 1, March 3, 1983, 383; *Congressional Record*, June 23, 1982, S7363, September 10, 1982, S11252.
16. Subcommittee on Transportation, *Hearings*, FY 1987, pt. 2, April 16, 1986, 213-216.
17. Martin Tolchin, "Where the Budget Cutters Didn't Want to Cut," *New York Times*, October 3, 1982.
18. DMI, *North Dakota Survey*, March 1982.
19. *Washington Post*, May 25, 1982.
20. Mark Starr, "How Congress Slices the Pork," *Newsweek*, August 2, 1982.
21. On the Cardinal, see the *Congressional Record*, November 18, 1981, S13616-13619; Howie Kurtz, "Budget Knife Only Nicks Road and Harbor Projects," *Washington Post*, January 26, 1982.
22. Dick Dobson, "Young Could (Kind of) See the Future," *Minot Daily News*, March 23, 1986.
23. James McGregor, "Andrews, Dorgan Prepare to Meet Head-On," *Grand Forks Herald*, March 24, 1985.

24. "North Dakota Media Don't Do Very Good Job of Covering Washington," *Devils Lake Journal,* December 3, 1985.
25. McGregor, "Andrews, Dorgan Prepare to Meet."
26. Dick Dobson, "Ebb and Flow of Mark Andrews' Washington Office," *Jamestown Sun,* May 23, 1985.
27. Dobson, "Ebb and Flow"; McGregor, "Andrews, Dorgan Prepare to Meet." The local pilot who regularly flew Andrews and Burdick around the state told me that he had dealt with the same local Burdick staffer for years, but that Andrews changed his contact person so often he never got to know any of them. Andrews had five different district staff directors in six years.
28. The most helpful source was the newspaper clipping file kept by his Fargo office staff.
29. "Andrews' Vote Shift Causes Cut in Weatherization Funding," *Grand Forks Herald,* July 20, 1983; *Forum* (Fargo), January 1, 1984; James McGregor, "Andrews Dickers on Budget Issues," *Grand Forks Herald,* May 2, 1985.
30. *Grand Forks Herald,* November 25, 1984; *Bismarck Tribune,* November 29, 1984; Jacqueline Calmes, "Angry Senate Republicans Bear No Grudges," *Congressional Quarterly Weekly Report,* August 3, 1985.
31. "Senator Andrews Selected to Head Committee on Indian Affairs," *Grand Forks Herald,* January 7, 1982.
32. Chet Gebert, "Indian School's Future Assured in Wahpeton," *Forum,* March 23, 1983.
33. Carl Flagstad, "Thurmond Had Good Reason to Help Minot AFB Project," *Minot Daily News,* May 31, 1984.
34. *Minot Daily News,* August 16, 1984, July 19, 1984. On the completion of the project, see Carl O. Flagstad, "Andrews Final Letter Notes Highlights," *Minot Daily News,* December 24, 1986.
35. "Andrews Endorsed for Election to U.S. Senate," *Sunday Forum* (Fargo), October 12, 1980.
36. Al McConagha, "Mark Andrews Gets Senate Reputation By Riding Lone Trail," *Minneapolis Star Tribune,* May 8, 1983.
37. Transcript, "McNeil-Lehrer Report," October 28, 1981, 2.
38. Also, no times in 1981, ten in 1984, and sixteen in 1985. The papers covered are: *New York Times, Washington Post, Wall Street Journal, Los Angeles Times,* and *Christian Science Monitor.*
39. Stephen Hess, *The Ultimate Insiders* (Washington: Brookings Institution, 1986), Table 2-2; in August 1985, Andrews's picture covered 20 percent of the page in *Newsweek's* lead story of the week—on divisions within the Republican party. His picture was labeled "Sen. Lawton Chiles"! *Newsweek,* August 5, 1985, 14.
40. Richard Cohen, "Senate Republican Control May Be Put to Test by Tough Issues This Fall," *National Journal,* September 10, 1983, 1827; Norman Ornstein, Robert Peabody, and David Rohde, "Party Leadership and the Institutional Context: The Senate from Baker to Dole" (Paper presented at the Annual Meeting of the American Political Science Association, August 1986, Washington, D.C.), Table 2.
41. Ward Sinclair, "Rural Development Being Neglected Under Reagan, Hill Critics Assert," *Washington Post,* August 7, 1982; Ward Sinclair, "Rural Aid Plan Hit by Unexpected Flak," *Washington Post,* March 12, 1983.
42. Helen Dewar, "2 in GOP Rap Trims in Budget," *Washington Post,* February 23, 1983; Helen Dewar, "Senate Republican Class of '80 Starting to Grow

Restive," *Washington Post,* March 7, 1983; "More Dumb Cuts," *Washington Post,* February 28, 1983; Tom Raum (AP), "Mark Andrews: GOP Critic of Reagan Administration," *Williston Daily Herald,* March 7, 1983; Tom Raum (AP), "A Rousing Reagan Critic," *Grand Forks Herald,* March 7, 1983.

43. Dewar, "2 in GOP"; see also his criticism of Stockman in the *Congressional Record,* September 10, 1982.

44. Dewar, "Senate Republican Class of '80."

45. "North Dakota Media Don't Do Very Good Job of Covering Washington," *Devils Lake Journal,* December 3, 1985. The ten daily papers are: *Bismarck Tribune, Devils Lake Journal, Dickinson Press, Forum* (Fargo), *Grand Forks Herald, Jamestown Sun, Minot Daily News, Valley City Times Record, Washington Daily News, Williston Herald.*

46. Raun, "A Rousing Reagan Critic."

47. AP, "Andrews in No Disfavor with Senate Republicans," *Dickinson Press,* April 19, 1983. The remainder of the paragraph is taken from this article.

48. McConagha, "Mark Andrews Gets Senate Reputation." The next two paragraphs are taken from this article.

49. *Congressional Record,* June 22, 1983.

50. *Minot Daily News,* October 18, 1984.

51. Dresner, Morris and Tortorello Research, *North Dakota Survey (2053),* March 1982.

52. DMI, *North Dakota Survey,* March 1982.

53. Joseph A. Davis, "The Garrison Diversion in North Dakota, A Case Study in Water Politics," *Congressional Quarterly Weekly Report,* July 30, 1983; Carl Flagstad, in *Minot Daily News,* July 1, 1985; Ward Sinclair, "Water Projects Are Drying Up as Lawmakers Feel Budget Heat," *Washington Post,* June 22, 1983; "The Death of a Dinosaur," *Washington Post,* June 11, 1984; Paul Starohin, "Pork: A Time Honored Tradition Lives On," *Congressional Quarterly Weekly Report,* October 24, 1987.

54. Howie Kurtz, "Congress' Budget Cutters Protect the Home Folks," *Washington Post,* January 25, 1982. The "amendment" was attacked in the committee, not on the Senate floor.

55. "Worms in the Pork," *Time,* January 3, 1983, 43.

56. AP, "Andrews Says Actions Aided N.D.," *Bismarck Tribune,* January 4, 1983. The remainder of this paragraph relies on this AP story.

57. Peter Grier, "Garrison Diversion: Needed, or a Clear Case of 'Pork'?" *Christian Science Monitor,* May 4, 1983.

58. Jim Neumann, "House Rejects Garrison Amendment," *Forum,* November 21, 1981. See also AP, "Dorgan Denounces Criticism," *Forum,* December 2, 1984; *Congressional Record,* December 14, 1982, H9757-H9767.

59. Neumann, "House Rejects Garrison Amendment."

60. "Garrison Vote in House Vital," *Forum* (Fargo), November 19, 1981; AP, "Head of Panel Says Garrison Not Dead," *Forum* (Fargo), November 22, 1981.

61. *Congressional Record,* June 22, 1983, S8889-S8909, see also June 13, 1984, S8241-8244; Davis, "The Garrison Diversion"; and David Rogers, "Senate Votes Down Limit on Tax Cut," *Boston Globe,* June 30, 1983.

62. Jeffrey Frank, "A 50,000 Mile Warranty for Pentagon Weapons," *Las Vegas Sun,* November 14, 1983 (reprinted from *Congressional Quarterly Weekly Report*); Pat Towell, "Pentagon Takes Aim At Warranties Law," *Congressional Quarterly Weekly Report,* March 10, 1984.

63. AP, "Andrews Attacks Army's New Gun," *Grand Forks Herald*, March 6, 1985.
64. "Andrews Wins Battle Not War on Arms Warranty," *Grand Forks Herald*, February 7, 1984; "Andrews Prepares to Fight Arms Warranty Effort," *Forum* (Fargo), February 12, 1984.
65. Editorial, "North Dakota Logic in the Pentagon," *Forum* (Fargo), February 15, 1984.
66. Editorial, "Andrews Fights the Pentagon," *Grand Forks Herald*, February 20, 1984.
67. Four in the *New York Times*; two in the *Washington Post*; one in the *Los Angeles Times*. These articles were in the staff clipping file.
68. Dick Dobson, "Andrews Draws Notice," *Minot Daily News*, February 18, 1984.
69. Derek Leabery, "Andrews' Role in Senate Expanding Greatly," *Washburn Leader*, March 28, 1984; Carl Flagstad, "Editorials Back Andrews' Warranty Law," *Minot Daily News*, February 24, 1984; and Mike Jacobs, "Populist Seen From the Potomac," *Grand Forks Herald*, March 31, 1984.
70. Respondents were asked to indicate on a 5-point scale the degree to which the statement fit or didn't fit the individual politician. I have construed the top 2 points on the scale as "high marks" and the bottom 2 points as "low marks."
71. Telephone interview, January 23, 1990.
72. Steve Blakely, "Senator's Mail Costs Disclosed," *Congressional Quarterly Weekly Report*, December 14, 1985, 2626-2627.
73. AP, "$17 Million Sought by Andrews," *Bismarck Tribune*, December 24, 1981; Kevin Wymore, "Andrews Medical Suit Set for Trial in Fargo Monday," *Grand Forks Herald*, April 15, 1984.
74. Jim Corcoran, "Victory for Defendants, Major Loss for Andrews," *Forum* (Fargo), June 16, 1984; Jeff Meyer (AP), "Andrews' Verdict Shows No Damages," *Grand Forks Herald*, June 16, 1984, same AP story carried in nine other papers; AP, "Jury in Andrews' Case Never Came Close to Awarding Damages for Negligence," *Williston Daily Herald*, June 18, 1984; Ellen Crawford, "Andrewses File for New Trial," *Forum* (Fargo), July 10, 1984.
75. Jim Corcoran, "Sen. Andrews Testifies in Malpractice Case," *Forum* (Fargo), April 19, 1984; AP, "$17 Million Sought by Andrews"; Corcoran, "Sen. Andrews Testifies"; Jim Corcoran, "Both Andrewses Dispute Doctor's Prior Testimony," *Forum* (Fargo), May 12, 1989; Jeff Meyer (AP), "Andrews: I've Lost My Wife, My Friend," *Bismarck Tribune*, April 19, 1984; Jim Corcoran, "Mary Andrews Testifies in Suit," *Forum* (Fargo), April 20, 1984; Jeff Meyer (AP), "Mrs. Andrews Repeats Husband's Story at Trial," *Williston Daily Herald*, April 20, 1984; Jim Neumann and Kevin Murphy, "Both Sides Win and Lose in Wake of Andrews' Verdict," *Forum* (Fargo), June 16, 1984; and AP, "Andrews Calls Doctor's Reaction 'Tough To Take,'" *Bismarck Tribune*, June 20, 1984.
76. Larry Batson, "Fargo Split over Senator's Lawsuit," *Minneapolis Star Tribune*, May 24, 1984.
77. Ibid.
78. Ibid.
79. Letter to the editor, *Grand Forks Herald*, April 28, 1984; see also note 75.
80. Mike Jacobs, "Andrews: Person, Politician," *Grand Forks Herald*, July 6, 1986; Neumann and Murphy, "Both Sides Win and Lose."

81. Editorial, "Politics, Pursuit of Damages Just Don't Mix," *McLean County Independent*, June 12, 1985.
82. *Bismarck Tribune*, April 28, 1984.
83. Neumann and Murphy, "Both Sides Win and Lose"; Jim Corcoran, "Andrews Says Suit Could Hurt Politically," *Forum* (Fargo), May 17, 1984.
84. Neumann and Murphy, "Both Wides Win and Lose"; McConagha, "Mark Andrews Gets Senate Reputation"; Jacobs, "Andrews: Person, Politician."
85. Jeff Baenen (AP), "Andrews Misses Wife's Help in '80 Senate Race," *Jamestown Sun*, October 11, 1980.
86. McConagha, "Mark Andrews Gets Senate Reputation."
87. Batson, "Fargo Split."
88. AP, "$17 Million Sought by Andrews."
89. *Congressional Record*, June 21, 1984, S7922-S7927; AP, "State's Only Option: Back Plan," *Minot Daily News*, December 31, 1984.
90. Editorial, "Politics, Pursuit of Damages."
91. Carl Flagstad, *Minot Daily News*, circa November 25, 1984.
92. "Andrews Says He Didn't 'Sell Out' ND," *Valley City Times Record*, November 30, 1984 (Andrews's only electoral defeat had come at the hands of William Guy, in their race for the governorship in 1962, by 2,000 votes.); *Bismarck Tribune*, November 30, 1984.
93. "Andrews Says He Didn't 'Sell Out' ND."
94. Mike Jacobs, "Guy Grows More Visible," *Minot Daily News*, December 1, 1984.
95. The groups involved were the North Dakota Water Users Association and the North Dakota Water Resources Districts (on the importance of Lonetree, see Carl Flagstad, "Supporters Insist on Retaining Lonetree," *Minot Daily News*, December 14, 1984); and "Andrews Fires Garrison Aide," *Grand Forks Herald*, March 16, 1985.
96. "Andrews Refuses to Sign Garrison Note," *Grand Forks Herald*, December 11, 1984; and "Andrews Declines to Sign Pro Garrison Telegram," *Minot Daily News*, December 11, 1984.
97. James McGregor, "Andrews at Risk on Garrison," *Grand Forks Herald*, December 9, 1984.
98. Ibid.; James McGregor, "Andrews: 'I'll Insist on Reservoir,'" *Grand Forks Herald*, December 14, 1984.
99. McGregor, "Andrews: 'I'll Insist'"; Jack Zaleski, "Andrews: I'm Getting a 'Bum Rap,'" *Devils Lake Daily Journal*, December 20, 1984; and Zaleski, "There is No 'Magic Bullet,' Says Andrews," *Devils Lake Daily Journal*, August 9, 1985.
100. McGregor, "Andrews: 'I'll Insist'"; Zaleski, "Andrews: I'm Getting a 'Bum Rap.'"
101. McGregor, "Andrews at Risk."
102. Jacobs, "Guy Grows More Visible."

Electoral Vulnerability

A BLACK BOX

The six-year period from the election to the reelection of a U.S. senator is a political lifetime. Wars begin and end, recessions come and go, presidents win or lose, legislation passes and fails, popular preoccupations ebb and flow. Incumbent images get reshaped; and incumbent fortunes rise and fall.[1] A lot can happen to make the circumstances at the time of reelection vastly different from the circumstances of the previous election. Sometimes what happens has the effect of rendering an incumbent senator vulnerable to electoral challenge. We are not at a loss for measures that attempt to capture vulnerability—previous election margins, partisan constituency makeup, incumbent voting scores, changing economic conditions. But we do not yet understand the *process* by which incumbents—especially well-entrenched incumbents—become vulnerable. For political science, the long, six-year interelection period remains, for the most part, a black box.[2]

In Chapter 4, we traced Mark Andrews's constituency career as he moved through the middle years of his incumbency. We did it not through continuous monitoring—which would have been preferable—but by taking occasional soundings at points where local or national media attention attracted ours. And we tried to link his reputation at home to his governing style in Washington whenever that linkage seemed helpful in explaining his behavior or his reception at home. During 1981-1982, we had found a good deal of adjustment-time stability. For the years 1983-1984, we found a period of positive reaction at home followed by a period of troubles. The last six months of 1984 recorded a steady stream of negative publicity for the incumbent. But if his fourth year in office ended on a downbeat note, the beginning of his fifth year found his political fortunes at an all-time low.

THE MARCH SHOCK

On March 5, 1985, the North Dakota political community was shocked by the publication of statewide poll results. The respected State Poll, by the University of North Dakota's Governmental Research Bureau, reported that in a head-to-head trial heat with Rep. Byron Dorgan, *Senator Mark Andrews would lose by 64 percent to 30 percent.* Beneath the headlines "Poll: Dorgan Would Bury Sen. Andrews" *(Forum)* and "Dorgan Picked over Andrews: Democrat Given Decisive Edge" *(Minot Daily News),* the two papers that sponsored the poll publicized the enormous statewide, across-the-board popularity of Byron Dorgan.[3] Andrews's persistent interest in the state's only congressman had not been misplaced.

For an incumbent of twenty-two years, the poll portended electoral trouble in 1986. Nothing was inevitable. But well-entrenched, well-known incumbents are expected to run comfortably ahead of all comers in the period before any challengers have declared themselves. A sitting senator once thought to be invulnerable was now shown to be extremely vulnerable. The shock was mitigated only slightly by the poll's other results, showing Andrews winning head-to-head trial heats with State Tax Commissioner Kent Conrad (57 percent-32 percent) and former governor William Guy (56 percent-35 percent). Andrews seemed to be so vulnerable to a challenge by Dorgan that there was nothing to feel safe about in a contest against the other two potential challengers.

Indeed, the Democratic party newsletter trumpeted, "Perhaps as many as a dozen Democrats could mount formidable challenges to the graying, paunching junior senator from Mapleton." Beyond any doubt, Andrews had lost support at home; and he would have to campaign uphill all the way. Columnist Dick Dobson predicted that if Andrews had to defend his seat against Dorgan, "We can expect to see one of the bloodiest campaigns in North Dakota history."[4]

REACTIONS: NORTH DAKOTA AND WASHINGTON

To anyone privy to Andrews's December 1983 poll, the March poll would not have been a shock. Rather, it would have been a public confirmation of a private worry. But no one knew, at the time, of the incumbent's weaknesses. Early public efforts to explain the startling poll results centered on Andrews's troubles of 1984. While noting that the poll provided no substantiation for such speculation, Dobson nonetheless concluded that "Andrews may have been hurt politically by his role in formulating a compromise on the Garrison Diversion project or by the lawsuit he and his wife filed against the medical establishment."[5]

A newspaper from the area in which the Garrison Diversion project was situated editorialized similarly about the reasons why "Andrews' support had faded so badly compared to Dorgan's popularity." First was Andrews's "identification as a leader of the Garrison compromise with environmental interests." On this question, the editor faulted Andrews's political instinct. "[We] look at Andrews' role in seeking a compromise as one of practical, reasonable politics," he said. "But Andrews could well have erred by failing to build a base of support for his position among water development leaders." However, the editor deemed the second reason far more important. "It's the multimillion dollar medical malpractice lawsuit," he wrote, "that will probably be Andrews' undoing as a political leader of North Dakota (and one of the best we've had when it comes to influence and ability to lead). . . . His defeat at the hands of Dorgan . . . if Dorgan, of course, seeks the Senate seat—would seem assured now that the Andrewses have filed for a retrial."[6]

A columnist from Eddy County, in central North Dakota, emphasized the same two problems. He wrote:

> An ill-advised malpractice suit . . . cost him dearly in public support. He alienated nearly all those who had been unwavering in their loyalty throughout the 17 years he served in the House. Then he antagonized the water development people with his Garrison Diversion proposal.[7]

But this columnist added a third explanation for the senator's difficulties. His reasoning commands special interest because the columnist was Edward Doherty, Andrews's former campaign manager and former executive secretary in his Washington Senate office. This longtime, but now thoroughly alienated, sidekick represented the conservative wing of the Republican party in North Dakota. And he spoke for that group when he wrote: "While he may not know or care, the Senator's also in deep trouble with many of his own party because of his constant criticism of President Reagan. He alibis that we didn't send him there to be a rubber stamp. Nor did we send him to be a 'Mr. No.' " He ended by suggesting that an independent conservative Republican candidate run in the general election.

This ideological problem was not new. Andrews's entry into electoral politics in 1962 had been as a "self-described 'Young Turk' [who] successfully fought the Republican establishment for a gubernatorial nomination." And throughout his career, "he seemed to find an understandable joy in rattling the bars of his party's fairly rigid ideological cages."[8] In my 1982 trip (see Chapter 2), I had heard intimations of his unhappiness with the narrow outlook of the Republican party organization.

In retrospect, evidence had been surfacing regularly to fuel ideologically oriented speculation. In the summer of 1984, just prior to the Republican National Convention, for example, Andrews and four other "moderate" Republican senators decided to hold their own, unauthorized set of public hearings on the party platform, in Washington. The event became an AP story in North Dakota, and gave wide, but brief, circulation to his disagreements with the conservative wing of the Republican party. An attack on the hearings by party conservatives helped to raise Andrews's maverick profile back home.

For a few days, Andrews's dissenting comments appeared in the North Dakota papers.

> Historically, the Republican party has been creative, innovative, thoughtful and progressive. Complacency, self-satisfaction and the desire for ideological purity threaten the majority status of the GOP.[9]

> I don't think we can crawl in a hole and pull the hole over us and say "we are pure."[10]

> The toughest tax we face today is the tax of high interest rates. Unless we respond to the issue of deficits—and the deficits are the causative factor in those high interest rates—you're simply not going to see many farm families survive.... We're not trying to pick a fight with the White House. We're just ... saying we think we ought to have open and public hearings.[11]

He did not go to the Republican National Convention. "I spend enough time with that bunch when I'm down in Washington," he said.[12] Instead, he held some highly publicized agricultural hearings in Minot, Dickinson, and LaMoure.[13] The sum total of these activities, together with the press coverage of them, cannot have increased his popularity with the conservative Republican faithful in North Dakota.

The fact of Andrews's vulnerability was quickly picked up by Washington observers. Their speculations centered on the ideological and partisan concerns. How much, they wondered, did Andrews's frequent policy disagreements with the president account for his vulnerability, and how much of a factor would his maverick voting record become at election time?

Evidence of his independence had continued to accumulate. At the end of the 1984 budget season, for example, *Congressional Quarterly*

Weekly Report had noted that Andrews "increasingly has joined forces with other GOP moderates in the Senate in resisting Reagan's policies on higher defense spending and reducing the deficit." In a study of 1984 voting patterns, *U.S. News and World Report* had fingered Andrews as the freshman Republican whose support for presidential initiatives "showed the most change . . . favoring Reagan 77 percent of the time in 1981 but only 61 percent last year [1984]—a 16 point drop." In a study of 1985 voting patterns, Andrews ranked as the fourth most "liberal" Republican on a battery of economic—taxing, spending, and budget—votes. In 1986, he would be called "a conspicuous exception" to the loyal Republican foot soldiers of his 1980 class.[14]

In February 1985, he "helped lead the fight for an emergency farm credit bill, which Mr. Reagan then vetoed." [15] His fight delayed Senate confirmation of Reagan's choice for attorney general. "The White House wants Ed Meese confirmed and that's what gives us leverage," he said. "This is our chance to get the farm problem resolved." [16] The move was vintage Andrews hardball, even though it eventually failed. Later in the year he learned that the Agriculture Department was discretely checking into the benefits he received from the farm program. Denouncing the investigation by turns as "a sophomoric attempt to intimidate me" and "big brother gestapo tactics," he defended the $18,000 to $20,000 worth of benefits allocated to his farm. "If you're going to have a representative government, you need some farmers in office." And he gave the attempt to embarrass him a farmer's brush-off. "Out where I come from, you look a man in the eye and ask him what you want to know. . . . As they say in farm country, it's small potatoes and there aren't many in the hill." [17]

In April 1985, a reporter wrote of Andrews, "In the past two months, he has voted against the Reagan administration on the three most important votes of the new Senate session." His headline captured the interest of the national press: "Sen. Mark Andrews, a Farm State Republican, May Stray Too Far—Even for a Maverick." [18] For some administration supporters the answer was clear—that he had strayed too far already. Even before the March poll was announced, Chairman Howard Phillips of the National Conservative Caucus took note of Andrews's votes and denounced him as one of five Republicans "who ought to be targeted for defeat in 1986 . . . for failing to measure up to true-blue conservative standards. . . . Conservatives have no stake in the reelection of Mark Andrews. If he thinks he can take conservatives for granted, he's making a mistake that will cost him his seat." [19] Like his other 1984 difficulties—his lawsuit and his Garrison compromise—Andrews's maverick Republicanism was the result of a characteristic independence when it came to decision making.

The North Dakota Democrats saw in the senator quite a different vulnerability. The Democrats attributed Andrews's March poll results to the lawsuit, to the Garrison blowup, and to "his association with the Reagan administration." Not too little, but *too much* association was the senator's political problem, as they saw it. In the words of the party's executive director, "His president is pretty unpopular out here. He's made a pretty good effort to distance himself from the president, but he's still his president." [20]

Andrews's problem was to keep his distance and keep his loyalty at the same time. Verbally he kept the balance by saying:

- "My people did not send me down here to be a rubber stamp for any president, even one they like as much as President Reagan."
- "The White House knows me. They aren't trying to beat me up. I'm not a rebel. I'm just independent."
- "Everyone wants to make a deal of it [that] because you fight for farm programs you're on the outs with the White House. The White House understands that." [21]

In May, he announced formally for reelection, at a fund raiser attended by Vice President George Bush—who had come he said, to show his "enthusiasm for Mark Andrews." [22]

In the aftermath of the March 5 shock, with explanations and speculations reverberating in North Dakota and in Washington, the principals went their separate ways. Dorgan pondered the pros and cons of making the race. He was being heavily courted by the Senate's Democratic establishment, anxious to capture a Republican seat in the impending battle for Senate control. He admitted to being interested in running for the Senate some time; he acknowledged that it would be fun to defeat Andrews; he affirmed that he did not like to lose; and he declined to make his decision anytime soon. [23]

Andrews accelerated his organizational activities. "I've been putting together a record that will stand up well in any kind of campaign when you go head to head and start talking about records and what's been accomplished," he said confidently. "When it comes time to campaign, I know how to campaign." He quickly hired a political consultant, a media specialist, and two North Dakota political operatives. He held two $100,000 fund raisers, one in Washington and one in North Dakota. And he went on television in the four largest cities for two weeks in June, urging people to "join the A team for North Dakota." The ad featured George Bush's endorsement, which called Andrews "special" and said, "He's there to represent the people of North Dakota and has never forgotten it and never will." Nationally, Andrews became only the second Senate candidate to air commercials; North Dakota observers called them the earliest ever in the state. In September, he ran a second set of television ads, which touted him as "one of the best senators North Dakota ever had." "Remember," the ads said, "it's never too early to go for the best." [24]

THE APRIL 1985 POLL

In April 1985, the senator commissioned a poll of his own, to give him a baseline from which to work in the upcoming campaign. The poll assumed that Rep. Byron Dorgan would run, and its questions focused exclusively on an Andrews-Dorgan contest.[25] It was an extensive voter survey, two volumes that totaled one thousand pages. Since I obtained the poll only after Andrews's defeat, I can provide only my outsider's reactions and interpretations—and guess, occasionally, at what the senator might have seen.

The result of the April poll's snapshot, horse race question—"If the election were held today, for whom would you vote?"—was almost identical to that of the State Poll, 63 percent to 32 percent in Dorgan's favor. The embellishments of the poll, moreover, carried forward the patterns revealed in the December 1983 poll. Overall, they revealed a virtually unrelieved picture of Byron Dorgan's extraordinary statewide popularity. By every standard of comparison and in every direct comparison, Dorgan received higher marks than Andrews. The poll left little doubt that if the congressman decided to run, the senator's political life was in grave danger. For Andrews, the problem was to figure out how much of this evidence pointed to Dorgan's strengths and how much to his own vulnerabilities.

On the plus side—and in the pattern of the earlier poll—there were some findings from which Andrews could take heart. While it was true that voters' judgments about Dorgan consistently outranked their judgments about Andrews, the incumbent nonetheless retained a substantial base of voter approval. His favorable/unfavorable opinion ratio was a very good 80 percent to 17 percent, and his approval/disapproval job rating was a strong 86 percent to 14 percent. (Dorgan's scores were 90 percent to 9 percent and 92 percent to 7 percent respectively, on the two measures.) When asked to agree or disagree with the statement "Before he was elected to the Senate, Mark Andrews was a good congressman for North Dakota," voters agreed by an 86 percent to 8 percent margin. When asked to agree or disagree with the comment that "When Mark Andrews became a senator, he forgot about the people of North Dakota," 73 percent *disagreed* and 26 percent agreed. Seventy-four percent of the respondents said they preferred two senators from different parties to any other arrangement. And by a margin of 56 percent to 41 percent they preferred that Dorgan not run against Andrews, but run two years later to replace a Democratic incumbent. By these several measures, Andrews showed a good deal of residual strength. He was in trouble, but he was by no means down and out— especially if Dorgan honored majority sentiment and declined to run.

On the matter of the likely policy issues in his reelection campaign, the April poll left little doubt about what the overriding one would be— the farm situation. North Dakota's farmers had been in a period of low prices and high interest rates, credit crunches, and farm foreclosures. Of the 26 percent of the respondents who were at least quarter-time farmers, 47 percent said that without help they doubted they could survive beyond five more years. When asked to name "the most important problem facing North Dakota or America," 32 percent of the respondents chose farm problems and most of the rest chose related economic problems—the deficit (12 percent), unemployment (10 percent), the economy (7 percent), and taxes (5 percent). Asked whether they approved or disapproved of Andrews's handling of "the most important problem," however, 58 percent approved and 31 percent disapproved. Andrews seemed to be holding his own on farm and economy issues. Still, no one could predict just how farm issues would play out at reelection time.

Whatever the pluses of the poll might be, the consistency with which North Dakotans found favor with Dorgan and the margins by which they registered their favor conveyed (to an outsider, at least) an alarming message. When, for example, voters were asked whether a battery of statements best described Andrews or Dorgan, they associated Dorgan strongly with all the favorable statements and Andrews with all the unfavorable ones. Table 5-1 displays the results.

Quite apart from the lopsidedness of these pro-Dorgan judgments, some of the answers in Table 5-1 pointed to serious—and surprising— campaign problems for Andrews. Voters' responses, for example, to the question, "Who has done the best job for us in Washington?" must have been extremely upsetting to a man who had spent nearly a quarter of a century in Congress giving topmost priority to helping his home state. Similarly, it must have been disappointing to see such support for the implication that Andrews "doesn't really accomplish much" or the implication that he already gets "enough credit for what he's doing." The problem was that voters' perceptions undercut Andrews's own sense of his many legislative accomplishments and his belief that his home state voters would support him on those grounds.

His pollsters searched hard, in the April survey, for evidence that

TABLE 5-1   Public Perceptions of Sen. Mark Andrews and Rep. Byron
Dorgan, 1985

"Does this statement best describe Mark Andrews or Byron Dorgan?"	Andrews	Dorgan	(Volunteered) Both	Neither
Has best solution to problems facing me and my family in future	25%	59%	6%	7%
I have my doubts about him	49	20	6	24
Competent and knowledgeable	22	44	32	1
Cares about people like me	20	59	19	4
Talks a lot but doesn't really accomplish much	45	20	7	25
Energetic	11	69	17	2
After all is said and done has done the best job for us in Washington	28	56	12	2
Makes me feel proud to be a North Dakotan	23	48	22	6
Does not get enough credit for what he is doing	24	42	13	18
Can best solve farm problems	29	49	12	8
Strong and forceful	28	53	15	3

Source: DMI, North Dakota Survey, April 1985.

the voters understood the difference between a legislator who got
things done and an issue activist who got public notice—for some
glimmer of a differentiation that might give Andrews an opening
wedge in coping with Dorgan's popularity. What they found, instead,
was overwhelming evidence that voters' perception of Byron Dorgan
was exactly opposite to Andrews's perception of Dorgan and, hence, to
the view of Dorgan's performance that Andrews had hoped to exploit.

Table 5-2 displays voters' responses to a series of questions probing
for Dorgan's legislative vulnerabilities. In the eyes of North Dakotans,
Byron Dorgan—not Mark Andrews—was the very model of a hard-
working, productive legislator. At another point in the poll, voters were
offered the argument, "There have been too many times when Mark

TABLE 5-2   Public Perceptions of Rep. Byron Dorgan, 1985

"Are the following statements about Byron Dorgan believable or important?"	*Believable and Important*	*Believable but Not That Important*	*Not Believable*	*No Opinion*
He has not been able to get any of his legislation passed	24%	15%	56%	5%
He cares more about getting the credit than doing the work	15	13	71	1
He's doing in Washington what you would if you were there	55	15	26	4
He's a lightweight in Washington	23	22	52	2

Source: DMI, North Dakota Survey, April 1985.

Andrews did the work, but Byron Dorgan has taken the credit." But, again, they disagreed—by a margin of 77 percent to 14 percent. If Mark Andrews was planning to make the case that he was better equipped than Byron Dorgan to govern in the interests of North Dakota, he could not draw much aid or comfort from the April 1985 survey.

Dorgan's alternative style had given the congressman the best of both worlds, home and Washington. He had introduced to North Dakotans, it appears, a new and appealing set of stylistic standards against which the old style incumbent senator was finding it hard to compete. Indeed, Dorgan's popularity seemed so great that it was producing favorable opinions on all questions. Yet it is hard to believe that Dorgan's popularity explains everything about the results in Table 5-2. These survey results also indicate that Mark Andrews had not secured as formidable a reputation for his legislative prowess as he would have liked or as he thought he had. At the very most, as we have been suggesting, he was habituated to a governing style—pork-producing, deal-making, low profile—that was becoming less than sufficient to his constituents. At the very least, the survey reviewed in Table 5-2 indicated that the incumbent senator faced a heavy burden of explanation back home concerning his governing activity in Washington.

We would expect the incumbent to have been engaged in explanation—which provides the connecting tissue between governing and campaigning—to a great extent. In their answers to the question "What do you like most about Mark Andrews?" voters seemed to acknowledge that he had, indeed, done a good job of explaining. Their answers fell into four broad categories. They "liked" certain personal qualities— appearance, honesty, intelligence, decisiveness, experience (32 percent). They liked him because he was, in vague terms, "doing a good job," "trying his best" (8 percent). They liked him more specifically because he was "doing a good job for North Dakota" (10 percent) and "helping the farmers" (10 percent). And they liked him because he "represents," "helps," and "communicates" with "the people" (13 percent).[26] If we combine the last three items, we get a picture of someone whose identification with North Dakota—the basis of his longtime political strength—remained recognizable, valued, and close.

On the other hand, a different open-ended question—asked much later in the survey—provided evidence that a fair number of voters wanted an even stronger and steadier sense of identification. They were asked, "If you had the opportunity to give Mark Andrews some anonymous advice—such as suggestions on how he could improve— what advice would you give him?" Only 62 percent of the respondents offered advice. The three largest categories—of the twenty-five coded by the pollsters—were Help the people/Communicate with the people (12 percent), Support the farmer (11 percent), and Stay in touch with North Dakota problems (7 percent). No other category exceeded 4 percent.

Although one cannot quantify the comments recorded by the pollsters, the first and third categories are loaded with advice such as:

- "Spend more time listening to the people"
- "Be a little more visible and accessible"
- "Hold more home forums where people can express their opinions"
- "Get back to grass roots and find out what's going on"
- "Tell us what he's been doing"
- "Spend a little more time in the state"
- "Come to North Dakota more often and talk one on one to the people"
- "Come back and meet more with your constituents"

Even with respect to helping the farmers, he was told to "get more involved in the farm situations in North Dakota, be more visible," and to "work more with the farmers."

From other answers in the April poll one could infer the same desire on the part of constituents for more attention from Andrews than they had been getting. Recall, for example, that only 20 percent, compared with Dorgan's 59 percent, associated Andrews with the description "cares about people like me" (Table 5-1). Respondents were later asked similarly, "If Mark Andrews, Quentin Burdick and Byron Dorgan were your neighbors, which man would you be most comfortable talking to about your personal worries?" Fifty-one percent said Dorgan, 28 percent Andrews, and 20 percent Burdick. These answers continued the gradual slippage in answers to the similar, caring-type questions we saw in Chapter 4.

Off and on, too, in their verbatim replies to various open-ended questions, voters expressed a sharpened sense, as one put it, that "he's too distant, he doesn't communicate with North Dakotans." Andrews was described as "pompous," "cocky," and "arrogant." It was said that he "thinks he's God and above everyone," that "he should come back to earth and stop being so arrogant," that he should "get off his high horse" or "shut [his] big mouth and listen" and "not be so high and mighty sometimes."

These private comments of voters were being echoed concurrently in the North Dakota press. They fit, for example, with the opinion of a *Grand Forks Herald* reporter that Andrews's "political negatives . . . include his infrequent public appearances in the state." And with the opinion of the *Bismarck Tribune* editor that "Andrews has let himself drift a little too far from the political spotlight in North Dakota the last few years." And with the editorial comment in the *New Rockford Transcript* that "for reasons known only to him, he's lost touch with the folks back home." "He is gradually becoming known as less of a people's advocate," wrote one editor, "and more of one who has chosen to move from the ranks of the ordinary North Dakotans, an aristocrat." [27]

Again, although we cannot assign weights to these constituent comments, they certainly do not portray a member of the "family" or a person who is "one of us." Perhaps Andrews had heard all this before and could discount it as minority sentiment. Undoubtedly, for someone who had built a political career on attentiveness to his constituency, it was a hard message to accept. But the portrait assembled from a combination of closed- and open-ended questions surely presented a reason to worry that his constituent support might be narrowing. Whether it was due to a declining attentiveness on his part, or Byron Dorgan's newly established standard of attentiveness, or something else, a perception seemed to be dangerously present back home that Mark Andrews had gotten somewhat out of touch.

On casual inspection of House and Senate records, it does not appear that Senator Andrews was any less personally attentive to his home state than Representative Andrews had been. At least he spent as much time in North Dakota in one job as on the other. If anything, he went home more often as a senator. Table 5-3 compares number of trips

TABLE 5-3   Mark Andrews's Attentiveness to North Dakota: House and
Senate Career

Chamber, Year	Trips Home	Days Spent at Home
House, 1973	13	58
House, 1974	13	86
House, 1977	20	155
House, 1978	17	86
Total	63	385
Average	16 trips/year	96 days/year
Senate, 1981	11	84
Senate, 1982	19	87
Senate, 1983	24	114
Senate, 1984	24	112
Total	78	397
Average	20 trips/year	99 days/year

Sources: Clerk of the House reports and Secretary of the Senate reports.

home and days spent at home for four of his (randomly chosen) at-large
years in the House and for his first four years in the Senate. Assuming
that the two chambers keep similar reimbursement records and assuming that Andrews's filing pattern was the same, the comparisons
between House and Senate visits show more consistency than disparity.
Certainly there is not enough of a difference to indicate any decline in
the senator's attentiveness.

The four House years show an average of sixteen trips home and
ninety-six days at home per year; the four Senate years show an average
of twenty trips to North Dakota and ninety-nine days spent there per
year.[28] The Senate years 1981-1984 were those in which dissatisfaction
with Andrews—or approval of Dorgan—had been building. But it is
hard to find any basis for voters' dissatisfaction in Table 5-3. It may be,
of course, that the senator's constituent contact was lower in quality. He
had given up his regular rounds at the county courthouses, a routine of
immense help in developing what one of the pre-1980 pollsters described as "that tremendous depth of intimacy that he had." It may be
that he suffered without the reinforcement of a well-publicized reelection campaign every two years. On the evidence we have, and at this
point in our discussion, however, the idea that Andrews had gotten out
of touch seems to have owed more to the persuasiveness of Byron
Dorgan's high-profile alternative style than to any change in Mark
Andrews's own attentiveness to North Dakota.

Our speculations on whether, why, and how much the senator might be thought to have gotten out of touch with his constituents have been based on fairly general data. However, the April 1985 poll did reveal one unmistakable vulnerability—voters' reaction to Andrews's malpractice lawsuit. This specific vulnerability was most likely related to the general picture we have been painting. Respondents were asked to agree or disagree with this statement: "Mark and Mary Andrews did the right thing when they sued her doctors." The results were: Agree strongly, 13 percent; Agree somewhat, 19 percent; Disagree somewhat, 26 percent; Disagree strongly, 32 percent; No opinion, 10 percent.

Voters' replies to other open-ended questions made clear their considerable disapproval. When asked, "What do you like least about Mark Andrews?" far and away the largest number, 17 percent, mentioned the lawsuit. It was the only specific item that received mention from more than 3 percent of the respondents. Reading the replies as reported verbatim by the pollsters, it is striking how unspecific voter "dislikes" were—*except* for the lawsuit. On the comparison question, "What do you like most about Mark Andrews?" not a single voter, as reported, mentioned the lawsuit. In other words, voter opinion on the lawsuit was specific; it was sizable, and it was a dead-weight negative.

On another open-ended question, "What in particular would you like to tell him [Andrews]?", 7 percent of the respondents mentioned his "handling of the malpractice suit." It was a number second only to the 8 percent who said, "help the farmers." Again, one can get only an impression from the reported comments. But the striking characteristic of these recorded comments, compared with all others, was their emotional content:

- "I'd like to express anger"
- "I'm very unhappy"
- "He made a big mistake"
- "He's trying to put one over on the people"
- "[He] went too far"
- "Drop the damned suit"

In answer to the earlier "dislikes" question, several of the comments had described Andrews's actions in the lawsuit as "unethical." Others called it "unpopular" and "repulsive." It seemed likely, therefore, that not only was the lawsuit a negative, but it had enough emotional content to have considerable staying power.

When asked in April 1985 why they planned to vote against Andrews, 15 percent said they would vote against him because of the lawsuit. Whether or not this meant they would act on their response nineteen months later could not be known. But the lawsuit had produced *controversy* where none had existed before. Because of the lawsuit, Mark Andrews had become controversial; and that condition opened up other, previously "undisturbed," perceptions of him to renewed scrutiny.

Because of the publicity given to the lawsuit and because of the less public talk that accompanied it, it seems likely that negative attitudes toward it colored many of the other performance judgments registered in the April poll. Political scientists Shanto Iyengar and Donald Kinder have developed a theory linking publicity, controversy, and voter scrutiny. They call it *priming*.[29] When voters judge the performance of public officials, these researchers argue, they give special weight to whatever information on whatever subject is publicly at hand. Voters are primed by the mass media to consider and to weight heavily some performance criteria and not others. We can conjecture that the respondents to the April poll were primed to give special weight to the lawsuit in answering questions about Mark Andrews's performance. More specifically, his behavior on the lawsuit as widely reported in the media—the controversial "way it was handled," as constituents often put it—subsequently influenced all those judgments suggesting that he was out of touch. His behavior on the lawsuit could be interpreted as a departure from acceptable community—or "family"—norms, thus priming voters to judge him more generally in outsider terms.

Similarly, the widely publicized brouhaha over his heavy-handedness on the Garrison Diversion project could be interpreted—as it was in the press—as a failure on his part to calculate with his customary care the allowable distance between independent action and constituent support.[30] Respondents may have been primed by this event, too, to think of Andrews as having lost touch and, hence, to render broader judgments in that same vein. Judgments expressed in April 1985 might or might not hold up until election day. But they might remain influential—in a second stage of priming—by predisposing voters to interpret later events as further evidence of Andrews's lack of contact with the folks back home.

To an outsider viewing the April poll in retrospect, its overall tenor is decidedly downbeat for a putatively popular incumbent. No one answer to any one question captured that tone. One that came closest, perhaps, was the 49 percent who said, "I have my doubts about him" (Table 5-1). Solidly entrenched incumbents will have developed a degree of voter trust that translates into the benefit of the doubt. People vote on the basis of the information that is at hand and on the credibility they attach to that information. Credibility is increased where the benefit of the doubt exists. Credibility was what I thought I saw during the meeting in Lehr. Now, however, Mark Andrews seemed to be receiving as much doubt as benefit.

Andrews's own campaigners surely assigned the greatest significance to a different bellwether survey question: "Do you think Mark Andrews has performed his job as Senator well enough to deserve reelection or do you think it is time to give a new person the chance to do better?" On this question, 46 percent answered "reelect," 38 percent favored "a new person," and 15 percent were undecided. Andrews's "reelect number" had never before fallen below 50 percent. In December of 1983, it had been 60 percent. The decline of 14 percentage points was both abrupt and large. It suggests, certainly, that the events and the interpretations of 1983-1984, as we have traced them, had an independent impact on the decline.

The decline in voters' readiness to reelect was simply one more indicator that in a contest with Byron Dorgan, Mark Andrews would be in difficulty. In that sense it was redundant. But the reelect number was a favorite of professionals because it tracked incumbent popularity against a generalized "new person." In recent years, it had become the pollsters' preferred measure of incumbent vulnerability. According to one national polling organization, "An incumbent is considered politically weak when support on the reelection question dips below 50 percent. But when the number dips below 40 percent, analysts [say] it 'is nothing short of a political earthquake.' "[31] Andrews's support figure was in dangerous territory. On the off chance that Dorgan might not run, other potential new persons would be watching. And they would find much hope and encouragement in the 14 percent drop and in the 46 percent to 38 percent reelect numbers of April 1985.

OBSERVATIONS AND REFLECTIONS: NORTH DAKOTA, NOVEMBER 1985

I made my third visit to North Dakota in early November 1985, to travel with Senator Andrews in the eastern part of the state. The dominant substantive focus of the trip was agricultural policy. But talk of the political situation was a constant companion. Acknowledgment of the incumbent's vulnerability had profoundly altered the tone and the substance of political conversation from my earlier visits. I had not been in his Fargo office for an hour when a friend of his dropped in. "How is Mark?" "He's fine and getting around—to Lakota, Cooperstown, and Valley City tomorrow." "He'd better. And when is the trial [that is, the appeal] coming up?" The quick exchange was an early clue to what people were thinking about. It was my first taste of the change in atmosphere since my last visit. In 1982, there had been confidence; this time there was worry. The fact of the worry, added to the published results of the March poll, moved me toward a somewhat altered view of

Mark Andrews's underlying strength with the voters of North Dakota.

It was my first chance to hear the senator's own interpretation of the public polls and his own outlook on the situation confronting him. In early October, a second State Poll pitting the senator against the congressman found Dorgan leading by 52-41—a substantial narrowing of the gap from 34 points to 11. The local consensus was that Andrews's early television ads had been helpful.[32] He was encouraged by this recent recovery.

> Things are looking up. I gained 24 points in the last poll. When the first poll came out I was 34 points behind Byron Dorgan. He was just coming off an all-out election campaign. . . . Now, in the second poll, it's been cut to 11 points, and it will keep coming down as he gets further away from his campaign.

He explained the first poll primarily in terms of disadvantages faced by any senator running against an incumbent House member.

> Bob Dole came up to me after the [March] poll and said to me, "Mark, your problem is that you are too liberal. You voted against the rest of the Republicans and the president too often. You should vote with us more." I said to him, "Bob, you're crazy. You should take a look at how well you run against [Rep.] Dan Glickman in Glickman's own district." Well, he did, and it turned out that Glickman beat Dole worse than Dorgan beats me. A congressman always runs better against the senator in the congressman's own district.

Even if Andrews was right, however, state size made a large difference between Dole's situation and his own. There were four other congressional districts in Kansas in which Senator Dole could make up ground in a head-to-head contest with Representative Glickman. Andrews, on the other hand, had no place else to go for support. He and Dorgan represented identical geographical constituencies. If Dorgan had been doing a better job of cultivating support within its boundaries, Andrews could be at a serious disadvantage in a head-to-head contest.

It was not state size that dominated Andrews's explanation of the first poll. It was another House-Senate institutional explanation— involving the inherent advantages of the House electoral cycle over the Senate electoral cycle for the business of cultivating constituency support. Andrews's idea was that the two-year cycle provided an automatic discipline that kept House members in touch with constituency thinking, whereas the six-year cycle relaxed that discipline.

> The congressman runs twice while the senator is not running at all. That's a big advantage. A student who gets one report

card at the end of the semester is a lot worse off than one who gets several grades during the semester. The more often you get graded, the more you learn how you are doing. Some people say it's easier to be a senator than to be a congressman. That's flat wrong. It's much harder to be a senator.

To the absence of a biennial report card, Andrews might well have added the absence of the biennial publicity generated by a campaign.

In his study of media coverage of selected Senate campaigns, Mark Westlye discovered that in 1976, Mark Andrews's House reelection campaign generated more newspaper coverage in North Dakota than did the reelection campaign of the incumbent U.S. senator during the same period. This was true even though the Andrews campaign was lopsided and easy. In 1974, Andrews's more difficult campaign had produced as many headlines as—though less total coverage than—the other incumbent senator's reelection campaign of that year.[33] Campaign-induced publicity surges of this sort give the incumbent House member a chance every two years to speak his or her mind, explain his or her actions, and reinforce favorable voter recognition. If the unpaid newspaper coverage does not do all that the candidate might like in this regard, the candidate will make certain that his or her paid media advertising does.

One of Andrews's veteran consultants believed that "five years without paid media" had seriously hurt his client.

> There was no change in what he did. But I think people got used to seeing him campaign every other year. When he didn't do it, they saw it as getting out of touch. We can't discount the effort of having five weeks of paid TV every two years and more weeks of paid radio. It meant that physically the congressman was there; and his absence was noticeable. We urged him to do video reports each year, but he thought it would be interpreted as too political.

"Whatever people thought about him," he added optimistically, " we could have changed if we had been able to dump media on them."

Successful House members-turned-senators find ways to compensate for the loss of their biennial report cards and their biennial publicity surges. When he first entered the Senate, Mark Andrews had professed his love of campaigning and vowed to campaign just as much as he always had. His later complaint about the absence of a biennial report card could be read as a tacit admission that he had not campaigned as much as he had intended and, consequently, that he was not, at that point, as closely in touch with his North Dakota constituency as was Byron Dorgan. In October, a top Republican party official had commented that Andrews "was the originator of all these town meetings across North Dakota when he was a congressman. His problem is that he hasn't had much of a chance to get back to the state as often during the last several years." [34]

The senator seemed willing to concede that he had not maintained his congressman's level of attentiveness to home. But he also took the view that the perception was worse than the facts. "When I first got elected," he reflected,

> I spent most of my time looking after Mary and I don't think I paid as much attention to the North Dakota operation as I should have.... Several of the editors said the reason [for the first poll] was that I just hadn't been around enough. So we checked and we found that I had been in Grand Forks twenty-one of the last twenty-four months. The problem was that no one knew about it. I would meet with fifty people, but the word never got out that I was there. The staff wasn't doing their job. So I had to clean out the staff.

That meant firing his field director, the person who managed his four-office, seven-person North Dakota staff and directed his constituency operation at home. He did.

In late 1985, Andrews made a personal effort to repair whatever the reality or the perception of his inattentiveness might be. First and foremost that meant courting the party faithful. One of the party organizers hired after the March poll explained.

> After the big defeat of 1984 ... Mark was the only statewide official left. There was a tendency to focus the blame on him—not directly but just because he was there. When the March poll came out, the party had sunk even lower. When I first started meeting with party leaders in Bismarck ... they were down on him. Secretary of State Ben Meier wrote a scathing letter against Mark saying that he was too liberal, that he opposed Reagan too much. But since the September poll, I noticed a big change of attitude in our meetings. Now Ben Meier says, 'We've got to get behind him.' They are just now beginning to come around to help him. It took a long time for their attitude to change.

It was, he concluded, an attitude strengthened by desperation. "If the party does not work together and we lose this election, we will become a Democratic state and we will be a long time recovering."

He went on to say that Andrews's own efforts had helped bring about that change.

> He knew he hadn't been around the state as much as he used to be. In March and April he went to the largest cities in the state

and talked to all the people we knew.... 'Tell me what you hear, what's wrong, tell me what I can do better.' People liked that. They had never seen him open up like that. It helped a lot in bringing party people back behind him.

The change in party attitude was a reason to be optimistic, said Andrews when we talked.

The senator also set the context for his campaign in terms of the party's crushing defeat in its most recent effort.

The Republican party was nearly wiped out in the 1984 election. We lost the governorship and all but two statewide offices. When the poll came out showing me 35 points behind, it shocked the party people.... People who thought I was a horse's ass, began to realize that I was their horse's ass, that I was the most important elected official they had. So they got up off the mat and started to work. George Bush came here in May, and we had the biggest party rally in North Dakota history.

As Andrews spoke, he was on his way to a small luncheon in Cooperstown to recruit campaign workers.

About twenty people joined Andrews for lunch and political talk at a local restaurant. He discussed his own race, but tied it to the welfare of the party whenever he could. He emphasized the perilous state of republicanism in North Dakota since 1984, but he described the situation as one that could be turned around. He told them, for example, of the promising effort underway—and financed by $60,000 of his own campaign money—to upgrade the statewide, computerized voter identification program. While it would help to get out the vote for him in 1986, it would also be of great long-term benefit to party revival in the state's own 1986 elections. Andrews spoke optimistically about his own race.

Party polls showed that when you combined the positives and the negatives, my ranking was fourth best among all twenty-two Republicans running for reelection. And yet Dorgan was even higher. He's never been pushed hard or had any strong competition. He's *never done anything* and yet he was 35 points ahead of me. That has come down to 11 points now. And it will keep coming down. The first poll was taken right after he had made an all out effort to get reelected and had been everywhere in the state.

He added, "You can't pick your opponent, but it might be best for me to run against Dorgan—the toughest opponent—so that our people will get out and work hard and we can prove how strong we are." There was nothing of the maverick Republican here—only an incumbent in trouble who knew he would have to pull the party together and energize it if he were to win reelection.

Andrews gave the party political ammunition to use against Dorgan, beginning with his own exploits on farm legislation.

> Target price is the name of the game now. I got us a sweetheart deal on a target price for wheat. But feed grains—uh, uh. I figured wheat was more important to North Dakota than feed grains. [Everyone nodded.] I worked with Bob Dole. He's from Kansas, the only state that grows more wheat than North Dakota. I don't think the president will veto a bill with Bob Dole's name on it. I made such a racket on wheat that they must have figured if they got me, they'd win.

It was a vintage description of a vintage Andrews legislative maneuver on behalf of North Dakota. His listeners seemed to appreciate it. He went on to tell them that the target prices in the bill Byron Dorgan had supported were not as favorable for wheat farmers as the prices he had negotiated.

His listeners reminded him how tough an opponent Dorgan would be. The local International Harvester dealer spoke up. "Dorgan is always in the papers. People think he's doing things. . . . You should get in the papers all you can." Everybody nodded again. This was not news to Andrews. He had recognized it, worried about it, and made sporadic efforts to compete with it from the beginning. But he had apparently not succeeded. When the March poll results came out, Andrews had already fired the press secretary he had hired in 1982. He had only recently hired a new one, and that press secretary would soon be gone, too. Andrews did not directly answer the farm implement dealer.

> Dorgan has never done anything. In four years, he did not get one cent appropriated for the Garrison project. We put the money in the Senate, but we never got one penny in the House. *He's never done anything.*

No one argued with him.

Andrews's oblique reply to the farm implement dealer reflected both an acknowledgment of Dorgan's public relations skill and a belief that in the final analysis getting things done in Congress was what really mattered—and he was prepared to pit his legislative prowess against Dorgan's publicity prowess. Andrews believed that in such a contest he would win, and comments from staffers during the trip confirmed this view. Describing Andrews's initial reaction to the March poll, a top member of his North Dakota staff said, "He couldn't understand it. He thought he had done so much for the state and had gotten so much for the state that: 'How could they feel that way about me?' "

The campaign staff person who organized the luncheon in Cooperstown commented afterward on the prospect of an Andrews-Dorgan race. "Everybody I talk to thinks it would be as close as you can get, but that in the end Andrews would win because of all he has done for [North Dakota]." However discouraging the April poll results might have been on this score, Andrews and his campaigners were operating on the assumption that there was or could be created, a close, positive connection between governing style and electoral payoffs.

In November 1985, no one knew whether Byron Dorgan would run for the Senate or not. Some of Andrews's optimistic and tough public talk was designed to make Dorgan think twice about running. At the same time, an opinion being expressed in newspapers around the state was that Dorgan should not run for the Senate in 1986. The belief was that an Andrews-Dorgan contest would cost North Dakota one of its two first-rate, popular public servants, and the state could not afford such a loss.

The original, publicly available March poll had showed what Andrews's own April poll had showed—Dorgan ranked higher, but both officeholders had highly favorable ratings. In the March State Poll, Dorgan's approval/disapproval rating had been 63 percent to 3 percent, while Andrews's had been 54 percent to 17 percent. In May, Andrews leaked his April poll result showing that 74 percent of the state's voters preferred one senator from each party. In November, a poll of subscribers to ten rural newspapers, the North Dakota Poll, asked people how they felt about an Andrews-Dorgan contest—"good," "a mistake," or "no opinion." Fifty percent said, "a mistake," and 33 percent, "good." Wrote columnist Dobson, "the full message of the poll seems to be: We like you Byron but don't run against Mark." [35]

Editorial writers in the *Forum* (Fargo), *Williston Herald, Beulah Beacon, Walsh County Press,* and *Grand Forks Herald* voiced the same conclusion.[36] In a column suggesting that Dorgan not run, the editor of the *Grand Forks Herald* editorial page summed up the argument.

> North Dakota could be better off if Dorgan stays in the House and Andrews stays in the Senate. . . . If all we've been hearing about the dismal rural economy is right, North Dakota simply can't afford a full blown battle for a Senate seat. Nor, with the rural political bloc eroding as it has been in Washington, can North Dakota afford to lose either of the two able members of Congress it now has in Dorgan and Andrews. . . . As far as North Dakota's general interests go, what's the sense of having our two crackerjack politicians go for each other's throats. . . . The bottom line is that both Dorgan and Andrews do a pretty fair job representing the people back home.[37]

Everyone's proposed solution was that Dorgan should replace the aging Quentin Burdick in 1988. Whether or not such sentiments would affect Dorgan, they did bring out an underlying appreciation of Mark Andrews as a public servant. The *Walsh County Press* commentary, from a staunch Democrat and Dorgan admirer, said: "Andrews has shown me a lot of moxie and brains in the last two or three years [and] has been representing me good enough. . . . Senator Andrews ain't that bad a guy for us people of North Dakota. I've been quite impressed by the way he's been sticking up for this state."[38] It was a picture of himself that the farmer-senator would recognize and embrace.

The luncheon I attended in Cooperstown was sandwiched between two community forums, in the morning at Lakota (pop. 900) and in the afternoon at Cooperstown (pop. 1,200). As we flew into Lakota, the senator articulated the trip's rationale.

> This is a Democratic town. It's Farmers Union country. But they vote for me by about 70 percent. It's not a very big town, but if you neglect towns like this, you'll be in big trouble. They want to see you. If you don't come, they'll say, "He spends all his time in Fargo and Bismarck."

He reminisced about his last visit to each town—the heavy rainstorm in Lakota two months earlier, the rally which the governor had left without shaking hands in Cooperstown two years earlier. In Cooperstown, he circled the Griggs County Courthouse twice, explaining how he held office hours in the courtroom there meeting constituents one by one when he was in the House, and how he dedicated it in 1974. "I know all the courthouses because I met constituents there for twenty years." Since he had been in the Senate, that old system had meant "too many people, too little time." And so he had substituted community forums.

The two forums reminded me of my experience in Lehr, except that they were a little larger—forty and thirty people, respectively—a little more formal, and a little more focused on the current plight of the farmers. The *Griggs County Sentinel Courier* summarized the Cooperstown forum:

> The forum touched on such topics as military spending, health care costs, a freeze in government spending, Great Plains coal gassification plant and social security, *but always the questions and discussion returned to the subject of farm problems.* (Emphasis added.)[39]

At Lakota, Andrews fielded questions such as:

- "We've had farm programs for fifty years. I've been a farmer all my life, and the farmers are in worse condition than when

we started. So how is a new farm program going to help?"
- "Is the credit system slipping into socialism?"
- "How are we going to clean up the tank cars so our grain won't get so dirty?"
- "Us young guys are having a hell of a time. How do we get a price for a product?"
- "Will it all go corporate agriculture?"
- "Why don't we export processed cereal so we can add the extra value ourselves?"
- "How do we cut everything out of there that allows the farmers to farm the program?"
- "What do we do in the short term to help family farmers who are overleveraged? How do we keep them on the farm?"
- "Why do we forgive loans to other countries like Mexico and subsidize Egypt?"
- "Why should we feed Russia grain and help our enemies?"

Andrews answered them all in a careful and knowledgeable way, not playing to prejudices against foreign aid, and trying to be constructive and informative whenever possible.

As far as I could tell—and this was my main preoccupation at both events—the sense of identification between Andrews and his constituents was as strong as it had been in Lehr six years earlier. They treated him as if they valued his ideas and his representation; he treated them as if he understood their problems and was working hard to alleviate them. "My corn froze just the way your corn froze," he said in Lakota. "That was the biggest mess I ever saw, 35 percent moisture in corn." "I like to think people in North Dakota, Republicans and Democrats, elect me because I am a farmer and I understand farm problems," he said minutes later. To which a farmer replied "You aren't using farming as a tax write-off?" To which Andrews exclaimed, "I sure am not!" And a few minutes later came the comment, "When you were farming, things were going good." He replied, "I'm still farming; I know things are a lot worse than in the '50s and '60s."

There seemed to be no exaggerated or mismatched expectations on either side. The constituents did not expect easy solutions; the senator did not expect any letup in their tough questions. When he asked for a show of hands on various questions, their sentiment accorded with his actions in Washington. In neither forum—nor at any other public function—was there the slightest hint of any interest in or opinion of his lawsuit. At one point in Lakota, Andrews commented in passing "I had to sell some land to pay for Mary's illness." That was all. Some private thoughts, undoubtedly, were kept private.

He kept to twin themes in both meetings: "Good ideas don't come from Washington, they come from right here in North Dakota." "I'm casting your vote, not mine. If you were down there, what would you do? Tell me so I can do it." He opened up each meeting with a detailed reminiscence of his last visit to the town and the county. Briefly, he gave his views on the deficit and the farm bill currently in the Senate before opening up for questions. His remarks on the deficit were keyed to a six dollar tractor part which a farmer presented to him in Lakota with the question: "Why in the dickens are we buying parts that are made in Japan? Can't we make 'em ourselves?"

It's nice when your friends bring you your props. It makes the point of what's wrong with our economy today. This part can be made in Japan and shipped over here and sold cheaper than it can be made right in this country. Part of the reason is the fact that our dollar is 35 percent higher in value than the yen, and that's killing us—from the standpoint of making this part in the United States or from the standpoint of those of us who raise wheat and have to export. Three out of every five bushels of grain you produce have to find a market in a foreign country, and when our dollar's 35 percent more valuable than it ought to be, it just prices us out of the market. How did we get that way? Well, we got that way because of spending, deficits, all the rest. That $184 billion deficit last year, we weren't willing to finance ourselves. In fact we had to go out hat in hand or tin cup in hand and ask foreigners to cover $83 billion worth of that deficit. How do you get them to do it? Well, not just by saying please. You get them to do it by kiting interest rates and having a superpowered dollar. And that ruins us in agriculture because the two things we need in farming are lower interest rates and higher prices for our products. . . . That's why I introduced a balanced budget proposal calling for a budget freeze across the board.

Regarding the farm bill, his opening remarks elaborated on the package he had mentioned at lunch. "Dole and the rest of us kind of put together a package" he told his listeners.

This is the package that has now been voted on once in a test vote and has survived. It's kind of interesting. For 1986, wheat prices would be $4.38 if you set aside 20 percent [of your land]. You set aside 30 percent, they'd be $4.85. If you set aside 40 percent, they'd be $5.50. It continues into 1987 [and 1988] and drops off in 1989. . . . You can have your own vote in your farm kitchen and decide what you are going to do, and you get a better target price if you set aside more land. . . . In three years we're going to know whether agriculture's working its way out or whether we've got to revisit. I think it's a pretty good bridge. . . . So we are making some progress, not enough, but moving in the right direction.

In Cooperstown, people kept coming back to the plan. Each time, the senator became more expansive about his own activity as an inside Senate player and more forthcoming about his views. One lengthy exchange near the end went as follows:

CITIZEN A: Do you really, honestly, senator, do you believe you'll be able to raise the support price on these grains with the budget problem? There seems to be a great budget problem.

SENATOR ANDREWS: I don't know whether we got Dole in a weak moment, but this is it. This was put in; it's got his name on it. In fact we put it together Thursday night late and he said, "Do you want your name up there next to mine?" I said, "No way. You put mine up there, they're all going to think there's something suspect about it. . . ." Now, remember Harkin and Dorgan, they were going to set aside 50 percent to get $5.25. Heck, we got $5.50 for 40 percent set aside. . . . Whether we're going to get it through, I don't know. . . . They say they're going to veto it. But can you imagine the fun things they're going to have advising the president to veto the thing that the majority leader has his name on. . . . That's what you send me down for is to negotiate. I think we negotiated a pretty good package.

CITIZEN B: On that bill, where will the opposition come from, if there's opposition?

SENATOR ANDREWS: Well, when people wake up and start reading it, I think they're going to say "Hey, what . . . it doesn't track feed grains. Feed grains got to go down. Rice goes down. Cotton freezes in 1986 and then goes down in the out years. Wheat's the one that's got the stuff." Quite frankly, they needed to get two or three of us to come along with them; and they did a special good deal for wheat. As far as I'm concerned, I think I know North Dakota, and North Dakota needs wheat. Our feed grain price support is not nearly as important. Our wheat price support is where it's at and that's why we've got it. I don't know. I think we've got a better than 50-50 chance of keeping it. But those figures, I showed them to young Mark out at the farm. . . . and he said, "Dad, you must have waved your magic wand. I haven't heard anything like that for a long time." But it's not bad.

CITIZEN C: Is there going to be any dollar or bushel limitation per farm?

SENATOR ANDREWS: A $50,000 payment limitation, same one that we had in the past [with] a provision to preclude hobby farming by the guy who's the banker in town or the head of a plant in St.

Louis. . . . But all this in and of itself isn't going to be enough. I think if farmers are given a $4.50 per bushel target price for wheat, I think we can kind of hold it together if we get good crops—but only if interest rates go down. So what I'm saying is we have to address the issue of the deficit. And we've got to get away from these politicians who make these great speeches of "Elect me and I'll cut back this foreign aid and we're going to get these deficits under control." The whole foreign aid budget is only $13 billion. The deficit is $180 billion. So it isn't going to be done that way. You've got to hold down defense spending. You've got to freeze entitlements. You've got to get an across-the-board freeze, and you're going to have to get some revenue enhancement from the people who are using these loopholes. We can do it; we have shown the way. Your North Dakota delegation, Quent Burdick and I, voted for that freeze. Neither one of us have voted to freeze Social Security if everything else isn't frozen. We balk at that. . . . Defense could stand it. Just as when I talked earlier on, good ideas come from North Dakota, not Washington. That little farmer concept of the warranty in the defense system is now the law, and we're saving $18 billion a year. Just because I figured if I can get a warranty on my Allison transmission on an M-1 tank. . . . These ideas that we generate from meetings like this, they work. They are working; they're saving us money.

In this exchange Andrews presented himself as someone who was working both to get the best possible short-term deal for the wheat farmers and to help agriculture in the long run by reducing the deficit. He presented himself as an active legislator with a thorough view of the needs of his state. He was beginning to campaign, as he had said he would, "as a legislative infighter who is independent of the Reagan administration and able to protect home-state interests." [40]

The forums at Lakota and Cooperstown took place in the context of increasingly hard times on the farm. That same month, a series of articles on "North Dakota's ailing farm economy" in the *Forum* concluded:

Dropping commodity prices, overproduction, declining land values, the strong dollar and high interest rates have cut into profits and driven some farmers out of the business. As many as 8,000 of the state's 35,000 farmers have a negative cash flow. [41]

In both forums, discussion centered on farm credit problems and on the current request of the privately managed Farm Credit System (FCS) for a multibillion dollar federal government bailout to maintain its lending capacity. [42] The sense of both meetings was critical of the FCS for its own management extravagances and wary of any bailout that would give advantages to farmers in debt to FCS as opposed to farmers who had obtained credit elsewhere. Andrews raised several questions in Lakota about how to keep farmers on the land while ensuring the equitable treatment of those in debt. But there seemed to be no consensus. He admitted to them, "I don't have any answer I'm comfortable about" in dealing with farmers forced to quit. There was agreement among citizens and senator that the eventual solution to the farm problem depended less on credit than on better prices and higher income. The solution was left for him to work out.

There was much speculation brewing among national political observers in 1985 that conditions in the farm states would pose serious problems for Republican incumbents in the 1986 Senate elections. In articles with headlines like "Reagan Farm Policy Makes Political Fodder in the Midwest," "Incumbency May Save Farmbelt GOP Senators," and "Mood of Rural Midwest Keeps GOP on Edge," political reporters weighed the power of incumbency against the electoral force of a dominating regional issue. As one journalist wrote in November:

> Already, Democratic rhetoric reflects the belief that farmers will take out their frustrations with President Reagan's farm policy on the GOP. Farm state Republicans counter that while the mood back home may be turning ugly, their well publicized agitation on the farmer's behalf should be enough to ward off attacks on GOP candidates.[43]

In his local meetings, Andrews was picking up plenty of dissatisfaction. As we left the Lakota meeting, Andrews exclaimed: "Boy, they sure are down on the Farm Credit System. You'd sure know there was a farm problem. They don't want to talk about anything else." The farm revolt question had to be a large and continuing one for the incumbent as he contemplated his forthcoming campaign.

In November, despite his position in the polls, there were positive indications for the campaign. There was his own feel for farmer sentiment after face-to-face meetings. "The main thing is," he said after the Cooperstown meeting, "that you want to see how friendly they are. I had a good feeling from both meetings. People aren't blaming me for the farm problem—and they will know I came." His prospective opponent showed no inclination to blame him either. "If I run," stated Dorgan, "the race won't be on farm policy, but on Mark Andrews and Byron Dorgan. There are not a lot of major differences between us." [44] As Andrews's private polls showed, of course, Dorgan had outflanked Andrews on every nonpolicy performance measure offered to the voters.

Evidence of Andrews's constructive efforts to help the farmer continued to accumulate. The week after I left, the *Forum* in Fargo carried a long, laudatory front page story taken from the *New York Times*—about his efforts on the farm bill. Under the headline "Farmers Count Thrice in Andrews' Priorities," the article by *Times* Capitol Hill correspondent Steven Roberts said, in part:

> The North Dakota Republican has three items at the top of his priority list: farmers, farmers, and farmers. . . . Andrews played a key role earlier in fashioning a farm bill that the Reagan administration strongly opposed, calling it a budget busting boondoggle . . . [and] last month, the North Dakotan helped lead the fight against efforts to trim it, and his side prevailed by three votes. "I've been around a long time," said Andrews. . . . "They know where I'm coming from. I'm trying to beat them if I can, and I did." [45]

Comments from his Senate colleagues elaborated on his single-mindedness. "He's just the same old Mark he's always been," said one. "He thinks the budget really doesn't pertain to agriculture." [46] He could hardly have asked for a more helpful portrayal.

When the Senate finally passed the farm bill at the end of November, Andrews extracted one last side payment from the majority leader. "In a final bow to Andrews," wrote one observer, "Dole added $35-per-acre payments to sunflower producers, most of whom are in North Dakota." Back home, the senator claimed credit for engineering another bargain on behalf of his constituents. "That's $73 million for North Dakota," he told a group in Dickinson. "If they're going to do it for soy beans, we ought to do it for sunflowers." He explained his support for the Senate bill: "It isn't a perfect bill, but I think we've come as close as we could to a good bill." [47]

This pattern—a quid pro quo bargain struck, followed by support for the end product—exemplified, once again, Mark Andrews's governing style. He would work stubbornly and skillfully to get everything he could by manipulating the legislative process; and he would, in the end, respect the results of that process. When the 1985 farm bill finally emerged from conference and was signed by the president, Andrews's sliding scale for target prices on wheat and his subsidy for sunflowers had been deleted. But, true to his acceptance of the legislative process, he supported the final product. "I have never yet voted for a farm bill that was good enough in my estimation," he told the Senate. "Yet I have voted for every farm bill that came along because it represents the very best product that we could put together. This [bill] again, Mr. President, is the best product we could put together." [48] He played the game hard and he accepted the outcome—as he always had done.

As he once told me:

When I first came to Congress—a young guy all fired up—Page Belcher [R-Okla., ranking Republican on the House Agriculture Committee] said to me, "Don't ever vote for a farm bill. No matter how good they are, they aren't good enough. It will be much easier for you if you vote against it. Then go home and say it should have been better." Well, I never did that. I always voted for the farm bill because there were so many things in there for North Dakota. North Dakota needed it. With nothing at all, you'd have to go back to the Organic Act, and then North Dakota would be kicked in the ass.

As I reflected on what I had seen of Mark Andrews in his home state since his election—in 1982 and 1985—it was hard to imagine a more determined, more consistent partisan of American agriculture. On the other hand, Mark Andrews was not a crusader. From the beginning, at Lehr, he traded on competence and respect rather than inspiration and direction. He never delivered a lot of emotion to his listeners; and he had never sought or commanded a high public profile. He was first and foremost a legislator; and he emphasized his legislative business when he talked to his constituents. His businesslike performance at Lehr, the contrast with Dorgan during their joint 1982 appearance, and his low-key performance in his 1985 community forums were all cases in point. The contrast suggested, however, a possible vulnerability, that Andrews might be thought of as too much the legislator and too little the ideological crusader, too much the establishment insider and not enough the antiestablishment outsider.

Listening to him, the thought recurred that, in terms of North Dakota's special political tradition, Andrews might be leaving himself vulnerable to an opponent who delivered a broad, populist, grass-roots, "us little guys against them big guys" message. And Byron Dorgan looked like just that kind of an opponent. Political writers in Washington who searched the United States for examples of populism—defined as "the voice of ordinary citizens against the impersonal institutions of society"—found North Dakota to be "unusually fertile ground for a modern populist" and found Byron Dorgan to be the exemplary populist.[49]

In the words of one journalist: "The state has a populist past that has never really died out and a suspicion of powerful economic interests bubbles just under the surface among its farmers and ranchers, small town businessmen and laborers." The author described Byron Dorgan as "perhaps the Democratic party's most visible and articulate symbol of [left-of-center] populist thinking." He quoted Dorgan: "People out there feel powerless because they're preyed upon by bigger interests. . . . The farmers that I know . . . are the Johnsons and the Olsons and the Larsens.

I don't want to see farmers that are named Chevron, Tenneco and Prudential."[50]

On the campaign trail, another journalist commented:

Dorgan knows ... the awesome power that populism still holds as a means of building and maintaining a political career. Talking to his rural constituents ... all across his state, Dorgan pounds away at Eastern bankers, the Federal Reserve lawyers, agribusinesses, the railroads and all the large institutional enemies Midwestern populists have fought since the turn of the century.[51]

In his 1984 campaign brochure, the congressman presented himself as the keeper of the populist flame: "The *Washington Post* called Byron 'a prairie populist straight from the tradition of [Sens.] William Langer (R-N.D.) and Hubert Humphrey [D-Minn.]. He makes good sense and he also makes waves!'" Dorgan could, and he later did, ostentatiously eschew locally beneficial pork barrel projects, in pursuit of a larger vision—and receive credit for it back home.[52]

To be sure, Mark Andrews had imbibed some of the populist tradition, too. His emphasis on a "commonsense" approach to problems, his theme that "good ideas come from North Dakota, not Washington" suggested it. And he certainly did his share of attacking various special interests. He could scarcely contain his delight over his successful battles with big institutions—with the Burlington Northern Railroad over branchline abandonment and with the Pentagon over his defense warranty law. Indeed, national political reporters attributed his defense warranty bill to "a prairie populist's skepticism" or to "genuine prairie populism."[53]

Some local observers, however, found the label wide of the mark;[54] and my reaction was the same. For one thing, Andrews never used explicit "us against them," "little guy, big guy" rhetoric. Indeed, one of the "dislikes" in the April poll was the assertion—among a small minority—characterized in statements like: "He helps the big businesses more than the smaller ones," "He's more in favor of big industry than the little guys," and "I don't think he supports the middle class, he's more for the high class." He did not champion "the little guy" by regularly attacking "the big guys." He was known as a big farmer, not a small one. And his big farmer, wealthy farmer image had almost surely hurt him in the matter of the malpractice suit.

More important, from the perspective of our study, Mark Andrews was too much of an inside player, too accepting of the negotiating and compromising governmental process to adopt a full-blown outsider, antiestablishment mentality. A more accurate label for Andrews would be simply "independent," "maverick," or, as one reporter called him, "all-purpose maverick." [55] One electoral question, however, was whether the incumbent might have become vulnerable to an argument made by a populist-style challenger that this Washington legislator was not as close to ordinary people as his challenger might be.

The question seemed worth pondering in 1985 because of the kind of criticism of Andrews that surfaced in North Dakota in the wake of the March poll. Explanations of the poll results picked up some threads of criticism we noted in the early reaction to Andrews's activities in the lawsuit and in the Garrison Diversion matter—that he had "alienated" or "offended" some of his constituents and that he had "assumed godlike powers." These 1984 scorekeeping hints that Andrews might be getting somewhat out of touch fed the same 1985 post-poll suggestion. "While Andrews has been one of the state's most effective legislators in Washington," wrote one editor in June:

> he has neither the charisma of Byron nor the strong committed political base of his junior in Congress. A good share of Andrews backers have been less than enthusiastic about the Mapleton Farmer ever since his political career began. And now those people particularly appear to be leaving him. [56]

This argument, that Andrews's acknowledged legislative prowess might not be sufficient to hold constituent support was, if true, particularly troublesome. And in the April poll, we recall, there was plenty of evidence that it might be true—at least if the challenger were Dorgan.

The thought that Andrews might be vulnerable to an ideological populist broadside could be extended to another thought about vulnerability—that he might be coming across to voters as too much the piecemeal producer of pork and too little the bearer of some larger message. As Chapter 3 demonstrates, his established reputation as "one of the state's most effective legislators in Washington" went well beyond his proven devotion to agriculture to embrace the cornucopia of benefits he delivered to his North Dakota constituency. Our working assumption has been that his constituents expected nothing less. After all, that is precisely the kind of performance they had been rewarding at the polls for more than twenty years. We assume that they did expect him to "bring home the bacon" and that he struck a pleasing chord when he accepted the title "King of Pork." Once he became vulnerable, however, the question arose whether even his pork barrel prowess might yet be insufficient to pull him through at election time. The possibility arose that—in the presence of Byron Dorgan's outstandingly popular political style—keeping in touch might require more than producing home state legislative benefits.

In August, the *Grand Forks Herald,* the state's second largest paper, raised exactly this possibility by launching a frontal attack on Mark Andrews's legislative activity. In an editorial entitled "Andrews' Secret Deals," the paper sharply criticized his negotiations in Washington on Garrison Diversion and on North Dakota's coal gassification plant as "practicing a curious kind of statecraft . . . secret deals affecting the state's future [which] left others to carry out their terms." The editorial said, in part:

> We have to wonder about how the deals were made and about the political judgment of the man who made them. These secret deals haven't won the senator any political friends, since he left the hard task of making them work to others. . . . Still, he claimed credit in both cases. . . . It looks as if Andrews enjoys throwing his weight around. *Political effectiveness is more than the ability to cut deals in Washington,* however. It requires carrying through on the deals. *And it requires getting along with the home folks.* In both of the secret deals Andrews made, the home folks deserved the courtesy of being informed, even if they could not be involved in the deal making. (Emphasis added.)[57]

The editorial was the harshest kind of indictment since it took his two most important assets, "political effectiveness" and "getting along with the home folks," and interpreted them as potential deficiencies. The paper was suggesting, if not asserting, the proposition that Mark Andrews's governing style was making a sizable contribution to his electoral vulnerability.

Not surprisingly, the *Herald's* editorial produced a quick and detailed reply from the senator, who called it fiction.[58] Whoever was right on the facts, the willingness—indeed, the eagerness—of the paper's leaders to strike so directly at the heart of Andrews's political image indicates either that he had grown apart from his constituents or that his newfound vulnerability made him fair game for everyone or that he was an increasingly tempting target for this particular paper.[59] Whatever the case, the wound was real. To the degree that the editorial played down his senatorial accomplishments and played up his distance from "the home folks," it softened him up for an opponent who would claim the very closeness to North Dakota that the Washington dealmaker was said to have abandoned. It also pointed up the special necessity for a Washington dealmaker to rely on constituents' trust. An open, continuously communicative legislative style provides the opportunity, at least, for interested constituents to observe. A less visible style must rely more on the willingness of constituents to believe in the value of the deals. As long as the willingness exists, the legislator is safe. Once it begins to be questioned, in the manner of the *Grand Forks Herald*, its fragility is exposed and undermined.

The idea that anyone could credibly argue that Mark Andrews was out of touch had heretofore seemed to me to be utterly preposterous. My 1985 visit to North Dakota, however, caused me to reconsider my Lehr-based assumptions and to modify my views—and not only because of the poll results or because of the *Herald*'s critical editorial opinion. A change in my own firsthand observations also suggested a degree of vulnerability I had not seen in my earlier visits. It is virtually inevitable that in the wake of a downturn in a politician's fortunes some personality-related notions will be offered in explanation. In Andrews's case, the publicity surrounding the March poll seemed to have brought to the surface criticisms concerning his "shyness," or—more strongly—his "aloofness," or—most strongly—his "arrogance." Staff aides who had worked with him over a considerable period of time in North Dakota offered to me—as they had not done in 1980 or 1982—observations to support the picture of a politician who could, indeed, get out of touch with constituents. "People [fellow Republicans] think he's aloof and arrogant," one staff aide said.

> His physical presence makes him seem standoffish. He's a celebrity, and people are reluctant to approach a celebrity. There is also a shyness there. I have to keep reminding him to go and shake hands all around when we enter a room. He's good about it and he's good at it. But he's shy about it, and that makes him standoffish.

Somewhat later, a second staffer said: "People aren't really comfortable around Mark. People in North Dakota expect their officials to sit down with them so they can call them by their first names. People call him 'Mark,' but they aren't sure they should." An editor wrote, after the election, "I never have felt really at ease around him." [60]

I saw a little of that standoffishness at a Republican rally and dinner dance in Valley City. But, since I had never thought that the strength of his constituency relationships depended on a back-slapping, "one of the boys" style, I thought little of it. He did not table-hop, but sat in the corner with Mary, who was in a wheelchair, and waited for people to come up to say hello. He seemed pleased that many did; on the other hand, many did not.

Another of the senator's Fargo aides struck an even more negative note during a discussion of the lawsuit and its reception locally.

> He's very good when he's talking business, whatever the subject. He's bright and quick and impressive. He plays the role

of senator beautifully. He looks and acts like a senator. But he is not good at making small talk. He does not meet people on their own level. He acts like he is above others. He seems arrogant and aloof. He's that way with staff, too. Many people do not like him and never have liked him. He's not popular and he never has been. You can know him as a senator; but to know him as Mark Andrews would be like breaking down the Kremlin wall.... People refer to him as God.

In context, the idea was that the lawsuit reflected his arrogance and that many local people were happy to see him get his comeuppance. The commentary also echoed the notion that he might be a lot less personally popular—locally at least—than his postelectoral victories would indicate. Located at the center of his original House constituency and being his virtual hometown, Fargo had long been a crucial element in his electoral base.

The undercurrent of criticism I encountered during my 1985 visit had been totally absent from my visits of 1980 and 1982. The April poll indicates clearly that it was present among the citizenry, too, in late 1985. Perhaps the criticism had been there in earlier years, and I had not seen it. More likely, I think, the criticism had grown and come into the open as Andrews became first publicly controversial and then publicly vulnerable. First came the lawsuit and Garrison, then the March poll. And these events, we now know, occurred well *after* the first blossoming of the voters' love affair with Byron Dorgan.

We might conclude that a little perceived vulnerability is a dangerous thing. Once recognized, vulnerability encourages criticism, suggesting an even greater vulnerability, encouraging further criticism, and so on. Editorial writers and staffers conceded Andrews's prowess as a working senator but had begun to question whether these abilities outweighed certain political or personal faults. Thus, even strength gets pushed aside in a concentration on weakness—which is, no doubt, why politicians work so hard to create impressions of invincibility.

Whatever the dynamic, the March poll results, the ensuing public interpretations, and the undercurrent of private criticism forced me, at the end of 1985, to acknowledge the fact that Mark Andrews—a man whom I had previously thought to be solidly entrenched as "one of us" at home and solidly productive as "working for us" in Washington—was in serious electoral difficulty. I had at that point no knowledge of the stylistic insufficiencies that had been revealed in the Andrews-Dorgan comparisons in the polls of December 1983 and April 1985. Even so, I had been forced to entertain the general idea that he was not as closely in touch with his constituents as he needed to be. Up to that point, I could not imagine such a possibility.

Whether Mark Andrews could survive in 1986 had to be treated, now, as an open question.

THE CHALLENGER

If political scientists have learned anything recently about incumbent advantages in congressional elections, they have learned that the quality of the challenger is the threshold requirement for a competitive contest.[61] As political parties and the distribution of constituency party strengths decline in electoral importance, the experience, talent, and presentational capacity of the individual candidates increase in importance. Without a quality challenger running against them, most incumbents will win easily and by a large margin. Incumbents, of course, know this. That is why they work hard between elections to show a degree of political strength that will discourage potentially strong challengers.

In the House of Representatives, this preemptive strategy seems increasingly to work, as ever greater numbers of incumbents win reelection, win by large margins, and run unopposed. The proportion of Senate incumbents following this pattern, however, is markedly smaller. In a typical election year, that is, a higher proportion of senators than House members face strong challengers, win by small margins, and suffer defeat.[62]

In the case of the Senate, the prospect of capitalizing on incumbent vulnerabilities tends to attract quality challengers; and, reciprocally, the perceived vulnerability of an incumbent depends heavily on the presence of a serious and formidable challenger. So it takes time for potential challengers to assess the likelihood of making enough of a difference to turn senatorial vulnerabilities into an individual victory. But until the potentially strong challenger decides, nothing of importance can be said about the reelection contest.

That was the situation in North Dakota in December 1985. Byron Dorgan was, by virtue of his position, a formidable challenger. Poll results seemed to indicate that he could, indeed, turn the incumbent's vulnerabilities into victory. Mark Andrews, who had been preoccupied with the prospect of a Dorgan challenge for four years, geared up for a tough reelection battle. In mid-December, the presumptive challenger announced his surprise decision: he would *not* run for the Senate in 1986. In an instant, Andrews's reelection contest took on a new focus and a new shape. Dorgan, no doubt, had his reasons; but to Andrews he was no longer of interest.[63] The focus shifted to a different potential challenger and to the shape of a race involving him. And a new question supervened: Is Mark Andrews vulnerable only to a challenge from Byron

Dorgan, or does his vulnerability extend to other challengers as well?

Kent Conrad was the thirty-eight-year-old North Dakota state tax commissioner. He had succeeded Byron Dorgan in that position; and he had won three successive statewide elections by huge margins. He was Dorgan's close friend, political ally, and favorite candidate. From the time speculation began, he had been considered a potential challenger, a possible backup if Dorgan did not run. In the March 1985 State Poll, his name, too, had been run head to head against Andrews. But in the months that followed, he and his prospects had been eclipsed by the intensive and suspenseful Dorgan watch. Andrews's own benchmark April poll had been devoted exclusively to Dorgan. When I visited North Dakota in November, Andrews's staffers mentioned Conrad as a likely candidate. Dorgan, they said, had not been raising money. Andrews's consultants were preparing an early December poll that would include both Dorgan and Conrad. So, privately, the odds had begun to change. But, in my two days with him, Andrews talked only of Dorgan. Not once did he mention Conrad's name.

By the standards used in political science, Kent Conrad was a "quality challenger." He held statewide office and he was experienced. From the earliest handicapping nationally, he was viewed, should he run, as "a strong candidate." By local standards, he had a reputation as "a smart, aggressive challenger." In his first and losing challenge, in a race for state auditor in 1976, his tough campaign tactics earned him a reputation within his own party as "Hacksaw" or "Chainsaw" Conrad. As soon as he surfaced nationally, he was described as "mounting an aggressive challenge," as "a hard-charging, fast on his feet challenger," and "an aggressive prairie populist." [64] He may not have been the Democrats' first choice, but his ideological and stylistic preferences were the same as Dorgan's. And he could capitalize, therefore, on the ground-breaking popularity of the congressman. He was, by any reckoning, a challenger to be taken seriously.

He *was* taken seriously. But observers read the polls, and they did not predict that he would win. All the polls showed him trailing. The State Poll had Andrews leading Conrad 57 percent to 32 percent in March 1985, 58 percent to 33 percent in October 1985, and 55 percent to 36 percent in April 1986. An early ranking "from least vulnerable to most vulnerable" placed Andrews as the sixth least vulnerable of the thirty-four Senate seats. A later rough consensus of political professionals picked eleven Republican seats that were "most vulnerable," and Andrews's seat was not among them. In the precampaign speculations of 1986, Conrad was treated as "a long shot" and North Dakota was rated as "leaning Republican." One January handicapper, who rated North Dakota as "likely Republican," wrote: "Private polls do show Andrews as vulnerable, and neither side says Andrews is a shoo-in. Had Conrad been able to enter the race back in August or September, though, Andrews may well have had his hands full." [65]

In head-to-head contests, Andrews's December poll showed him losing to Dorgan by 39 percent to 59 percent but defeating Conrad 66 percent to 28 percent.[66] Other parts of this short survey, however, indicated that voters had not yet fully focused on Conrad, and that when they did, he might show considerable strength. To the degree that people knew him, his ratings were strongly positive. Conrad's favorability/unfavorability ratio was 60 percent to 11 percent, with 29 percent having no opinion. His job rating showed 72 percent approval, 13 percent disapproval, 15 percent no opinion. The comparable figures for Andrews were: opinion favorability 79 percent, 17 percent, 3 percent and job rating approval 83 percent, 15 percent, 2 percent. Andrews's ratings remained strongly positive, but so did Conrad's. Moreover, Conrad had room to grow.

Last, the poll showed that Andrews's reelect number had dropped further—from 47 percent in April to 43 percent in December. And the number favoring a new person stood at 37 percent. For anyone who had followed that interelection trend line, those numbers severely undercut the head-to-head numbers. One person who looked carefully was the prospective new challenger. "The polls showed him clobbering me," said Conrad afterward. "But I looked at the numbers behind the numbers. I looked at his reelect numbers—38 percent [for a new person]—and I knew that he was beatable. I knew I could beat him. I was the only one who thought so." [67]

Kent Conrad's decision to challenge the incumbent senator was not a hasty or ill-considered one. It reflected a degree of calculation and determination that added an immeasurable but crucial increment to challenger quality. For as long as Mark Andrews had served in the U.S. Congress, Kent Conrad had wanted to serve in the Senate. In response to a question put to him long afterward: "How and why did you decide to run?" he answered:

> You would have to start when I was fourteen years old. I came to Washington when Kennedy was president, and I visited the Senate. When I got home, I said that I wanted to be a senator some day; and I figured out that the best time for me to run would be in the late 1980s or early 1990s. Everything I did afterward pointed toward that goal. I decided to start with a statewide office to build up my name recognition, and then to run for the Senate. Which is what I did. I know that sounds crazy, that no one could have that kind of confidence. But I always had the confidence. I believed it was my destiny.... I

lost some races. But I always believed I would win, whenever I ran. I think you have to have that kind of confidence, especially when you were like I was [in the Senate race]. I had absolutely no money, and no one thought I could win.

On January 27, 1986, he formally announced his candidacy for the U.S. Senate. "What would you have done if Dorgan had run for the Senate?" I asked. "I'd have run for the House—but only to get to the Senate." Conrad was no Dorgan. But the experience, plus the ambition, the confidence, and the determination of the new challenger promised a competitive campaign for an incumbent who had shown numerous signs of his vulnerability.

NOTES

1. See Gary Jacobson and Raymond Wolfinger, "Context and Choice in Two Senate Elections" (Paper presented at the Annual Meeting of the American Political Science Association, Chicago, 1987); Richard F. Fenno, Jr., *The United States Senate: A Bicameral Perspective* (Washington, D.C.: American Enterprise Institute, 1982).
2. Four exceptions: Mark Westlye, *Senate Elections and Campaign Intensity* (Baltimore: Johns Hopkins University Press, 1991), chap. 8; Gary Jacobson and Raymond Wolfinger, "Information and Voting in California Senate Elections," *Legislative Studies Quarterly* (November 1989); Edie Goldenberg and Michael Traugott, "Mass Media Effects on Reorganizing and Rating Candidates on U.S. Senate Elections," in *Campaigns in the News: Mass Media and Congressional Elections*, ed. J. P. Vermeer (Connecticut: Greenwood Press, 1987); and John Zaller, "Information and Incumbency Advantage in Congressional Elections" (Paper presented at the Annual Meeting of the American Political Science Association, Washington, D.C., August 1991). Of the four, only Westlye conceptualizes the notion of the prior vulnerability of the incumbent as an analytic variable. He uses it to predict the likelihood of a divisive primary. He measures vulnerability in terms of (1) scandal involvement or old agedness, (2) prior election margin, and (3) ideological distance from the state electorate.
3. Dick Dobson, "Dorgan Picked over Andrews," *Minot Daily News*, March 7, 1985.
4. Dick Dobson, "Andrews Jumped on by Almost Everyone," *Minot Daily News*, March 18, 1985.
5. Ibid.
6. Editorial, "Politics, Pursuit of Damages Just Don't Mix," *McLean County Independent*, June 12, 1985.
7. E. W. Doherty, "Eddy's 4th Estate," *New Rockford Transcript*, March 20, 1985.
8. Dale Wetzel, "Long Political Career May Be at End," *Minot Daily News*, November 6, 1986; Reed Karaim, "His Color, Corn and Contrariness Made Mark a Memorable Player," *Grand Forks Herald*, November 16, 1986.
9. *Bismarck Tribune*, July 3, 1984; see also "6 GOP Moderates Hold Own Platform

Hearings," *Boston Globe*, July 31, 1984.

10. *Jamestown Sun*, August 1, 1984.

11. *Minot Daily News*, August 1, 1984.

12. *Bismarck Tribune*, August 19, 1984.

13. *Bismarck Tribune*, August 26, 1984; "Farmers Take Aim at Interest Rates, Support Prices at Farm Bill Hearing," *Grand Forks Herald*, August 25, 1984; "Interest Rates Top List of Farm Concerns," *Minot Daily News*, August 25, 1984.

14. *Congressional Quarterly Weekly Report*, October 27, 1984, 2789; Greg Sellnow, "White House: Andrews Is Vulnerable," *Bismarck Tribune*, August 8, 1985; William Schneider, "A Year of Continuity," *National Journal*, May 17, 1986; and Jack Germond and Jules Witcover, "The New Senators Intend to Be Heard," *Grand Forks Herald*, November 22, 1986 (see also Dick Dobson, "Mark Andrews Is No Reagan Loyalist," *Minot Daily News*, May 11, 1986).

15. Steven V. Roberts, "Republican Family Feud Deepens as 1986 Looms," *Washington Post*, August 1985.

16. UPI, "Filibuster Threat Hangs over Meese," *Rochester Democrat and Chronicle*, February 20, 1985.

17. Reed Karaim, "Andrews Says USDA Tried to Intimidate," *Grand Forks Herald*, October 30, 1985; Ward Sinclair, "Senate Farmers in a Snit," *Washington Post*, October 29, 1985; AP, "Andrews Says USDA Trying to Intimidate Him," *Jamestown Sun*, October 31, 1985.

18. David Shribman, "Sen. Mark Andrews, a Farm State Republican, May Stray Too Far—Even for a Maverick," *Wall Street Journal*, April 11, 1985.

19. Dobson, "Andrews Jumped on."

20. AP, "Andrews to Run in Senate Race," *Jamestown Sun*, May 8, 1985; Shribman, "Sen. Mark Andrews."

21. Edward Walsh and Helen Dewar, "Farm-Belt Republicans Face Their Own Winter of Discontent," *Washington Post National Weekly Edition*, December 16, 1985; Shribman, "Sen. Mark Andrews."

22. Shribman, "Sen. Mark Andrews."

23. Richard Cohen, "The Two Dakotas," *National Journal*, April 20, 1985; Jeff Meyer (AP), "Andrews' TV Spots Organizational," *Minot Daily News*, June 15, 1985; AP, "It Never Hurts to Be Prepared," *Bismarck Tribune*, March 25, 1985; James McGregor, "Andrews, Dorgan Prepare to Meet Head-On," *Grand Forks Herald*, March 24, 1985; and Cohen, "The Two Dakotas."

24. AP, "It Never Hurts"; McGregor, "Andrews, Dorgan Prepare"; Meyer, "Andrews TV Spots Organizational"; Stuart Rothenberg, "Prime Time Politics: Early Returns on Early Media," *Public Opinion*, February/March 1986; Sidney Blumenthal, "Senate Candidates Rush to Television to Define Their Images," *Washington Post*, July 24, 1986; Dick Dobson, "Poll Fallout," *Jamestown Sun*, October 15, 1985; and Bill Kling, "Senate Race Opens Early with TV Ads for Andrews," October 7, 1985.

25. DMI, *North Dakota Survey* (2 vols.), April 1985.

26. The rest were scattered, with 14 percent voicing negative or no opinion.

27. McGregor, "Andrews, Dorgan Prepare"; Editorial, *Bismarck Tribune*, April 2, 1985; Doherty, "Eddy's 4th Estate"; and editorial from *Emmons County Record*, reprinted in *Bismarck Tribune*, April 28, 1984.

28. Compiled by the author from Clerk of the House reports and Secretary of the Senate reports.

29. Shanto Iyengar and Donald Kinder, *News That Matters* (Chicago: University

of Chicago Press, 1987). See also Jon Krosnick and Donald Kinder, "Altering the Foundations of Support for the President Through Priming," *American Political Science Review* (June 1990).

30. In the April poll, the Garrison project was supported by a 53 percent to 36 percent margin. But it never received more than 1 percent of the mentions in any open-ended question. Those comments produced confusingly divided opinions of Andrews's performance. The project was certainly not the net asset it had once been.

31. The firm was KRC Communications Research. John Robinson, "Bush's Popularity Falls to 16-Month Low of 68%," *Boston Globe*, July 26, 1990. See also Barbara Salmore and Stephen Salmore, *Candidates, Parties, and Campaigns: Electoral Politics in America* (Washington, D.C.: CQ Press, 1989), 116-117.

32. Dobson, "Poll Fallout"; Kling, "Senate Race Opens."

33. Westlye, *Senate Elections and Campaign Intensity*, 56.

34. Kling, "Senate Race Opens."

35. Dick Dobson, "Survey Results Eyed by Andrews, Dorgan," *Minot Daily News*, May 28, 1985; Dobson, "Dorgan Wins but When?" *Jamestown Sun*, November 20, 1985.

36. Dobson, "Survey Results Eyed."

37. Steve Schmidt, "How to Show Appreciation," *Grand Forks Herald*, November 16, 1985.

38. Henry Kelly, "Kelly's Korner," *Walsh County Press*, May 1985.

39. *Griggs County Sentinel Courier*, November 6, 1985.

40. McGregor, "Andrews, Dorgan Prepare."

41. Philip Brasher (AP), "N.D. Economy Must Look to Federal, Overseas Help," *Forum* (Fargo), November 30, 1985.

42. "Farm Bailout Is Hot Issue," *Forum* (Fargo), November 3, 1985.

43. Milton Coleman, "Reagan Farm Policy Makes Political Fodder in the Midwest," *Washington Post*, April 12, 1985; Jack Germond and Jules Witcover, "Incumbency May Save Farmbelt GOP Senators," *National Journal*, March 16, 1985; quotation from Rob Gurwitt, "Mood of Rural Midwest Keeps GOP on Edge," *Congressional Quarterly Weekly Report*, November 16, 1985.

44. Cohen, "The Two Dakotas."

45. Steven Roberts *(New York Times)* "Farmers Count Thrice in Andrews' Priorities," *Forum* (Fargo), November 11, 1985. *The Grand Forks Herald* printed the same story under the title "Andrews Plugs Away on Farm Bill Debate." The paper had it on page 11. This drew Republican complaints and a defense by the editor, Mike Jacobs, "Is Andrews in the Times News in the Herald?" *Grand Forks Herald*, November 11, 1985. "The story only recited Andrews' activity on behalf of farmers—and North Dakotans know about it already."

46. Roberts, "Farmers Count Thrice."

47. David Rapp, "Something-for-Everyone Breaks Impasse on Farm Bill," *Congressional Quarterly Weekly Report*, November 23, 1985; Jay Ulku, "Bill Satisfies Andrews," *Dickinson Press*, November 28, 1985.

48. *Congressional Record*, December 18, 1985, S17945.

49. Alan Ehrenhalt, "Populism Today: The Politics of the 'Little Guy,'" *Congressional Quarterly Weekly Report*, September 17, 1983.

50. Rob Gurwitt, "Left and Right Compete for Populist Mantle," *Congressional Quarterly Weekly Report*, April 21, 1984.

51. Ehrenhalt, "Populism Today."

52. Dan Morgan, "It's Like a Man Biting a Dog: A Lawmaker Turns His Back on

Pork Barrel Politics," *Washington Post National Weekly Edition,* April 2-8, 1990.

53. Pat Towell, "From Senator Andrews, a Populist's Skepticism," *Congressional Quarterly Weekly Report,* March 10, 1984.

54. Mike Jacobs, "Populist Seen from the Potomac," *Grand Forks Herald,* March 31, 1984.

55. Walsh and Dewar, "Farm-Belt Republicans."

56. Editorial, "Politics, Pursuit of Damages Just Don't Mix."

57. Editorial, "Andrews' Secret Deals," *Grand Forks Herald,* August 20, 1985; on the coal gassification plant controversy, see David Lindley, "Congress OK's UND Money, Liquor Bill," *Grand Forks Herald,* December 20, 1985; AP, "Federal Bill Includes N.D. Provisions," December 21, 1985.

58. Mail Bag, "No Secret Deals, Sen. Andrews Says," *Grand Forks Herald,* August 24, 1985.

59. See *Griggs County Sentinel Courier,* November 6, 1985; see also Editorial, "Bomber Fuel Idea Won't Save Plant," *Grand Forks Herald,* November 3, 1985.

60. Henry Kelly, "Kelly's Korner," *Walsh County Press,* November 10, 1986.

61. See especially Gary Jacobson and Samuel Kernell, *Strategy and Choice in Congressional Elections* (New Haven, Conn.: Yale University Press, 1981). See also Peverill Squire, "Challengers in U.S. Senate Elections," *Legislative Studies Quarterly* 14 (1989): 531-547; and Sandy Maisel, "Congressional Elections: Quality Candidates in House and Senate Elections" (Paper delivered at a conference at the Carl Albert Congressional Research and Study Center, University of Oklahoma, April 1990).

62. For a review of these propositions, see Melissa Collie, "Micropolitical Research and Congressional Elections," in *Research in Micropolitics,* vol. 2, ed. Samuel Long (Greenwich, Conn.: JAI Press, 1987).

63. Interestingly, he did not follow the polls. One assessment is Frederick Smith, "Did Dorgan Duck Andrews Because He's Chicken?" *Bismarck Tribune,* December 16, 1985.

64. "Wrap-up of 1986 Senate Races," *Congressional Quarterly Weekly Report,* July 20, 1985; Dick Dobson, "Andrews Confident of Reelection," *Jamestown Sun,* May 7, 1986; Dick Dobson, "Mark Andrews Is No Reagan Loyalist," *Minot Daily News,* May 11, 1986; Paul Taylor, "In a Time of No Issues, the Issue Is Mood," *Washington Post National Weekly Edition,* June 23, 1986; and Taylor, "Those Independent Senate Republicans," *Washington Post National Weekly Edition,* April 14, 1986.

65. Greg Turosak, "Conrad Even with Andrews in New Poll," *Grand Forks Herald,* September 18, 1986; William Schneider and Eileen Quigley, "GOP Senators May Avoid Six Year Itch in 1986," *National Journal,* May 25, 1985; Jack Germond and Jules Witcover, "Inside Politics: Big Stakes," *National Journal,* December 7, 1985; Paul Taylor, "The Democrats Can Recapture the Senate—If Anybody Will Run," *Washington Post National Weekly Edition,* January 20, 1986; Taylor, "In a Time of No Issues"; and the *Cook Political Report,* January 3, 1986.

66. DMI, North Dakota Survey, December 1985.

67. Interview with Sen. Kent Conrad, May 10, 1990. Other comments of his in this section are from the same interview.

Electoral Defeat

THE CONTEXT

Senate elections are both collective and individual events. As collective events, they determine the partisan control of the Senate. As individual events, they shape the careers of individual senators and would-be senators. Each of these electoral aspects produces its own distinctive mode of analysis.

For political scientists who focus on the collective event—that is, on party control of the Senate—the most common aim is the prediction, for a given election year, of the overall partisan outcome. In pursuit of this aim, analysts typically measure and manipulate a set of aggregate, across-the-board, national-level factors, including the state of the national economy, the president's public popularity, the number of seats each party has at risk, and whether the election occurs in a presidential or midterm year. The result is a prediction in terms of seats gained and seats lost, of party swings, party majorities, and party control.

In 1986, there was more interest than usual in the collective event and in predictions about it. The Republicans clung to a 53-47 majority, and control of the Senate clearly hung in the balance. Some analysts worked with a hybrid factor especially suitable for 1986—the "six-year itch"—a factor derived from the historically poor performance of the president's party in the sixth year of his presidency.[1] Analyses of the collective events of 1986 were based on these national-level factors; and most of them predicted, well in advance of the election, a sufficient net shift of Republican to Democratic seats to give Senate control to the Democrats.[2]

Political scientists who focus on Senate elections as individual events engage in a different kind of research. Their most common aim is to produce empirical generalizations about the conditions under which Senate elections are won or lost. Analysts in this mode are more interested in after-the-fact explanations than in before-the-fact predictions. To the degree that they are interested in explaining partisan outcomes, they disaggregate before they aggregate. That is, they collect their data from the universe of individual Senate elections and they fashion their generalizations from this large evidential base.

These political scientists, too, are interested in national-level factors. But they add numerous other factors to their analyses, factors that can vary widely in their impact from one race to another in the same election year. Such local-level factors include the quality of the challenger, the performance of the incumbent in office, the statewide economy, the partisan and cultural predispositions of the electorate, the size of the state, the conduct of the campaign, and personal matters.[3] Analysts who focused on the thirty-four individual events of 1986 worked to assess the relative impact of these many national and local factors on the winners and on the losers. Those who attempted before-the-fact handicapping did so only on election eve; and their horse race analyses betrayed a considerable uncertainty.[4]

These two modes of analysis introduce an array of relevant electoral factors, and both end up making generalizations about Senate elections. Both leave to others the residual task of explaining the outcome of any single Senate election contest. In this chapter, we undertake that leftover task. We begin by scanning the array of national-level and local-level factors used by the generalizers. The purpose is to narrow our focus to the factors that seem to fit the case at hand. To anticipate the main conclusion to be drawn from this introductory exercise, we shall maintain that local-level factors, not national-level factors, were decisive in the 1986 North Dakota contest between Mark Andrews and Kent Conrad.

Nineteen eighty-six was not a presidential election year. If there was one observation about the 1986 elections—House and Senate—on which experienced observers agreed, from beginning to end, it was the absence of overriding national factors and the dominance of local ones. The following commentaries, therefore, help to set the context for our locally based examination of the North Dakota election:

> The 1986 election . . . is an effort to find reliable leadership, to place or keep in office officials the voters feel they can trust. It is not a referendum on President Reagan, on national issues or where the country is going next. (David Broder, *Washington Post*)[5]

The battle for control of the Senate will be fought out on a state by state basis. (Richard Cohen, *National Journal*)[6]

This year's congressional election is not one contest but several hundred—each different, each demonstrating that, this year at least, all politics is local. (David Shribman, *Wall Street Journal*)[7]

This year's battle for the Senate is a subtle, state by state struggle to define each campaign in local terms. This year, there is an absence of a crosscutting theme. (Rob Gurwitt, *Congressional Quarterly Weekly Report*)[8]

The 1986 election campaign . . . is developing into a contest with few national issues. (E. J. Dionne, *New York Times*)[9]

I've been involved in professional politics for over 16 years and I have never seen an off-year election as denationalized as this one. (Lee Atwater, Republican official)[10]

I don't think there will be any national issues . . . that will cause any Democrats or Republicans to lose. I think it will be 34 personality contests in the Senate races. (Edward Rollins, Republican consultant)[11]

From the beginning we have said that there's not a set of overarching issues. (David Johnson, Democratic official)[12]

You can't track this election; it's a series of local elections. (Victor Kamber, Democratic consultant)[13]

By all informed estimates, the thirty-four 1986 Senate elections had to be treated separately by analysts. And, for candidates, it would be everyone for himself or herself. With this encouragement, therefore, we feel safe in isolating the North Dakota contest for examination.

The observations listed above should not be taken to mean that the state of the economy—which was stable—or the president's popularity—which was high—would have no effect on election outcomes. What the commentators meant was that these sorts of national factors would not determine the outcome for any large set of races. Their comments left plenty of room for each candidate to manipulate such factors, or not manipulate them, in ways that local conditions encouraged or permitted. In the case at hand, Mark Andrews could use the popularity of the president to gain visibility for his maverick independence; and Kent Conrad could use the disparity between the national and the local economies to highlight his call for change. While no single factor would be compelling nationwide, all factors would be available for interpretation by local candidates performing before local electorates in locally oriented campaigns.

THE SUMMER CAMPAIGN

DYNAMICS

In a campaign that pits challenger against incumbent, the challenger gives voters reasons to change officeholders while the incumbent makes an argument for being kept in office. The incumbent's best opportunity to take the offensive occurs in the period before the campaign becomes a contest. It takes the form of creating a record, raising money, and tending the home state in ways that ward off all serious challengers. Preemptive strikes of this sort are frequently successful. But failing this early offensive victory and, therefore, facing serious competition, the incumbent is most likely to be thrust into a defensive posture during the campaign. Such was one major dynamic in the North Dakota case. Because of his various perceived vulnerabilities, the incumbent was unable to scare off quality competition. So he had to confront an aggressive challenger who went quickly on the offensive by criticizing the incumbent's performance in office and by touting himself as the agent of change. The dominant pattern of the North Dakota campaign, therefore, found Kent Conrad attacking and Mark Andrews defending.

The other major campaign dynamic found the challenger starting out far behind in the polls and gradually closing the gap until, at election time, the race was a tossup. In the end, it became the closest (50.4 percent-49.6 percent) of the thirty-four Senate races in 1986.[14] Figure 6-1 shows the change in candidate fortunes as registered in the University of North Dakota's State Poll. Figure 6-1 suggests a way of thinking about campaigns that become increasingly competitive over time. Candidates who begin a campaign far behind have a large potential for growth in strength if, as, and when the electorate gradually gains information about them. This potential makes possible the kind of positive momentum that can produce eventual victory. Candidates who begin the campaign far ahead, on the other hand, face the task of preventive maintenance. They need to inoculate themselves against the onset of serious voter doubts about them, lest an electorate that has begun to doubt becomes increasingly receptive to further doubts. That condition makes possible the kind of downward spiral in support that can end in defeat. Normally, of course, incumbent candidates who begin

FIGURE 6-1 Candidate Preference: North Dakota Senate Race, 1986

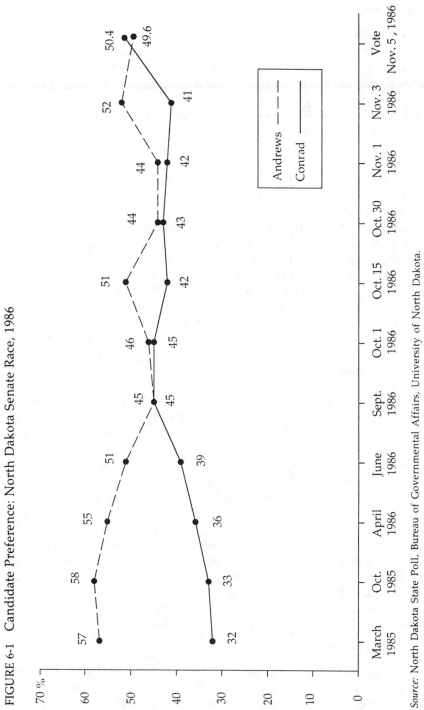

Source: North Dakota State Poll, Bureau of Governmental Affairs, University of North Dakota.

the campaign with a large lead can capitalize on their resource advantages, hold their lead, and win. Sometimes, however, they cannot prevent slippage in their lead; hence, they open up an opportunity for their opponent. In this situation, quality challengers can come from far behind, gather strength, and win.[15]

Whether the dynamic of such increasingly competitive contests is viewed as the fall of the incumbent or the rise of the challenger depends a good deal on the viewer's perspective. Since our perspective comes from over the shoulder of the incumbent, we shall treat the North Dakota campaign of 1986 primarily as the decline and defeat of Mark Andrews and only secondarily as the victory of Kent Conrad.

As the campaign began in the spring of 1986, the underlying condition was the vulnerability of the incumbent. His vulnerabilities were of two sorts—contextual and personal. Contextually, there was the state of the farm economy. In this, the most agricultural of states, the farm economy was in deep difficulty. In the six years since Mark Andrews had been elected to the Senate, land values had plummeted, and more than 3,500 farmers—11 percent of North Dakota's farmers—had gone bankrupt. Unemployment was the highest it had been in more than ten years. And observers spoke of "the wave of discontent that is sweeping across the agricultural states of the Midwest as the farm economy continues to deteriorate."[16] It was a prime example of a national factor that was locally interpretable.

Indeed, almost every national observer who discounted the economy as a national issue followed up immediately with the comment that in the farm states it would be a major issue. "Today apart from the farm revolt, which could help Democrats in one or two Senate races, there is not much evidence that the voters want a major change," wrote one national observer. According to another, "Whatever the health of the economy overall, a number of states with competitive contests are struggling through regional recessions. The poor condition of the farm economy has affected Missouri, the Dakotas and Wisconsin."[17] The day after the elections, an analysis of exit polls nationwide confirmed that "Americans who went to the polls yesterday said they were generally upbeat about the nation's economy despite pockets of deep distress in some farm and energy states."[18] As we have seen, the concerns of North Dakotans about the farm economy came through loud and clear in Andrews's own polls. The local economy provided the crucible for the electoral blending.

On the personal side, there was the accumulation of actions taken and actions not taken—by Andrews and by others, in Washington and in North Dakota—that had diminished the sense of identification and trust previously developed by the longtime incumbent. These factors have been described at length in the preceding chapters. When Kent Conrad's campaign manager described his strategy to a reporter, she stressed both the contextual and the personal vulnerabilities.

> [She] read the early polls and felt Andrews' support was "soft." Farm folks were hurting. A two-pronged strategy was mapped. Conrad would present himself as the candidate willing to fight for changes, and *Andrews would be attacked as the senator who had lost touch with the state*, she said. *People wanted a senator who was going to be one of them*; a senator who would talk with them, not at them, she said. (Emphasis added.)[19]

The challenger tested this strategy with the voters in his first election-year poll in March 1986.

Respondents were given the following instructions and question:

> I'm going to read you a very brief description of a Democratic candidate for U.S. senator and then I'll ask you to say who you would vote for in an election between this Democratic candidate and Mark Andrews.
> "This candidate is known for being close to the people of North Dakota, and he is someone who has stood up to the special interests on behalf of the average person. He would bring fresh approaches to dealing with the problems facing the state. By electing him, voters would send a strong message to Washington that we need new policies to help our economy and our farmers."
> If the election for senator were between this Democratic candidate and Mark Andrews the Republican, for whom would you vote?[20]

The response was 41 percent to 41 percent, with 18 percent undecided. For Conrad, it was a very encouraging result. And he set out to fill the prescription he had written for himself.

THE CHALLENGER'S PROGRESS

Kent Conrad's first concern was to convince people to take his campaign seriously. "You have no idea what it's like," Conrad recollected,

> when nobody thinks you can win. You endure a thousand insults. I remember once I was in Boston. I had an airplane ticket to get home and that was all—no money. My first appointment stiffed me and I had to walk to my next appointment halfway across town—in the pouring rain. I remember walking along in the rain and saying to myself, "What in God's

name are you doing this for?" I had $126 or $176 in the bank, I can't remember which. And the incumbent had hundreds of thousands of dollars. No one but me thought I could win.

He chose as his campaign slogan, "Yes, we can."

Six months into his campaign, Conrad had raised $192,000. He had spent $130,000 of it to give initial visibility to his candidacy.[21] "I put all the money I had into television before the June 10 primary," he recalled. "I know people said we should save it till later, but I didn't believe it. Our campaign needed credibility."

His introductory TV commercials were soft and positive—partly biographical and partly policy-oriented. They were designed to bring name recognition to Conrad and populist definition to his candidacy. As tax commissioner, he had pressed out-of-state corporations to pay their "fair share" of taxes to North Dakota. "We don't like big economic sources from outside trying to dominate us," he told his audiences. "We won't be dictated to. We're not doormats." His earliest commercials continued this populist theme.[22] They reminded the voters of his Fair Share Program in "getting the big tax evaders to pay what they owe." They played off the dismal farm situation, "businesses closing, farmers going under and many of our families leaving the state" and argued, as a remedy, that "we need to target the farm program to the family farms instead of to the corporate conglomerates." Each ad ended with: "Kent Conrad for the change we need," or "Kent Conrad, he'll fight for the change we need."

He even put this last refrain to music. "We put a lot of money early on into the song, $5,000 or $6,000," he said. "People criticized that, but I thought it was important to credibility and morale—the feeling that we could do it." In commercials for the public and in music for his workers, he presented himself as an aggressive agent of change in a context where change was needed.

Poll results on June 3 indicated that he had surmounted his first hurdle. He was now running 39 percent to 51 percent behind Andrews, a net gain of 7 points in two months. "I don't think I'm a long shot anymore," he said. "It's still uphill, but I no longer would put it in the long shot category."[23] The June 10 primary, in which both candidates were unopposed, delivered another boost to Conrad's candidacy. He outpolled Andrews by 12,000 votes, "the biggest lead any Democratic Senate candidate has ever had in a primary." Conversely, Andrews's totals were "the party's third lowest in primary history." Local observers read the primary results as signifying that Conrad was "a real contender" and that Andrews "seems to be vulnerable." Further, the low turnout was taken as an indicator of overall Republican party weakness and, therefore, as "bad news for the Republicans," as "trouble for the Republicans" and as a warning to that party organization "to go on 'red alert.' "[24] By mid-June Conrad had become a credible challenger for Andrews's job.

In the summer, from June to September, he gained 6 more percentage points. The gain brought Conrad into a 45 percent-45 percent tie with Andrews. Doubtless, some of this resulted from his own visibility, organizational strength, and message. On the summertime stump, for example, he pressed the farm economy as "the driving, overriding issue" and linked Andrews to the administration's farm policy. "Mark Andrews will have to explain administration farm policy," he said. "No state has been more affected by it." [25] "He's one of the architects without any question," Conrad charged. "He's on the Budget Committee, he's on the Appropriations Committee, he's on the Agriculture Committee, and he has gone along with the larger economic policies that have put this state in a deep hole." [26] The challenger advertised himself as the messenger who would carry his state's urgent economic message to Washington.

THE INCUMBENT'S PROBLEMS

Looking from the outside at media coverage, however, the summer campaign was only partially under Conrad's—or Andrews's—control. Every campaign produces unexpected events; and every campaign team lives in fear of the potential for adversity hidden in these "uncontrollables." In the North Dakota campaign, the uncontrollables of July and August had the effect of keeping the incumbent on the defensive and, thus, contributing to the challenger's strong summertime momentum.

The first series of events involved renewed public agitation of the malpractice suit. In May, the North Dakota Supreme Court denied the Andrewses a new trial. The news was carried in all the papers; and so was the senator's response: "No jury, no judge and no court will ever compensate for the pain Mary and I have suffered. I only thank God she is alive. Her good spirits and courage serve as an inspiration to us all." Senator Quentin Burdick expressed the opinion that Andrews's springtime slide in the polls began with this news.[27]

In early July, an AP reporter opened up the malpractice suit to overt political commentary with a long story in which he predicted that it "could be a pivotal issue" in the campaign. He reported, for the first time, results from a Democratic poll of June 1985, which showed that

51 percent of all voters surveyed said they "tend to think less of Mark Andrews for the way he handled his lawsuit"; 37 percent

did not think less of him and 12 percent were unsure. Among just Republicans, 46 percent disapproved of the lawsuit. Those surveyed also thought the damages sought in the lawsuit were excessive.[28]

This story, too, was widely printed in the state, often on the front page.

The state's two largest papers editorialized at length—as they had not done earlier—their conviction that the lawsuit ought not to be an issue. But at the same time they acknowledged its presence and its potency. "We are concerned about the direction the race has taken," said the *Forum*. "Unfortunately," the editorial continued, "[the suit] is being discussed more than any of the issues by many in North Dakota . . . we hope the malpractice whispers will stop. . . . The fact that Andrews and his wife exercised their rights as citizens really has nothing to do with Andrews' campaign for reelection to the U.S. Senate." [29]

The editor of the *Grand Forks Herald* called the lawsuit "an unspoken part of the election campaign until last week" and agreed that the assumption of the AP story was "probably right." "It may be that the lawsuit has hurt Mark Andrews as a politician." He also noted that Kent Conrad had not raised the issue, "at least in public." "Sometimes though," the editor wrote, "it's the things that fester below the surface, outside the campaign rhetoric, that most influence the voters. That could be the case this year." He concluded, "I'm afraid this doesn't speak too well of us." [30] The Democratic poll only confirmed what we learned from Andrews's own April poll, that the lawsuit was a deadweight detriment to his cause. Reviving the issue, however sympathetically, could only keep it rattling around the state and in so doing could only hurt the incumbent.

The second uncontrollable of the summer campaign was a sudden and potentially scandalous early August disclosure—the kind that produces a classic nightmare for one candidate and a classic windfall for the other. The matter was not by itself major, but its emergence in the middle of the campaign season and its hints of personal wrongdoing attracted major attention. The overwhelmingly negative attention kept Mark Andrews on the defensive for most of August. "It was one of the few times in Sen. Mark Andrews' political career" wrote a political reporter, "during which his down home charm and jaunty self-confidence gave way to visible distress and a confused groping for explanations." [31]

A Washington lawyer who was an old friend of Andrews hired a North Dakota detective to investigate the lobbying activities of Byron Dorgan's wife, and, by inference, Dorgan himself. The lawyer then mailed some of his documentation to several North Dakota newspapers.

The papers—especially the *Grand Forks Herald* and the *Bismarck Tribune*—
plunged eagerly into a dirty tricks investigation of why the lawyer did
it, for whom, with whose help, and with what results. Their reporters
produced an extraordinary output of lengthy articles, detailed chronolo-
gies, photocopied documents, person-in-the-street interviews, and eye-
catching headlines. The clear suggestion in many of the early accounts
was that Senator Andrews might have been involved in the investigation or known about it. Conrad jumped in to join Dorgan in a request to
the FEC to get to the bottom of the matter and suggested: "This may be
all right in some places. But in North Dakota, when you hire somebody
to investigate private lives, you have gone beyond the pale." Andrews
expressed total surprise at the revelation and denied any knowledge of
or involvement in his friend's activities. A week later, his friend
corroborated Andrews's denials.[32]

For ten days, however, Andrews had to endure a painful succession
of local headlines:

- "Andrews Friend Hired Agency to Probe Dorgan"
- "Poison Pen Trail Leads to Andrews' Pal"
- "Andrews Says He Had No Part in Investigation of Dorgan"
- "Andrews Repeats Denial of Involvement"
- "Andrews Has Some Explaining to Do"
- "How Reporters Tracked Down Secret Source"
- "Chronology of the Year's Best Political Who-Dun-It"
- "What People Say About the Dorgan Investigation"
- "Conrad Wins in Dorgan Probe"
- "Conrad, Dorgan Consider Requesting Inquiry of Probe"
- "Probe May Break Law Experts Say"
- "ND GOP Sweats It Out"
- "Involved or Not, Andrews May Be Bruised" [33]

"With friends like that," said Andrews of the lawyer "one hardly
needs enemies." [34] It was probably the understatement of the summer.
For a candidate who was already suffering from a diminution of
constituent trust and whose campaign had already taken on the tone of a
credibility check, a week of headlines questioning his integrity was
extremely troublesome. Poll results indicated that Andrews's denials
might not catch up with the adverse publicity. In the September State
Poll, the voters split into thirds when asked whether they believed
Andrews (35 percent), did not believe him (31 percent), or did not know
(34 percent). Nineteen percent said the dispute made them less likely to
vote for Andrews; 4 percent said that they were more likely to vote for
him; and the rest said it made no difference.[35] These opinions added up
to one more public airing of doubts about the incumbent. National news

sources reported that "the matter has gripped the state, as newspapers worked to ferret out the details of the case." And national handicappers wrote that it had helped "to turn a lopsided election into a horse race." [36]

The investigation controversy posed the same kinds of character-related questions about the incumbent as the lawsuit had generated. Because of the similarity of the two "scandals," it is likely that citizens for whom the lawsuit had already raised doubts concerning Andrews's personal behavior were more receptive than otherwise to this second wave of negative publicity. Put differently, it was harder for Andrews to contain the new spate of adverse publicity—despite the lack of corroborating evidence—than it would have been were he not already facing disapproval for a previous matter of personal propriety. The accumulation of negative information put him in a downward spiral, further preventing him from taking the offensive—and keeping open the challenger's possibilities for growth.

MEDIA STRATEGIES

Another contribution to the challenger's summertime momentum was his own television campaign—which changed from positive, pro-Conrad commercials to negative, anti-Andrews commercials. In late August and early September, Conrad launched a television barrage— one part planned, one part unplanned—that worked to undermine Andrews's credibility and all but eliminate his lead. The planned commercial accused the senator of "double talk." Andrews was pictured saying, "I have never voted for a pay raise yet," when in fact he had voted for something like it. He was also pictured saying, "I've always thought deregulation was a negative for North Dakota; in fact I voted against it," when in fact he had once voted for deregulation. The ad closed with these words: "It's time to stop the double talk. It's time for a change." Again, Andrews was thrown on the defensive, explaining that his "pay raise" vote had involved only honoraria and that his one early vote for deregulation was succeeded by several votes (and, as we saw in Chapter 3, many attacks) against it. His all-purpose rebuttal was to charge Conrad with "distortion" of his record.[37]

As it turned out, Conrad's first attack ad was merely an appetizer for a more consequential and damaging one. When some 1986 farm legislation passed the Congress, in August, Andrews produced a television commercial in which he said, "We passed that amendment, as you know, just a few days ago. And the price of wheat went up." The fact was that the price of wheat did immediately rise a few cents, but only briefly, then it resumed its steady slide downward from over $3.49 average per bushel in May to $2.22 average per bushel in October.

Furthermore, the 22 percent drop in the market price of wheat between May and June had been the largest one month drop in fifteen years. Andrews had kept his ad running even after the price had resumed its slide.[38]

Conrad recalled:

> I remember I was watching TV one night when I heard him say that as a result of the farm bill wheat prices had gone up. I couldn't believe he had said that. They hadn't gone up, they had gone way down. When I heard that I said to myself *[snapping his fingers]*, "I've got him now." I went right down to the local people and we did a spot that showed enough of the interview to remind people of what he had said. Then I said that Mark Andrews was wrong, prices hadn't gone up, but had gone way down. And I said, "That's not the kind of message we ought to be sending to Washington." I didn't tell my paid TV consultants about it because I didn't want to take the time to discuss it. I knew I had him. Besides, they were charging $2,500 a pop and we did this ad for $400.

Andrews's press secretary protested at length that Conrad had not interpreted Andrews's meaning correctly or fairly. And the Andrews campaign ran a radio spot deploring Conrad's negative campaign: "Negative campaigns may be a sad fact of modern politics. But they aren't a substitute for positive ideas. . . . Mark Andrews' opponent is already on TV, tossing out one insult after another, criticizing everything and proposing nothing." Conrad's campaign manager replied: "The incumbent runs on his record, and the challenger challenges it. That's what Kent Conrad is going to do day after day after day." [39] With respect to the wheat ad in particular, she said, "If your opponent has given you—on a silver platter—the opportunity to show that he has been double-talking, then grab that opportunity." [40]

Sensing that he had his opponent on the run, Conrad produced an even more explicit TV spot on Andrews's wheat price statement. "Andrews wanted to debate the thing," Conrad recalled,

> So I did a second ad locally. I had a chart made up showing wheat prices dropping over the past ninety days. In the middle of the big drop was a tiny little blip in the middle. I drew a big blue circle around it and said, "This tiny rise is what he's bragging about."

Verbatim, the ad went as follows:

> I'm Kent Conrad. I said it was double talk when Mark Andrews said wheat prices were going up. Here are the facts. In late May wheat prices were $3.30 a bushel. They declined sharply to just

over $2.00 in early September. Mark Andrews is trying to claim credit for this slight increase of a few cents for a few days, without accepting any responsibility for the steep decline caused by the farm bill he helped write. That's not straight talk.

"He'll fight for the change we need," read the final words on the screen.

For two weeks in early September, Conrad spent "much of his campaign treasury" on his television attack. Conrad's fund-raising efforts may have seemed unimpressive—$496,000 to Andrews's $1,345,000 as of September 30.[41] But here, too, Andrews was on the defensive, in a posture well described by Gary Jacobson, in which large, reactive expenditures by an incumbent signify challenger strength. "What I spend," said Andrews, "depends on what my opponent spends."[42] But Conrad was aiming only for $750,000—a figure beyond which, he believed, money would be wasted. He based his calculation on the low cost of television in North Dakota. For $800, he could buy thirty seconds on "The Cosby Show." For $20,000, he could blanket the state with one television ad for one week. For $40,000, he could run an ad that all TV viewers would, theoretically, see ten times. He sought money from Democratic sources with the argument that North Dakota gave them a greater bang for the buck than elsewhere.[43] And he had sufficient funds in September to keep several television ads going at once.

On September 18, the State Poll reported that Conrad had finally caught up with Andrews, and was now in a dead heat at 45 percent support for each candidate. "Those ads boosted us 17 [sic] points in the polls," Conrad said later. "That was a major turning point in the campaign. It gave us credibility. It was such an increase that it bothered me. I said, 'We've got to slow this down. It's going too fast.'" But the increased credibility of his campaign helped enormously in fund raising. "The Democratic Senatorial Campaign Committee sent a newsletter containing the poll results to political action committees and other money givers," wrote one observer. "Democratic fund raisers who have been assisting Conrad said the [September] poll results could turn a trickle of contributions into a roaring river." Another explained, "All the people in this town [Washington] go on is polls."[44]

The poll results were, of course, more bad news for the incumbent. One newspaper that sponsored the poll contributed a downward shove by interpreting the results as, once again, challenging Andrews's credibility.

Andrews has lost ground steadily in the poll since last fall. Part of that has to be credited to the Conrad campaign.... But it's fair to surmise that one of Sen. Andrews' weaknesses is

Andrews himself. His credibility is on the line with a large group of voters, the poll shows.[45]

This was exactly the interpretation Conrad's "double talk" charge was designed to generate. And it was exactly the same loss-of-credibility interpretation that Conrad's campaigners were emphasizing.[46]

The summertime surge of his challenger posed a problem of strategy for Senator Andrews. His basic campaign plan had long since been fixed by his service in Congress. He would run on his positive legislative accomplishments on behalf of North Dakota and on his maverick independence in decision-making generally. His campaign slogan was "Leadership, Experience, Independence." "I'm consistently in the middle and I'm consistently for North Dakota," he said in April. "It makes it easier for me to save rural electrification, education, health care, and transportation programs that are important to my state." [47] He would defend his record on farm issues in exactly this way, that he had always worked for the best farm bill he could negotiate on behalf of his home state farmers. He believed that he had worked hard for his constituents and that they would reciprocate with their support. He was confident that his positive record would stand up against any competition.

The senator believed, as he had expressed it six years before, that North Dakotans would not respond favorably to negative campaigning. When he first came under direct challenge by Kent Conrad, as one who "helped write" the 1985 farm bill, and as "one of the architects" of the administration's economic policy, his basic response was to picture himself as someone who gets things done and to ask what his critics would do in the Senate. "Where are their ideas? Where are their suggestions? They're doing an awful lot of bellyaching." Or "What we're saying is let's look for constructive answers. Everything's not going to go down the tubes." [48] His main reaction to Conrad was the same as it had been to Dorgan: "What's he ever done? He hasn't *done* anything."

His first reaction to Conrad's attack ads was not to go after Conrad in kind. He did not want to, and he did not believe he had to. But by the time of the September poll results, he was being pushed to rethink his posture. "If it's an example that the negative campaign works," he said of the poll, "then who knows, maybe that's something new. I'd rather talk about what I've done, [but] this is the day of the negative campaign." [49] It was one more example of a change to which an old style politician might have to adjust.

During the preprimary, May-June season, Andrews's television advertisements were warm and low key, designed to reinforce the sense of identification with the voters that had long been his stock in trade. He began with a couple of man-and-woman-in-the-street collage of testimonials: "We've got a great senator. I say keep him." "It's just gotta be Mark Andrews." They were punctuated with a couple of jabs at Conrad in response to his early ads: "Conrad knows as much about farmin' as I know about tax collection." "Conrad says we make taxes more fair by hiring more tax collectors. Baloney." Because Andrews's own poll results had indicated some slippage on the personal-caring dimension, his media advisers ended each of his next series of [seven] ads with, "Mark Andrews, Nobody Has Ever Cared More."

Two of these "he cares" ads were testimonials—one from a woman whose home he had saved and another from a disabled female veteran whom he had helped to get medical care. Several others featured the senator sitting at home by the fire, in an open shirt, talking in calm, conversational tones either to someone off stage or to the camera with Mary beside him. Two examples:

> North Dakota's a very special state. It's like one big family. They don't call us Senator this and Senator that. It's Mark and it's Quentin. And you have that personal relationship of knowing those people you're privileged to represent. And they call you when they've got a problem. One of the big satisfactions you get is when you're able to help out, help someone save their home or save their farm or get a passport in a hurry or get Aunt Minnie's Social Security check. That's what it's all about.

> Mary and I want to take a moment out to say thanks. Thanks for all the wonderful moments we've shared in your homes and on your farms. The great thing about a state like ours is that folks get to know each other in personal ways, and you've given us memories we'll never forget. And you've given us ideas, too, of how to make those Washington bureaucrats sit up and take notice of the problems we face in North Dakota. Well, we made 'em take notice all right. We got those extra billions for education, we made a bad farm bill a whole lot better, and we fought and won the battles for rural health care, day care centers, and for services people need when they're old or poor or handicapped. Serving you is not a job but a privilege. Fighting for North Dakota is everything I'm all about. I want to keep the experience I've had in Congress and in the Senate working for you over the next six years and make North Dakota a better place for all of us.

Other ads featured his legislative battle for the rural electric co-ops and his reaction to Mary's illness. In all of these commercials, Andrews's

TABLE 6-1   Mark Andrews's Favorability Ratings

	April 1985	*December 1985*	*September 1986*	*Overall Change*
Very favorable	31%	28%	22%	−9%
Somewhat favorable	49	51	40	−9
Somewhat unfavorable	11	12	17	+6
Very unfavorable	6	5	16	+10
No opinion	2	3	5	+3

Sources: DMI, North Dakota Surveys, April 1985, December 1985, and September 1986.

demeanor was comfortable and confident. There were no shots of him in Washington. The assumption seemed to be that he was senatorial enough, that what he needed was more of the "one of us" and "cares for us" themes.

These down home, old-shoe presentations of self were launched before the events of the summer put him so overwhelmingly on the defensive. Toward the end of the summer, he changed campaign consultants and began giving his new consultants more of his media work. When, however, the newer specialists produced the troublesome wheat prices ad, he veered back toward the group that had produced his first series.[50] These changes reflected some disorganization and uncertainty on his part—not an unfamiliar condition in his staff relations. It is quite likely, therefore, that he looked to his own September poll for direction. It was taken in the week (September 13-15) before the State Poll results were announced. Its questions reflected something of Andrews's campaign worries at the time; and its answers confirmed the need to worry.

THE SEPTEMBER POLL

The Andrews September poll registered the same trend in voter intentions as the State Poll—though it did show Andrews still ahead. In his December 1985 poll, the senator had led his newly prospective challenger by 62-26 with the rest undecided. Now, the split was 48-41-12. Table 6-1 indicates that whereas nothing changed during 1985, a very sizeable downturn in his favorability/unfavorability ratio had occurred during 1986. The strong indication is that the Conrad campaign and the damaging uncontrollables of the summer had taken a considerable toll. As the editor of the *Bismarck Tribune* wrote, "Andrews has developed a real image problem."[51]

Further evidence for this conclusion appears elsewhere in the

September poll. On the question, "What has Mark Andrews done or said during the campaign that you particularly *dislike?*", 63 percent of the respondents offered a criticism. Seven percent of them mentioned the Dorgan investigation; and 20 percent—far and away the most focused criticism—mentioned Andrews's policy on farm prices. Of the eighteen comments reported verbatim from that subset, fourteen of them mentioned his wheat price comment, along these lines:

- "He said something about farm prices and they went up for a day."
- "He's taken the business of wheat prices and making it a big deal. They didn't go up enough to make it significant."
- "I dislike when he said wheat prices went up, then prices fell."
- "He took credit for a slight increase in wheat."
- "He said the price of wheat was up and it was down."

His challenger had clearly gotten unusual mileage out of his wheat price commercials.

On the other hand, when asked the same "dislike" question about Conrad, nearly a third of those (58 percent) who had a criticism mentioned his negative campaigning. And of the twenty-six comments reported verbatim, five mentioned the wheat price ad specifically. On a separate question—whether negative campaigning best characterized Andrews or Conrad—respondents picked Conrad by a 2-1 margin. By the same margin they picked Conrad over Andrews for "criticizing but proposing no solutions." So Andrews had some basis for retaining his belief that North Dakotans did not like negative campaigning. But only within limits. When asked point blank whether they thought Conrad was "legitimately criticizing" Andrews's record or "distorting" it, the first option received more support, 46 percent to 37 percent.

The poll contained evidence, too, of Andrews's residual strength, based on his long service and experience. Voters would not, for example, agree when offered serious criticism of Andrews's performance. By a margin of 78 percent to 22 percent, they called "unbelievable" the statement that "Mark Andrews doesn't really care whether or not farmers get higher prices." And they found the statement that "Mark Andrews is doing all he reasonably can do to solve farm problems" "believable" by 65 percent to 33 percent. The statement that "Mark Andrews doesn't have as much clout as the average U.S. Senator" was judged "unbelievable" by 62 percent and "believable" by 35 percent. The voters seemed not to want to beat up on Andrews. On the other hand, their doubts about him seemed to have grown—enough for an opponent to make headway with a series of criticisms focused on Andrews's credibility.

TABLE 6-2   Public Perceptions of Mark Andrews and Kent Conrad

"Does the following statement best describe Mark Andrews or Kent Conrad?"	*Andrews*	*Conrad*
1. Has best solution to problems facing me and my family in the future	36%	38%
2. Cares about people like me	37	31
3. I have my doubts about him	35	38
4. Sometimes I don't really trust him	32	26
5. Deep down I know he will do the best job for North Dakota in Washington	45	38
6. Can best solve problems facing agriculture today	46	35
7. I would really feel bad if he loses	35	29

Source: DMI, North Dakota Survey, September 1986.

This ambivalence is portrayed in Table 6-2, which displays the results of the question, "Does the following statement best describe Mark Andrews or Kent Conrad?" Comparing Table 6-2 with Table 5-1, it appears that Andrews's "Nobody has ever cared more" commercials had registered favorably with the electorate (question 2). It is also worth noting that Andrews's "always in the middle" had not put together an overall view of things that could dominate the populistic message of Conrad—and his mentor, Byron Dorgan (question 1). At the risk of overinterpreting these imprecise numbers, it would seem that the voters of North Dakota retained a good deal of respect for Mark Andrews's experience, his knowledge, and his ability (questions 5 and 6) while at the same time withholding from him a measure of personal approval and trust that he needed if he was to withstand the criticism of an aggressive challenger (questions 3 and 4). That was the essential problem he had to cope with in the six weeks of campaigning that remained. A visiting reporter wrote during the first week of October, "Both Republicans and Democrats here say that Mr. Conrad, who still faces formidable obstacles . . . has been able to turn the economic issue to his advantage only after other issues of a more personal nature made Mr. Andrews vulnerable." [52] It was a fair summary of the sequence of events and of the situation I found when I journeyed to North Dakota to see things for myself.

OBSERVATIONS AND REFLECTIONS:
NORTH DAKOTA, OCTOBER 1986

When Mark Andrews was visiting fifty-seven North Dakota towns on his two "neighbor to neighbor" trips during July and August—in a mobile van accompanied by a five-piece band—he protested, "Actually we're not really campaigning.... We just had a week off, and you just can't block off all your time for campaigning until the last month of the campaign." He responded similarly to the unwelcome State Poll of September: "The real campaign will begin when we're able to get home when Congress adjourns." [53] He estimated that date to be October 12.

I arrived in North Dakota for a four-day visit—my fourth—on October 11, so I was there to observe the beginning of what Andrews deemed to be the crucial stage of the campaign. "Right now, it's a tossup," he said when we met. "It could go either way, depending on what happens from now on. We think we have things falling into place, but who knows?" To the degree that the horse race was neck and neck, the outcome did hang in the balance. It was perfectly possible, therefore, that what he did in the next four weeks would make the difference. To the degree, however, that the campaign had already developed its own dynamic, and to the degree that the momentum was now on the side of the challenger, there was an open question whether the campaign Andrews thought was just beginning might not be very nearly over. The six-week campaign, that is, may have already been overwhelmed by the events and trends that preceded it.

When I left North Dakota in November 1985, I had come to believe that Andrews was not strong enough to ward off a serious challenge. And I had come to believe that there had been a gradual slippage—over a period of years—in the closeness of his identification, in his caring/trusting, "one of us," family-like relationship with the electorate. When I learned that Byron Dorgan would not be his opponent, however, I thought that he might have an easier time of it. It was Dorgan who was the state's most popular politician, and it was Dorgan who had popularized the alternative home style that had been so vexing to Andrews. As I began my 1986 visit, I knew about the September State Poll results. I knew that the contest with Conrad was going to be very close. And I knew, therefore, that Andrews's vulnerabilities were not about to vanish with the appearance of a new challenger.

On the trip out, I entered these thoughts in my notebook:

One of the things, if not *the* thing I'm looking for as I start is: what happened to the man who had it so easy in 1980 and who seemed so closely identified with North Dakota? He once told me that "it's easy when they accept you as family." Is he still family? Or has something happened to that relationship? Are they "disciplining" him? A small state can be like a small town—negatives have a way of spreading fast and taking hold. Or, think of the emotion that accompanies "family" betrayal of some sort. *If* Mark has lost the trust of his constituents, it happened over six years, and it is a *big, big change.* A loss would be quite a story. . . . So the question, as I fly over this familiar flat land, is whether that will be my story or not. What, if anything, has happened to the man from Lehr?

The answer to the last question did not come quickly or easily—and not during my visit. In a sense, it is the question of this book.

What did become clear during my trip was that the 1986 campaign was totally different from that of 1980. I never saw Andrews in a context comparable to the meeting at Lehr. There was simply no time for a leisurely trip to a few small towns, for informal exchanges with small groups, for the subtle swapping of North Dakota values, for the easy reinforcement of "family" ties. Mark Andrews had become vulnerable; he was running for his political life. If he was to survive, he would certainly have to depend on the continued existence of the sense he evoked in 1980, that "he is one of us and he is working for us." But in 1986, it would have to exist as an implicit underpinning, less visible to the observer and obscured by the surface demands of a difficult campaign.

The difference between 1980 and 1986 was reflected in his campaign literature. Both years' brochures were self-conscious about the matter of representing a small state. But the 1980 brochure, "Mark Andrews and the People of North Dakota," had featured nineteen pictures of the congressman, each with a different group of constituents. Its emphasis was on "one of us." In his 1986 brochure, the emphasis was on "works for us." It carried the cover slogan: "For a small state like North Dakota, it's good to have a big man working for us." The inside pages featured Andrews at work. The brochure had eight pictures, five of them of Andrews in Washington. And it had twenty-two separate paragraphs—including eight on his activity on behalf of agriculture and ten on other specific Washington accomplishments. The rest of it makes much of the idea that "Washington pays attention to North Dakota because we've got Mark Andrews on the job for us." The campaign literature stressed achievements, not relationships. The brochure reflected a senatorial outlook, more than a congressional one. But it assumed that the strength congressman Andrews had as "one of us" remained.

I traveled with the senator to seven events: two party rallies (in New Rockford and Wahpeton), two talks to community groups (in

Minot), and three ceremonies celebrating his governing accomplishments (in Fargo, Grand Forks, and Minot). I also caught occasional
glimpses of the media campaign being waged by the candidates. To a
greater degree than I had observed before, Andrews had been put on the
defensive by his opponent and had lost control of the dialogue with his
constituents. In his speeches he was being forced to spend the lion's
share of his time defending his vote in support of the 1985 farm bill—as
he had not had to do, for example, when we visited Lakota and
Cooperstown the year before. In the media, he was struggling to blunt
the effects of Conrad's summertime attacks on his credibility. Only at
the celebrations for his legislative accomplishments in Washington was
he clearly in control of his campaign agenda.

All in all, I found him frustrated by the development of the
campaign. I found him presenting himself to the voters in the same way
as always. He remained in the protectionist phase of his constituency
career. There was no visible outreach to new supporters; there was only
the collection of IOUs from old supporters. I found Andrews believing—or so I thought—that when all was said and done, he would collect
the IOUs and he would win. To put it somewhat differently, my sense
was that deep down Mark Andrews could not imagine himself being
turned away by constituents for whom he had done so much for so long
and for whom he had continued producing benefits to the very last
moment of his Senate service.

THE FARM PROBLEM

A visiting reporter opened an interview: "How's it going?" Andrews answered, "It's going all right. We've got a farm problem in
North Dakota that's causing a lot of frustration; and we've got an
opponent who is capitalizing on it." He elaborated with a sensitivity to
farming that I had long since become accustomed to.

> People are frustrated and hurting. Farming is not just a way to
> make a living; it's a way of life. People feel they are not
> recognized for the solid contribution they make to a strong
> America. There's a lot of pride and emotion tied up in the
> family farm. It's almost like belonging to a church. They will
> listen to people condemning the administration for what
> they've done for agriculture and then they say, "The hell with
> them." It's a hard backdrop to campaign against.

To the reporter's follow-up question, "How do you make your pitch?"
he described himself as "the most prominent spokesman for the farmer's
point of view." He continued:

Vote for me because I'm a farmer, an acknowledged fighter for the farmer. I'm on key committees and I've got a lot of seniority. I can work our way out of this problem better than someone who knows nothing about farming. We need a balanced delegation of Republicans and Democrats. If you send a message by knocking off a Republican who has been voting and working his tail off for the farm program, the Jesse Helmses and the Dick Lugars [the two top Republicans on the Agriculture Committee], who are opposed to the program anyway, will say, "There's no sense in doing anything [for the farmers]. . . . It doesn't pay to be like Mark Andrews."

It puzzled him—and galled him—that someone so personally inexperienced in farming (Conrad) should be able to make so much headway on the farm issues against someone with so much personal experience in the vicissitudes of that occupation (Andrews).

On four occasions during my visit, I heard the senator explain his actions on the 1985 farm bill. Self-justification had become a necessity of his campaign. "Andrews has been forced to be apologetic about the farm bill," wrote a local reporter who had been following him since summer. "[He] has to explain, in effect, 'I admit I voted for the bill, but you have to understand why.' . . . For months, Andrews has had to keep explaining what he did and why." [54]

Once again, as in Lakota and Cooperstown a year earlier, the explanation I heard centered on the legislative process—on how he had manipulated it and on what he had accomplished in so doing. The difference, of course, was that during my 1985 visit, the farm bill had not yet taken its final form, he had not yet voted on it, and no one was challenging his performance. So he had been in control of the dialogue. Still, in 1986, he showed the same devotion to the process and offered the same explanation for his actions—that he had gotten the best deal he could for North Dakota under the circumstances and that all the alternatives would have been worse.

His speech at New Rockford was my introduction to the latest Andrews campaign. Much of it was very familiar. "I've been coming to towns like New Rockford for twenty-five years," he said as we flew in. He was introduced as "one of us"; and he told his seventy-five listeners that "tonight, we're kind of talking among family." He began with a self-deprecating story, with a multitude of local references and reminiscences, and with praise for the suggestion of a local legislator that Andrews had written into the farm bill. "Good ideas don't come from Washington; they come from right out here in North Dakota." He took a quick swipe at "our tax collector, that great and knowledgeable farm expert," and at people who "grow three extra fingers on each hand, to point at somebody else and to blame them for the problems without having any solutions." He briefly assessed the ongoing U.S.-U.S.S.R. summit meeting in Iceland as a lead-in to a discussion of the 1985 farm bill.

> Both are heads of nations that can put a man in space; only one speaks as the head of a nation which grew some food and had enough left over to share with others. That's truly the strength of America. . . . That's why we have to have a farm program, not just for the economic benefit of North Dakota, but for the future of our country in a troubled world where 300 million people go to bed hungry every night. Then how do we do it? What kind of a farm program do we get?

At this point he launched into a long explanation of his performance on the farm bill, which in substance, in tone, and in its various references was a vintage Andrews performance:

> All through the debate on the farm program—and I'm a member of the Agriculture Committee—I was part of a bipartisan coalition, Republicans and Democrats, that was working for a marketing loan concept. I thought it was a whale of a good concept, and it was backed by such 'nonfarmer' organizations as the North Dakota Farmers Union, the North Dakota Farm Bureau, and the NFO [National Farmers Organization]! All three of these organizations were backing me on what I was trying to do. You know, we kept that concept going right up until about a month before the final decision was made, when we brought it to a vote and it lost by one vote—we lost by one vote—because two or three cotton state senators went the other way. If they'd been with us we would have gotten it.
> Now what do you do at a point like this? You know what you do—a lot like the farmers, Greg, that you're advising. Do they lay down and quit? Or do they stay and fight and stay on the farm? My dad died when I was twelve. And when I started farming, my mother and uncle only had a contract for a deed, because the mortgage had been foreclosed on our family farm in the thirties. We know what it's like to stick it out. North Dakotans bend but they don't break. They fight back. And that's precisely what we did in trying to put together a farm program when we didn't get it our way. I couldn't have served you by going back and pointing a finger and blaming somebody else that our one vote lost. That wouldn't have done our economy any good.
> What did we do? We built on the concept Milt Young put together years ago. Milt, as you know, was the father of the target price concept. He said we need target prices because you

never can tell when world conditions are going to come along and the price of wheat is going to be way below the cost of our producing it. . . . We won. We kept the $4.38 target price. And I'm getting darned sick and tired of listening to Democratic candidates saying that the price of wheat is $2.00. Baloney! It's $4.38. . . . This year it will bring into our state $672 million. That's a thousand dollars for every man, woman, and child in this state. Now you're telling me I shouldn't have worked for something like that? I shouldn't have worked for that kind of a safety net? It's not what I wanted in the first place; it's not what we were fighting for in the first place; but it's sure an awful lot better than nothing else. . . . It's the Milt Young target price concept backed up and kept by some darn tough last-ditch struggles that has given us the safety net that is giving our farm economy and our main streets in New Rockford, Carrington, and the rest—$240 million more this year than last year.[55]

This talk was the explanation of a man steeped in farming, steeped in associations with North Dakota, and steeped in the business of legislating in Washington. It was the voice of experience and of expertise. It was a perfectly plausible explanation of his behavior on the 1985 farm bill. But it was, as always with Mark Andrews, a Washington-centered explanation: detailed, complicated, and narrowly drawn. It was heavily dependent for its success on his audience's appreciation of his insider's legislative philosophy—"be a player," "get the best you can," "something is better than nothing." And it was an explanation of his behavior rather than an explanation of what had happened to the state's farmers. It contained no easily grasped denunciations of national policies—or of any single national policy—which might be responsible for the state of the North Dakota economy. And it left him open to Kent Conrad's question on nightly TV: "If he's got so much clout, how come we're in such trouble?"[56]

On the ride in from the airstrip, the Republican district leader, a farmer, had said, "It would be a damn shame if we sent that phony [Conrad] to Washington in place of Mark Andrews. . . . [But] the farmers are mad at everything right now, and every district will be tough." One has to wonder how receptively farmers who were "mad at everything" would listen to Andrews's explanations of his various legislative exploits. Perhaps his talk was more inside baseball—more a rehash of the problem—than many of them wanted to hear. Perhaps the farmers were more in a mood to question his gaffe on wheat prices than to credit him for fighting on their behalf in the Senate. "It was," he said later, "a good crowd and they looked happy." But he also said, "Two guys came up afterwards and said, 'You've got to answer the

Conrad ad about the pay raise.' " They were listening to the challenger's attacks.

Rep. Byron Dorgan had faced the same decision on the 1985 farm bill as Andrews and had decided to lend a populist voice to the farmers' anger by voting against it. Kent Conrad was following his friend and mentor along the path of protest, denouncing the farm bill, associating it with the farmer's woes and associating Mark Andrews with it. Andrews, of course, could have ridden on the back of the discontent. But he was too much a child of the process to abandon or deny his legislative handiwork. In conversation, he associated himself even more closely with the farm bill.

> I made a big difference. I was the maverick raising hell, putting together the coalitions to save the target price concept and the safety net for farmers. . . . Some of the most bitter words in the Agriculture Committee were between [Republican chairman] Jesse Helms [N.C.] and myself because I was lined up with the Democrats in order to get the $240 million for North Dakota. If I hadn't broken off and joined the Democrats, the economy— which has been tough—would have been totally disastrous.

Mark Andrews, we have said, was a maverick but not a populist. He had worked with the Democrats; the farm bill had passed with two-thirds support from both the Democrats and the Republicans in both houses; and he would, of course, support the results. He always had. "It isn't just election politics with me," he said, "I did the same thing [joining with the Democrats] in 1981 and four years before that when I was in the House. That year, I had to get time to speak on the floor from the Democrats. I couldn't get it from the Republicans." This deeply ingrained insider's governing style dictated the content of his explanations at home.

Andrews's defense of his actions on the farm bill was only one part of his campaign. It was the part that depended most on his longtime reputation as a farmer and friend of the other North Dakota farmers. To this point in his career, that reputation had been reassuring and sufficient. But he had not been put under so much pressure or appeared so vulnerable before. This time, doubt had been created and he was seeking the benefit of the doubt. His campaign posture, on the defense, was not exactly a winning posture. But, as preventive maintenance, it was not necessarily a losing posture either. In the end, he would need a cushion of trust—to shield him from blame if not to credit him with victory. He had always had that trust. The big question was whether enough of it was left to pull him through in November.

ATTACK AND COUNTERATTACK

Throughout my visit, the television campaign was in full swing. Conrad was attacking on several fronts. He had revised and strengthened his "double talk" TV ad. And he was running a populist-style ad tying Andrews's vote for the farm bill to the payment of subsidies to agribusiness:

> I'm Kent Conrad. This year one California corporate farm will receive farm program payments totaling $20 million. That at a time when family farms are failing in record numbers. That's wrong. The reason is the new farm bill. Mark Andrews helped write it and voted for it. It's right here in the *Congressional Record.*

Like each of his other ads, it was designed to put and keep the incumbent on the defensive.

Conrad's ads were a reminder that incumbents cast votes in Congress and that each vote represents potential ammunition for a challenger. Andrews ventured, "I've cast probably 10,000 votes, more or less, in the years I've been privileged to represent North Dakota." A challenger can spotlight any one of them for scrutiny and attack. When that happens, the incumbent has to explain directly or rely on an established reputation to turn aside the attack—or launch a counterattack. Mark Andrews wavered among these strategies, and he adopted a little of each. But he reacted slowly; and he placed the greatest reliance, throughout, on the force of his established reputation.

On the matter of his pay raise/deregulation votes as described in the "double talk" ad, I listened to him, in private, decide against a televised explanation. Yet he had a lengthy record, detailed in Chapter 3, of *opposition* to the proderegulation position Conrad was attacking him for holding. "I don't want to get into any of that nit-picking stuff" he told his campaign manager. He did, however, respond to these and other Conrad charges in his luncheon talk to the Minot Kiwanis Club— and, I assume, to anyone else who might ask.

> I heard that I voted for a pay raise. Actually, that was called pay reform by everybody in Washington. Even Common Cause ... urged us to vote for that, as pay reform. What it did was it set
> . the pay of senators the same as House members and sharply limited honorariums. ... I think deregulation stinks now, and I've introduced legislation to correct it. Heck, even the *Grand Forks Herald* had a full-page deal on that. ... But it's also true that in 1978 ... when the issue was totally different, I voted like everyone else for deregulation. ... The one that's really

intriguing is when he goes full face on camera and says, "Mark Andrews is in favor of lower farm prices." My whole family laughed when they saw that. And I would hope that not too many people in North Dakota would believe that. . . .

I've got to have confidence in the people of North Dakota realizing that I don't talk in double talk, that I've never had anybody investigated in my life, and that I'm surer than heck not in favor of lower farm prices. In fact, I've been the principal architect of higher farm prices for twenty years. And if that kind of a record hasn't penetrated the consciousness of North Dakota, then we haven't told our story. We'll be telling more of our story. But again, I've told our people that I don't want to get into that kind of a nit-picking contest.

It was an explanation that relied, in the end, on his established reputation and on the benefit of the doubt that followed from that reputation.

In private, the senator spoke similarly, but with more emotion and more embellishment. "I've never had a campaign that was such a nit-picking campaign," he said when we first talked.

He said I said the price of wheat went up and yet it went down. Well, it had gone up when I said it did. Then he said I voted for a pay raise. I never voted for a pay raise. I voted to cut the honoraria and bring our pay up to the level of the House. For most senators, that meant a loss in pay. Then there was the business about the private investigation into Dorgan's wife. . . . I called [my friend] and I said, "What the hell are you doing messing around in my state?" He said, "Don't worry, it's not political." I said, "Why didn't you tell me first?" He said, "I didn't want to worry you." Now the son of a bitch is on the West Coast, he won't make a statement, and some people think I was connected with it. How crazy can you get! I suppose he thought he was trying to help me. Conrad and Dorgan have milked that for all its worth. They even filed a complaint with the FEC [Federal Election Commission]—after they knew it was too late for the FEC to do anything. That's the way it's gone. It's been all nicking picking bullshit. He hasn't said one damn thing.

What Conrad *was* doing, however, was sowing doubts about the incumbent. And the incumbent was running a risk by not going on television to answer back.

Andrews was not unaware of the problem. "When they ran that negative barrage about the wheat situation," he told a reporter during my visit, "we didn't respond and we probably should have." [57] But when he talked about that decision to me, he emphasized his lack of money at the time.

> It's the first time I've ever had a campaign where the opposi-
> tion had plenty of money to put into the campaign and we
> couldn't go after them. I can't get [Chairman John] Heinz [R-
> Pa.] of that great and glorious Senate Campaign Committee to
> give me any more money. He says, "You're not in trouble; you
> don't need it." He's looking backwards. We had a 15-point lead,
> or a 20-point lead, in June. Conrad began his negative cam-
> paign in August, and they didn't give us any money to answer
> him. We don't have that lead any more.

It is a reasonable guess that if Andrews had understood the gravity of
what Conrad was accomplishing with his wheat commercials, he would
have moved heaven and earth to find some more money. Since he did
not, our further guess is that Andrews believed, in August at least, that
he did not need to reply, that his profarmer reputation would surely
deflect this "nit-picking" charge.

There is some evidence that prior to the September polls, Andrews
was slow to realize how much trouble he was in. One of his campaigners
noted "the complacency that developed when Byron Dorgan decided
not to run." "When Kent Conrad became the opponent," he said,
"everyone heaved a sign of relief and assumed it would be easy."
Reporters, too, found the Andrews camp "breathing easier" about his
seat. That early judgment was supported by a big lead in the polls and
by his fund-raising success. Given his incumbency and given his quid
pro quo legislative style, Andrews had no difficulty raising PAC money
early on. Between January 1985 and June 1986, he had amassed a state
record $1,140,000. When Dorgan declined to run, wrote one reporter,
Andrews's PAC fund raisers put out the message to "the PAC community that Andrews is not in serious trouble, . . . to forget the North
Dakota race, Andrews is home free." Even after the September poll,
Republican party leaders sounded no alarm.[58] From my own observation, sitting in Andrews's Fargo district office, it seemed that the
Andrews enterprise was conducting business as usual—a leisurely pace,
little activity, long lunch hours, early closing times, closed on Saturday. I
felt no sense of urgency, anywhere, to match the September poll results.

By the time of my visit, Andrews had realized that he would have to
help himself—by dealing, somehow, with the challenger's aggressive
television campaign. To deflect pressure on the farm issue, Andrews ran
a commercial with a strong endorsement from a former Democratic
secretary of agriculture, Bob Bergland of neighboring Minnesota. "Every
year," said Bergland, "Mark Andrews fights to keep money for rural
electrification in the budget. I'm from a different party . . . but if you
want to keep rural electrification, vote for Mark Andrews."[59] The
senator showed a lot of reluctance—for whatever reason—to plunge

wholeheartedly into a negative shoot-out-style confrontation. But he had decided to go on the attack. "There has been a lot of mud slinging," said one of his top campaigners, "and the senator has just stood back and said nothing. Our strategy was not to dignify it. But now our ads will start taking it to him, criticizing Conrad."

He produced two attack ads—one criticizing Conrad for claiming to have reduced the tax commissioner's budget when he didn't and another criticizing Conrad for claiming to have rejected a pay raise when the money remained available to him. "This is the type of campaign that seems to be waged," he said, in defending the ads. "This is what Kent calls his 'chainsaw' campaign style. I don't think chainsaw campaigning is where it's at, but we can play that game, too. If it works for him, it might work for us, too." The first ad produced a quick and persuasive rebuttal. The second ad kept Conrad busy near the end of the campaign.[60] In both cases, the arguments were arguments about accounting—hardly enough to alter the dynamic of the campaign. They also indicated, it seemed to me, how little Kent Conrad had by way of a public record to shoot at—certainly when compared with Mark Andrews's 10,000 votes. The tax commissioner gave his opponent very little by way of ammunition with which to launch a retaliatory counterattack. In this respect, strange to say, Byron Dorgan might have been an easier opponent than Kent Conrad.

The other negative Andrews ad that ran during my visit linked Conrad with the "gloom-and-doom" Democratic ticket of Carter and Mondale in 1980. Like them, said Andrews, Conrad "ridicules," "criticizes," but puts forward "no solutions" and "no plans." The ad touts the need for "experience" and "clout," and ends: "We've got one who gets things done." This mildly negative ad was totally incapable of reversing the "I challenge, you defend" rhythm of the campaign. Like the other ads I saw, it seemed remarkably punchless. Taken together, they did not come close to constituting an effective counterattack to the strongly negative campaign being waged against him. Interestingly, the senator was far more reluctant to play hardball at home than in Washington.

When he commented on his television battle with Conrad, Andrews criticized the local media for their reluctance to blow the whistle on his opponent. Speaking of Conrad's wheat price commercials, he exclaimed:

> You'd think that the press would say, "Andrews was absolutely correct. Wheat was up—seven cents, for ten days. When the House didn't pass the bill, the price of wheat went down." I'm looking for the guys in the striped shirts to point a finger and say "Andrews was right." If we had any good reporters out here they would say that.

To a visiting East Coast reporter, he complained similarly:

> The press isn't playing the role of traffic cop. In the East, the
> press is experienced enough to call politicians on it when they
> don't tell the truth. Out here, political opportunists can knock
> farm programs and the press doesn't get in there and say,
> "They have no alternatives" or ask, "What would we do
> without it?"

The press, he said later, should have helped him explain the positive
features of the 1985 farm bill.[61]

The Conrad campaign, as might be expected in a tight race, had its
own criticisms of the local media. We cannot keep score in these matters.
It is certainly a debatable question whether, in a time of negative
campaigning, the press ought to take on a more active refereeing role in
political campaigns.[62] Andrews's complaint was one more reflection of
the trouble he was having with the explanatory task faced by every
incumbent. He was embattled; he was losing the television contest; and
he was looking for a little outside help.

Andrews's complaints also reflect the closeness of the contest—a
contest in which each candidate works for the slightest advantage.
Viewed this way, Andrews and his campaigners felt very strongly that
they were not getting any breaks from the North Dakota press. "Our
biggest problem is press," said one campaigner. "We have a lot of
trouble getting any press. They are so biased." The campaign press
secretary pointed out that the morning's page 1 story in the *Grand Forks
Herald* about a major project, for which Andrews was responsible, failed
even to print Andrews's name.[63] "The editor [of the paper] is hung up
on what he calls Mark's arrogance," said the press aide. "They know he's
accomplished a lot for North Dakota, but they can't bring themselves to
admit it. You see lots of articles in the paper like this, reporting things
Mark has done without mentioning Mark's name." A third campaigner
was still upset about the degree to which coverage of the Dorgan
investigation had been manufactured by the press. He singled out the
lurid headlines of the *Bismarck Tribune*. "One of their reporters even said
to me, 'Now I'll get that fat son of a bitch's ass.'"

To me, these particular complaints seemed to be valid. Indeed, I
could understand why the local media might be taking a fresh and
vigorous interest in Conrad's strong challenge. It was a good news story.
Mark Westlye writes in his analysis of media campaign coverage about
"the need of reporters and editors to find controversy in, and to make a
horse race out of, a political campaign."[64] I could understand why the
media people might feel that they already had given the powerful
incumbent plenty of coverage. He was an old story.

The tenor of the complaints from the Andrews camp suggested something more, however. They suggested a general deterioration in press relations which might, indeed, be costing the senator the small advantage he now sought from the media. To me, the complaints suggested that Andrews was reaping at home what he had sowed in Washington by his inattention to the press operation in his office, including the revolving door for press aides. Although his press operation was probably competent at issuing press releases, neither he nor his staff had ever established good, personal working relationships with the everyday North Dakota newspeople. Perhaps, it seemed to me, that large failure was responsible for the animus contained in reporters' private descriptions of Andrews. Most likely Byron Dorgan's earlier, press-cultivating, style was ultimately responsible for Andrews's exasperation with the home state press—not the later television ads of Kent Conrad.

CELEBRATION OF ACCOMPLISHMENTS

In their own unemotional and uninspiring way, many of Mark Andrews's ads conveyed his fundamental view that he, unlike his opponent, was "one who gets things done." It was, indeed, the comparison he made between his record of accomplishment and Conrad's lack of same that led Andrews to think of Conrad's criticisms as nitpicking. During my visit, his self-perception was reinforced again and again as he went about the celebratory activities associated with his governing accomplishments in Washington. These occasions found him in his element and in control.

In Grand Forks, there was the formal announcement of a joint flight training and research venture between Northwest Airlines and the University of North Dakota's (UND) Center for Aerospace Sciences. In Fargo, there was the presentation by the American Public Transit Association of its Distinguished Service Award. This ceremony included the signing of a contract worth $69 million to a bus manufacturing and assembly business in North Dakota, followed by a tour of Fargo's brand new bus station. In Minot, there was the presentation by the president of the North Dakota Educational Association (NDEA) of the 1986 Education Leadership Award from the National Committee for Educational Funding.[65] In Chapter 2, we detailed the manifold legislative efforts that produced such home state recognition in the fields of aerospace, transportation, and education. To witness these payoff campaign events was to see Mark Andrews at the top of his form.

"We call this 'Andrews Alley.' Mark Andrews is responsible for this facility," exclaimed a university official as we entered UND's aerospace complex—after a short ride in from the Mark Andrews International

Airport in Grand Forks. The senator responded in kind. "Isn't this something," he exulted.

> I'm responsible for all of it. It's all federal money—three buildings, one every year for three years. I haven't missed a year yet. And I think we'll get a fourth one next year. . . . I got [Sen.] Jake Garn [R-Utah] to come out here and dedicate the second building a year ago. When he saw it, he said, "Mark, I had no idea you were putting all this money into aerospace here." I said, "I know you didn't, Jake, and I didn't want you to know." He said, "If I'd known, I'd have tried to get it for Utah." I said, "I know it, and it's too late!"

The thought of his legislative coup produced a satisfied chuckle.

At the ceremony that followed, the dean of the college introduced the senator:

> Mark Andrews is the captain of our team. He has put the infrastructure in place for us. Mark and I have a dream of filling the valley with aerospace facilities—a kind of aerospace valley to go with silicon valley. . . . Mark lobbied actively with Northwest Airlines to help convince them to locate [the training facility] here.

After Northwest's CEO had acknowledged the senator's "gentle pressure" as "go between," Andrews told the audience, "If that kind of pressure is what brought this infrastructure, I'm proud to have been a part of it. That's what you hired me for." He added:

> I started two projects when I went to the Senate—an agricultural project at NDSU and an aerospace complex at NDU. You are on your third or fourth building here and we just broke ground for the first building at NDSU a few months ago.[66]

In Fargo, Andrews was introduced by the executive vice president of the Public Transit Association:

> As chairman of the Subcommittee on Transportation he has been a fighter, and I mean a very successful fighter for rural transit and for the special services on which our elderly and disabled citizens depend. . . . Time and again, Senator Andrews has risen on the Senate floor . . . to defend public transportation [and done] one heck of a sales job.

He praised Andrews for engaging in the "kind of behind-the-scenes activity of an elected official which doesn't always get the attention it deserves."

Andrews, in turn, attributed his success to "the blowtorch factor," to "the fact that we have people in our communities like Walter sitting out there who when I was a newly hatched senator said, 'We've got this concept for this downtown bus depot. What are we going to do about it?' So we had to go out and get the money." Which, of course, he did. Referring to the bus contract soon to be signed with the state of New Jersey, Andrews talked about his close relationship with the ranking Democrat on his transportation subcommittee—Frank Lautenberg of that state.

> Frank Lautenberg sits on the committee with me, and we've concocted a little deal of moving some Red River Valley potatoes down to New Jersey. . . . We got together a group of people, this again, is the blowtorch factor . . . to have a trailerload of potatoes delivered next door to Frank Lautenberg's [*laughter*]. Frank said he got more press and more TV off our Red River potato event than he has out of most anything else. You know, it's amazing how interested New Jersey was in placing this contract for the tens of millions of dollars for New Jersey buses that are going to be built just downstream in Pembina.

Again it was a vintage Andrews use of his legislative connections in Washington to improve his electoral connections at home.

At his press conference with the president of the NDEA, there was more praise for his governing skills, specifically for "the Andrews amendment" increasing the federal budget for education. "The point is," said the NDEA leader, "Mark Andrews opposed his own president, worked hard to build a bipartisan group to pass the increased education funds and stuck with the job until the actual appropriations were authorized. He did extremely well for education." [67] Andrews took the opportunity to repeat his theme that "good ideas don't come from Washington. They come from North Dakota." He told the educators, as he had told the nurses in 1982:

> The ideas that I've had in education and the success I've had in being a champion for education [have come] because of the amount of information our educators . . . here in North Dakota have shared with me. So on the floor of the Congress I can make the argument . . . based on fact rather than just so much hoop-hurrah.

Once more—as in each of the other cases—Andrews's inside legislative style was praised and Andrews had the opportunity to publicize his resultant legislative accomplishments.

In each of these settings Andrews was on the offensive. He could talk aggressively about his record of tangible, beneficial legislative accomplishments brought about by the prowess of an effective legislator. As he said later about the aerospace center, "It was good for North Dakota, but it was also good for the nation. It had to go somewhere;

where better than here? That's what I'm all about and that's what I'm doing." Conrad, he believed, could not match this kind of performance—indeed, didn't even understand it. "When I mentioned all the things I had done for North Dakota," Andrews recalled from a recent joint appearance, "Conrad's only answer was, 'That's what senators are supposed to do.' He thinks that's all there is to it." [68] The veteran legislator shook his head in disbelief. And he hoped the voters would react similarly. For the time being, at least, these ceremonial events gave him the opportunity, in front of local audiences, to capitalize on his legislative "experience" and "clout."

Referring to the matter of what he had done for North Dakota, I reminded him later in the visit of the "What have you done for me lately?" syndrome and asked whether "bacon" was not a highly perishable commodity. He countered with the notion that what he had done in the past was a warrant for what he could do in the future and that he was seeking reelection on that basis.

> None of these things is finished. In the areas I'm talking about—the aerospace center, the farm program, branchline abandonment, education, health care—the job still needs to be done. With my track record, who better to have in the arena scrapping to rewrite the farm bill and update it to provide export markets? I'm an effective legislator. I have the experience. The areas of my expertise are all ongoing concerns. It's not like the guy who got a dam built or a school constructed— when it's done it's done. My job is not done.

The idea of an unfinished home state agenda was an appealing one. But I did not hear it expressed in public.

What I did hear expressed during his celebratory events—much as I had heard in 1980—were sentiments designed to strengthen the bonds of community. In Fargo, speaking of the bus depot, he said:

> It is fitting that this facility be right next to the main line of the old Northern Pacific, where more than a hundred years ago they laid the track to come out and develop what we're proud to call North Dakota. Until that track came, until that transportation system was in place, people couldn't come to till the soil, build their homes, and build the community structures that we need. Transportation has changed. Now, more than a hundred years later, we have the great need for the kind of bus system and the handicap vans that are here and can move our people freely among our communities.

To the group of educators, he expressed his own attachment to this statewide community.

That's the great thing about North Dakota; you're not known as Senator this or Governor that. It's always been Quentin and Mark and Byron and Bud. That's the way we want to keep it in North Dakota. It's part of our tradition. And we talk about our problems together.

To someone who had observed the senator at home in earlier years, his rhetoric and his effort to identify with his statewide community were very familiar.

But the context now seemed very different. The closeness of his relationship to the community was being questioned. The insinuation was abroad that he had gotten somewhat out of touch. And, despite Andrews's frequently stated opinion that "he doesn't know what he's talking about," Conrad's attack was making headway. I asked the senator why he thought Conrad's "nicking picking bullshit" was nonetheless taking hold with the electorate. "I think it's partly the sourness of the farm economy. There's a lot of frustration," he began. But he moved quickly to something else he had not discussed publicly. For the first time in our conversations, he talked about the lawsuit.

> I think some of it goes back to the lawsuit, to Mary's meningitis, and to the misdiagnosis and the trial. . . . I thought people would praise me for sticking up for my wife. I thought they would say that family comes first. But instead of that, they criticized me for going after the doctors. What kind of reaction is that? This is supposed to be a family-oriented state. I was acting in the best interests of my family. I couldn't have lived with myself if I hadn't. But people were critical. If that's the kind of people I've been working for and living with all these years, then the hell with it. I don't want the job.
>
> [Is North Dakota still "family"?] I always thought it was until I ran into this attitude. We did a TV spot featuring our "neighbor to neighbor" campaign this summer. It showed Mary campaigning with me as we always have, as a team, Mark and Mary. Yet the most important Republican woman in the state sat right in my office and berated me for putting Mary on TV. What did she want me to do, put her in a closet? I would have thought she would have said what a wonderful thing it was to see the family together again, campaigning as a team. But she was attacking me for protecting my family. If that's the way they feel, I'll get the hell out of this business. There's just a lot of sourness all around.

When, in 1982, he had described North Dakota as "family," he had acknowledged the possibility that they might "discipline sternly" someone who had violated family expectations. At the time, he could not imagine such an eventuality in his case. Now, in 1986, he could.

One instinct was to confine the problem to a small group. "I offended the country club set when I stood up for my wife," he said privately. "It's all right for a Democrat but for a Republican to challenge the establishment—terrible, terrible." Another instinct was to refuse to explain his actions publicly or to solicit public understanding. There was, in his comments about the lawsuit, a combination of disappointment, disbelief, and weariness—as if he couldn't believe that any large number of voters would turn on him for fighting for his own family but that he was resigned to the consequences if they did. As he put it publicly, "If the people in North Dakota hold it against you for standing up for your family, then I don't know the people of North Dakota very well." [69] He seemed markedly disinclined to dig in and fight for his political life with every weapon and with extra enthusiasm or determination. Again, I felt that deep down, he believed that he *did* know the voters of North Dakota and that he did not have to undertake a fresh and extraordinary explanatory effort to convince them of his worth.

THE REPUBLICAN PROBLEM

From the beginning of the campaign, Andrews had hoped that the harder he was challenged, the more his supporters would get out and work. In April, when he led Conrad 55-36 in the polls, he took the view that "anything that gets friends to say, 'By gosh, Mark needs some help' is worth it. I can lose an election by myself. But I can't win an election by myself. The best way to get friends to be supportive is to get 'em a little scared." When the September poll showed him in a dead heat, he reiterated that "the challenge is to make sure that people go to work." [70] In October, I heard him tell a reporter that "our friends are concerned now, and that may be the best thing of all. We have volunteer phone banks going now. It's the first time the Republicans have made this kind of effort in North Dakota."

He compared his situation to that of a Kentucky colleague who had been defeated two years before.

> I ran into Dee Huddleston in Washington a little while ago. He asked me how it was going, and I told him about the latest poll. He said that he had been ahead by 25 points, that his opposition had sneaked up on him, and by the time his supporters took it seriously it was too late and he lost. He said to me, "The best thing that could happen to you is to have the trouble come early enough so you can do something about it."

The question, of course, was whether the tightening race had produced more effort on the part of Republican campaign workers.

In our conversation, Andrews was gloomy.

> My situation is made worse by the absence of any Republican party in this state. They are inept and incompetent and almost nonexistent. They can't get together to do anything. You ask them to write a letter; finally they get around to it and it's time for the next letter. They are useless. I've put $200,000 of my money into voter identification. No one else would do it. And we have set up our own phone bank. We have a new, young campaign group that is shaping up and is good. The trouble with the party is that they are so used to my having 40-point leads that they don't know how to get off their backsides and fight. I'm the only Republican on the statewide ticket. They should be working hard but they aren't. I don't even know if they can.

As I left, he noted, "The key is to motivate my supporters to get out and work, to get out and vote. Hopefully they are not going to sit back and relax. . . . I'm the only major Republican officeholder left in the state." In the background, of course, was the senator's independent brand of Republicanism, prominently displayed via his frequent disagreements with President Reagan. In April, he had been described as one of the two Republican first termers "most independent of the party leadership," and second highest of the group in the number of anti-Reagan votes in key issues during his five years in the Senate.[71] All of Andrews's political experience and all of his polls told him that his maverick Republicanism was an essential source of his political strength. "They call him a maverick because he votes for you," was the headline of his campaign literature. Every newspaper endorsement he would receive would praise him for it. But, as he put it, "I get a lot of static from the Republican party." One campaign worry was that his party's conservatives, who might have nowhere else to go, would nonetheless sit on their hands at election time.

Until the middle of August, Andrews was threatened with a primary opponent from the party's conservative wing—from his one-time campaign manager and executive assistant. Edward Doherty saw the Andrews-Conrad campaign as "a contest to see who could criticize President Reagan the most." Doherty decided not to run. But while he threatened to run, he articulated the view that Andrews's "liberalism" was "not in the political mainstream of this state."[72] It was a view held by others, people from whom Andrews would eventually need both organizational work and votes.

One event that held out some potential for help was the October 17 visit of President Reagan to Grand Forks to stump for Andrews.[73] In the fall of 1986, there was a good deal of media speculation whether or not, in general, a presidential visit would help Republican candidates. In Andrews's case, the benefits of such a visit were not clear. His opponent had been trying to tie Andrews to Reagan's economic policy; and Andrews had been trying to assert his independence. When national commentators discussed Reagan's visits, they saw it as an effort to "nationalize" the election, to superimpose a common referendum-like theme on local races.[74] But that was not what Mark Andrews needed. If anything, the "nationalization" of the North Dakota race would fit with Conrad's themes.[75]

In Andrews's September poll, respondents were asked, "If Ronald Reagan came to North Dakota, would it make you more or less likely to vote for Mark Andrews?" The result was a wash—32 percent "more likely," 30 percent "less likely," and 38 percent no difference. By the time of the visit, the campaign had crystallized to the point where very few voters expected to be affected one way or another. To the question, "Will President Reagan's visit to North Dakota make a difference in how you plan to vote in the U.S. Senate race?" 94 percent answered no and only 4 percent yes. Among the small number, slightly more conservatives and Republicans said yes; and they overwhelmingly said they would be more likely to vote for Andrews. The tendency was welcome, but the numbers kept things inconclusive.[76]

Perhaps because of this uncertainty, Andrews played down the potential impact of the impending visit when we talked. "The president's visit is not an unmixed blessing," he said. "It will just take people away from what they should be doing." He also commented, "We aren't paying much attention to it. But it will let people know that there's a campaign going on." Out of that stimulation might come not greater nationalization of the race but some added local enthusiasm for Mark Andrews. "I asked him to come because in an off-presidential year turnout is low and I want to stimulate interest," he said publicly.[77] It was, of course, the same maverick-loyalty tightrope he had been walking all along in the Senate. And Conrad went on the attack immediately. "[He's] claiming he's a maverick, but when he gets into trouble, the first thing he does is bring in the president."[78] From Andrews's comments at the time, however, I carried away the impression that while he held no great hope for the visit, he believed he could continue to avoid the downside risk. And he believed it might help to shore up some elements of his support.

First, Reagan's presence would affirm Andrews's Republicanism and help him with his party. "The White House came around nine months ago, and asked us all if we wanted the president," he said.

> I said "sure," and they were surprised. . . . I'm proud to have the
> president come to North Dakota. He did sign off on a tripling
> of FmHA [Farmers Home Administration] loans. He did sign
> the farm bill. He's accused of being worse than he is for the
> farmers. . . . The president understands that senators vote for
> their states. You don't have to be disagreeable when you disa-
> gree. I've never been out here ripping the president up and
> down.

The president, he thought, would make it clear (which he did) that he
needed and wanted Andrews back in the Senate. And that might
motivate some Republican partisans to work and to vote.

A second benefit would come from the simple fact that the
president of the United States, with all of his prestige, actually came to
North Dakota—courtesy of North Dakota's senator. Andrews, I thought,
talked about the visit as if it were one more demonstration of his
personal clout. Three days before the president's visit, the chairman of
the Joint Chiefs of Staff came, at Andrews's invitation, to Minot to
address the Chamber of Commerce.[79] The Minot Air Base "has a large
economic impact" on the area, said Andrews. The dinner was heavily
attended by people in uniform. So the tangible importance of Admiral
William Crowe's visit was not lost on the citizenry. When we first talked
and Andrews asked me how long I planned to stay, he was enthusiastic:
"I've got the chairman of the Joint Chiefs coming on Tuesday and the
president coming on Friday. That's pretty good, I'd say." He, of course,
would introduce both guests. He lumped the two visits together as
personal accomplishments, as two more examples of his ability to bring
home the bacon to his constituents. He hoped thereby to buttress his
provider's image among the home folks.

The president's visit came and went, with net effects that were
difficult to fathom.[80] But the discussion of Andrews's Republicanism
produced one irritating by-product that added to the frustrations of the
Andrews campaign. Former aide Doherty—presumably informed by his
inside experience—embroidered his criticism of the senator's liberalism
with the charge that he had come under the "considerable influence" of
his third, and (according to Doherty) excessively liberal, administrative
assistant. Jacqueline Balk-Tusa had been Andrews's ally in his truck
width fight (Chapter 2). She was characterized by Doherty as "a big city
liberal from the East Coast," "an eastern liberal feminist from the East
Coast," and "an eastern liberal feminist from New York." For a
candidate already facing criticism for something less than total devotion
to the sensitivities of his constituents, this gossipy charge was extra
baggage. It played upon and evoked the traditional suspicion of "outsiders" among North Dakotans. "She has," said Doherty, "demonstrated a

very unwholesome attitude toward North Dakota people." [81] She was clearly not "one of us." And the implication was that her employer might be less so, too, than he once was.

Ed Doherty quickly disappeared, and his rhetoric was deplored by at least one newspaper. But that did not mean that the suspicions he planted would be without effect.[82] By the time of my visit, Balk-Tusa had been staunchly defended by Andrews and was running his campaign. The senator who knew all about the propensities of his neighbors had decided that the positive value of her talents outweighed the negative value of her outsider status. In the context of lavish praise for her talents, one Andrews campaigner fretted that "North Dakotans hate anything or anybody who comes from the outside." When asked who was advising the senator, he replied, "Only Jacqueline." It was likely that a number of North Dakotans would react unfavorably to Andrews's staff chief/campaign chief and that their whispers, like the lawsuit, would rattle around informally in the small town atmosphere of the state. It would be one more "out of touch" straw-in-the-wind that Andrews did not need.

POSTSCRIPT

I left the campaign trail with the embattled incumbent anticipating the president's visit and three more weeks of campaigning. From the few accounts I saw afterward, the horse race continued neck and neck to the end. The dynamic of the campaign never changed.

The challenger stayed on the attack with a hard-hitting television accusation that Andrews had missed a vote of special consequence to North Dakota in order to collect a speaking fee in Florida. The charge again portrayed an incumbent less than fully devoted to his constituents. Against pictures of the *Congressional Record* and a picture of a beachside swimming pool, the following words were printed and spoken:

> March 10, 1983. The Senate votes on whether $2.2 million in North Dakota job creation funds should be given to big states like Pennsylvania and Ohio. But one senator is missing. And North Dakota ends up losing by a single vote. The one missing senator—Mark Andrews. He was collecting a $2,000 speaking fee at a fancy Florida hotel. A $2,000 fee that cost North Dakota $2.2 million. It's time for a change.

Another of Conrad's final commercials accused Andrews of voting for a $40 billion cut in Social Security. Andrews responded verbally, in meetings, to both these commercials. Of the first, he declared: "It's a flat out lie, and they know it is." To the second, he countered, "I never voted against Social Security in my life." [83] But, as before, he did not go on television to answer either charge. "They dumped the Social Security thing on us at the very end," he said afterward, "so that we had no time to answer it." Whatever other effect the charge had, it kept the incumbent on the defensive.

After I left, Andrews ran a low-key, reputation-centered rebuttal to Conrad's attacks. Dressed in a windbreaker, leaning on a feedlot fence, and looking into the camera, he said:

> I get a lot of calls and letters complaining about the Conrad campaign. They say some folks might be swayed by the kind of political campaign Kent Conrad is running. One thing you know about me. I don't speak in double talk; I've never had an opponent or anyone else investigated; and I've never been for lower farm prices in my life. Matter of fact, I'm for raising 'em as high as I can get 'em. We've fought and won many battles for North Dakota together, and I'll never believe all we've worked for will be undone by somebody who's never cast a vote in his life, who will say or do anything to get elected. We know each other too well to let that happen. We've had too much success winning Washington over to what North Dakota needs and wants to see it suddenly taken from us. So don't worry, folks. With your help we're going to keep moving full steam ahead and keep North Dakota the state we want it to be.

It was his most direct televised effort—in the context of his challenger's charges—to reinforce his credibility and his identification with his constituents. In this respect, the commercial was vintage Andrews, expressing the sense that "he is one of us" in reassuring and quietly emotional tones. When he spoke the sentence, "I'll never believe . . . ," the voice was from his heart. He honestly couldn't "believe" that his constituents would "undo" his record of service. As a campaign vehicle, however, the commercial was mild-mannered and without fire. It was business as usual. It seemed out of sync with the life-or-death situation he confronted.

At the very end of the campaign, Andrews attacked his opponent for a variety of outside associations that suggested that Conrad was not entirely "one of us." He criticized Conrad as "a favorite of the East Coast limousine liberals," as a supporter of "the paper [*Village Voice*] of New York City's radical chic," and as the beneficiary of a contribution from the Council for a Livable World, described as so liberal that Quentin Burdick had refused to accept its money when offered. Burdick denied the last allegation. And Conrad referred to his opponent's eleventh hour barrage privately as "nasty" and publicly as "everything but the kitchen sink." On election eve, Andrews ran a Ronald Reagan testimonial on "a number of state radio stations." [84]

This entire last-ditch effort signaled a radical departure from his traditional election eve "Mark and Mary Show," with its warm, reassuring portrayal of community attachments and values. It is not clear whether the senator lacked the money for this commercial or decided not to revive memories of the lawsuit. [85] But the package of late campaign decisions was one more indication that the campaign had been thrown off stride. Conrad ended his campaign on the same note with which he had begun: "North Dakota needs a change in the Senate. We need someone who will fight for us, for our way of life." [86]

The polls wobbled inconclusively at the end (see Figure 6-1); but all indications were that the outcome was in doubt and too close to call. From all that we could surmise from afar, however, the momentum remained as it had been, from the beginning, with the challenger. [87] Andrews seemed to agree with this reading when he talked afterward about his own lack of money at the very end. "Conrad outspent us 3-1 in the final week," he said.

> He had an insert in the paper the last weekend, a good insert. I wish we could have had one, but we couldn't afford it. The Republicans gave Abdnor hundreds of thousands more than they gave us. The papers were full of stories that we had all this money to spend at the end. We didn't. We ended up with a $100,000 debt.

While in retrospect he wished for more money, it is not clear what he could have done to make a difference. He had already spent $1.7 million, more than twice what Conrad had spent. [88] Furthermore, it is not clear what Andrews would have done with more money. As it turned out, he thought he was ahead. "We were 4 or 5 points up [in the polls] before the last weekend," he said to me after the election, "then it just disappeared—pffut!" Because he believed he would win, it seems unlikely that he believed that any last-minute attack on Conrad would have much effect.

Just before I left the campaign trail, Mark Andrews discussed his situation in the terms I had viewed it in from the outset of my visit. Thinking back six years to "the man from Lehr," I asked him flatly whether the essence of his relationship to the North Dakota voters was not a matter of "trust" and whether the challenger's campaign against him was not, fundamentally, an effort to undermine that trust. "Yes, it is," he replied.

> Peter Hart has advised the Democratic candidates to make the issue one of credibility and of character. [89] And that's what all

this nit-picking is about, all that stuff about double talk. That's what the talk about the malpractice suit is all about—to suggest that it reflects some character flaw or a lack of credibility.

You would think that people would approve of the way I have stood by my wife. I spend my life standing up for other people's families; why can't I stand up for mine? But if we believe the polls, a lot of people are buying their campaign. . . . It's very frustrating. I've worked for twenty years and I've built up a reputation. But people seem to be believing all the snarf that's being thrown around now. . . .

We could have gone negative—just as they have—but we had to make a basic decision. We decided not to. Maybe we made a mistake. . . . We could have made some pretty basic comparisons.

When people begin to think in the last couple of weeks and when they get into the voting booths, they will ask themselves: "Which person do I want to represent me in the Senate?" At that point we'll see whether all the good will I've built up over all these years is still there, or whether it's gone.

He was saying, I thought, that he needed a cushion of voter trust if he was to withstand the assault of his challenger. In Lehr, in 1980, he had had it. He saw the election of 1986 as a test of whether he still did.

His candidacy was endorsed by newspapers in each of the state's four largest communities: Fargo, Grand Forks, Bismarck, and Minot.[90] Each one of them praised his institutional experience, his policy independence, and his ability to "bring home the bacon." For varying combinations of those reasons, and with varying degrees of enthusiasm, they all declared him to be deserving of reelection and/or too valuable a resource for North Dakota to lose. They all praised Kent Conrad, but none of them blamed Andrews for the state of the farm economy. In one or another of the six endorsements I examined, Andrews was given credit for all the legislative accomplishments detailed in Chapter 3. To a large degree, therefore, the editorial boards saw Mark Andrews as he wanted his constituents to see him—as a good legislator; and they judged him the way he wanted to be judged—on his record.[91]

These endorsements must have been encouraging to the embattled candidate. At the least they were a testament to his very considerable strengths. But to an outsider remembering the man who campaigned in Lehr, something seemed to be missing. The endorsements were calculating but not warm. They acknowledged and valued his political strengths; but they did not say that they liked him or that they trusted him. Only one conveyed any sense of his being "one of us": "Like the state he represents, Andrews is a fighter against odds," wrote the *Forum*. "He has hauled his big frame around Washington for 23 years doing battle for the farmers of North Dakota, of which he is one." On the other hand, another paper offered criticism on this score: "Andrews must recognize that he has suffered a loss of credibility in this state," wrote the *Bismarck Tribune*, and "[he] will have to work hard to regain the confidence of North Dakotans." [92]

For the most part the endorsements did not deal with the emotional side of his constituent relations or with the whispers that questioned the depth of his community attachments. By what was not said, therefore, there remained room for opinions focused on allegations of aloofness, of arrogance, and of personal transgressions to flourish. There remained the possibility that, despite his legislative successes, the accumulation of difficulties he had experienced since 1984 had taken a heavy toll. In what was not said, therefore, one could sense that the close, nearly ideal relationship between representative and constituency I had detected in 1980—and the cushion of trust he needed in 1986—might no longer exist. As the election result of November 5 demonstrated, it didn't.

NOTES

1. Rhodes Cook, "Will the 'Six-Year Itch' Strike Again in 1986?" *Congressional Quarterly Weekly Report*, June 29, 1985; William Schneider, "1986: The 'Six-Year Itch,'" *National Journal*, December 7, 1985.
2. See Michael Lewis-Beck, "A Model Performance," *Public Opinion*, March/April 1987, and the studies cited therein.
3. Gerald Wright and Michael Berkman, "Candidates and Policy in United States Senate Elections," *American Political Science Review* (June 1986); Alan Abramowitz, "Explaining Election Outcomes," *American Political Science Review* (June 1982).
4. For example, R. W. Apple, Jr., "Looking Ahead," *New York Times*, November 2, 1986; Barry Sussman, "And the Winner Was. . . ," *Washington Post National Weekly Edition*, November 10, 1986; Colman McCarthy, "Wrong from the Start," *Washington Post National Weekly Edition*, December 15, 1986.
5. From David Broder, "A Season of Personal Politics," *Grand Forks Herald*, October 12, 1986. See also David Broder, "Campaign Time: Here We Go Again," *Washington Post*, January 1, 1986.
6. Richard Cohen, "Running Without Reagan," *National Journal*, December 7, 1985.
7. David Shribman, "Regional Politics: Congressional Election in '86 Will Be Largely a Series of Local Races," *Wall Street Journal*, May 30, 1986.
8. Rob Gurwitt, "Many 1986 Senate Candidates Tailor Bids to Fit Local Moods," *Congressional Quarterly Weekly Report*, August 23, 1986.
9. E. J. Dionne, Jr., "Election '86: Uncertainty on Issues Clouds Races," *New York Times*, August 31, 1986.
10. Quoted in Gurwitt, "Many 1986 Senate Candidates." See also Atwater's comments in Sidney Blumenthal, "So Far This Year, GOP Strategists Can't

Find a Reason for Running," *Washington Post,* March 16, 1986.

11. Quoted in Dick Kirschten, "An Uncertain Transition," *National Journal,* December 7, 1985.
12. Quoted in Gurwitt, "Many 1986 Senate Candidates."
13. Quoted in Dom Bonafede, "Midterm Election Puzzle," *National Journal,* October 8, 1986.
14. *Public Opinion,* January/February 1987, 22.
15. This dynamic is discussed, in the presidential context, in Larry Bartels, *Presidential Primaries* (Princeton: Princeton University Press, 1988).
16. Keith Schneider, "GOP Anxious on Dakota Senators," *New York Times,* October 17, 1986; John Dillon, "States' Economic Woes Cloud GOP '86 Outlook," *Christian Science Monitor,* May 1, 1986; Edward Walsh and Helen Dewar, "Farm-Belt Republicans Face Their Own Winter of Discontent," *Washington Post National Weekly Edition,* December 16, 1985.
17. Michael Barone, "Six-Year Itch," *Washington Post,* March 21, 1985; Gurwitt, "Many 1986 Senate Candidates"; see also Shribman, "Regional Politics"; and David Shribman, "Economic Conditions in States Vary Dramatically," *Wall Street Journal,* August 26, 1986.
18. Ellen Hume, "Americans Voice Optimism on Economy in National Poll Taken During Election," *Wall Street Journal,* November 5, 1986.
19. AP, "Architect of Conrad Victory Receives Flood of Lucrative Offers," *Forum* (Fargo), November 10, 1986.
20. Peter D. Hart Research Associates, Inc., "Study #2370, North Dakota Poll," March 22-23, 1986.
21. Dick Dobson, "Andrews, Conrad Hunt for Dollars," *Minot Daily News,* August 17, 1986.
22. Dennis Farney and David Shribman, "The Dakotas Emerge as Vital Battleground in Senate Elections," *Wall Street Journal,* October 23, 1986; see Sidney Blumenthal, "The Democrats Are Going Back to Populism," *Washington Post National Weekly Edition,* September 15, 1986.
23. Bob Laux-Bachand, "Conrad Trims Andrews Lead in Poll," *Minot Daily News,* June 7, 1986; Richard Vernaci, "Senate Race May Hinge on Andrews' Malpractice Suit," *Bismarck Tribune,* July 2, 1986.
24. Mike Jacobs, "Primary Political Signals," *Grand Forks Herald,* June 22, 1986; Dick Dobson, "Advice to GOP: Don't Ignore June Vote," *Minot Daily News,* June 15, 1986; Jacobs, "Primary Political Signals."
25. Greg Turosak, "Conrad Even with Andrews in New Poll," *Grand Forks Herald,* July 13, 1986; Ronald Brownstein, "Mark Andrews," *National Journal,* April 4, 1986.
26. Greg Turosak, "Candidates Ride Hard on the Campaign Trail," *Grand Forks Herald,* July 13, 1986.
27. AP, "Supreme Court Denies Trial for Mark and Mary," *Dickinson Press,* May 8, 1986; William Robbins, "Dakota Senator Sees His Lead Slip," *New York Times,* September 7, 1986.
28. Vernaci, "Senate Race May Hinge on Andrews' Malpractice Suit."
29. "Let Issues, Not Lawsuit Concern Us," *Forum* (Fargo), July 7, 1986.
30. "Andrews: Person, Politician," *Grand Forks Herald,* July 6, 1986.
31. James McGregor and Reed Karaim, "Dorgan Investigation Raises Many Questions," *Grand Forks Herald,* August 10, 1986.
32. Robbins, "Dakota Senator Sees His Lead Slip"; AP, "Sen. Andrews Not Involved with Dorgan Investigation," *Jamestown Sun,* August 15, 1986; Gerry

Gilmour, "Lawyer 'Clears' Andrews in Dorgan File," *Bismarck Tribune,* August 19, 1986.

33. *Grand Forks Herald,* August 7, 1986; *Bismarck Tribune,* August 6, 1986; *Williston Daily Herald,* August 7, 1986; *Valley City Times,* August 13, 1986; *Grand Forks Herald,* August 10, 1986; *Grand Forks Herald,* August 10, 1986, *Grand Forks Herald,* August 10, 1986; *Grand Forks Herald,* August 13, 1986; *Grand Forks Herald,* August 10, 1986; *Forum* (Fargo), August 8, 1986; *Grand Forks Herald,* August 13, 1986; *Grand Forks Herald,* August 13, 1986; and *Forum* (Fargo), August 13, 1986.

34. Frank Strom, "Andrews Wishes 'Hyped-Up' Story Would Just Disappear," *Minot Daily News,* August 19, 1986.

35. Turosak, "Conrad Even with Andrews."

36. Gurwitt, "Many 1986 Senate Candidates"; Robbins, "Dakota Senator Sees His Lead Slip"; see also Dionne, "Election '86: Uncertainty on Issues."

37. See Janelle Cole, "Conrad: Andrews Lied About Voting Record," *Bismarck Tribune,* September 12, 1996, and "Andrews: Recent Record Different," *Bismarck Tribune,* September 13, 1986; Greg Turosak, "Andrews and Conrad Bicker About Issue of Credibility," *Grand Forks Herald,* September 13, 1986.

38. Figures are from "Prices Received by Farmers: Item, Spring Wheat," North Dakota Agricultural Statistics Service, Fargo, May 18, 1988; Jack Germond and Jules Witcover, "TV Ad Blunder Could Hurt Andrews," *National Journal,* September 13, 1986.

39. Philip Brasher (AP), "Conrad Claims Andrews Goes Back on His Word for Debates," *Williston Daily Herald,* September 4, 1986.

40. John Vanrig, "Senate Race Heats up the TVs," *Grand Forks Herald,* September 3, 1986.

41. James McGregor, "D.C. Democrats Celebrate Poll Results," *Grand Forks Herald,* September 19, 1986; *National Journal,* October 25, 1986.

42. Gary Jacobson, *Money in Congressional Elections* (New Haven: Yale University Press, 1980); *Grand Forks Herald,* July 2, 1986.

43. George Will, "So Much Cash, So Few Ideas," *Newsweek,* November 10, 1986; Paul Taylor, "In the Fight for the Control of the Senate, Only One Thing Is Certain," *Washington Post National Weekly Edition,* September 15, 1986; Germond and Witcover, "TV Ad Blunder"; Vernaci, "Senate Race May Hinge"; McGregor, "D.C. Democrats Celebrate."

44. McGregor, "D.C. Democrats Celebrate."

45. Steve Schmidt, "Close Poll Results Will Heat up Senate Race," *Grand Forks Herald,* September 19, 1986.

46. Greg Turosak, "Senate Contenders Won't Pull Punches," *Grand Forks Herald,* September 19, 1986.

47. Ronald Brownstein, "Mark Andrews," *National Journal,* April 12, 1986.

48. Turosak, "Candidates Ride Hard."

49. AP, "ND Poll Indicates Tossup in Andrews-Conrad Race," *Forum* (Fargo), September 19, 1986.

50. "The Politics Page," *National Journal,* September 6, 1986; McGregor, "D.C. Democrats Celebrate."

51. DMI, North Dakota Poll, September 1986. This is the only available trend line from the three DMI polls; editor's comment quoted in E. J. Dionne, Jr., "Democrats See Economy as Emerging Issue," *New York Times,* October 4, 1986.

52. Dionne, "Democrats See Economy."

53. Turosak, "Candidates Ride Hard"; AP, "Farm Woes Hurt Andrews," *Forum* (Fargo), September 19, 1986.
54. Greg Turosak, "Farm Bill Central to Race: Andrews Wrestles with Vote," *Grand Forks Herald*, October 14, 1986.
55. The same figures can be found in AP, "N.D. Crop Payments Increase 63%," *Forum* (Fargo), October 11, 1986.
56. Farney and Shribman, "The Dakotas Emerge."
57. Terry Greenberg, "Andrews Admits the Pressure Is on," *Minot Daily News*, October 15, 1986. He expressed the same regret after the election was over: Dale Wetzel, "Conrad Has Slim 'Miracle' Lead over Andrews," *Minot Daily News*, November 5, 1986.
58. Philip Brasher (AP), *Williston Daily Herald*, December 27, 1985; Dobson, "Andrews, Conrad Hunt for Dollars"; McGregor, "D.C. Democrats Celebrate"; AP, "Farm Woes Hurt Andrews"; Greg Turosak, "Poll Spurs Questions About Election Coattails," *Grand Forks Herald*, September 19, 1986.
59. Rich Jaroslovsky, "Washington Wire," *Wall Street Journal*, October 31, 1986.
60. Kevin Murphy, "New Andrews Ads Use Double Talk Motif," *Forum* (Fargo), October 14, 1986; Dick Dobson, "Should North Dakota Dump Experience?" *Minot Daily News*, October 26, 1986.
61. Patrick Springer, "Mark Andrews," *Forum* (Fargo), November 7, 1986.
62. See Sarah Williams-Berg, "Conrad and Andrews: It's Time to Grow Up," *Walsh County Press*, October 13, 1986; see David Broder, "Negative Campaigning Revisited," *Washington Post National Weekly Edition*, September 10-16, 1990.
63. Marian Young, "Northwest to Announce Deal with UND," *Grand Forks Herald*, October 10, 1986. Andrews's prominence in this deal is discussed earlier in this chapter.
64. Mark Westlye, *Senate Elections and Campaign Intensity* (Baltimore: Johns Hopkins University Press, 1991), 13. With respect to Westlye's judgment about challengers, see page 45.
65. Young, "Northwest to Announce Deal"; "U.S. Transportation Association Gives Andrews '86 Service Award," *Forum* (Fargo), October 14, 1986, and Peg Portscheller, NDEA president, press release, October 15, 1986.
66. On the NDSU project, see "New Research Facility to Be Built," *Jamestown Sun*, August 19, 1986.
67. Portscheller, press release.
68. Accounts of this debate said: "Andrews plugged his ability to bring home projects to North Dakota" and "Andrews emphasized his experience and seniority in Congress and mentioned projects he's helped obtain for North Dakota." Greg Turosak, "Farm Differences Mark Debate," *Grand Forks Herald*, October 11, 1986; Randy Bradbury, "N.D. Candidates Square off in Grand Forks Debate," *Forum* (Fargo), October 11, 1986.
69. Jim Neumann, "Andrews Sees Gas Plant Purchase," *Forum* (Fargo), August 20, 1986.
70. *Walsh County Press*, April 21, 1986; McGregor, "D.C. Democrats Celebrate."
71. Ronald Brownstein and Richard Cohen, "Senate GOP Class of 1980: Making the Grade," *National Journal*, April 12, 1986.
72. Wire report, "Ex-Andrews Aide Eyes Senate Run," *Forum* (Fargo), July 4, 1986; Greg Turosak, "Ex-Aide Won't Run for Senate," *Grand Forks Herald*, August 14, 1986.
73. John Vanrig, "Reagan Plans for Visit Vague," *Grand Forks Herald*, October 9,

1986.

74. For example, E. J. Dionne, Jr., "2 Parties Mount Final Offensives: Democrats Approach Is Local—GOP Relies on Reagan," *New York Times*, October 24, 1986; Lou Cannon, "Reagan to Aid GOP Candidates," *Philadelphia Inquirer*, October 23, 1986; Tom Wicker, "Battle for the Senate," *New York Times*, October 31, 1986; and Dick Kirschten, "Reagan on the Road," *National Journal*, October 18, 1986.

75. One analysis described Reagan's visit to North Dakota as an effort "to nationalize the Senate race by couching it in terms of continuing or stalling the Reagan revolution." Jack Germond and Jules Witcover, "Taking Voters Minds off the Farm Crisis," *National Journal*, October 25, 1986.

76. State Poll, Governmental Research Bureau, University of North Dakota, September 15, 1986.

77. Greenberg, "Andrews Admits the Pressure Is on."

78. Farney and Shribman, "The Dakotas Emerge."

79. See Debbie Sandvold, "Reagan Adviser Positive About Summit," *Minot Daily News*, October 15, 1986.

80. A *Wall Street Journal* article said, "*After* Mr. Reagan's recent visit to North Dakota, GOP analysts assert, support for embattled Sen. Mark Andrews shot up nine percentage points in tracking surveys." Jane Mayer, "Nevada Race Turns into Acid Test of Ability of Reagan to Win Votes for Senate Candidates," *Wall Street Journal*, October 30, 1986. On the other hand, North Dakota's State Poll (see Figure 6-1) shows Andrews gaining 7 points *before* the president's visit and falling back into a dead heat thereafter. There is no obvious explanation, other than a skewed sample, for Andrews's October 15 surge.

81. Randy Bradbury, "Ex-Andrews Aide Won't Run," *Forum*, August 14, 1986. See also Dick Dobson, "Doherty Could Spice up Senate Race," *Minot Daily News*, July 13, 1986; E. W. Doherty, "Eddy's 4th Estate," *New Rockford Transcript*, June 7, 1986.

82. Steve Schmidt, "No Regrets," *Grand Forks Herald*, August 15, 1986. In midsummer, this sensitivity to outside influence had surfaced when Andrews had been roundly criticized—and roundly defended—for going to "a big fancy corporate headquarters in San Francisco" to raise money. Wade Williams, "Sen. Andrews of California?" July 26, 1986; Wesley Belter, "Andrews' Work on Transportation Good for N.D. as Well as Frisco," *Forum*, August 17, 1986; Dobson, "Andrews, Conrad Hunt for Dollars."

83. Howard Fineman, "How the Vote Brokers Operate," *Newsweek*, November 10, 1986; Bob Laux-Bachand and Carl Flagstad, "Andrews, Conrad Both Claim Lead on Last Day," *Minot Daily News*, November 4, 1986.   .

84. Sidney Blumenthal, "Populist TV Ads Sold 3 Democrats to Voters," *Washington Post*, November 6, 1986; Jim Neumann, "Conrad Ousts Andrews," *Forum* (Fargo), November 6, 1986; Dale Wetzel, "Conrad Shocks Andrews with 'Miracle,'" *Minot Daily News*, November 5, 1986.

85. Laux-Bachand and Flagstad, "Andrews, Conrad Both Claim." According to published reports, Andrews spent nearly $700,000 between October 16 and November 24. It is not clear what he did with all that money. AP, "Many N.D. Candidates Ended Campaign in Debt," *Forum* (Fargo), December 9, 1986.

86. Blumenthal, "Populist TV Ads."

87. Republican pollster Richard Wirthlin, also from afar, credited Conrad's last-

minute Social Security commercials as having an important effect. Basil Talbot, "Social Security Jabs at GOP Tied to Key Dem Wins," *Chicago Sun Times*, November 12, 1986.

88. AP, "Many N.D. Candidates Ended Campaign in Debt"; Thomas Edsall, "The Republicans Found out That Money Can't Buy You Love," *Washington Post National Weekly Edition*, November 7, 1986.

89. For Hart's own expression that character would be—and was—the "overarching" issue of 1986, see Paul Taylor, "In a Time of No Issues, the Issue Is Mood," *Washington Post National Weekly Edition*, June 23, 1986; and Paul Taylor, "Accentuating the Negative," *Washington Post National Weekly Edition*, October 20, 1986.

90. "Andrews Is Endorsed," *Forum* (Fargo), October 12, 1986; "Re-elect Mark Andrews," *Minot Daily News*, October 26, 1986; "Andrews Has Earned Trip Back to Senate," *Grand Forks Herald*, October 26, 1986; and "Seniority Counts in the Senate," *Bismarck Tribune*, October 30, 1986.

91. I came across two other editorial endorsements, both favorable, and one favorable column—at random. They are: "Now Is Not the Time for Change; Andrews Is Best for North Dakota," *Devils Lake Journal*, October 28, 1986; "N. Dakota Needs Mark Andrews," *Williston Daily Herald*, October 14, 1986; and Dobson, "Should North Dakota Dump Experience?".

92. "Andrews Is Endorsed," *Forum*; "Seniority Counts in the Senate," *Bismarck Tribune*.

Post-Mortems

When I walked into Senator Andrews's Washington office two weeks after the election, the first thing he said was, "These things happen. It's a disappointment, but you can't cry over it. Trying to figure out what happened is about as profitable as looking up a dead horse's ass." But he talked about the election anyway, punctuating each effort to explain with the plaint, "Who knows?" Halfway through our seventy-five minute conversation he said, "You're the political scientist. Perhaps you, in your analysis, can tell me when the love affair with the people of North Dakota stopped." His comment came about as close as he could have to my own point of view—that something had happened between 1980 and 1986 to change the relationship of close identification and rapport between an incumbent and his constituents.

Andrews's immediate reaction had been: "It looks like my love affair with the people of North Dakota is over, but now I'm going to have a love affair with my family." For so many years he had savored his assumed place in the bosom of his North Dakota "family," and he had just been ejected from that place. Publicly, he acknowledged his disappointment. "You've got a love affair going with the people of North Dakota you've served for two decades and they say, 'You're not doing as well as the other guy can.' "[1] For him as well as for me, the question, "Why did Mark Andrews lose the election?" could be answered with only another question: "How did Mark Andrews lose his longstanding relationship of trust and support with his constituents?"

The most general answer, as it has evolved in this study, would be that the deterioration was gradual. Whatever happened to the incumbent took several years to happen. We have conceptualized the Senate campaign and election of 1986 in North Dakota as the culminating event in the long political career of a member of Congress. We have sought answers to our central puzzle by tracing and interpreting the events and decisions of his six-year Senate career as it unfolded in Washington and at home. The analysis rests heavily on a narrative account of the development of his governing style and his governing accomplishments in Washington and of the sequence that linked triumph-to-weakness-to-vulnerability-to-defeat at home. The eventual outcome was not foreordained, nor was it foreseeable when Rep. Mark Andrews became a senator. I could not have imagined it until four years later. The incumbent himself did not believe it would happen until it actually did. We can expect, therefore, to find a number of factors and contingencies under consideration as we assess the post-mortems that followed his career-ending defeat.

However it is calculated, the margin by which Andrews lost the election was the smallest of the 1986 Senate season: 2,135 votes and a single percentage point. With .5 percent change, or a switch of 1,068 votes, he would have won.[2] In an election that close, numerous factors can be decisive and yet no single factor is *the* decisive one. We shall devote most of our analysis to four factors—the farm issue, the lawsuit, incumbent credibility, and incumbent governing style. And we shall treat a couple of others—party and campaign—less extensively. All of these commanded attention in the various post-mortems. We shall try to weave them together into an analysis that is consistent with the story presented in the earlier chapters of this book. For the most part, as we would expect, post-mortem discussions echoed the themes developed in Chapter 6. But they were delivered after the fact, with the benefit of hindsight and with a freedom of expression that would not have been possible beforehand. As such, they deserve separate treatment in this concluding chapter.

THE LOCAL CONTEXT

First, it should be noted that national factors were not judged to be important in determining the North Dakota outcome. Indeed, they were not judged to be important anywhere in the election year 1986. As we reported in the previous chapter, national observers expected the Senate contests to be candidate-centered and locally driven. When it was over, everyone agreed that they had been. *Newsweek's* headline read: "The Results: All Politics Is Local." Columnist Edwin Yoder wrote, "Election day saw the American electorate wallowing as usual in localism. From a national point of view, the 1986 elections were the most themeless, even mindless, in half a century."[3]

Collectively, of course, the Senate elections of 1986 did produce a nationally important result: the Democrats gained eight seats and took control of the Senate. All postelection stories dwelled on that fact. None of them argued, however, that party control had been an issue in several campaigns. If anything, observers attributed President Reagan's speechmaking on behalf of Republican candidates as a failed effort to make party control an overriding national issue.[4] Furthermore, no one argued that the result was attributable to any nationwide issue or national tide. "Democrats' Win, Sans an Agenda, No Help in '88" was the headline of Albert Hunt's interpretation in the *Wall Street Journal*. E. J. Dionne, Jr., wrote in the *New York Times* that the victorious Senate Democrats were "without a clearly defined mandate for a new political agenda."[5] The nature of the election, therefore, left the observers of national tides and national agendas with very little to say about the North Dakota contest.

THE FARM ISSUE

The one local factor everyone recognized was the depressed state of the farm economy. All observers knew that trouble on the land meant trouble for incumbents, and, therefore, that any farm state Republican incumbent in 1986 was positioned squarely in harm's way. When Andrews lost, the farm economy served as everybody's basic explanation. When CBS declared Conrad the winner, commentator Bill Moyers explained:

> I think the conclusion is inescapable [that] in the farm belt where prices are low, foreclosures high, credit tight—across the farm belt—the Reagan farm policy was an albatross and Republican candidates could not shuck it. Let's take North Dakota, for example—Mark Andrews versus Kent (Chainsaw) Conrad. In the exit polls, 45% of North Dakotans said farm policy was the leading issue, and of those who felt that way, by a margin of 6-4 they went for Mr. Conrad. The second most important topic at 27% was the economy . . . there again, Conrad favored by 3-2.[6]

His was the fairly conventional view that the farm issue would overwhelm everything else in a farm state. The final CBS exit polls for North Dakota were a bit less overwhelming: they showed that 36 percent had chosen "farm policies" as one of the "issues that mattered most in your vote," and that Conrad's margin among those voters was 54 percent to 46 percent. And among the 25 percent who chose "the economy" as one such issue, Conrad lead by a similar 56 percent to 43 percent.[7]

To buttress his opinion that the farm issue had overwhelmed all else in North Dakota, Moyers made Mark Andrews the extreme case.

> Look, the farmers have no better friend in the Senate than Mark Andrews, the Republican who got beat tonight. He had three planks in his platform—farmers, farmers, farmers. This is North Dakota. He had three answers for those problems— money, money, money. He was a big spender for farms.

If Mark Andrews could not stand against the tide, he implied, no farm state Republican could. The post-mortem in the *New York Times* took a similar view.[8] For national observers, then, the farm issue was sufficient explanation for the North Dakota outcome.

All the evidence we have amassed in the preceding chapters—poll data, campaign advertisements, candidate rhetoric, newspaper commentary—points, also, to the farm economy as the dominating policy issue of the campaign. The substantive attacks of the challenger and the substantive defenses of the incumbent centered on farm matters. If, as political scientists now fully recognize, the content of Senate campaigns influences voter response, there is little doubt about the potency of the farm economy issue.[9]

Both contestants gave it a prominent place in their earliest post-mortems. "I think very clearly the dominant issue was the economy," said Conrad on the morning after. "Agriculture is in trouble, Main Street business is in trouble. People wanted a change in direction." [10] "We got caught up in the same kind of storm that a number of the Republicans did," Andrews told reporters. "The farmers felt that the economy was against them and they wanted corrections made and they felt the way to make them was to change the people who were in office." [11] Other local observers acknowledged the explanatory power of the farm economy. "While Conrad's narrow victory . . . can be attributed to a variety of factors, the main one was undoubtedly the farm recession," wrote the editor of the *Forum*. Political journalist Dick Dobson pointed to "the rural vote" as a "mega factor"—one of the two—in Conrad's victory. "Conrad effectively exploited voter discontent with the farm recession." Dobson further noted that "Conrad carried 35 [of 53] counties, including several small farming communities that normally go Republican— Emmons, Grant, Kidder, Logan, Wells, etc." [12]

Two of the counties Dobson listed—Emmons and Logan—were sites of my first 1980 campaign swing. Indeed, the town of Lehr is located in Logan County. Andrews's comments, too, triggered my memory of Lehr. In his morning-after reflections, he spoke of the votes he had lost in his home territory because of the lawsuit: "We could have overridden [it] if we would have had the support that I normally get in the rural areas. When I started reading those returns coming in from LaMoure County and Logan County and all the rest [of the rural areas], I knew that the farm economy [had] really done us in."[13]

In October 1980, on our way to Emmons, LaMoure, and Logan Counties, he had said, "If I don't get at least 70 percent of the vote in these counties, I'm in trouble." In 1980, he had carried those three counties by 73 percent, 73 percent, and 77 percent, respectively. His performance at Krueger's Cafe in Lehr had seemed to me to seal that kind of margin, in those places, forever. It hadn't. His 1986 percentages in the three counties were 43 percent, 44 percent, and 47 percent—an average drop of 19 percent. It was eerily symbolic that the Logan County/Lehr connection had come to assume the same large place in the post-mortems of local observers and of the candidate himself as it had assumed in my thinking for six years.

By everyone's account, then, the farm issue was an important factor in the election outcome. But the question arises: How important? As decisive, for example, as Bill Moyers's explanation seemed to make it? Or is there more? In the story as we have told it in this book, the farm issue is a necessary part of any explanation. But it is not, by itself, a sufficient explanation of what happened.

As a mild caveat to the Moyers view, we should note that in the exit polls "farm policies" was only one of several policy areas among which voters were allowed to choose as being important to their vote decision. Because they were allowed to choose more than one, it is not clear which one dominated their vote decision. Conrad did about as well in some of these other issues as in "farm" and "economy." The 19 percent who chose Social Security gave Conrad a 53 percent to 46 percent lead; among the 17 percent who picked "federal spending," Conrad led by 51 percent to 47 percent. Among the respondents (nearly half the sample) classified as "farm," their top issue choice, selected by 62 percent of them, was not surprisingly, farm policies.[14] But their second and third choices, at 52 percent each, were foreign trade and family values, two issues where Andrews led Conrad overall. The economy was their fourth most popular choice, picked by 46 percent of the respondents.

A stronger caveat comes from the presence in the CBS exit poll of a menu of candidate-centered factors. Again, voters could choose more than one. And several of these vote determinants attracted levels of support for Conrad that were just as strong as the 54 percent level he reached among voters who emphasized "farm policies"— albeit among fewer voters. Among the 17 percent of the respondents who chose "will work harder" as a factor that "mattered most," Conrad's margin was 78 percent to 32 percent. Among the 16 percent who picked "character" and among the 10 percent who picked "dislike the other candidate," Conrad led by 53 percent to 42 percent and 58 percent to 43 percent, respectively.

Thus, candidate-related factors may have been just as important to some voters as policy-related factors. Preelection campaign wisdom held that there was no partisan tide running against Republican candidates in the farm belt, and that individually attractive incumbents would survive discontent on the farm.[15] Postelection summaries concluded that things had turned out exactly that way.[16] Other midwestern farm state Republican freshman senators did, indeed, survive in 1986—Charles Grassley of Iowa and Robert Kasten of Wisconsin, for example.[17]

As a final caveat to the Moyers view, it should be noted that Andrews had weathered other downturns in the state's farm economy during his career in the House without apparent difficulty. Net farm income in North Dakota registered a 30 percent decline from 1973 to 1974; yet he was reelected in 1974 (against Byron Dorgan) with 56 percent of the vote. Similarly, his 63 percent election margin in 1976 was preceded by a 69 percent drop in net farm income from 1975 to 1976. By the same aggregate measure of agricultural well-being, the decline from 1985 to 1986, preceding Andrews's defeat, was only 8 percent.[18] To be sure, other measures—especially, as we have noted, the precipitous 1986 fall-off in wheat prices—would spotlight 1986 as an especially bad year on the farm. We are only pointing out that although Andrews had had plenty of farm-related explaining to do in other years, he had enjoyed some countercyclical success in holding the confidence of his constituents. Clearly we will need to look beyond the farm to analyze what happened in 1986.

THE LAWSUIT

When we turn to the post-mortems emanating from North Dakota, the farm issue takes its place within a greater complex of factors, including some candidate-centered ones. One of the state's top Democratic officeholders explained Conrad's victory as "to some degree . . . a repudiation of some of Reagan's policies; but, it gets more complex. In some ways, it's a repudiation of Mark Andrews."[19] Most prominent on the list of factors to explain the repudiation of Mark Andrews was the lawsuit.

In the account of the state's top political columnist, Dick Dobson, the first mega factor mentioned was Andrews's first-ever defeat in his home county stronghold. Dobson began his analysis there. "What probably was the mortal blow," he wrote, "was that for the first time

Mark failed to carry Cass County." [20] Containing, as it does, the state's largest city, Fargo, Cass County is the most populous, most urbanized of the state's counties. Conrad carried the county, Dobson observed, by more than enough votes (1,161) to have elected Andrews, had the margin been reversed. Indeed, had Andrews carried Cass County by his normal 66 percent of the vote, he would have amassed a 14,400 victory margin there in 1986.[21] Why didn't he? "The reason is obvious," Dobson wrote.

> Cass County residents disapproved of the multimillion dollar malpractice lawsuit that Andrews and his wife (disabled by meningitis) had filed against the Fargo medical establishment. In other words, Fargo's doctors were out to dump Andrews. . . . Once the Cass County returns were in, that was it; it was all over. Andrews' neighbors had voted him out of the Senate.[22]

Among newspaper and other local accounts, everyone mentioned the lawsuit as a factor—sometimes "a big factor"—in Andrews's defeat. Sen. Quentin Burdick was reported as saying that "when he was out campaigning for Conrad, people often mentioned Andrews' decision to sue Fargo doctors and medical establishment." [23] The lawsuit, like the farm issue, appears to be a necessary part of the explanation we seek. But is it sufficient?

Mark Andrews understood the special force of these two mega factors as well as anyone. When I asked him afterward where, in retrospect, he might have gone looking for 1,200 votes to switch, he answered, "There were two things that hurt us. One was the farm bill. . . . Then I lost Fargo by 1,000 votes. That was the lawsuit." What he understood less clearly was *why* these two things should have hurt as much as they did.

With respect to the farm bill, he believed that he had given a satisfactory accounting to the voters of his legislative activity. With respect to the lawsuit, he believed the voters would not punish him for what he had done. And, finally, he believed that whatever negative reaction these two factors had provoked, they would be outweighed by a positive reaction to his governing performance in Washington. An examination of the voters' responses in these three areas will help us to explain what happened.

EXPLANATION AND CREDIBILITY

When in the campaigning-governing-campaigning sequence the incumbent turns his or her attention from campaigning to governing, the linking activity is explanation—the incumbent's explanation at home of his or her governing behavior in Washington. As a candidate for reelection, the incumbent seeks voters' approval or satisfaction with his or her record in office by explaining that record. This explanatory effort involves the transmission of information on the part of the incumbent and receptivity to that information on the part of the voter. Receptivity, in turn, is crucially affected by the candidate's current level of credibility, by the voters' willingness to believe the candidate's explanation, and by the voters' inclination to give the candidate the benefit of the doubt when information and explanation are ambiguous.

We can think of the benefit of the doubt as a matter of trust. And we can think of the candidate's credibility and constituents' trust as a relationship that grows out of the sum total of an incumbent's activities over a long period of time. Incumbents build up, or try to build up, a cushion of trust that will ensure voters' receptivity to their explanations—especially when they are put in harm's way. Mark Andrews faced this kind of explanatory task with respect to his behavior on farm policies. In 1985 and 1986, I had watched the senator explain his governing activity on the farm bill. He believed that his constituents would be receptive to his explanation and would approve of his performance. After all, he had always been successful in the past.

After the election, he told reporters that although he had expected the lawsuit to cost him 5,000 votes in Cass County, "we thought we would cover it up in farm votes and other votes across the state." [24] In retrospect, however, he realized that there had been no covering votes from the farm, and he wondered about the adequacy of his explanation. "When you see rural counties that I've carried by two to one [in] election after election after election going after the idea that the farm bill is no good, obviously either the farm bill isn't good or I did a lousy job explaining it." [25]

Privately he was more expansive—and more upset.

> I thought we explained the best we could that the bill meant $1,000 for every man, woman, and child in North Dakota. I don't know how else we could have done it. Maybe I should have emphasized the target price of $4.38 [they got in the 1985 bill] as an increase over $3.81 [which they had in the 1981 bill]. Nobody else ever fought harder for the farmers than I did. Bill Moyers said on election night that I was the best friend the farmer ever had. I was the best. But the exit polls showed people concerned about the farm issue going 60-40 against Andrews. That's tough to take. What happened? Who knows?

The magnitude of the rural defection obviously puzzled him.

I didn't lose it in the cities. I lost it in all the little towns I
always carried by two to one. That was the farm thing, I guess.
There was that ugly feeling out there that things are bad, so
we'll beat up on Mark Andrews. Why? Who knows? I could
have gotten up and criticized the farm bill. But I didn't think I
had to distance myself that much from the administration. And
I think it was a good farm bill.

By the standards of almost any outsider—political scientist or
reporter—Andrews's legislative record on agriculture policy showed
him to be a formidable player, extraordinarily well informed, and
immensely helpful to his state. And certainly, by outsider standards, his
explanation at home of his governing activity in Washington was
knowledgeable, skillful, and sincere. A North Dakota reporter who
spent a year following the senator's activity on Capitol Hill set down
some "farewell observations" that dovetailed with my own conclusions.

It is particularly ironic that Andrews should lose his election
partially because of voter discontent with current farm policy.
There probably was no Republican senator who fought the
Reagan administration harder over farm policy than did Andrews. Andrews is a political realist, and he knew that the
President would veto any farm bill that strayed too far from
Reagan's commitment to reduced agricultural price supports.
But within that boundary, Andrews made the White House pay
dearly for his support every step of the way during the tortuous
farm bill debate. He probably got about as much for North
Dakota farmers as was possible. Of course he voted for the bill
in its final form. That is the price you pay for striking deals. It's
how business is done in Washington. He was honoring commitments that had benefited his constituents.[26]

If ever a record and an explanation should have been persuasive to
voters, they should have been persuasive in Mark Andrews's case. But
they were not. Why?

His explanations were not easy to grasp. As I had observed in 1985,
and again in 1986, most of his explanations were Washington-oriented,
calling for voters' appreciation of his insider perspectives and his insider
performance. Voters can appreciate the broad targets or the concrete
results of the legislative process much easier than they can the bargaining process itself. Legislative negotiation—of the sort described in the
truck width fight, for instance—remains invisible to the naked eye. The
voter always lacks information about what goes on in Congress, but the
deficiency is doubly hard on the voter when the activity being explained is so heavily freighted with the kinds of inside, out-of-sight
maneuvering with which Mark Andrews was so enamored and at which

he was so talented. Under the best of circumstances, that is, his governing style made explanation difficult. Explanation normally required a strong predisposition on the part of his constituents to believe what he said about what he had done in Washington and how his behavior had redounded to their benefit. We can assume that voters had remained favorably predisposed for seventeen years when he needed them—in good times and in bad.

In 1986 in North Dakota, the best of circumstances did not prevail. The farm recession was sufficiently serious and widespread and exploitable that Andrews needed an abnormally robust predisposition on the part of his constituents to believe his explanations and to give him the benefit of the doubt on his farm policy activity. He didn't get it. It was Mark Andrews's underlying weakness that he had lost that crucial cushion of credibility when he most needed it. That is where the lawsuit problem interacted with the farm problem. Simply put, the lawsuit had severely damaged his overall credibility with his constituents. For them, the lawsuit had raised troubling questions of adherence to community norms and, hence, of character. He might be "working for us," but he might not be "one of us." And there is plenty of evidence from the poll results that constituents' doubts were not limited to Cass County. To some degree, therefore, any kind of explanation that Andrews might undertake of his farm bill behavior in 1985 and 1986 would encounter more suspicion and less receptivity.

The bewilderment expressed in Andrews's post-mortems about the lawsuit echoed the bewilderment he had expressed during the campaign. "I'll never understand that," he said afterward.

> I just don't understand what gets into people, how they think. I had an Air Force F-4 retrofit contract all ready to come into Fargo. That meant $400 million and a lot of jobs for the area. They won't get it now. They want me to help them, protect them, stand up for them, but when I help my family, protect my family, stand up for my family, they turn against me.

He did not believe—could not believe—that voters would punish him at the polls for the lawsuit. His only explanation, therefore, for the fact that they did was that *they*, not he, had abandoned their longtime love affair and the community values on which it rested.

"It's courage and determination, North Dakota style, and all that," he said of his wife's fight. "Geez, we got phone calls saying we don't want to see people in wheelchairs. And that really cut, because what do they want me to do, put her in a closet someplace? That's the one that probably hurt more than anything else." Later he said, "Somehow or another, North Dakota just never understood Mark Andrews if they figured he was going to back away from supporting Mary. I would think North Dakota would think less of me if I didn't stand up for my family." [27]

One of his consultants believed that Andrews should have explained the lawsuit more than he did.

> There was a negative reaction to the lawsuit. But to those of us who knew him, what happened to Mary was the result of negligence, and he had suffered a terrible blow and he deserved all the sympathy in the world taking on the medical establishment. I always thought he should have been much more straightforward and detailed in his advertisements about the terrible things that had happened to Mary. But he did not want to do it.

It was a private matter; he expected the voters to understand; and he did not believe he should have to make a public play for their sympathy. He said afterward:

> If I had not fought for my wife, it wouldn't have been me. You have to be who you are. If people don't like it, so be it. But you ask yourself: Are these the people I've worked so hard for for twenty-three years? If that's so, maybe I'm better off out of here. . . . I never regretted suing those bastards. The judge found them guilty; but the jury handed down an outrageous ruling.

That very private decision was every bit as crucial to his career as his very public decision to support the 1985 farm bill.

Not only did the lawsuit diminish incumbent credibility by itself, it also diminished incumbent credibility by reinforcing the negative effects of certain controversial events that followed. One was his role in the Garrison Diversion compromise with the Audubon Society. An even more serious case was the summer investigation of Byron Dorgan and Andrews's possible association with it. Because this investigation, like the lawsuit, involved a matter of personal propriety, the two subjects were coupled in many post-mortems as having made a joint, cumulative contribution to the "erosion of polling strength" suffered by the incumbent. Provided that voters reacted the way observers thought they did, then the two matters were mutually reinforcing in the stimulation and perpetuation of voters' doubts and suspicions.

On election night, the Republican state chairman paired the lawsuit and Dorgan investigation in observing that Andrews had begun the fall campaign "with a couple of strikes against him." A reporter mentioned the same pair of "incidents" in his post-mortem. "While Andrews' slip in the polls was unexpected, it was attributed both to Conrad's campaign and to a couple of incidents in the past couple of years that may have hurt Andrews' credibility [and] his popularity." A month later, another reporter wrote that Andrews's "evident frustration" with the same two problems "still bubbles to the surface." [28] A third reporter's post-mortem was similar, but included the Garrison contretemps.

> Andrews suffered from something called the "character" issue. This seems to be a collection of voter suspicions about his motives in a wide variety of areas: his medical lawsuit, his possible involvement in an investigation of Rep. Byron Dorgan, D-ND, his wheeling and dealing on Garrison diversion and other matters. [29]

It is our guess that of the three sources of "suspicion," the lawsuit was the most damaging and most likely to have a negative multiplier effect on the others.

Mark Andrews's weakness as it derived from a loss of credibility was no political secret. His challenger knew it. And on one matter, postelection observers expressed little disagreement. Kent Conrad had been extremely effective in exploiting the doubts that existed about Andrews's trustworthiness. As one of Andrews's campaigners put it:

> A couple of years ago, the idea began to get around that Mark Andrews was aloof—you know, the arrogance thing. I don't know where it came from. People may not have been able to put their finger on it. But people were just waiting for something concrete to come along; and Conrad gave it to them. First there was the double-talk ad, and then the wheat ad. And people said, "See, I told you, there was something wrong with Mark Andrews."

Another said, "Conrad ran a good negative campaign and people believed it or accepted it. They were ready to accept anything bad about Mark." The challenger had a similar view of his success. "I couldn't have done it without the antipathy that had built up toward Mark Andrews in North Dakota," Conrad said afterward. He recognized vulnerability, and he exploited it—especially on television.

Conrad called his commercials "attack" ads—"hard on the issues, nothing personal," as he put it. The Republicans labeled them "negative advertising." "Conrad carried on a hard-hitting, aggressive, largely negative campaign," wrote one pro-Andrews observer, "[and] it is doubtful that the tax commissioner would have won if he had not employed the negative campaign." [30] A Republican leader said simply, "It came down to the effectiveness of their media. Their slick advertising was better than Andrews' slick advertising." There was a general agreement locally with this sentiment. [31] Andrews agreed that Conrad's negative campaign was a major factor in his defeat. "This was the year the negative campaign was in vogue," he said. "The in-thing seems to be who started negatives early enough and did them long enough. We should have done them a lot earlier. I just didn't like the negatives. We should have started whacking them in August." [32] A Republican leader echoed that "the lesson to be learned is that negative advertising works." But long afterward, Kent Conrad's television consultant had the last word. "The wrong lesson is that negative campaigns work," he said. "The right lesson is that if you stand up and fight back, you can beat them. If you don't you'll lose." [33] Mark Andrews didn't fight back, and it cost him.

Looking back, Andrews commented that Conrad had presented a very elusive target: a "tougher opponent than Dorgan would have been." [34] "If Dorgan had stayed in the race," he repeated privately, "I think we would have won. We had some better issues against Dorgan than against Conrad." Conrad, he said, "got 80 percent of the vote in 1984, had as much name familiarity as Byron did or I do, and he had no voting record. All he'd been known as was the guy who spent his time bashing corporations." [35] When Andrews did try to go negative against Conrad for misfeasance in the tax commissioner's office, the effort, as we saw earlier, seemed feeble, refutable, and doomed. So the elusiveness of the target may have helped to deter a strong counterattack.

But Andrews never seemed to have his heart in any such tit-for-tat strategy. He had never liked negative campaigning; he had never believed that North Dakotans liked it; and he approached the 1986 campaign with the same mindset. When the election was over, one of his media advisers recalled Andrews's reluctance.

> We didn't answer Conrad's wheat ad for a long time. There was the idea that we shouldn't stoop to answer him. Finally, we did have an ad that showed Mark leaning on a fence post, looking straight into the camera, saying, "I'm not for lower wheat prices, I don't double talk." It was a good ad. People liked it.

As we described it earlier, this ad seemed much too gentle to spur a reversal of his fortunes.

Later in the campaign, another hard-hitting television ad (also described earlier) accused Andrews of missing a vote that cost the state $2 million in unemployment funds, while he sought an honorarium for speaking at a posh Florida watering hole. Again the incumbent did not counterattack. "Everyone I talked to two weeks before the election was talking about it," said one Andrews campaigner. "But we didn't answer it. The argument was that it wasn't showing up on our tracking polls. Yet on the street, everyone was talking about it." Surely the incumbent did not help his cause by his tardy response to these attacks. But he seemed almost resigned to this shortcoming. "We didn't do as good in writing nasty thirty-second commercials," he summed up. "If you have to go that far to win an election, I'm probably better off at the farm." [36]

This last comment fit with his reaction to his difficulty with the lawsuit. Andrews couldn't believe that he would have had to behave differently in order to win. And if that was so, well, then, he would probably "be better off out of here" or "better off at the farm." Since Mark Andrews was an ambitious politician and since he obviously enjoyed his work in the Senate, we conclude that the real meaning of these comments was that he did not believe he had to behave differently in order to survive. From beginning to end, that is to say, his fundamental calculation was that his record of accomplishment would matter most and would, in the final reckoning, carry him to victory at the polls.

GOVERNING STYLE AND PORK BARREL PRESENTATION

Having watched and studied Mark Andrews's governing exploits, it is impossible to believe that any legislator in the history of the state could have worked any harder for, or delivered any more federal money to, North Dakota than Mark Andrews. Surely he was the most dedicated, most single-minded, most successful procurer of grants, projects, and protective legislative language I have ever encountered. From its most heroic to its most parochial connotations, *Time* magazine's title, "King of Pork," seemed appropriate. What is more, Andrews funneled federal dollars to a citizenry that placed an abnormally high value on precisely that kind of constituent service. He believed that when all the shouting was over, his legislative reputation as a provider of government largess, "working for us," would reelect him. He believed he could convince voters that, in the postelection language of the *Forum*, "North Dakota needs competency as well as clout in its congressmen. We had both of these attributes in Andrews." In his own public post-mortems, Andrews emphasized his legislative success. "We brought the bacon home," he stated as he ticked off "a long list of federal projects and farm bill supports." In whatever he did, he said, he "put North Dakota's interest first. And while we haven't won all our legislative battles, we have won the major share of them." [37] He had always thought of himself primarily as a legislator; even after his defeat, he wanted to be remembered for his legislative accomplishments.

But it was not easy for him to comprehend, or to accept, the electoral failure. Just as in the case of the farm bill and the lawsuit, the voters' reaction to his legislative accomplishments left him puzzled.

Privately, he described his feelings as "disappointment" or "hurt," over what must have seemed like lost love. As he recited his long list of tangible, job-producing accomplishments, he said, "I got more things for North Dakota than anyone in the history of North Dakota. That's part of the hurt." Later he repeated the sentiment: "It was a disappointment. . . . I got so much for North Dakota. That's the hurt of it." In our conversation, he told about a reporter from the *Christian Science Monitor* who had come from another farm state to do a story on his campaign.

> She said to me, "I've just been in state X. Everybody knows that the senator up for reelection there is a klutz; but in that state they love him. Everybody in Washington knows you are one of the best legislators on Capitol Hill; and back home everyone is mad at you. I don't understand it." I told her, "I don't either."

His puzzlement colored his discussion of election specifics.

> I lost Jamestown. I lost the Republican precincts there, but I won the Democratic precincts. . . . Maybe a lot of Republicans said, "I'll just send a protest vote against Mark Andrews, teach him a lesson." Well, they got more than they wanted. Who knows? I lost Jamestown, even though I saved Western Gear [Company] and a lot of jobs in that town.

No one else, he believed, was likely to be able to legislate in so beneficial a fashion for the people of North Dakota.

> I don't know what will happen to the state now. Milt Young carried Quentin Burdick for years. I carried Quentin Burdick for six years. Dorgan never got anything, never did anything except issue press releases. I'm afraid Conrad will do the same. They're out of the same shed.

He paused, then completed his valedictory. "At our farewell luncheon today, Bob Dole said, 'Now that Mark Andrews is gone, some of the rest of us may get some of the money—especially Kansas.'"

His remarkable pork barrel prowess was his trump card. Surely it helped. After all, he nearly won. But legislative accomplishments proved insufficient to pull him through. Why? The main answer, as we have developed it in this book, is that the voters of North Dakota had become gradually responsive to a more expansive governing style—one exemplified by Byron Dorgan and one they could imagine getting from Dorgan's protégé, Kent Conrad. The signs of this new attraction were written all over Andrews's midcycle polls, well before the malpractice suit was filed and well before the farm bill became an issue. In March of 1982, the incumbent senator had already begun to receive lukewarm reactions to his "leadership on national issues." And by December of

1983—despite favorable voter reaction overall—the underlying poll results made it clear that North Dakota's hottest love affair was with Byron Dorgan, not Mark Andrews. By all measures of identification at home and legislative prowess in Washington—Andrews's twin strengths—Dorgan already ranked higher with the voters than did the incumbent senator. Andrews's popularity—and probably his credibility as well—was being undercut well before the lawsuit hit the electorate. Public reaction to that event served only to cripple further an already threatened incumbent.

It was not that Dorgan and Andrews differed fundamentally on policy matters. They did not. Their differences were mainly stylistic and presentational. The voters were becoming increasingly attracted by Dorgan's vigorous attention to national issues and his equally vigorous cultivation of personal publicity. If, therefore, Andrews had wanted to strengthen his hand for a run against Dorgan—or to fortify himself against later adversity—he would have been well advised to move in the direction of the stylistic patterns so heavily favored by his constituents. But, as we have seen, he did not. He worried about it; but he did not change his governing style.

He never developed a broad legislative agenda designed to resonate beyond North Dakota. He did take one notable legislative initiative of this sort: the defense warranty proposal (Chapter 4). It was a natural for a populist-leaning state, and it brought him the most flattering press treatment he ever received in North Dakota. The idea that one of their own might be on a path to national leadership seemed exhilarating to the home folks. Indeed, it was the only specific legislative accomplishment that voters could recognize. But in Andrews's hands, the warranty proposal became more of an isolated accomplishment than part of a broad legislative crusade against Pentagon waste. Thus its potential impact on the electorate was dissipated. His fellow farm state freshman, Charles Grassley, had successfully "inoculated" himself against the effects of the farm recession by launching and escalating just such a broad-gauged anti-Pentagon spending crusade.[38]

The North Dakota senator was certainly proud of what he had done with his defense warranty proposal. But he let it lie, as another piece of evidence that he was an effective inside legislator, and as a notice to the Pentagon that he was a force to be reckoned with. He seemed, therefore, to be storing up chits for future use in making deals for North Dakota, rather than pushing a large policy question onto the national agenda. Accordingly, the matter soon disappeared from public view. As we have already emphasized, it was not his habit or his instinct to think nationally. And he never did surround himself with a staff of legislative activists who would push him to change.

A North Dakotan who returned from a Washington research organization to campaign for Andrews offered the suggestion, in a postelection memo, that pork barrel politics might not have produced a sufficient legislative profile to hold the state's voters. Having listened to Andrews tell a large audience how much bacon—sometimes "the whole hog"—he had brought home, and having watched the audience sit emotionless while the senator listed the many local groups to whom the federal dollars had flowed, the expatriate campaigner speculated about the limited appeal of such legislative exploits.

> By telling them all the things the federal government had done for them, he seemed to be saying they were unable to fend for themselves. . . . Mark Andrews was telling his people the truth, but they did not want to hear it. He was telling them they can't make it on their own, despite their frugal habits, good intentions and work ethic. While the senator was telling the Minot folks that they couldn't do without him, his young opponent was in Fargo saying, "If Mark Andrews is so influential back in Washington, why are we having such a tough time in North Dakota?" He [Conrad] ran a campaign that helped North Dakotans maintain their pride. That's real important. I'd forgotten just how important. And I'm afraid Senator Andrews forgot it, too.[39]

The author's suggestion was that Mark Andrews needed to convey some larger vision than that of a successful inside negotiator, some broader mission than bringing home the bacon—what we have called a "pork barrel plus" performance. The further suggestion is that Conrad, like Dorgan, had already preempted the broader, populist vision that had been at the heart of North Dakota's politics for so long.

In fairness to Andrews, his reputation as a legislative operator had always involved more than an ability to get grants and projects. He had made substantive contributions to agricultural legislation; he had authored important amendments on education and health care; he had taken an independent stand on civil rights; and he had displayed streaks of populism. To some degree, therefore, "King of Pork," while accurate, was also an oversimplification, a caricature. On the other hand, it was a caricature for which Andrews himself was primarily responsible. For he presented his other legislative accomplishments as bits and pieces of legislative effort and not as an identifiable whole. His pork barrel performance was what he thought would reelect him; that was what he campaigned on; that is what he emphasized when it was over; and that was what he wanted to be remembered by.

This narrow perspective was displayed in the following postelection outburst by one of his closest advisers: "If Mark Andrews had not been there the last six years, the North Dakota economy would have been devastated—utterly devastated. Wait till the pork stops coming in! It has begun to stop already. Then maybe people will know what they have lost." It was not the most inspiring view one might have taken of the aspirations of North Dakota voters. Without any doubt, they expected, appreciated, and valued the flow of federal dollars. But their favorable appraisal of Byron Dorgan indicated some desire to render judgments on a basis that would incorporate rather than isolate pork barrel prowess.

The North Dakota senator adapted no more easily to the publicity-seeking element of the new legislative style than to its issue activism. But he recognized and worried openly about his shortcoming from the very beginning of our association. Public relations ability was the special political strength he saw in Byron Dorgan. In his post-mortems, Andrews recalled his troubled relations with the press. "I had a lot of trouble with my staff in the early days. . . . My press people were not very good. And I wasn't watching them as closely as I should. I was learning my Senate duties and spending a lot of time worrying about Mary. I had to clean them out a couple of times." Not until his last year did he express satisfaction with his press operation. But by that time, he admitted afterward, it was too late. "Just when I've got the best staff on Capitol Hill, I won't need them anymore." But, he explained, "even when I had the best staff on Capitol Hill, the press still wrote that I had a lousy staff." The fact is, he suffered from poor press relations throughout his term.

Afterward, he rehearsed some of his difficulties—inaccurate investigative reporting and a negative spin on breaking news.

> A couple of years ago, articles started appearing that I had gotten out of touch with North Dakota, that I hadn't been home as much as I used to. We checked and found it was not true . . . but the criticism took on a life of its own. . . . The press wrote some outrageous stories about how I berated my staff. They wrote that I had a candy box on my desk and that when they snitched candy, I screamed at them. You've been in my office many times. Have you ever seen a candy box in my office? ["No."] People believe these stories. Since when can the press print stories like that with impunity?[40]

"Unfair press treatment," he said, "continued into the campaign—especially their coverage of the Dorgan investigation. I think they were looking for sensationalism. About the only thing I could say was that I didn't know anything about it because I didn't."[41] When the facts came out and proved him innocent, he said, "It all made perfect sense. But nobody believed it, so the story stayed around." Unfavorable media treatment that "stayed around" or "took on a life of its own" or was "believed" by people could only contribute to an atmosphere of doubt that was harmful to the incumbent.

Whether or not all of Andrews's complaints were valid, there is little doubt that credibility can be weakened or strengthened by media treatment. There is also little doubt that elective politicians work hard to ensure favorable treatment. And there is little doubt that Mark Andrews was not very successful in this endeavor—not during his six-year term and not during his reelection campaign. He knew that his credibility had suffered in both respects—starting before constituents' doubts peaked over the lawsuit and continuing throughout the campaign. When I asked a close Andrews confidant what happened, the answer was, "There's not much to talk about. The campaign was one of innuendo, lies, distortions, and half-truths fueled by a virulent anti-Andrews media. That was the campaign." At the very least, the vehemence of this broadside indicates how poor his press relations had become and how central various perceptions of Mark Andrews's credibility had become to the explanation of the electoral outcome.

With better public relations, Mark Andrews could have added to or shored up his public credibility—when that was what he most needed. Certainly the presence and the polling prowess of Byron Dorgan gave him every incentive to do so. Still, the matter puzzled him at least as much as it stirred him to action. And when the campaign was over he recorded, once again, his familiar ambivalence on the subject.

> My wife says my problem was that I spent too much of my time doing it and not enough of my time talking about it. I'm not good at grandstanding. And I think the people of North Dakota are getting used to people who put a lot of effort into press releases. They have been "Dorganized." Dorgan has brought about a change and there has been a slow erosion in that direction. My relations with the press aren't as good as they once were. Maybe there's a new generation of press people. Maybe I've gone beyond my time. Who knows?

The comment was characteristic. Mark Andrews was not a talking or a publicizing legislator. He was a doing legislator. He knew that for many legislators, setting forth a national agenda or vision means little more than talking about it and publicizing it, not doing anything about it. But he believed that doing—however narrow its scope might be—was better than talking and publicizing. His attitude toward Byron Dorgan, and toward Dorgan's "clone," Kent Conrad, remained to the end: "What has he ever *done*?" It was one more expression of his unwavering belief that governing accomplishments ought to carry the day.

Andrews's question, "What has he ever done?" was, by 1986, an anachronism. Halfway into Andrews's Senate term, twice as many North Dakotans were crediting Representative Dorgan as were crediting Andrews for securing federal funds for the state (Table 4-1). By 1985, solid majorities of North Dakota citizens were giving Dorgan high marks and high credibility on a whole battery of questions, including some about his legislative accomplishments (Table 5-2). Dorgan was outpolling Andrews, too, on all measures of effective communications and public relations practices.

Since the congressman was, after all, his prospective opponent, these various comparisons constituted a virtual invitation to change. They should have stimulated some movement toward the stylistic preferences of the voters, a move to preempt some of the stylistic territory occupied by Dorgan. But, as we have seen, Andrews did not respond to the "Dorganization" of North Dakota, not with respect to issue activism and not with respect to publicity seeking.

A midcourse correction would surely have helped him; it might even have saved him. So why didn't he do it? Why didn't Mark Andrews change his governing style? The answer, as we have developed it through our narrative account, is simple: *he couldn't.* Whether he wanted to or not, he couldn't.

We have been arguing throughout the book that Mark Andrews's perceptions, decisions, and behavior patterns must be understood as the products of a long political career. That career took shape and flowered in the House of Representatives; Andrews became a very late-blooming phenomenon in the Senate. In the sequence of his career experiences, we suspect, lies much of the explanation of why he behaved as he did and why he didn't behave differently. Our earlier description of Andrews's transition from House to Senate emphasized the persistence of the congressman's perspectives and behavior in the work of the senator. Our explanation of his unreconstructed pork barrel presentation to the voters in 1986 forces us back to that long-term, career-oriented explanation of the senator's behavior.

The distinctive governing style of Mark Andrews took shape during his House career, when he was a minority member of a powerful money-allocating committee. During his fifteen years in that position, he learned how to negotiate behind the scenes and across party lines within a small working group in order to win tangible, incremental benefits for his state. He became a legislative insider; he learned how to bring home the bacon; and he became an enormously skillful deal cutter in that particular legislative domain. This was the established governing style he brought with him to the Senate.

The change from one institution to the other might, by itself, have produced an incentive to change his governing style. After all, he was now a member of the majority party, holding a leadership role. Besides, many senators could be seen exemplifying the newer activist legislative style. There is some evidence that Andrews thought about changing his pattern of behavior, at the beginning with his committees and from time to time with his staff. But whatever efforts he undertook were half-hearted and met with questionable success. In the end, the governing style he exhibited in the Senate was the governing style he had learned and followed for a long time in the House. Ultimately, it constrained and shaped his 1986 presentation to the North Dakota electorate.

Even Andrews's campaign conduct demonstrated his lack of receptivity to newer political styles. The national press described the 1986 Senate elections as "ugly, unedifying and unprecedentedly expensive," as "the nastiest, silliest, most vacuous, vicious campaign year in history." [42] By national standards, the Andrews-Conrad campaign was relatively tame. It was, accordingly, swamped by the publicity given to a number of other campaigns. [43] But North Dakota observers judged it to be, by local standards, both unusually negative and something of a turning point in statewide politics. They wrote that "in employing the so-called negative campaign, Conrad was bringing to North Dakota politics [a practice] that is accepted in other states." They wrote about the state's 1986 campaign experience as if it signaled the end of North Dakota's "retail politics, the art of campaigning in small town cafes and barbershops"—"a change, alas, [that] has been for the worse."

A national reporter, surveying the 1986 Senate elections, generalized that campaign consultants "have discovered that it almost always pays to attack an opponent on television. This is a reversal of the accepted wisdom of the 1960s and 1970s, when attack ads were considered a high risk tactic, prone to backfire." [44] In this light, Mark Andrews's reluctance or inability to embrace hard-hitting television tactics stands as one more instance in which the old style politician of the 1960s and 1970s had been caught on the cusp of change. It was all of a piece with his lagging performance in other aspects of public relations and public presentation.

In the days following his defeat, the senator himself brought up these career-long constraints on his senatorial performance. A staff member who accompanied him to a postelection meeting reported:

> On Tuesday, Strom Thurmond had a meeting to talk about how the Senate could be made to run better. Mark may have put his finger on something when he spoke up and said that he had been too long in the House, and that he had acted too much like a House member, like a minority House member. He said that he didn't develop a national point of view; that he didn't become senatorial. Everything he did, he said, was directed at North Dakota.

It was ironic that a man who had devoted every legislative moment of his career to helping North Dakota should have reflected that it might have been, in the final showdown, a liability. The voters, we have suggested, had signaled a readiness for something more, for "pork barrel plus," in 1986. But he could not give it to them. And for that inability, the timing and the unfolding of his career were largely responsible.

In our conversation, too, Andrews engaged in some career-oriented analysis. He remarked that with the Democrats having taken control of the Senate, his reelection would have put him back in the minority again. He reconfirmed his attachment to his longtime governing style when he reflected that minority status might, indeed, have been more suitable to him.

> I might have been more effective in the minority, because I have so many friends on both sides of the aisle. At our transportation [subcommittee staff] guy's farewell luncheon today, [Sen.] Dan Inouye was there, [Rep.] Jamie Whitten was there, [Sen.] Lowell Weicker, and [Sen.] Ted Stevens. There were as many from the Democratic side as the Republican side. I can screw something up or put something together as well as anyone in the Senate. I could have done it in the minority as well as I could in the majority. I know what I'm doing. I know how to legislate.

The presence of Jamie Whitten—the chairman of the House Appropriations Committee, the chairman of that committee's agriculture subcommittee (on which Andrews sat for so long), and a Mississippi-agricultural pork barreler par excellence—was a visible reminder of the circumstances under which Andrews's governing style had been molded and of the time in his career when he had learned how to legislate. It seemed incredible that he could think of himself as being quite comfortable in the minority party again—willingly relinquishing his chance at policy leadership to pursue tangible benefits for his North Dakota constituents.

In sum, Mark Andrews's career carried him across a changing political landscape. He could not adapt to that change. And his failure to adapt helps us explain his campaign behavior and his campaign defeat.

PARTY AND IDEOLOGY

In light of the senator's maverick independence in Washington and his career-long problem in relating to his party's conservative establishment at home, it was natural that some postelection speculation should have centered on the party-and-ideology factor as a possible contributor to his defeat. At the general level of organizational strength, there was little disagreement that the Republican party was in decline. Its statewide ticket had been decimated in 1984; and the loss of Andrews meant that for the first time, there would be no North Dakota Republican legislator on Capitol Hill. "It's obvious the party is down and out," wrote political analyst Dobson when it was over. "The Democrats," he wrote later, "have been the ascendant party, especially over the last four years. They have the better party organization both at the headquarters and at the grass roots level." Andrews, too, called them "a well oiled machine." Observers noted that both parties had invested heavily in voter identification programs and that "the success of those voter ID programs was expected to factor heavily in the outcome." Kent Conrad's reaction to his victory as "a miracle," in which "we absolutely could not have done any better than we did," his naming of "the Democratic party" as his strongest base of support, and his reference to "my very dear friend" Byron Dorgan made clear the importance of the party organization, or "the team," to his success.[45] On the other side of the fence things were, as they always had been, a lot more problematic.

In his public post-mortems, Andrews said simply, "The party has grown progressively weaker and weaker."[46] Privately, he expanded on his relationship to the organization. He went out of his way to praise— as his own creation—the voter ID program of 1986.

> I have never been able to get control of the party machinery. When Milt Young was senator, he wouldn't let anyone touch it. But he didn't do anything with it. When I finally got to the Senate, the governor was a Republican. He did nothing with it; and he was the only Republican governor to get beaten in 1984. By that time, the thing was in shambles. We spent a lot of money getting phone banks and voter identification organized. And they did a terrific job. . . . We would have lost by a lot more if we hadn't had the phone bank operation.

He was speaking favorably, of course, about a collection of Republicans and others who had worked hard on his behalf.

With the party's conservative establishment, however, relations remained strained, if not positively unhelpful. As previously noted, some national conservatives had openly declared their nonsupport; and some local conservatives had threatened him with a primary. "I have never been a favorite of the Republican party—or what passes for the Republican party," Andrews reminisced after the election.

> Yet I'm the only one who survived. They seem to hold that against me. It's been that way for a long time. I remember in

> 1964 when we went to receive the endorsement of the state
> convention out in Dickinson. Don Short represented the west-
> ern part of the state and I represented the eastern part. He
> voted against the Civil Rights Bill. I voted for it. He voted
> against the farm bill. I voted for it. We were good friends; and
> we agonized over our votes together, even when we differed.
> But he was a real right winger. I remember when he and his
> wife walked down the aisle to the stage, everyone at the
> convention stood up and cheered and clapped and whistled.
> Then, when Mary and I walked down the aisle, two people
> belched and one yawned, and that's about it. Well, it wasn't
> that bad; but I'll never forget that cold reception. Don Short got
> beat—it was the Goldwater year. And I won. The party people
> never got over that and never forgave me for that victory.

He had spent a career at home and in Washington, alternately "rattling
the bars of his party's fairly rigid ideological cage" [47] and attending to
his party functions at home. He was more independent than loyalist; but
he tried, where possible, to be both.

One diagnostic factor for the 1986 campaign was the question of
President Reagan's visit to North Dakota. From the beginning, and with
no public hesitation whatever, Andrews declared his desire to welcome
the conservatives' hero to the state and to solicit his assistance. The
president came on October 12, late in the campaign. Other farm state
senators had played it differently. Charles Grassley had kept the
president out of Iowa; Bob Kasten had invited him to Wisconsin a year
earlier. [48] Andrews's stated hope was that the visit would stimulate
public interest. But it could also be interpreted as a gesture toward party
solidarity that might mollify the conservative wing. When the election
was over, he wondered about the wisdom of that decision: "We were 12
points up in our polls the week before the president came, and 7 points
up in the North Dakota poll just before the president came. Maybe that
was a mistake. Maybe I would have been better off not having the
president come. . . . I don't know. Who knows?"

Kent Conrad thought Andrews's decision had been extremely
harmful, because it had sent precisely the wrong signal to the electorate.
"Bringing in Reagan was a mistake. Reagan's policies had been a disaster
for our state. It made people wonder, 'How independent is this guy?' It
was another turning point for us, I think." Conrad's argument was that
the president's visit turned away independent voters.

It is impossible to know whether the president's visit helped
Andrews with conservative Republicans. Since turnout was the highest,
for a nonpresidential year, in North Dakota history (and the highest of
all Senate races in 1986, at 58.3 percent), we can assume that it did

"invigorate state Republicans," and that conservative Republicans did not sit out the election.[49] The CBS exit poll shows that Conrad won some votes from Republicans (13 percent), from conservatives (32 percent), and from people who approved of the president's job performance (32 percent). But one cannot know what these numbers mean, either in terms of conservative defections or in terms of the effect of the president's visit. The CBS exit polls do show Conrad winning 54 percent of the self-styled independent voters. By the time the president came to North Dakota, however, the dynamics and the course of the campaign were fixed. So the visit probably had only the most minimal of effects.

One possible effect of the visit, however, was to remind North Dakota's conservatives that they had a Republican president of their common persuasion and that their senator had been one of his most frequent Republican opponents. That reminder could only have aggravated their unhappiness with the incumbent. When reporters solicited an election post-mortem from the state's top-ranking Republican officeholder, the staunchly conservative secretary of state, he commented:

> There's things I don't like that Mark did. But one thing about him, he fought for the farm price. He lost for several reasons. He lost the conservative vote because he lambasted President Reagan. And the lawsuit. Then, of course, Kent Conrad accrued some extra points with his ads.[50]

Similarly, national conservative Republican leader Paul Weyrich attributed Andrews's defeat partly to the fact that "movement conservatives in North Dakota were treated by the senator with arrogance and contempt. The senator went out of his way to antagonize conservatives."[51] It seems likely that conservatives who were irreconcilable before the president's visit remained unreconciled when it was over.

In the Andrews camp, a bitter campaigner exploded in anger at the Republican establishment's lack of campaign assistance.

> They did everything in their power to defeat Mark Andrews. The Democrats didn't have to do a thing. Any excuse, any reason they could find to strike at Mark Andrews, they did. They resented him because he was too successful, because he turned on the [medical] establishment, because he cared for his wife, because he had an eastern staff. They did it any way they could.

The rocky relationship of the onetime "Young Turk" with the conservative regulars of his party—"the bellyachers, the bitchers, and the right wingers," as he called them—accompanied him to the end of his career. Whether, however, this difficulty was on balance any more costly in 1986 than it had been in ten previous elections we hesitate to guess.

OUT OF TOUCH: THE ROAD FROM LEHR

When a longtime legislator is defeated for reelection, the most common all-purpose explanation is that a once popular, solidly entrenched incumbent had gotten out of touch with constituents. Our central puzzle has been to explain that kind of defeat of a veteran legislator who had appeared six years earlier (and before) to be enjoying an ideal representational relationship with his constituents and an impregnable elected position. What happened, we have asked, to the man from Lehr?

As we cautioned earlier, this question assumes both the accuracy of our initial observations at Lehr and the reasonableness of the interpretations drawn from the entire 1980 (and 1982) visit. While recognizing the uncertainties involved, our stance has been to assume both accuracy and reasonableness, to assume that things happen to turn an invulnerable incumbent into a vulnerable one, and to analyze the slice of Mark Andrews's career that took him from Lehr in 1980 to election night six years later. A helpful way of summing up much of our analysis of what happened during that interelection period is to say that somehow or other Mark Andrews got out of touch.

Successful incumbents develop and display a keen sense for how intensely their constituents will respond to their activities—what constituents will approve of, put up with, criticize, and oppose. Without accurate judgments about the metes and bounds of constituent sentiment, no incumbent can survive in a representative system. Miscalculations about voter sentiment can be taken as evidence that the incumbent has, indeed, gotten out of touch with those sentiments. We have already caught glimpses of this condition in Andrews's case—the reaction to his commission proposal in the Garrison controversy and his own admission that he needed a disciplinary biennial report card.

From his own post-mortems we have learned that several of his crucial calculations concerning constituents' reactions—to his farm bill explanations, to his lawsuit, and to his governing accomplishments—proved to be inaccurate. And in each case, he later expressed some mystification about why his constituents had not reacted as he thought they would. He could not, he said, understand why they did not accept his explanations on the farm bill, or respect his private action on the lawsuit, or, most important, support him on the basis of his legislative accomplishments. During the campaign, his slowness to recognize the damage that Conrad's commercials were doing to him only compounded these more basic miscalculations. The point is not that he ignored voter sentiment; it is that he misread voter sentiment. He thought he knew how they would act. He didn't.

When we say that a veteran incumbent has gotten out of touch over time, one problem that suggests itself is the generational one. Elected officials with a lengthy tenure in office run the risk of losing contact with the newest, youngest members of their constituency. They may continue to rely on the people who originally elected them and kept them there; but those people in turn may have lost their vigor or their cohesion or their interest well before the incumbent wants to leave office. Meanwhile, the incumbent may fail to replenish his or her coalition from the next generation of voters and lose disproportionately among the young. Since this syndrome presents itself as a possibility in Andrews's case, it is worth noting that the CBS exit poll, at least, gives little evidence that it was a problem for him.

The youngest, 18-29, group voted for him in exactly the same proportion (49 percent-49 percent) as the electorate as a whole; and they differed very slightly (49 percent-51 percent) from the oldest, 60 and over, group. They also gave Andrews the same 50 percent favorable job rating as the 60 and over group did. These results are more interesting in the light of one student's conclusion, drawn from a larger selection of 1986 exit polls, that "in the Senate races, they [the 18-30 age group] proved to give stronger majorities to the Democrats nationally than any other age group." [52] Whatever other problems Mark Andrews had, the youngest North Dakota voting cohort doesn't seem, on early inspection, to have been one of them.

From other sources of postelection interpretation, however, there accumulated another bit of evidence that he was out of touch. The problem centered on the changing North Dakota sensitivities of the Andrews staff. The change from his first (1981-1983) administrative assistant, William Wright, to his last (1985-1986) administrative assistant, Jacqueline Balk-Tusa—from someone who had been administrative assistant to Andrews's predecessor, Milton Young, to a Washington lobbyist who helped him engineer his truck width victory—was a visible reminder of this problem. One Andrews consultant said: "With regard to his staff work, . . . Bill Wright . . . was never replaced. He was a North Dakotan. He had a very good feeling for North Dakota. Those that came after him did not, and that hurt."

As previously noted, Balk-Tusa became an early target of North Dakota conservatives as a liberal outsider. She increased her local visibility as the effective manager of the Andrews reelection campaign. Kent Conrad volunteered after his victory that it was a major mistake for Andrews to have given her such a prominent role in the campaign. And a former Andrews staffer, a North Dakotan, summed up his post-mortem: "I joke with people and say I'm going to write a book about Mark called *The Tale of Two Women*—his wife, Mary, who got him to Congress and the one from New York who got him out of there."

A reporter who followed Andrews in Washington wrote a more general explanatory post-mortem.

> In the end, Andrews' greatest weakness was probably his staff. He could have used more people from North Dakota who had an understanding of the state's attitudes and values. The North Dakota electorate is small enough to function as a community. We are still a state of small towns, with a shared identity, in a way, as one big small town. We are comfortable with our level of intimacy and courtesy in our political debate that is hard for someone from somewhere else to understand. Andrews had people on his staff in important positions who could not comprehend the nature of our politics. He paid a stiff price.[53]

This reporter's view of North Dakota as a supersensitive cultural entity corresponds exactly to my own. To the degree that his assessment is valid, it is additional evidence that Mark Andrews had not remained as closely attuned to his constituents as he needed to be.

As if to prove the case, one of those staffers hired from outside the state delivered this parting shot at Andrews's constituents in the aftermath of the campaign.

> They wanted her [Mary] to die for him or for him to put her away. They didn't want to see her. It was a story about a family fighting back after a tragedy, and the people of North Dakota turned ugly when confronted with it. They romanticize their small town life, but they are ugly small town.
>
>   They have taken crap from their legislators for years and they love it. Langer was nothing, absolutely nothing. Young was not much better. Burdick has been brain dead for years. Dorgan just prints press releases. But they love all these people. There isn't one legislator in the lot. There has only been one legislator in North Dakota history, and that is Mark Andrews. North Dakota is an intellectual gulag. They get what they deserve.

Even discounting for postelection trauma, staffers with underlying perceptions such as these could not help Mark Andrews cultivate that sense of close identification and trust with his constituents on which his representational relationship had, for twenty-three years, depended. His later hiring practices were based on yet another miscalculation—and the man who did the hiring was not the man from Lehr.

In all these cases, Andrews miscalculated the credibility and the cushion of support he retained with the voters. At the very end of our last preelection conversation in North Dakota, he had put the problem squarely in these terms: "We'll see whether all the good will I've built up over all these years is still there or whether it's gone." He believed it was still there. It wasn't—not enough of it, anyway.

Our study traces the gradual slippage of that strong sense of identification between representative and constituency with which Andrews began his Senate career. As landmarks, there were the early unfavorable comparisons with Byron Dorgan on matters of contact and trust; there was the costly casting of Andrews as an outsider in the malpractice drama; there was a good deal of unfavorable press treatment relative to attentiveness at home, to dealmaking on Garrison in Washington, and to the scandalous Dorgan investigation; there was voters' willingness to entertain challenger-inspired doubts about his vote on the farm bill, his "double talk" on issues, and his devotion to high wheat prices; there was Andrews's own admission that the lack of a biennial campaign and a biennial report card had deprived him of the discipline that had kept him close to his constituents as a House member; and there was Andrews's further admission that some of the staffers in charge of monitoring and strengthening his home relationships were inadequate (even antipathetic) to the task.

Each of these conditions or perceptions was an indicator of a downturn in credibility, a weakening sense of identification, a leakage from the reservoir of good will that Andrews believed he had retained and that he so badly needed. Taken all together, these indicators pictured an incumbent who had, to a damaging degree, gotten out of touch with his constituents. Indeed, that picture was the most fundamental premise of the Conrad campaign.

In Andrews's case, the one word that unsympathetic observers most often used to encapsulate this description was *arrogant*. It cropped up repeatedly in voters' criticism, in press opinion, in interest group comments, and in staff reflections. It became so pervasive that in a conversation in Indiana that fall, I heard Republican pollster Robert Teeter exclaim: "Our problem in North Dakota is the incumbent—his arrogance." Kent Conrad used that word to describe what he thought was his opponent's Achilles heel. "Mark Andrews had gotten so that he believed everything he said was right, not because it was right, but because he said it. . . . He thought he knew more than anyone else; and he had stopped listening." It was another example of the personalized criticism that was so easily generated and circulated in a small state like North Dakota.

Arrogant was not a word I had heard or read until the last year and a half of his term. As carried into the post-mortems, the word refers more to an accumulation of difficulties than to any single one. It seems to have come into use as an all-purpose characterization after Andrews's vulnerability was publicly revealed in the March 1985 State Poll. It certainly suggested vulnerability. Whatever it meant—personal aloofness, political unresponsiveness, maverick independence, unwillingness to change, violation of community expectations—it was the opposite of the reputation Andrews had long nourished as "one of us" and as "family." It was shorthand for "out of touch."

Arrogant was not an adjective I would have applied to the man I saw in Krueger's Cafe. And it was a far harsher term than I would have applied to the man I found campaigning six years later. During his reelection campaign and afterward, I did sense an attitude, however, that might be interpreted as aloofness, if not arrogance. It was a certain war weariness that expressed itself in a take-it-or-leave-it attitude about the process, together with a sense of resignation about the outcome. His campaign posture seemed to be: I deserve reelection because I've spent my political lifetime looking out for North Dakota and doing good for North Dakota; if, after all I have done, you won't support me, there's nothing else I can do or say now. Furthermore, if, after all I've done, you won't support me, then you aren't the family I thought you were and I'd rather be doing something else than trying to represent you.

As a campaigner, the incumbent lacked, I thought, enthusiasm and aggressiveness. His television campaign was neither imaginative nor combative. Everyone seemed to be going through the motions of a thoroughly protectionist campaign. They were relying on old constituencies to reward past performance and not reaching out for the support of new constituencies. One of Andrews's advisers had a similar post-mortem observation.

> He just got tired of running. After twenty-four years, he thought he should have been appreciated. He felt he had sacrificed so much and done so much that he ought not to have to run hard any more. I remember one day when I was briefing him, he said something to the effect that "if people don't know me by now and appreciate all I've done, what the hell am I doing in this job anyway?"

He did not look like a highly competitive politician under fire and fighting as hard as he could for his political life. His unwillingness or inability to court the voters assiduously one more time could be interpreted by them as something akin to arrogance. In the North Dakota community, such an interpretation would, of course, compound every other difficulty.

CONCLUSION

Why, then, did Mark Andrews lose? How can a political science observer answer Andrews's own challenge: "Perhaps you, in your analysis, can tell me when the love affair with the people of North Dakota ended." To the specific question, "when?" we can only answer: not all at once, but gradually over a six-year period. To the more general question, the answer lies in the detailed narrative account of the interelection period. Two crucial factors, the farm situation and the lawsuit, command initial attention quite apart from the six-year story. Two equally crucial factors, the eroding credibility and the hardening governing style, emerge only in the course of the six-year story. Had Mark Andrews been running for reelection to the House of Representatives in 1982 rather than for reelection to the Senate in 1986—with the same farm situation and with the same malpractice suit—it is our view that he would have been reelected. His credibility would have remained higher; his governing style would not have come under serious challenge locally; and he would not have had time to get out of touch to the degree that he had.

The knitting together of these four central factors requires, we have argued, a sense of sequence that only a narrative account can provide. For example, weaknesses in Andrews's credibility, by comparison with Dorgan, appeared well before the lawsuit came along to give his standing as "one of us" its biggest single downward push. The early comparisons with Dorgan also revealed weaknesses in governing style that would persist over time unless tended to. As another example, the lawsuit appeared before farm issues came to the forefront; and it undercut, therefore, Andrews's ability to explain his farm-related actions. Had he not initiated the lawsuit, he might have been able to sell his farm-related explanations to the voters. He always had.

He still, however, would have had to cope with the waning of his credibility and the growing insufficiency of his pork barrel accomplishments. With or without the lawsuit, therefore, Andrews's best chance of repairing or reversing the erosion of credibility, identification, and trust was to alter his governing style. His best chance was to respond to the challenge of "Dorganization" with a broadened issue activism and a heavy concentration on public relations. To understand why he did not—indeed, could not—do this, it is necessary to understand the timing of his House-to-Senate career and the continuing reinforcement of his low-profile, inside-playing, pork-producing style. His only other survival chance—and a much slimmer one—was to have conducted a hard-charging, hard-edged, expansionist campaign in order to beat back his challenger and reverse voters' doubts. Miscalculations and battle fatigue—products of his own career-length experience—combined with a declining party organization to eliminate that alternative.

What the electorate of 1986 apparently preferred from their incumbent senator was the *same* representational relationship he had presented in 1980 and a *different* governing style. What he offered them, instead, was a *changed* representational relationship and the *same* governing style. It was the wrong combination. In a head-to-head contest with a challenger whose political associations and talents enabled him to exploit the mismatch, the incumbent lost.

While the central puzzle of the book has been the defeat of a successful incumbent politician, the narrative account emphasizes the importance of sequence and the theme of change. The story encompasses at least two decades of change in legislative styles in Washington and at least six years of change in constituents' receptivity in North Dakota. At the end of our postelection conversation, the defeated incumbent offered his own change-related interpretation of his defeat. "Maybe people just wanted a change," he said. "Maybe my time is over." A month later, he seemed satisfied with a similar wrap-up. In essence, what he felt the voters said on election day was, "Hey, Mark, you're a nice guy, but the other guy's a nice guy, too, and it's time to let someone else have a chance." It is the most personally comforting of Andrews's post-mortems—and, as far as it goes, it is accurate. He had gotten a little out of touch and it was time for a change.

For political scientists, our study of a single failed incumbency suggests that in other Senate reelection cases, too, it may be necessary to understand the journey in order to understand the outcome. The journey may be one of six years or more. Sequential impacts—of early career on later career, of campaigning on governing, and of governing on campaigning—take time to develop and can usefully be analyzed within a framework that emphasizes time.

One especially interesting question that flows from our analysis pertains to the incumbent's vulnerability. How, when, and by what means does electoral vulnerability or the perception of vulnerability get established? And what can be done about preventing it from happening or coping with it when it does happen? These questions are raised but must be left for future study.

In some respects, the study of vulnerability is the reverse side of the study of the advantages of incumbency. But it takes incumbent-related research in a somewhat different direction—toward a longer time span, toward the interelection period at least, and toward a career-long perspective if that seems relevant. This does not mean the abandonment of any of the explanatory factors that political scientists have traditionally employed to study election results—national and local issues, incumbent and challenger characteristics, ideological and partisan factors, and candidate-constituency relationships. It only places them in a longer time span to accommodate the changing perspectives of the incumbent and the changing influences on the incumbent over time.

Stories of individual incumbents such as this one can play a helpful part in such studies.

NOTES

1. AP, "Andrews Hurt by Conrad's TV Ads," *Bismarck Tribune*, November 5, 1986.
2. The official totals were: Conrad 143,932, Andrews 141,797. State Canvassing Board, "Official Abstract of Votes Cast at the General Election Held November 4, 1986."
3. *Newsweek*, November 17, 1986, 30; Edwin Yoder, "Not Really a Reagan Bashing" *Forum* (Fargo), November 17, 1986.
4. See, for example, David Broder, "Voters to Politicians: Guess Again," *Washington Post National Weekly Edition*, November 17, 1986; Editorial, "Reagan's Winter," *New York Times*, November 6, 1986.
5. Albert Hunt, "Democrats' Win, Sans an Agenda, No Help in 1988," *Wall Street Journal*, November 6, 1986; E. J. Dionne, Jr., "Democrats Rejoice at 55-45 Senate Margin, but Still Seek Agenda to Counter Reagan," *New York Times*, November 6, 1986. See also Hodding Carter III, "Senate Shift Will Make a Clear Difference," *Wall Street Journal*, November 6, 1986.
6. Bill Moyers, CBS election night television coverage (taped).
7. The total number of respondents in the poll was 976. "CBS News Exit Poll, North Dakota Election Night 1986."
8. Dionne, "Democrats Rejoice at 55-45 Senate Margin."
9. Gerald Wright and Michael Berkman, "Candidates and Policy in United States Senate Elections," *American Political Science Review* (June 1986); Gary Jacobson and Raymond Wolfinger, "Context and Choice in Two Senate Elections" (paper presented at the Annual Meeting of the American Political Science Association, Chicago, 1987); Alan Abramowitz, "Explaining Election Outcomes," *American Political Science Review* (June 1982).
10. Jim Neumann, "Conrad Ousts Andrews," *Forum* (Fargo), November 6, 1986.
11. Sid Spaeth, "Farm Economy 'Did-in' Andrews," *Forum* (Fargo), November 6, 1986.
12. Editorial, "Congratulations, Winners," *Forum* (Fargo), November 6, 1986; Dick Dobson, "Doctors, Farmers Unseat Andrews," *Minot Daily News*, November 9, 1986.
13. Spaeth, "Farm Economy 'Did-in' Andrews."
14. Respondents were classified as "farm" if they answered yes to the following question: "Do you or does anyone else in your household work on a farm or have a job that has anything to do with agriculture?"
15. Dennis Farney, "No Farm Belt Revolt Benefiting Democrats Has Crystallized Yet," *Wall Street Journal*, October 10, 1986; "Vox Populi: No Breakthrough on Farm Issue," *National Journal*, October 25, 1986; on Grassley and Kasten, see Chuck Raasch, "Farm Belt: A Strange Political Wind Rises over the Fields of the Heartland," *Democrat and Chronicle* (Rochester, N.Y.), October 25, 1986. Also, Richard Cohen, "Running Without Reagan," *National Journal*, December 7, 1985; Rob Gurwitt, "Many 1986 Candidates Tailor Bids to Fit Local Moods," *Congressional Quarterly Weekly Report*, August 23, 1986; E. J. Dionne,

Jr., "Poll Finds Voters Discount View Election Is Referendum on Reagan," *New York Times,* October 31, 1986.

16. See Broder, "Voters to Politicians"; "Reagan's Winter"; Hunt, "Democrats Win"; Dionne, "Democrats Rejoice"; and Carter, "Senate Shift." Also, Charles McDowell, "The Best Candidate Usually Wins," *Bismarck Tribune,* November 8, 1986.

17. On Grassley, see James Dickenson, "Breaking Rules, Flying High," *Washington Post,* March 25, 1985; Jack Germond and Jules Witcover, "Down at the Barn, Reagan's No Laughing Matter," *National Journal,* April 20, 1985; Farney, "No Farm Belt Revolt." On comparisons between Grassley and Andrews, see E. J. Dionne, Jr., "Democrats See Economy Emerging as Big Issue," *New York Times,* October 3, 1986; "ND Race Draws Ink Across U.S.," *Grand Forks Herald,* October 12, 1986. On Kasten, see Julia Malone, "GOP Deficit Fighter Woos Voters with Federal Funds," *Washington Post,* September 26, 1985; James Dickenson, "In the Farm Belt, Seeds of Political Irony," *Washington Post,* July 20, 1986; Jack Germond and Jules Witcover, "Character the Issue in Wisconsin," *National Journal,* October 25, 1986. The race in Missouri can be seen similarly. See Rob Gurwitt, "Many 1986 Candidates Tailor Bids to Fit Local Moods."

18. Data from "Farm Income Indicators for North Dakota, 1949-1990," North Dakota Agricultural Statistics Service, Fargo, North Dakota, September 11, 1991.

19. Stacy Herron, "Has Tide Turned for Republicans?" *Bismarck Tribune,* November 5, 1986.

20. Dobson, "Doctors, Farmers Unseat Andrews."

21. His most recent vote percentages in Cass County were: 1974, 54 percent; 1976, 67 percent; 1978, 72 percent; 1980, 69 percent.

22. Dobson, "Doctors, Farmers Unseat Andrews."

23. Don Gackle, "Here and There," *McLean County Independent,* November 8, 1986; Randy Bradbury, "Conrad's Advertising Gets Credit for Victory," *Forum* (Fargo), November 6, 1986.

24. AP, "Suit Hurt Andrews," *Grand Forks Herald,* November 7, 1986.

25. Dale Wetzel, "Conrad Outlines Plans, Andrews Bows Out," *Minot Daily News,* November 6, 1986.

26. Reed Karaim, "His Color, Corn and Contrariness Made Mark a Memorable Player," *Grand Forks Herald,* November 11, 1986.

27. AP, "Suit Hurt Andrews"; Patrick Springer, "Mark Andrews," *Forum* (Fargo), November 7, 1986.

28. Gackle, "Here and There"; Bradbury, "Conrad's Advertising Gets Credit"; Randy Bradbury, "Conrad Holds Lead," *Forum* (Fargo), November 5, 1986.

29. Springer, "Mark Andrews."

30. Karaim, "His Color, Corn and Contrariness."

31. Gackle, "Here and There"; Bradbury, "Conrad's Advertising Gets Credit."

32. AP, "Andrews Hurt by Conrad's TV Ads"; Randall Mikkelsen and Lance Nixon, "Andrews Clings to Hope, Conrad Forces Celebrate," *Grand Forks Herald,* November 5, 1986.

33. Bradbury, "Conrad's Advertising Gets Credit"; Paul Taylor, "The Trick Is to Get Vicious Carefully," *Washington Post National Weekly Edition,* July 16-22, 1990. The consultant is Frank Greer.

34. AP, "Andrews: Dorgan Would Have Been Easy," *Minot Daily News,* December 28, 1986.

35. Ibid.
36. Ibid.
37. Editorial, "Congratulations, Winners"; Randall Mikkelsen, "What's Ahead for Andrews? Probably Not Another Race," *Grand Forks Herald,* November 6, 1986; and Carl Flagstad, "Andrews' Final Letter Notes Highlights," *Minot Daily News,* December 24, 1986.
38. Gurwitt, "Many 1986 Candidates Tailor Bids." Bob Kasten, too, launched a broad-scale populist attack in his successful reelection campaign. Helen Dewar and Dan Balz, "Don't Be Surprised If the GOP Retains Control of the Senate," *Washington Post National Weekly Edition,* March 4, 1985.
39. Joe Schneider, "Aftermath," Council of Economic Development Research Memorandum, November 5, 1986. The story of a House incumbent's failure in 1986, with the suggestion that "pork-barreling" has its limitations, will be found in Paul Starobin, "Pork: A Time Honored Tradition Lives on," *Congressional Quarterly Weekly Report,* October 24, 1987.
40. When it was over, twenty-five of Andrews's Washington staffers wrote a letter to the North Dakota newspapers blaming disgruntled former staffers for criticism of Andrews and praising him as "a politician, a statesman, and a good, decent man." Letters to the Editor, "Andrews' Staff Gives Him Fulsome Praise," *Forum* (Fargo), December 14, 1986. See also Carl Flagstad, "Andrews Staffers Begin Hunt for New Jobs," *Minot Daily News,* December 24, 1986.
41. AP, "Andrews: Dorgan Would Have Been Easy."
42. David Shribman, "Costly, Negative Congressional Campaigns Spur Immediate Backlash, Legislative Calls for Reform," *Wall Street Journal,* November 7, 1986; Sandy Grady, "Night of the Video Monsters," *Bismarck Tribune,* November 5, 1986.
43. See Tom Morgenthau, "When in Doubt, Go Negative," *Newsweek,* November 3, 1986; Paul Taylor, "Accentuating the Negative," *Washington Post National Weekly Edition,* October 20, 1986.
44. Gackle, "Here and There"; Dick Dobson, "North Dakota Politics Have Changed," *Minot Daily News,* November 16, 1986; Taylor, "Accentuating the Negative."
45. Herron, "Has Tide Turned for Republicans?"; Dick Dobson, "Are We a Democratic State?" *Minot Daily News,* December 14, 1986; Bradbury, "Conrad Holds Lead"; AP, "Andrews Hurt by Conrad's TV Ads."
46. Springer, "Mark Andrews."
47. Karaim, "His Color, Corn and Contrariness."
48. "Reagan Has Hit the Campaign Trail," *National Journal,* October 18, 1986.
49. Bradbury, "Conrad Holds Lead"; Editorial, "ND's Record Vote Turnout," *Forum* (Fargo), November 8, 1986; "The Senate Turnout: Hardly a Groundswell," *Congressional Quarterly Weekly Report,* November 8, 1986.
50. Herron, "Has Tide Turned for Republicans?"
51. Paul Weyrich, "Ignoring the Right Cost GOP the Senate," *Wall Street Journal,* December 8, 1986.
52. Barry Sussman, "Guess Who Voted Democratic This Time—Young People," *Washington Post National Weekly Edition,* November 17, 1986.
53. Karaim, "His Color, Corn and Contrariness."

Index